D1547562

Designing For Science

Implications From Everyday, Classroom, and Professional Settings

Edited by

Kevin Crowley
University of Pittsburgh

Christian D. Schunn
George Mason University

Takeshi Okada
Nagoya University

 LAWRENCE ERLBAUM ASSOCIATES, PUBLISHERS
2001 Mahwah, New Jersey   London

The final camera copy for this work was prepared by the authors, and therefore the publisher takes no responsibility for consistency or correctness of typographical style.

Lawrence Erlbaum Associates, Inc., Publishers
10 Industrial Avenue
Mahwah, NJ 07430

Cover design by Kathryn Houghtaling Lacey and the editors. Photographs by Takeshi Okada.

Library of Congress Cataloging-in-Publication Data

Designing for science : implications from everyday, classroom, and professional settings / edited by Kevin Crowley, Christian D. Schunn, and Takeshi Okada.
    p. cm.

Includes bibliographical references and index.
    ISBN 0-8058-3473-7 (cloth : alk. paper)
    ISBN 0-8058-3474-5 (pbk. : alk. paper)
    1. Science—Study and teaching. 2. Science—Philosophy.
    3. Science—Methodology. I. Crowley, Kevin D. II. Schunn,
    Christian D. III. Okada, Takeshi.
    Q181 .D23   2001
    507´.1—dc21

                                                    2001016101
                                                    CIP

Books published by Lawrence Erlbaum Associates are printed on acid-free paper, and their bindings are chosen for strength and durability.

Printed in the United States of America
10 9 8 7 6 5 4 3 2 1

Dedicated to
Joseph and Barbara Crowley
Oswin, Ute, and Gabriela Schunn
Kahichiro and Eiko Okada

Contents

PART III: EVALUATING SCIENTIFIC THINKING

Preface

Since the 1980s, impressive progress has been made toward understanding how it is that people think, and learn to think, about science in each of three distinct contexts. These contexts are: 1) the practice of science by professionals pursuing research and development in laboratories; 2) the teaching and learning of science in elementary, secondary, and college classrooms; and 3) the informal science that children and adults explore in the course of everyday activities at home or at institutions such as museums. A major component of this progress has been an increased focus on the context-specific aspects of scientific reasoning. For example, a good understanding of science is not going to help you design a good science curriculum unless you also understand a lot about a school and about the way the teachers and students interact. The same can be said for professional science or everyday science.

Although specialization by context has been and will continue to be necessary for progress within each of these contexts, it also creates a potential problem. As current accounts of scientific thinking become increasingly embedded in specific contexts, it is possible that the study of scientific thinking, which has historically remained loosely unified, may in fact split further apart. It may fragment into three particular context-specific accounts of scientific thinking that do not make reference to each other and do not build off of each other's results.

Guided by the desire to explore connections between the three separate strands of scientific thinking research, we convened a conference in April 1998 at the University of Pittsburgh's Learning Research and Development Center. We invited leading researchers from each of the three contexts to discuss whether it was possible, whether it is a good idea at all, to consider everyday, instructional, and professional science together in a coherent view of the development and practice of scientific thinking. This book represents an extension and integration of the presentations and conversations of the conference.

To facilitate the finding of common themes while simultaneously reflecting the concern for context, we called the conference *Designing for Science* and encouraged participants to frame their presentations around issues of how their work was directly connected to practical applications within and between the three contexts. When we were first thinking of how to put the program of the conference together, the default notion was to do it by the contexts: First, everyday science; second, classroom science; and third, professional science. But it struck us that such an organization would reinforce any disintegration that was occurring rather than prompt us to think about integrative connections. Thus, we opted instead for a basic organization according to a simplified design cycle: Developing goals for learning and performance, designing an artifact or instructional experience to meet those goals, and evaluating whether it worked.

We chose a focus on design because we believe that practical application is the ultimate test of scientific theory. It may once have been commonplace—particularly among our fellow psychologists—to hear talk about how applications should follow only after respectable basic research had run its course. Essentially this is just one pass through a design cycle. We have been more interested in those who see repeated and cyclical synergy between the basic and applied; those whose basic questions are shaped by application and those whose applied research breaks and reformulates basic theory. These are the researchers who have contributed chapters to this volume.

In the first section of the book, we present research focused on extending our knowledge of the fundamental components of scientific thinking. In the second section, we present research focused primarily on how to build something for scientific thinking in classrooms, in museums, or for practicing scientists. Finally, in the third section, we present research whose focus is primarily on how to evaluate the effectiveness of artifacts in scientific settings.

We are grateful to the Mitsubishi Bank Foundation for their generous support of the Designing for Science conference and the Learning Research and Development Center at the University of Pittsburgh for providing matching funds. Chien-fu Chang, Michael Fender, Jodi Galco, and Leonard Tena did a fabulous job making sure that the conference went smoothly. Erin Guthridge, Roger Taylor, and Kelli Millwood provided proofreading assistance for the book. Finally, we thank Rose Russo, who has copyedited, tracked down errant citations, redrawn figures, and, as if that weren't enough, whipped up the pageproofs using FrameMaker on a Mac G3.

Kevin Crowley
Christian D. Schunn
Takeshi Okada

April, 2000

List of Contributors

John R. Anderson
Department of Psychology, Carnegie Mellon University, Pittsburgh, PA 15213.

Margarita Azmitia
Psychology Department, University of California, Santa Cruz, CA 95064.

Maureen A. Callanan
Psychology Department, University of California, Santa Cruz, CA 95064.

Zhe Chen
Department of Psychology, Carnegie Mellon University, Pittsburgh, PA 15213.

Clark A. Chinn
Department of Educational Psychology, Graduate School of Education, Rutgers University, 10 Seminary Place, New Brunswick, NJ 08901-1183.

Kevin Crowley
University of Pittsburgh, Learning Research & Development Center, 3939 O'Hara St., Pittsburgh, PA 15260.

Kevin Dunbar
Department of Psychology, McGill University, 1205 Docteur Penfield Avenue, Montreal, PQ H3A 1B1.

Daniel C. Edelson
School of Education and Social Policy and The Institute for the Learning Sciences, Northwestern University, 2115 North Campus Drive, Evanston, IL 60208-2610.

Jodi Galco
University of Pittsburgh, Learning Research & Development Center, 3939 O'Hara St., Pittsburgh, PA 15260.

Louis M. Gomez
School of Education and Social Policy and The Institute for the Learning Sciences, Northwestern University, 2115 North Campus Drive, Evanston, IL 60208-2610.

Jennifer L. Jipson
Psychology Department, University of California, Santa Cruz, CA 95064.

David Klahr
Department of Psychology, Carnegie Mellon University, Pittsburgh, PA 15213.

Richard Lehrer
Wisconsin Center for Education Research, 1025 W. Johnson St., Madison, WI 53705.

Ben Loh
School of Education and Social Policy and The Institute for the Learning Sciences, Northwestern University, 2115 North Campus Drive, Evanston, IL 60208-2610.

Betina A. Malhotra
Department of Educational Psychology, Graduate School of Education, Rutgers University, 10 Seminary Place, New Brunswick, NJ 08901-1183.

Sue Marshall
School of Education and Social Policy and The Institute for the Learning Sciences, Northwestern University, 2115 North Campus Drive, Evanston, IL 60208-2610.

Jim Minstrell
A.C.T.Systems for Education, 16549 SE 30th, Bellevue, WA 98008.

Takeshi Okada,
School of Education, Nagoya University, Furo-cho, Chikusa-ku, Nagoya, 464-8601, Japan.

David E. Penner
Department of Educational Psychology, University of Wisconsin, Madison, 1025 West Johnson Street, Madison, WI 53706.

Anthony J. Petrosino,
Sanchez Building, Room 462-A, University of Texas at Austin, Austin, TX 78712.

Josh Radinsky
School of Education and Social Policy and The Institute for the Learning Sciences, Northwestern University, 2115 North Campus Drive, Evanston, IL 60208-2610.

Brian J. Reiser
School of Education and Social Policy and The Institute for the Learning Sciences, Northwestern University, 2115 North Campus Drive, Evanston, IL 60208-2610.

Leona Schauble
Wisconsin Center for Education Research, 1025 W. Johnson St., Madison, WI, 53705.

Christian D. Schunn
Psychology 3F5, George Mason University, Fairfax, VA 22030.

Takashi Shimokido
School of Education, Nagoya University, Furo-cho, Chikusa-ku, Nagoya, 464-8601, Japan.

Jeff Shrager
Afferent Systems, Inc., 1550 Bryant Street, Suite 760, San Francisco, CA 94103.

Herbert A. Simon
Department of Psychology, Carnegie Mellon University, Pittsburgh, PA 15213.

Paul Thagard,
Philosophy Department, University of Waterloo, Waterloo, Ontario, N2L 3G1, Canada.

Eva Erdosne Toth
Department of Psychology, Carnegie Mellon University, Pittsburgh, PA 15213.

Ryan Tweney
Department of Psychology, Bowling Green State University, Bowling Green, OH 43403.

Designing For Science

Implications From Everyday, Classroom, and Professional Settings

I

Fundamentals of
Scientific Thinking

1

"Seek and Ye Shall Find"
How Curiosity Engenders Discovery

Herbert A. Simon
Carnegie Mellon University

For children to achieve an understanding of science and of the ways of doing science, and for them to be motivated to use these ways in coping with, understanding, and enjoying the physical, biological, and social world around them, it is not enough that they believe that science is practically important. They must also be curious. Curiosity calls attention to interesting, odd, and sometimes important items in the drama that is revealed to us through our senses. Idle or purposeful, curiosity is the motor that interests children in science; it is also the principal motor that energizes and steers the education of professional scientists and the conduct of their subsequent scientific work. A depiction of the workings of curiosity must form a central chapter in any account of how science is and ought to be carried on.

Philosophers of science have been prone to divide scientific activity into two components: the processes of discovery and the processes of verification. But instead of treating the two symmetrically, philosophy of science and the theory of scientific method (although not the history of science) have generally emphasized verification far more than discovery. "Somehow," theories and hypotheses are assumed to appear on the scene, and these are then tested to determine whether they should be accepted or rejected. Courses on research methods focus almost exclusively upon how experiments should be designed to test *given* hypotheses, and how statistical tests should be applied to evaluate the outcomes of such experiments. Experimenting without clear-cut hypotheses is dismissed as "counting bricks," and the origin of hypotheses is attributed to "intuition," or "inspiration," neither of which is then explained.

5

On the other hand, in psychology, processes of discovery have engendered much cognitive and developmental research, as witness the many interests in these processes that are represented in this volume. One important theme in the developmental research is that children are born with curiosity, which, if maintained and even stimulated, leads them to enjoy and understand science (and sometimes become scientists). I will explore this theme and use it to critique some widely held views about research methodology that are sometimes taught in science curricula, but that almost surely act to stifle curiosity, hence impede science education. When these views are held by working scientists, they also impede the progress of science. My purpose, of course, is not just to remove from our teaching what is harmful, but to review some of the things we know about discovery that are perhaps both teachable and worth teaching and practicing.

Curiosity

We start with the widely accepted generalizations that learning depends on time on task, that time on task requires sustained attention, and that attention can only be sustained if the stimuli are interesting,[1] or, in causal terms: *Interesting stimuli → attention → time on task →learning.*

Daniel Berlyne (1960) showed, with the help of extensive experiments with children, adults, and rats, that attention is sustained longest if the stimuli are neither too simple (boring) nor too complex (inscrutable). Our attention can be sustained as long as we can continue to find interesting pattern in the stimulus, but what is just complex enough depends on what we already know. After we have heard lots of music, the simple tunes that initially fascinated us no longer retain our attention very long; whereas music that was initially experienced as a jumble of raucous sound can now hold our attention for hours as we begin to discover the pattern buried in it. We pass gradually, one might say, from nursery songs to Bartok, if not, perhaps, to John Cage.

---

1. In every experiment on learning, time on task is either controlled or manipulated as an experimental variable. Large effects of attention are produced by the introduction of distracting tasks. The control of attention has been most thoroughly studied by Berlyne, whose work is cited in the next paragraph.

Children, left to themselves in a rich environment find, and attend to, stimuli that are at the right level of complexity for them—in which they can find interesting pattern. With experience, they learn to discover and enjoy more and more complex patterns. We say that they have curiosity, and we are concerned that this curiosity seems often to be burned out of them in the process of growing up and being schooled.

Although I know of only a little research that supports (and none that refutes) my conjecture, I would guess that curiosity—the habit of examining the environment for interesting pattern—can be learned. Extrapolating Berlyne's research, I would venture further that a reasonably rich environment, but one that does not continually force new stimuli on children instead of leaving the initiative to them in seeking pattern, is most conducive to encouraging active curiosity. I would venture a third guess that the environments that are best for this purpose respond to the child's exploration of them by revealing progressively clearer and more interesting patterns with each modest investment of new effort (Qin & Simon, 1990).[2] (These guesses would be at the core of my criticism of TV fare, which egregiously violates the second and third conditions.)

It has often been remarked (perhaps even shown empirically) that curiosity—wonder at all sorts of surrounding phenomena—is a common characteristic not only of young children, but also of good scientists. It is not unreasonable to suppose that this has something to do with their capability for doing good science, but it's not easy to run an experiment in standard form to prove this.

Experimental Method

Which gets me to the other half of my thesis: What is an experiment in "standard form?" And does skill in running such experiments produce good science?

Standard textbooks on scientific methodology, and on experimental method in particular, place controlled experiments (and especially critical experiments) at the center of the scientific stage. To design a controlled

---

2. A number of experiments in which students are presented with data and asked to discover scientific laws in them support these generalization. See, for example, (Qin & Simon, 1990), where children, presented simply with the distances of the planets from the Sun and their periods of orbit, were sometimes able to rediscover Kepler's Third Law, previously unknown to them, in less than an hour.

experiment, one needs a hypothesis: say, the hypothesis that the presence or absence of a particular condition causes a particular effect to occur or not.[3] Following Mill's canon of difference, the underlying logic is that: "If an instance in which a phenomenon occurs, and one in which it does not, differ in only one other circumstance, this circumstance is the cause, or the effect, or an indispensable part of the cause, of the phenomenon." What you get out of a controlled experiment is some evidence that influences you (or should) to have somewhat more or less credence in your particular hypothesis than you had before.

Of course, to make this particular rabbit stew, you have to catch the rabbit—to produce an effect. So you set up an "experimental" condition, in which the presumptively causal condition is present and a "control" condition in which it is not, and you measure the level of the phenomenon of interest in each condition. If the occurrence of the phenomenon is more frequent or more intense in the experimental condition than in the control condition, then it is a causal factor, otherwise it is not.

But how much more frequent or intense must it be? Nowadays, we are all sophisticated about the presence of random variables in the air and the wicked way in which they infect data. We require "significance"—that is "statistical significance"—of our differences, which brings us into the whole tangled and badly understood morass of modern statistics.[4] I'll say something later about what scientists do when they don't know statistics. For the moment, let's ignore this particular complexity, for there is another even more important one that hides in the usual notion of experiment.

To run the orthodox experiment, you have to have a hypothesis: that some specified variable is the causal agent for some specified phenomenon. You have to have a conjectured law of nature. It is generally regarded as bad form (often referred to as "counting the bricks in a wall") to run an experiment without a hypothesis. And that leads to the question of where hypotheses come from. A theory of the design of experiments and of statistical tests of the validity of hypotheses obviously does not fill this bill, for, according to orthodox doctrine, the design, execution and evaluation

3. This preoccupation with the methodology of controlled experiments and with the logic of testing hypotheses is a relatively modern development, as shown in Okada's chapter in this volume, where he traces its history in Japan and the United States.

4. For discussions of the common pathologies of statistical significance testing, see Gregg and Simon (1967), Grant (1962), or any modern textbook on testing authored by mathematical statisticians.

of experiments can only occur after the hypotheses are already in place. If running experiments to test hypotheses lies at the core of science, then a theory of how science works must include a theory of the origin of hypotheses. "Discovery" is the usual term for the crucial missing piece: We need a theory of scientific discovery as well as a theory of verification.

A "critical" experiment is simply a controlled experiment in which *two* hypotheses are already proposed, one of which is consistent with one outcome of the experiment, the other with another outcome. Thus, in the famous Michelson-Morley experiment, if the velocity of light were independent of the direction of a beam and its reflection relative to the Earth's motion, then the hypothesis that the Earth moved through an ether was refuted; if the velocity depended on the direction of the beam (*in a specific predicted way*) then the existence of an ether was supported. If the velocity were independent of direction, then there was no evidence of a stationary ether. If the velocity depended on the direction, but obeying a function incompatible with the ether hypothesis, then all bets were off—another contingency the textbooks commonly ignore. Does an experiment that refutes both hypotheses leave us without knowledge, or does it provide us with exciting new phenomena for our curiosity to explore? Let's look at some other examples.

The Curies were seeking to extract pure uranium from pitchblende. After some time they discovered that the substance they were obtaining had an intensity of radiation not only higher than that of their raw material, pitchblende, but higher than pure uranium. You might say that they had refuted both hypotheses, that the partly refined substance was pitchblende, and that it was uranium, and that the experiment had come to an end. Wisely, they did not abandon their effort but continued the process of purification until they had found a new element, radium. Were they wrong in continuing without a hypothesis? What was the rationale for what they were doing? One answer might be "curiosity," but that would not be accepted by most standard textbooks.

Scientific Discovery: The Origins of Hypotheses

We all "know" where hypotheses come from: We read last month's journals, find reports of some experiments, decide that if we did the experiments with better controls or with more subjects or with different instructions they would come out differently. Of course that explains some circumstances (probably not very productive ones) in which we think up hypotheses, but not what the process is of thinking them up. Perhaps they simply well up by intuition, insight or creativity from that mysterious region known as the subconscious—itself not a very interesting hypothesis, or one easy to test.

Is there a better answer to the question of the origins of hypotheses? Let's look again at some evidence from Nobel-level science. There's the notorious case of Fleming, returning from vacation to be greeted by a stack of dirty Petri dishes, which he had left unwashed in his laboratory sink. On one, he notices some very sick (lysed) bacteria, and just next to them some mold, which he recognizes as belonging to the genus Penicillium. Now he forms a hypothesis: the bacteria are dying because of something the mold is excreting.

Where does the hypothesis come from? Notice and recognize two words in the second sentence of the last paragraph: the words "notice" and "recognize." Forming a hypothesis, at least in this case, depends on noticing some phenomena, and recognizing some things about them. Both the noticing and the recognizing depend on prior knowledge: the noticing, because we mainly notice things that are unusual or surprising in their current surroundings: the recognizing, because there is very little we can say about things that we don't even recognize. (However, noticing something that is unrecognizable in a context where everything should be familiar is itself a source of hypotheses.)

Fleming is surprised, and surprise occurs only when we have expectations that are violated. Out of that violation of expectations, a hypothesis arises. In this case, Fleming's knowledge suggests no reason why the bacteria should be lysing, but they are lysing: Hence, he hypothesizes that the presence of the mold is a cause of the lysis of the bacteria. (Notice that he did not run the control condition, the test of whether the bacteria would lyse in the absence of the mold.) His knowledge also suggested to him that, if the hypothesis were true it would be interesting and important, for lysing bacteria is something we humans would like to be able to do in the interest of our health.

So hypotheses, at least in this case, come out of observations that occasion surprise; and to make such observations, there must be phenomena to observe, and knowledge of what to expect. If so, perhaps our account of scientific discovery should begin, not with the experiment, but with the processes of observing phenomena (of a familiar kind) that may produce surprises.

Are there implications for education from Fleming's experience? Train children not to wash the dishes? That may not be the right lesson to draw from the example. Perhaps more important for Fleming is that he was knowledgeable: He had put in his ten years acquiring expert knowledge about molds and bacteria. In this domain, he was Pasteur's "prepared mind" to which accidents happen. But "knowledgeable" is not enough either: He was also curious. He did not say, "Let's clean up that damned mess and get on with it." He asked, "What is causing that curious phenomenon?" Perhaps another observer, with a different background of knowledge, would observe, while counting the bricks in a wall, something unusual about their texture, or that alternate bricks in every third row had cracks. For the right person, that could be his or her path to the Nobel.

Is Fleming's case an isolated oddity? Decidedly not. I have identified more than a half dozen others whose surprises resulted in Nobel prizes, and I am certain that my list is very incomplete. I'll just mention Planck, the Curies, Krebs, Roentgen, Penzias and Wilson, and come to think of it, myself.[5] As Nobel prizes have been awarded in the hundreds, but not the thousands, this is not an uninteresting phenomenon, although I do not claim it is the whole story.

Planck was informed of data that decisively refuted a theory he had published a few months before. His immediate reaction was to modify the key descriptive law he had been using, extending it, *a posteriori* and *ad hoc,* to fit the new data as well as the old. Then he spent three months developing a new hypothesis to fit the revised descriptive law. In the course of doing so, he introduced, quite incidentally, and for quite pragmatic reasons, the concept of the quantum. It took 26 years for that concept to develop into the quantum mechanics of Heisenberg and Schrödinger. Here we clearly see observation of phenomena driving hypothesizing, not the converse.

I have already mentioned the experience of the Curies, and will describe Krebs' discovery a little later. As for Roentgen, it is well known that he discovered X-rays when, on opening a drawer in which there was an unused photographic plate with a key lying on top of it, he found a sharp image of the key on the plate. Penzias and Wilson, experimenting,

---

5. See my autobiography, *Models of My Life,* pp. 369-370.

mainly out of curiosity, with an instrument at Bell Labs, found unexpected low-frequency radiation in outer space. They had no idea of what might cause it, and had to inquire around among their physics colleagues for a possible explanation. (It turned out to be the background radiation from the "Big Bang"). With very high frequency, hypotheses arise from exposure to phenomena, with or without surprise. I'll return to that in a moment.

Observing Phenomena: The Case of Faraday

> *"It is quite comfortable to me to find that experiment need not quail before mathematics, but is quite competent to rival it in discovery."*

> Letter of Michael Faraday to Richard Phillips, 29 November 1831(on the occasion of his great discovery of magnetic induction of electricity).

There is no better example of observation driven by curiosity as a wellspring of science than the case of Michael Faraday, who was responsible for laying the empirical, and to a large extent, the theoretical, foundations of electromagnetism. Electricity and magnetism were subjects already steeped in mathematics by such imposing figures as Coulomb and Ampere at the time (about 1820) when Faraday began working in them. Faraday had no mathematics at all, nor ever acquired any. Such theories as he created were verbal and visual theories, particularly the latter, yet they included the basic laws of magnetic and electrical fields, later mathematized by Maxwell.

To emphasize, as I do here, Faraday's observations rather than his theories is not to discount his interest in theory and capabilities for generating it. Rather, it is to show how, in making his most important discovery, of magnetic induction of electricity, observation led the way to theory, rather than deriving from it. A second theme is to show that "theory" means many things, and that the "theories" that guide experimentation may be of a much vaguer and looser form than those that are discussed in the literature on experimental method and that are "tested" by controlled or critical experiments.

In its simplest terms, the story is this (Williams, 1965; Magnani, 1996):[6] The world of science was electrified (literally) in 1820 by Ørsted's demonstration that an electric current induced a magnetic field around it.

Until that time, electricity and magnetism were wholly distinct phenomena, although similarities in their laws of attraction and repulsion had, of course, attracted attention. Ørsted, starting out with no hypothesis more definite than that all forces in nature should be related, simply put a magnet near a live electric wire, and noticed that the needle was deflected. The experiment was immediately repeated all over Europe, and extended.

Faraday, upon learning of Ørsted's finding, also formed a hypothesis, based on a principle as vague as Ørsted's: that if electricity could induce magnetism, then, by symmetry, magnetism should be able to induce electricity. Beginning in 1821, he periodically conjured up observational situations that he thought might produce such induction. They generally involved bringing magnets and electricity into some kind of spatial proximity. They were also unsuccessful, as were those of other investigators playing a similar game. (The story is a little more complicated, Arago produced a partial effect that later proved important, but no one at first could make heads or tails of it.) From the summer of 1828 to the summer of 1831, Faraday, apparently discouraged by failure to produce induction, made no more experiments along these lines.

In 1831, on learning of the great progress that had been made by Joseph Henry in America and by Moll in the Netherlands in producing powerful electromagnets, Faraday decided to try with one of the new magnets essentially the same observations he had tried with weaker magnets, and without success, in 1825. Without specific reasons for acting in this order, on this occasion he closed the circuit, B, in which it was hoped a current might be induced, before he closed the magnet circuit, A, that was connected to the battery; and when the latter was closed, a momentary current was detected in circuit B. In all his previous experiments, it had happened that circuit A was closed before circuit B, and no current was detected.

Faraday quickly constructed a "theory" of the phenomenon he had produced: the battery current and its induced magnetic field created both an induced current and an "electrotonic state" in circuit B. The latter resisted the (steady) current that would otherwise have been induced in B, and permitted only a momentary transient. When the battery circuit, A, was opened, the pressure that had created the "electrotonic state" in B was

---

6. There is a large literature of Faraday studies, based on his publications, diaries, and correspondence. The Williams book and Magnini's thesis will provide some guidelines to this literature. See also Romo and Doncel (1994).

removed, and a transient in the other direction occurred. Although Faraday tried to find other evidences, physical and chemical, of the hypothesized "electrotonic state," he did not succeed; but he only gave up the hypothesis when he arrived at a more satisfactory (and operational) one some months later.

Within a month of this first induction of a surprising, if only transient, current, Faraday had extended his initial surprise to new observations in which he produced a continuous current by spinning a copper disk between the poles of a powerful magnet (an idea stimulated by his knowledge of Arago's experiment, mentioned earlier). In the course of his successive observations, he had to modify his theory of the phenomena he was producing, and by the end of the year, he had created his famous concept that current was produced when a wire cut the "lines of magnetic force" of a "magnetic field." The first of the quoted phrases had been occasionally used earlier by Faraday, on the basis of his observation of iron filings scattered on paper over a magnet, but these concepts essentially grew out of observations, and did not precede them. They gradually replaced the earlier "electrotonic state" hypothesis, for which he had found no converging evidence.

Did Faraday Perform an Experiment?

Let me raise next the question of whether what I have been calling Faraday's "observations," which led him to conceive his theory of magnetic fields, were or were not experiments in the modern sense. What was the experimental condition and what was the control in the crucial first experiment of 1831? One might suppose that the experimental condition was that in which the battery circuit, A, was closed and the control condition that in which it was open. But the effect (the momentary current in B) did not occur during the former condition, but only at the moment of closing (or opening) circuit A—a "condition" that, as far as we know, Faraday had not even conceived when he set up the experiment.

If we insist on calling this an experiment, then the phenomena observed created its design rather than the design creating the phenomena. Why not simply say that Faraday set up, during his ten years of intermittent curiosity, a whole series of situations in which he could observe various phenomena, and on the last occasion (through the accident of the order in which the two circuits were closed), he obtained an interesting effect—his curiosity was rewarded? Does this demean Faraday? Does it mean he was a mere brick counter?

Something even worse must be said about the crucial experiment. Faraday did have a galvanometer mounted in the second circuit, in order to measure any current that might be produced in it, but in the crucial event he provides no numerical reading of the galvanometer. The entry in his lab diary simply records: "…immediately a sensible effect on needle. It oscillated and settled at last in original position. On *breaking* connection of A side with Battery again a disturbance of the needle." He uses essentially the same statement in his published report of the event—the event that paved the way for the dynamo—and the referees of the Proceedings of the Royal Society did not blink.

If we see almost no numbers in this earth-shaking first paper, then of course we see no tests of statistical significance. Does that mean that scientists of that time were not aware that spurious effects might be produced by currents of air in the laboratory or dirty circuit connections or a thousand other unintentional irrelevancies? On the contrary, Faraday's diary is full of comments about precautions he took and possible causes of error in his interpretations. He simply felt no urge to quantify these disturbances. Instead, his reaction, and that of his contemporaries (and of most scientists today), was, when he obtained an effect he thought interesting, to consider how he could change the situation to magnify it. If you can magnify an effect enough it becomes significant—by any criterion. Before he communicated the first exciting finding, he worked for more than four months, successfully, to greatly magnify and clarify the original phenomena.

Hence, that first event was not all that he reported in his initial paper (which appeared in print, by the way, within about three months of submission). He reported the whole sequence of subsequent observations made over about four months. The success of his first act of curiosity suggested variants of the situation that gradually enabled him to magnify the effect in which he was interested and to transform a transient electrical impulse into a continuous current. Each change produced new phenomena and each phenomenon suggested new changes. The reports of these experiments occupy nearly fifty pages of the printed edition of his laboratory diary.

This does not sound like an inexorable logic of experimentation that begins with hypotheses, created in some unexplained way; leads to logically deduced predictions from these hypotheses; thence to controlled, and even critical, experiments; then to the torture chamber of significance tests; thence to acceptance of the hypotheses or oblivion. It sounds like a much more rambling (if highly exciting) walk through the woods in search of mushrooms, or rare flowers, or phenomena of any kind that excite surprise or one's sense of beauty or wonder or puzzlement—and motivate the search for more.

So perhaps we should say that Faraday did not perform experiments; he followed his curiosity. On the basis of very vague hypotheses (e.g., if electricity produces magnetism, then magnetism will produce electricity), he set up situations that he thought might reveal the conjectured phenomena, tried to build simple theoretical constructs that would explain (or, at worst, name) the phenomena actually observed, used these to suggest new situations that would produce new phenomena, etcetera. Perhaps this is the behavior that we should be studying when we study scientific discovery.

Perhaps this is also the behavior that we should be teaching when we try to preserve and enhance the curiosity of children. Perhaps this is the behavior we should be teaching our graduate students. Perhaps this is even the behavior we should be capturing when we rewrite our textbooks on experimental method.

Is Faraday Unique?

I should raise again, as I did with Fleming and Planck and Roentgen and Penzias and Wilson, the question of whether Faraday is unique. There is ample evidence that he is not. I should like to describe a final case providing an equally full record of the course of discovery: Hans Krebs' discovery of the reaction path for the synthesis of urea *in vivo*, a case examined in careful detail by the science historian, F. L. Holmes (1991), and simulated with some success by two distinct computer programs (Kulkarni & Simon, 1988; Grasshoff & May, 1995). Here again, the initial experimental or "observational" inquiry was conducted on the vaguest hypotheses (that the synthesis most likely begins with one or more of the twenty amino acids and/or ammonia as the source of the urea nitrogen). Again, the key observation was an "accident" that revealed that a particular amino acid, ornithine, was implicated in the reaction path, for when ornithine and ammonia were present (and only then), a large amount of urea was produced. This accident led, in turn, to the gradual discovery that ornithine served as a catalyst, not as the initial source of the nitrogen. The experiment that led to the key observation was therefore an accident, in that ornithine was selected for testing because it was a potential source of the nitrogen, whereas it served, instead, the catalytic function of releasing the nitrogen contained in the ammonia.

A similar example of curious attention to phenomena is provided by the acceptance of the theory of continental drift as a consequence of new evidence discovered, in the course of curiosity-driven search of previously unexplored ocean depths, of the upwelling of volcanic material in the mid-Atlantic Ridge and of reversals of the Earth's magnetic field in a Pacific trench outside Puget Sound. The explanation was provided after the observations were made, and the observations were made by scientists dubious of the continental drift hypothesis and not expecting to find phenomena that would test it, much less confirm it. I could go on with other examples, but perhaps these are enough to create a certain amount of curiosity about my hypothesis that will motivate others to pursue it.

Evidence from Psychometrics and Simulation

Before resting my case for curiosity and for the important role of hypothesis finding in sophisticated thinking, I may mention some evidence that is quite different from the historical cases presented so far, and which derives from psychometrics and computer models of scientific discovery. With respect to psychometrics, two tests that are widely used to measure "higher mental processes" are the Thurstone Letter Series Completion Test and the Raven matrices. Both of them present tasks of finding patterns in data: extrapolating letter series, like A B M C D M — — —, in the first case, or completing analogies among geometric forms, like b:d :: p:_, in the other. There is no inexorable logic to the process, nor any definitely "correct" answer; the task is wholly inductive. Success depends on marshaling the curiosity to seek for identities of symbols, symmetries, regular successions, and similar patterns (Simon & Kotovsky, 1963). Pattern finding is the name of the game.

In research on scientific discovery, the BACON program has been highly successful in finding, without the aid of prior hypotheses, scientific laws (that is, patterns) hidden in data. Presented with the data scientists used to discover some of the important laws of 18th and 19th century physics (Ohm's Law of current and resistance, Joseph Black's law of temperature equilibrium in liquids, Kepler's Third Law, and a number of others), BACON succeeded in finding the correct law, with a small amount of search and with no knowledge of any relevant theory (Langley, Simon, Bradshaw, & Zytkow, 1987).

Conclusion

The evidence is very strong, perhaps overwhelming, that curiosity leading to observation, and often to surprise, is a drive of central importance to the scientific enterprise. A major goal of science teaching in the schools must be to sustain and encourage the curiosity with which most children are endowed, and to help them learn how this curiosity can direct their attention to interesting, and sometimes surprising, phenomena in the situations they are observing, and these phenomena, in turn, to ideas about how the phenomena might be explained. These key methods for the discovery of hypotheses must not be too much diluted by preoccupation with formal "logical" and statistical methods of designing controlled experiments aimed at testing discoveries after they have been made. There can be no verification until a discovery has been achieved, no tests without fresh hypotheses.

Stating the matter in this way already suggests how we can approach our teaching of science. Using what we know, from the research of Berlyne and others, about curiosity, we create situations in which our students can look for patterns. We choose situations where patterns are neither too easy nor too hard for *these* children to find, and we provide the right level of hints, if they are required, to help them find them. We find suitable interesting situations in the world around us, in the laboratory, even in the library.

If we design the tasks correctly, our students are neither bored nor frustrated. They learn that the goal of science is to find pattern in the world, wherever they look, and they acquire some of the skills of finding it. We expose them to some of the pattern-seeking adventures in real science, perhaps largely through historical examples, so that they see that they are doing the same thing that scientists do, with the same prospects of finding new patterns.

As our students progress, we introduce them to situations where they may find apparent patterns that do not hold up under more extensive or careful scrutiny of the data, or that at least require revision and elaboration. In this way, they learn that science is concerned with verification as well as discovery, but that the former is always kept in the service of the latter. By maintaining the proper priority of discovery over verification, we nurture their curiosity and do not crush it.

All of this is a very obvious strategy. All good teachers know that students learn only when they are attending, that they attend only if their curiosity is aroused, that curiosity is sustained only if the right balance is maintained between simplicity and complexity. Nor is the application of these common ideas to science instruction in the schools a novelty. The literature reports significant numbers of successful science curricula at elementary and high school levels that are built on these principles. My purpose here has been, not to propose a radically new direction of science instruction, but to show that the best instruction models closely the actual practice of science. It places in the forefront the discovery of pattern in nature, for that is the central preoccupation of the scientist, the central task that she or he must learn to perform and to enjoy.

This is not to say that our main goal in elementary science instruction is to make scientists. Rather it is to help to make adult human beings who, whether scientists or not, will have some understanding of the nature of the scientific process and the ways in which, and the degree to which, it creates understanding of, and sometimes mastery over, the complex phenomena that we all encounter in the modern world, and which we must deal with effectively through all our lives.

In the first sole-authored monograph that I published, in 1943, with the formidable title of *Fiscal Aspects of Metropolitan Consolidation*, the dedication read:

> *To my mother and father,*
> *who taught me that curiosity is the beginning of all science.*

More than a half century later, that principle still seems to me to be sound.

References

Berlyne, D. E. (1960). *Conflict, arousal, and curiosity.* New York: McGraw-Hill.

Grant, D. A. (1962). Testing the null hypothesis and the strategy and tactics of investigation theoretical methods. *Psychological Review, 69,* 54-61.

Grasshoff, G., & May, M. (1995). Methodische Analyse Wissenschaftlichen Entdeckens. *Kognitionswissenschaft, 5,* 51-67.

Gregg, L.W., & Simon, H.A. (1967). Process models and stochastic theories of simple concept formation. *Journal of Mathematical Psychology, 4,* 246-276.

Holmes, F. L. (1991). *Hans Krebs.* Oxford, UK: Oxford University Press.

Kulkarni, D., & Simon, H. A. (1988). The process of scientific discovery: The strategy of experimentation. *Cognitive Science 12,* 139-175.

Langley, P., Simon, H.A., Bradshaw, G.L., & Zytkow, J.M. (1987). *Scientific discovery: Computational explorations of the creative processes.* Cambridge, MA: The MIT Press.

Magnani, G. (1996). Visual representation and scientific discovery: The historical case of the discovery of electromagnetic induction. M.S. Dissertation, Department of Philosophy, Carnegie Mellon University, Pittsburgh, PA.

Qin, Y., & Simon, H. A. (1990). Laboratory replication of scientific discovery processes. *Cognitive Science, 14,* 281-312.

Romo, J., & Doncel, M.G. (1994). Faraday's initial mistake concerning the direction of induced currents, and the manuscript of Series I of his Researches. *Archive for the History of the Exact Sciences, 47,* 291-335.

Simon, H.A. (1996). *Models of my life* (reissue). Cambridge, MA: The MIT Press.

Simon, H.A., & Kotovsky, K. (1963). Human acquisition of concepts for sequential patterns. *Psychological Review, 70,* 534-546.

Williams, L.P. (1965). *Michael Faraday.* New York, NY: Basic Books.

2

Explanatory Conversations and Young Children's Developing Scientific Literacy

Maureen A. Callanan
Jennifer L. Jipson
University of California, Santa Cruz

Child: *[age three years, 11 months] Where is my brain?*
Father: *Here. [Pointing to her head.]*
Child: *Why is there a bone in my head?*
Father: *Because your brain is an important organ and your skull protects it.*
Child: *Why is it important?*
Father: *Because it helps you think and become intelligent.*
Child: *If my brain gets hurt I won't be intelligent?*
Father: *No, if your brain gets hurt you won't be intelligent like you are now.*

When designing programs for science learning, it is important to consider that children's experiences with science begin years before they encounter science in the classroom. Children's developing understanding of science begins in their everyday activities and conversations about the natural and technical world. Children develop "scientific literacy" as they begin to learn the language of science (e.g., concepts such as "gravity" or "metamorphosis"), the kinds of causal explanations that are used in scientific theories (e.g., the day-night cycle results from the rotation of the earth), and the kinds of procedures that are used to answer scientific questions (e.g., testing hypotheses, controlling variables). Laboratory studies of children's scientific understanding have uncovered crucial information about the cognitive processes involved in learning scientific topics (Carey, 1985; Chi, Slotta, & de Leeuw, 1994; Rosengren, Gelman, Kalish, & McCormick,

21

1991; Vosniadou & Brewer, 1992) and scientific reasoning strategies (Schauble, 1990; Klahr, Fay, & Dunbar, 1993). These studies provide the kind of controlled manipulation of variables that allow precise inferences about how children reason on certain tasks. What these laboratory studies cannot provide, however, is an understanding of the natural contexts within which scientific literacy emerges. Because aspects of scientific thinking seem to vary depending on experience and cultural background (Kuhn, 1996; Samarapungavan, Vosniadou, & Brewer, 1996), there is reason to believe that socialization may play an important role in its development. In this chapter, we consider everyday conversations with family members as a context in which young children begin to develop scientific literacy well before they enter school.

In particular, we focus on a discourse style that we call "explanatory conversation." As illustrated in the example that begins this chapter, these conversations include "why" questions and/or causal explanations. Many researchers have noted the sense of wonder in young children's "why" questions about aspects of themselves and of the world around them (see Chukovsky, 1963; Piaget, 1974). As Simon suggests elsewhere in this volume, children's questions represent just the kind of curiosity that is fundamental to initiating the process of scientific discovery. Parents also offer causal explanations to their children for how things work and why things happen, sometimes in answer to children's questions and other times spontaneously (Callanan & Oakes, 1992; Crowley & Callanan, 1998; Callanan, Shrager, & Moore, 1995). These questions and explanations are components of the "explanatory conversations" that we consider in this chapter as social contexts within which children may be formulating and revising their understanding of scientific concepts.

Investigations of children's conversations about science differ from experimental work in important ways and provide a different sort of data that is equally crucial to a precise understanding of human scientific reasoning. If we understand how young children experience scientific concepts and explanations as they arise in their everyday lives, we will be better able to assess the relative importance of individual cognitive processes and social experiences in children's developing understanding of science. In this chapter we will discuss research exploring two main issues: (1) how children's curiosity leads them to ask causal questions about scientific phenomena; and (2) how parents, in everyday conversations, guide children in interpreting scientific information and model ways of thinking about scientific processes. Along the way we will address questions about cultural differences in the ways that children learn to think about science, and discuss ways to assess the impact of explanatory conversations for children's developing understanding of science. Finally, we will consider some theoretical ideas about how to integrate this type of research with the more traditional ways of studying scientific reasoning and ideas.

The study of explanatory conversations is motivated by several current approaches to the study of cognitive development, in particular, the "theory theory" approach, with its focus on the individual child, and the sociocultural approach, with its focus on the child in social context. The "theory theory" approach, presented by Gopnik and Meltzoff (1997) and Wellman and Gelman (1998) among others, focuses on how children's naive theories of important domains change across development. Gopnik (1998) argues that seeking causes and explanations is a basic and universal component of human cognition. Recent sociocultural views, in contrast, have emphasized the social context of cognitive development (Rogoff, 1990; Rogoff, 1998; Tharp & Gallimore, 1988) and called for a shift from the focus on *what* children know to a focus on *how* children come to know within activity settings of their everyday lives. We will argue that the social context of explanatory conversations may be an important arena for children's thinking about science. Within these conversations children and their conversational partners are creating the very settings in which children learn about the issues that are puzzling and interesting to them. We suggest that as a result of these conversations, children may develop and revise their "theories" about scientific (and social) domains. Parents' participation in these causal conversations may provide children with information not only about science content, but also about whether asking these sorts of questions is valued in the community, and about how to begin to find answers. Rogoff, Mistry, Göncü, and Mosier (1993) suggest that explanatory conversation is a discourse style that is not necessarily shared across cultural groups. In their study, for example, Salt Lake City mothers were about twice as likely to explain the workings of a toy to their toddlers as were Mayan Guatemalan mothers. It is clearly essential to explore what explanatory conversations look like across different families, communities, and cultures.

The study of causal conversations in everyday situations, then, is a window on children's thinking as well as on social contexts of learning. One challenge in this research, however, is that it is difficult to capture the moments of inquiry and discovery just as they are happening. Evidence suggests that explanatory conversations are likely to happen in the midst of everyday family activities, such as driving in the car or trying to cook a family dinner (Callanan & Oakes, 1992; Eisenberg, 1991), making it difficult for us as researchers to be in the right place at the right time. This also may mean that explanatory conversations are likely to occur outside of the settings where much of the research on parental input has taken place, largely experimenter-initiated tasks, free play, and book reading. For example, Gelman, Coley, Rosengren, Hartman, and Pappas (1998) found few explicit discussions about the underlying essence of category membership in their investigation of parents reading picture books with children. Gelman et al. found, instead, that parents used more subtle cues, such as gestures (e.g., linking two pictures with a sweep of the hand) and brief generic statements (e.g., "birds lay eggs") to guide children's understanding of shared category membership. It may be a mistake to conclude from this, however, that children's theory revision happens independently of explicit explanations from parents. Picture book reading is an activity with a particular structure and a typical discourse pattern that may not involve explanations. In the midst of other types of activities, however, children and parents may be likely to engage in explanatory conversations.

In this chapter, we will describe three types of studies using different methods to capture (for subsequent coding) the moments when natural explanatory conversations occur. First, we discuss studies using a diary method; second, we discuss a method of observing natural conversations in a museum setting; and third, we discuss a method in which we give parents and children a more focused task that is designed to elicit explanations about a particular domain. For each study we will describe the method and some of our findings regarding children's and parents' contributions to these causal conversations. Different methods emphasize different types of contributions. For example, the diary methodology we have used focuses on children's "why" questions as initiators of causal conversations. In contrast, when we explore parent-child conversations in a museum setting, the explanatory conversations we see seldom begin with a "why" question from a child. This underscores the importance of using multiple methods in order to obtain a more complete representation of the types of explanatory conversations in which parents and children are engaged. After discussing the three studies, we will consider a difficult open question regarding whether and how these conversations may have impact on children's cognitive development. We will explore both methodological and theoretical aspects of this question.

Children's "Why" Questions: A Diary Methodology

One method we have used to capture the moments when natural explanatory conversations occur is a diary technique, where we asked parents to keep track of their children's "why" questions and the conversations that followed. With this technique researchers are not present during the interaction to document all of the detail of the discussion, and we are limited by what parents remember or choose to report. But we do have the advantage with this technique of gathering data about the phenomena that puzzle and interest children enough for them to spontaneously seek explanations from the adults around them. Because children are creating these situations for themselves (rather than having them initiated by researchers, or even parents), they seem particularly revealing of children's own interests and motivations, and they may be particularly likely settings for conceptual change to occur.

The diary methodology also allows us to address two important methodological issues that arise in research with families from diverse backgrounds (for example, immigrant parents, parents with lower economic status, and parents with lower formal educational backgrounds). First, these parents may have a very different perception of the experimental setting than do middle-class, highly-educated white parents. We argue that looking at children's spontaneous "why" questions may be a method less prone to bias than other types of studies. Bringing a child and parent to a laboratory situation may be more uncomfortable for parents who are unaccustomed to university environments than asking them to keep track of their children's questions at home. Second, the diary reports can be collected through telephone interviews, eliminating potential difficulties related to parents' literacy.

The diary technique, by definition, focuses us on children's "why" questions. "Why" questions have been studied in great detail as a window on children's thinking. Piaget (1974) argued that "There is no better introduction to child logic than the study of spontaneous questions" (p. 171). In these diary studies, our focus goes beyond what children's questions tell us about what they are thinking, and also includes the conversational activities that emerge in response to these questions. Rather than focusing on what we can learn from children's questions, then, we focus on what children themselves might learn from having asked the question and engaged in the conversation that follows.

In previous work with mostly middle-income European-American families, we have found that preschool children ask "why" questions about complex scientific phenomena, and that parents'answers potentially offer guidance for children's theory development (Callanan & Oakes, 1992). (Children, of course, ask questions about non-scientific domains as well, but for the purposes of this chapter we consider only the questions about scientific domains.) Because some research suggests that scientific causal explanation may be more characteristic of middle-class western communities (e.g., Rogoff et al., 1993), it is important to explore conversations in families of different cultural backgrounds. Previous research has suggested that questions and causal conversations may not be as common for Latino children as for children from European-American backgrounds (Heath, 1986). Delgado-Gaitan (1994), for example, argues that Mexican immigrant children may be taught that questioning adults is a sign of disrespect. (However, Delgado-Gaitan also reports that in the Mexican-descent families she studied, there was a sharp division between school-related topics and other topics, with Mexican immigrant parents being very open to children's questions when they saw them as part of their schooling.) Other studies suggest that Latino parents with more formal schooling are more likely to use an "inquiry" style with their children (e.g., Laosa, 1980). This literature raises questions about whether the kinds of "why" questions documented in middle-class European-American families are likely to occur in Mexican-descent families, and whether they vary in frequency depending on parents' formal schooling. In an attempt to address these issues, we have been working with Mexican-descent families as well as European-descent families, and we have also looked at parents' educational background as a potentially important moderator variable.

In our diary study (Callanan, Pérez-Granados, Barajas, & Goldberg, 1999), forty-eight Mexican-descent families kept track of their children's "why" questions for two weeks. There were two groups, varying in years of mothers' formal schooling. The "higher education" parents had completed high school or completed at least some college (mean years of schooling=14). The "lower education" parents had not completed high school (mean years of schooling=seven). Willingness to participate in the study was high within both groups of parents. Parents from the "lower education" group were easier to identify because many of them lived in the same neighborhoods or attended Head Start programs. Families were also contacted through community groups, social service organizations, or word-of-mouth. Parents from the "higher education" group were contacted through a bilingual preschool, advertisements in a bilingual newspaper, and through word-of-mouth. Within each education group there were two age groups of children—a younger group (mean age=3;10, range 3;4 to 4;5) and an older group (mean age=5;2, range 4;7 to 5;11). For simplicity, we will refer to these two groups as three-year-olds and five-year-olds.

Considering our earlier data from Anglo families (Callanan & Oakes, 1992), as well as our data from higher and lower education Mexican-descent families (Callanan et al., 1999), we see a great deal of evidence that preschoolers' causal conversations exhibit curiosity and interest in making connections among things they experience in everyday life. Parents reported questions asked by their children on a wide range of topics, as shown by the examples in Table 1.[1]

Table 1. Examples of Diary Questions

MEXICAN-DESCENT FAMILIES; LOWER FORMAL EDUCATION
(from Callanan et al., 1999)

> *¿Cómo es que los pescados andan en el agua y no se ahogan?* (4;8)
> How come fish are in the water and they don't drown?

> *¿Por qué soñamos?* (5;8)
> Why do we dream?

> *¿Por qué el niño no tiene dientes?* (4;1)
> Why doesn't the baby have any teeth?

> *¿Por qué las nubes estan pintadas de negro?* (3;8)
> Why are the clouds painted black?

> *¿Por qué flotan los aviones y no se caen?* (5;3)
> Why do airplanes float and not fall?

> *¿Por qué llueve?* (3;11)
> Why does it rain?

---

1. All questions asked in Spanish are translated and presented in both languages. Questions asked in English are presented in English only.

MEXICAN-DESCENT FAMILIES; HIGHER FORMAL EDUCATION
(from Callanan et al., 1999)

¿Por qué la luna no más se mira cuando está oscuro? (4;1)
Why can you only see the moon when it's dark?

¿Por qué sale el sol? (3;4)
Why does the sun come out?

¿Por qué se nos pudren los dientes si comemos dulces? (5;8)
Why do our teeth rot if we eat candy?

¿Por qué la luna camina con nosotros? (4;11)
Why does the moon walk with us?

¿Por qué llueve? (3;7)
Why does it rain?

Why do people get cancer? (5;4)

ANGLO FAMILIES
(from Callanan & Oakes, 1992)

Where does rain come from? (3;5)

How those jets get up there? (3;0)

How does the fire go out in the candle? 4;2)

How do the firemen not get burned? (4;1)

How come the moon is big and orange now but other times it's little and white? (4;2)

Causal questions were not necessarily frequent events in all families (the average number of questions reported was approximately ten in a two-week period), but almost all of the children asked at least one of these questions. For this chapter, we consider a subset of children's questions that were identified as "science" questions, that is, potentially related to natural phenomena, biological processes, or physical mechanisms (as compared with "social" questions, which were related to human behavior, mental states, and cultural or religious traditions).[2]

---

2. The distinction between "science" and "social" topics is, admittedly, an arbitrary one. Children do not necessarily think of these as distinct domains, as suggested by Carey's (1985) work, for example. We would argue, however, that the distinction is a meaningful one for the parents who are answering the questions. The questions about the natural and physical world also touch on topics that are more relevant to the focus of this volume. Further, when all of the questions are included in the analyses, the patterns of results are virtually identical (see Callanan, et al., 1999).

Children's questions provide evidence of scientific thinking in several ways. They involve asking for causes of events, noticing patterns, and seeking definitions for new words. Sometimes children evidenced hypothesis-testing in their questions, as in the following example from Callanan and Oakes (1992):

Child: *Why does Daddy, James (big brother), and me have blue eyes and you have green eyes?*

Mother: *You got your eyes from Daddy. (Said goodnight, and left the room.)*

Child: *(Calling mother back into the room.) I like Pee-Wee Herman and I have blue eyes. Daddy likes Pee-Wee Herman and he has blue eyes. James likes Pee-Wee Herman and he has blue eyes. If you liked Pee-Wee Herman you could get blue eyes too.*

Mother: *It would take more than liking Pee Wee Herman to make my eyes blue. God gave me this color and it can't be changed.*

Child: *Could you try to like Pee Wee Herman so we could see if your eyes turn blue?*

This example is striking because, despite this four-year-old's naive understanding of the potential causes of eye color, she shows a strong grasp of scientific method and variable manipulation. Young children are not likely to carve up the world along the lines drawn by scientific disciplines. The questions reported in these diary studies do show, however, that preschool children show great interest in many phenomena that adults would categorize in the fields of biology, physics, and other scientific disciplines.

Interestingly, there is very little evidence of difference in the questions asked by children from different ethnic or educational backgrounds. Despite predictions drawn from the literature then, the Mexican-descent children in our studies asked virtually the same types of questions as the Anglo children, regardless of the educational background of their parents (Callanan et al., 1999).

Because our focus is on co-construction of scientific literacy, we are interested not only in the questions children ask but also in the parents' responses and the ensuing conversations. How might parents guide children's understanding and interest in science? While explanatory conversations may be relatively rare events, we have found that when children ask causal questions, parents are very likely to explain causal connections to them. Parents' responses were coded into four categories:

1. Causal, including causal mechanism, e.g., "He got hurt because he was hit by a car," as well as causal outcome, e.g., "You have a mouth so you can eat."

2. Religious, e.g., "God made it that way."

3. Unexplained essence, e.g., "That's how ducks are made."

4. Non-causal, e.g., in answer to "How are babies born?" the response was "The baby is in my stomach."

Parents of Anglo and Mexican descent, and parents from higher and lower educational backgrounds, were all likely to provide causal answers to their children's questions. For example, in the Callanan et al. (1999) study with Mexican-descent families, an average of 56% of parents' responses to children's questions were causal. The average percentage of the other response types were: religious responses, 2%; unexplained essences, 17%; non-causal responses, 25%. The pattern of responses was the same for the two groups of families, and similar to those found by Callanan and Oakes (1992) for Anglo families.

Although children asked questions about a wide variety of topics, we focus here on the conversations that emerged in our study of Mexican-descent children from questions about two particular sub-domains of biology: (1) human birth and (2) human anatomy. These two sets of questions contrast with one another in interesting ways. The birth questions represent cases where children are asking for a causal explanation for an event that is unclear to them (i.e., "Where do babies come from?"), whereas the anatomy questions seem somewhat more vague and open-ended (e.g., "Why do I have a mouth?"). At first glance, then, the birth questions may seem like better opportunities for parents to "teach" children something about biology. But, exploring these two sets of conversations revealed some unexpected patterns.

Birth Questions

Questions about how babies are born occurred in both education groups, but it is interesting that in the lower-education group they were asked roughly equally at both ages (33% of three-year-olds and 50% of five-year-olds), while in the higher-education group, they were somewhat more common in five-year-olds (50% of the children) than in three-year-olds (8% of the children). The parents' answers to questions about where babies come from varied in both groups. There were parents from both educational backgrounds who reported that they didn't know how to answer, or that they told children to "wait till they were older." There were also parents in both groups who gave children accurate information—as shown in the examples below, these answers usually did not provide very extensive information about conception or the birth process, but they provided some limited information about causal connections.

> Niño: *¿De dónde vienen los babies?*
> Madre: *Del estómago.*
> Child: Where do babies come from?
> Mother: From your stomach.

> Niña: *¿Por qué tanto tiempo tienen que estar ahí [en el vientre]?*
> Madre: *Pues dura nueve meses para que crezca el bebé.*
> Child: Why do babies have to be there so long?
> Mother: Well it takes nine months for the baby to grow.

> Niña: *¿Por qué cuando una persona está en la panza de la otra el bebé se hace una bolita?*
> Madre: *Porque los bebés son chiquitos y la panza de la mamá es aún más chiquita, y por eso se hace una bolita.*
> Child: Why is it that when a person is in another person's stomach they become a little ball?
> Mother: Because babies are little but their mom's stomach is even smaller and that is why a little ball forms.

These conversations about where babies come from may suggest that parents don't provide much guidance in children's theory building at this young age. However, parents' answers to this particular type of question may not be representative of their answers to other topics. Most parents reported that these were particularly difficult conversations, and that they were either uncomfortable about these questions or just confused about how much detail to provide.

Anatomy Questions

Parents' answers to children's questions about human anatomy provide an interesting contrast. These included questions about why people have certain body parts, (e.g., "Why do we have a mouth?") as well as questions about features of particular body parts (e.g., "Why do you have black hair and I have yellow hair?", "Why does her foot hurt?"). Anatomy questions were asked by 54% of the children with higher-education mothers, and 50% of the children with lower-education mothers (collapsed across age). The proportion of causal explanations given to these questions was not significantly different across maternal education levels, though there was a trend for more causal responses in higher-education families ($M=57\%$) than in lower-education families ($M=30\%$).

Despite the fact that the anatomy questions seem quite open-ended, it is striking that in answering these questions, parents often directed children toward biological content. As some of the following examples show, many of these questions seemed to arise from events that children were questioning in a more "social" way, but parents' answers seem to have been focusing them toward the biological domain, for example by introducing words like "grow" or by describing developmental processes.

Niño: *¿Por qué al bebé no le han salido los dientes y al otro niño sí?*
Madre: *Porque no todas las personas son iguales y porque a alguna gente les salen primero que a otros.*
Child: Why doesn't this baby have teeth and the other child does?
Mother: Because not everybody is the same and some people grow them sooner than others.

Niño: *¿Por qué a mi hermanito no le lavamos los dientes?*
Madre: *Hijo, el niño todavía no tiene dientes para lavarlos, está muy chiquito.*
Child: Why don't we brush my brother's teeth?
Mother: Honey, the baby still doesn't have any teeth to wash, he's too little.

Niño: *¿Por qué tenía pelo corto en esta foto?*
Madre: *Porque eras más pequeña, eras una bebita.*
Child: Why did I have short hair in this picture?
Mother: Because you were younger then, you were a baby.

Niño: *¿Por qué tenían los bebitos el pelo corto?*
Madre: *Cuando los niños nacen tienen poco pelo o nacen sin pelo.*
Child: Why do babies have short hair?
Mother: When children are born, they are born with little or no hair.

Child: How can I get boo-boos? [Breasts.] How come you have
              some and I don't?
Mother: You're still growing. As you eat better and get bigger, they
              will start growing.

While these questions focus on how things appear at the present time, it is interesting to see how often parents' answers draw children's attention to processes of growth, change, and birth. Using phrases such as "when you were a baby" or "you're still growing" may begin to help children delineate the domain of human growth and change. Because questions about body parts so often led to these sorts of discussions, children may learn from such conversations that body parts and appearance are connected to processes of growth and change. Although parents in this study did not report many complex scientific explanations, these anatomy conversations suggest that parents may guide children's theory development by helping them to pick out the relevant domain of explanation and by providing them with fragments of the puzzle of how to interpret different daily experiences in larger explanatory frameworks.

In sum, the diary studies provide us with some evidence that children's "why" questions invite parents to enter into explanatory conversations with them. These questions cover a wide range of topics that would fall into scientific disciplines. Parents and children from the different backgrounds studied so far seem to engage in very similar types of conversations. In addition to providing information about science, parents may also be guiding children's understanding of scientific domains by communicating to them evaluations about what kinds of things are important to know. In Goodnow's (1990) provocative discussion about the socialization of cognition, she suggests that researchers need to attend more to the subtle messages available to children regarding what are the appropriate and inappropriate things for them to know about. In responding to children's questions about birth, parents seemed to give the indirect message that children should not know much about this topic. When answering anatomy questions, however, parents seemed quite intent on having their children understand something about the process of human growth and development. There are likely to be differences across families and cultures regarding the kinds of knowledge that are valued. Interestingly, however, in the work we have done with European- and Mexican-descent families from different educational backgrounds, we have not seen differences in the value placed on the process of discovery. In informal interviews with parents as part of the diary studies, parents were virtually uniformly positive in their opinions about the value of children's questions and in their willingness to provide answers.

Parents' Explanations: Conversations in a Museum

The second technique we have used to "capture" explanatory conversations is to observe families in a setting that provides motivation for parents and children to talk about scientific events and their explanations. In collaboration with Kevin Crowley, we have observed and videotaped parent-child conversations in a hands-on children's museum, the San Jose Children's Discovery Museum. This collaborative work is described more fully in Crowley's chapter elsewhere in this volume. Our goals in videotaping conversations that occur while families interact with exhibits are to see how often explanations occur as well as to gain a better understanding of the dynamics of these conversations. While we don't expect every interaction in this setting to be focused on scientific explanations, the design of the environment may give us a better chance of capturing explanatory conversations here than in other settings. In our discussion we will refer to two data sets: one sample of 269 parent-child interactions across a variety of different museum exhibits, and a separate sample of 50 interactions at one particular exhibit, the "Take Another Look at Change" exhibit.

In the larger data set, the proportion of interactions in which parents gave an explanation was 25.6 % overall. Three different types of explanations were identified: scientific principles, causal connections, and connections to prior experience. In the museum setting, unlike in the diary reports, we found that parents' explanations most often emerged in the absence of "why" questions from children. Consistent with the diary findings, though, parents' explanations seldom gave full accounts of scientific principles. Parents explained abstract scientific principles, for example introducing concepts like gravity, in only 12% of the explanations they gave. Instead, most explanations were identified as causal connections, which involved giving specific information about causes of a particular event (54% of the explanations given). The following example was recorded at a zoetrope exhibit: "Each one of those pictures is a little different pose on the horse, and it makes it look like it is galloping." As in the diary data, then, there seems to be a focus on helping the child to understand the particular event as it is happening rather than a focus on more abstract reasoning.

In the third explanation type, connections to prior experience, parents connected the present experience to the child's previous experiences. This happened in 25% of the explanations in the larger museum sample. An example recorded at a heartbeat exhibit was: "Remember the stethoscope at the doctor's? We can listen to your heart beat." This strategy of connecting an explanation to a child's previous experiences was also apparent in many of the parents' responses in the diary study. This strategy may be a particularly effective way to engage children in science topics. In Tharp's (1997) discussion of five standards for culturally relevant pedagogy, he proposes *contextualization* as one of the standards, and argues that contextualizing new information in children's experience is a necessary component of effective teaching. Consistent with the work of Moll and Gonzalez (1994), Tharp also argues that contextualization may be particularly important when teaching children from culturally diverse backgrounds for whom middle-class schooling practices may be unfamiliar. Our data suggest that parents naturally use this effective strategy of contextualizing new information in children's prior experiences.

Beyond the explanations that have been discussed, another more subtle way that parents may guide children's developing scientific literacy is by helping children identify the domains of thought that are relevant to the events or activities in which they are engaged. Experience does not come parsed into domains. Within the context of the Children's Discovery Museum, parents have opportunities to help children interpret their experiences by guiding their attention to relevant features of novel and complex situations. In one exhibit (Figure 1), children and parents observe time-lapse photography of objects changing (e.g., plants growing, metal rusting, candles melting). As with most museum exhibits, and everyday life in general, the Take Another Look at Change exhibit affords multiple possible topics for engagement and conversation. In particular, parents can focus on the content of what is changing in the videos, or they can focus on the technology behind the production of the time-lapse videos. What parents choose to talk about is likely to influence children's focus of attention and their interpretation of what they are seeing. In other words, parents may be guiding children in terms of how to "parse" their experience at the exhibit.

Figure 1. The "Take Another Look at Change" Exhibit. **a)** This exhibit offers multiple possibilities for exploration and conversation. **b)** The video content component of the exhibit consists of several videotaped events depicting common objects undergoing changes-of-state (e.g., plants growing, metal rusting, bananas rotting). **c)** The video technology component consists of the use of time-lapse photography to capture these change-of-state events, allowing museum visitors to observe often lengthy processes in just a few seconds.

Our analysis of 50 interactions at this exhibit supports the idea that parents play a role in parsing and interpreting events for their children. Of the parents we observed, 56% chose to focus exclusively on the content of the videos, discussing what was happening to particular objects over time (e.g., "The plant is dying; that's what happens when we don't water our plants.") and treating the time-lapse photography as transparent. Another 32% of the parents discussed both the change-of-state events and the technological process by which these events were captured (e.g., "This is time-lapse photography, where they put a camera on something for a really long time and then they sped it up really fast."), and 12% of the parents did not engage in conversation while at this exhibit. None of the parents chose to focus on the time-lapse mechanism without mention of the change-of-state events. It is, perhaps, not surprising that parents found the content of the videos more salient than the medium that was used to present that content. The fact that some parents focused children on the time-lapse technology does illustrate, however, that events can be interpreted in multiple ways. Parents talk to children in ways that may help children to understand the abstract domains that are relevant to the activities in which they are engaged.

When we investigated the ways that parents talked about the change-of-state events, we again found considerable variability in the talk. Twenty percent of the parents merely labeled the objects that were changing. More commonly, parents used descriptive or explanatory language in addition to labels for the objects. Thirty-six percent of the parents used change-of-state verbs, such as "grow" or "rust," to describe the events. This level of information not only provides children with an appropriate verb for observed changes, but may also help children to distinguish among events that are perceptually similar but result from different causes (e.g., a melting candle vs. a withering plant). Thirty-two percent gave even more explicit information about causal mechanisms for the changes that were occurring in the videotapes. For example, one parent said, "The beans died because they didn't get enough water." These parents provided the most detailed differentiation of causes for different events. This causal information could be very informative to children as they are learning about physical vs. biological changes.

Most museum exhibits, like most events in everyday life, do not fall neatly into one particular scientific domain. Parents' explanations often specify the relevant domain and help children to focus on what is important within the domain. We are still at the beginning of the process of trying to understand how children may be learning from parents' explanations. Some conversations suggest that children may be learning new ideas from their parents, as in the example below:

Parent: *They stopped watering it. See what happened next, because there is no water.*
Child: *They all died?*
Parent: *Because they're not gonna get any water.*
Child: *Poor things!*

Whether this child is really learning something new cannot be determined with certainty in such cases, however, and experimental studies are needed to address these questions more directly. Other conversations suggest that certain explanations may not increase children's understanding of the phenomenon, as in the example below:

> Parent: *See that little clock in there? They're fast forwarding the growth of the potatoes.*
> Child: *So they can make them grow faster?*

This child's confusion was not cleared up in the conversation that followed. At times, parents may provide misleading or incorrect information to children.

This close inspection of parent-child interactions at a single exhibit not only demonstrates what parents do to structure the learning process, but also reveals ways that parents and children together co-construct understandings (or misunderstandings) within their interactions.

Parent-Child Discussions of Growth: Focused Parent-Child Tasks

The third technique we have used involves collecting data in more focused settings where parents and children are asked to engage in an activity where causal conversations are likely to take place. We will focus on one study in particular, in which we constructed a book that asked "What happened to the ...?" and showed various three-picture sequences of change-of-state events such as a mushroom growing, the moon changing shape, and a balloon deflating (Jipson & Callanan, 1999). The majority of the families in this study were from middle-income, European-American backgrounds. We expected parents and children to talk about causal explanations for the changes pictured in the book.

In this focused task, we found parents using many of the same strategies as in the museum study. Parents explained specific causal mechanisms rather than abstract scientific principles. Parents often referred to children's prior experience with similar events. And, parents often seemed to help children to identify the domain that is relevant to the events under discussion.

In an example from Jipson and Callanan (1999), a parent was helping her child explain changes of state, such as pictures of the moon in different phases:

> Parent: *Yeah, it's a full moon...Do you know why it's getting bigger?*

Child:	*Because it's growing.*
Parent:	*It's growing? Does this grow like mushrooms grow? [refer-ring to a picture seen earlier in the book]*
Child:	*Uh, yeah.*
Parent:	*It grows in the dirt? I've never seen the moon in the dirt!*
Child:	*No.*
Parent:	*No, the moon is up in the sky!*
Child:	*Yeah. Why did they grow up?*
Parent:	*You know why it looks like it's growing?*
Child:	*Um hm.*
Parent:	*You have asked me about this before. The earth is blocking it. It's a shadow so it gets bigger and bigger and bigger.*
Child:	*Where's the shadow?*
Parent:	*You can't see it…*

This parent seemed somewhat surprised that her child appeared to think the moon actually grows. In her conversation she seems to be trying to find out whether her child really misunderstands. In doing so, this mother contrasts the apparent growth of the moon with the more familiar event of mushrooms growing. As this conversation unfolds, the parent not only provides information about the process of growth (as related to dirt), but also offers an alternative explanation of the phases of the moon as related to the physical movement of astronomical objects. Despite the fact that this parent is technically wrong about the reason for the moon's phases (a topic that is often seriously misunderstood by many adults), she does give the child information about the correct general domain for this event.[3] Thus, as they negotiate meaning in a particular explanation, parents may guide children toward the "correct" domain by suggesting domain-appropriate forms of explanation. Further, as suggested by the above example, parents again connected the current discussion to the child's earlier experiences that were relevant.

In another example, Jipson and Callanan (1999) observed one mother attempt to explain crystal formation by saying, "It's kind of a rock that kinda grows. It doesn't really grow because it's not alive, but it grows

---

3. As this parent suggests, the way the Moon looks in the sky is related to its position in relation to the Earth and the Sun. However, the phases of the moon are not caused by the Earth's shadow. Instead, as the Moon moves in its orbit around the Earth, our view of the side illuminated by the Sun changes. For example, when the Moon is between the Earth and the Sun, we can't see it because the light from the sun is hitting the side of the Moon away from the Earth (New Moon).

because it adds more and more of the rock to it." In this example, the mother not only provides information about the ontology of crystals, but also suggests something about the domain-specificity of the process of growth. Interactions of this kind may help children negotiate their understandings of objects and events in the world, and consequently, can be considered to be a context for the construction and revision of intuitive theories.

Parents' conversations with children about scientific topics may vary in important ways depending on the activity setting in which the conversation takes place. This variability is very apparent in a comparison of the discussions of growth we observed in the museum vs. in the focused book-reading task. While 32% of the parents at the museum exhibit used at least one explanation, 98% of the book reading interactions involved at least one explanation. The explanations in the book reading task also tended to be longer and more involved. There are obvious reasons why parents focused more on explanations in the book-reading task, most notably because the book activity was defined by the researchers and the parents' goal was to participate in the research. In the museum, although they knew they were being videotaped, parents and children were negotiating their own goals and structuring multiple simultaneous activities. We see both activity settings as valid representations of some conversations that children engage in with parents. The book-reading conversations seem similar to some of the diary conversations, and may be representative of reflective situations in which children and parents focus on a particular topic for an extended time.

Of course, not all book-reading tasks are likely to elicit explanations, as mentioned in the earlier discussion of the work of Gelman et al., (1998). Our book clearly presented several phases in the change-of-state of an object and explicitly asked parents and children to discuss that change by asking "What happened to the...?" Gelman and her colleagues used a picture book that depicted objects varying in similarity, and did not provide text that would direct the conversation. Even within the genre of book reading, then, different kinds of conversational activity settings are encouraged depending on the content and goals of the book. In any case, taken together, the findings emphasize the importance of multiple methods in order to get a complete picture of the explanatory talk in which children and parents engage.

The Impact of Causal Conversations on Children's Thinking

Overall, the studies described show that while parents rarely articulate complex scientific principles, they are providing other sorts of information that may well contribute to children's developing scientific literacy. In all three types of studies, parents seem to be providing fragments of explanatory information about particular events as children experience them. These fragments could potentially be used by children to construct causal theories. What remains open, however, is the more intractable question of whether these conversations are in fact influencing children's (and perhaps parents') understanding of scientific phenomena.

There are several difficulties to consider when attempting to address this question. First, it is not obvious what one would predict in terms of measurable impact of a particular explanatory conversation. We would not necessarily expect that a simple pretest-posttest design would be an appropriate test, given the complexity of human cognition. Instead, sociocultural theory would lead us to think about children's science understanding as emerging and being revised over many such interactions. Second, it is difficult for correlational findings to be convincing evidence of impact. We can look at individual differences in parents' styles of explanation and correlations with children's understanding of scientific topics. Even then, however, the direction of effect cannot be disambiguated. Parents who explain often may influence children's understanding, or children who understand scientific concepts may encourage their parents to explain. One possible solution to these problems is to investigate parent-child conversations on a particular topic over a period of time in a microgenetic approach, looking at more detailed and specific connections between parents' explanations and children's understanding.

One might ask how likely it is that the kinds of strategies we have uncovered will be found to have an impact on children's science understanding. As we have said, these are often "fragments" rather than full-fledged scientific explanations. Recent studies of scientific thinking, however, remind us that adults, and even adult scientists, do not think in terms of flawless scientific theories (Kuhn, 1996; Dunbar, 1997; Tversky & Kahneman, 1990). These explanatory fragments could, in fact, be more helpful to children than more complete causal explanations. As mentioned earlier, Gelman, et al. (1998) report in their monograph that parents rarely discussed the nonobvious features that differentiate different types of objects (such as animals vs. machines). In his commentary on that same monograph, Keil (1998) argues that the indirect ways that parents in the Gelman et al. study discuss categories of objects may be much more appropriate to their children's level of understanding. Keil discusses the problem of "explanatory satiation," and argues that:

> Rather than try to load the child down with what would ultimately be an impossible burden of detail, the parent is instead showing the child how to approach various domains and allowing the child to proceed to discover the details at her own pace. (Keil, 1998, p. 152)

It remains to be seen what level of detail is most appropriate in explanatory conversations with children. Our findings seem to be parallel to those of Gelman and her colleagues, though, in that parents are providing systematic yet incomplete information about complex links among objects and events experienced by children.

Aside from the issue of the relative completeness of parents' explanations to children is the issue that parents sometimes even provide children with information that is incorrect or misleading. More research is needed to assess the potentially negative, as well as positive, effects of explanatory conversations. If our focus is on children's scientific literacy, rather than their knowledge of particular causal mechanisms, however, then the accuracy of particular comments may be less important than a discourse style that helps children figure out how to ask and find answers to questions. Even incorrect explanations may help children to explore their own ideas about a topic and to further their understanding in the long run.

Designing for Science

What can be learned from this research regarding the design of science education? Despite the open questions that remain, these findings are potentially relevant to early childhood educators, parents of young children, and designers of informal science education programs (e.g., museums).

There is a great deal of agreement among early childhood educators that academic skill-based instruction is not developmentally appropriate for young children (Elkind, 1986; Hirsh-Pasek, Hyson, & Rescorla, 1990). Instead, many educators prefer "developmentally appropriate practice" for preschool-aged children, which is defined by the National Association for the Education of Young Children (Bredekamp, 1987; Hart, Burts, & Charlesworth, 1997) as child-centered, exploratory, and contextualized. Our data support this approach to early education. In our studies, children's questions reveal their natural curiosity about the world (see also Gallas, 1995). Developmentally appropriate science instruction capitalizes on young children's natural curiosity; rather than focusing on the "right" answers, teachers engage children in the process of doing science. Interestingly, many of the authors of other chapters in this volume discuss models of science education that have much in common with this preschool model. While, traditionally, classroom science activities often convey a sense of science as objective and authoritative (Lemke, 1990), recent work on innovative science instruction shows that even adolescents' science learning should perhaps be more focused on students' spontaneous questions and process of discovery (e.g., Warren & Rosebery, 1996). Perhaps the design of science education programs, even for older children, should find better ways to make links with children's curiosity as a starting point for encouraging engagement with science topics.

Our findings speak to parents as well as teachers, suggesting that they can support children's science learning without intentionally focusing on instruction. Just by attending to children's spontaneous questions, and by commenting on their actions, parents may be making powerful contributions to their child's emerging scientific literacy. Consistent with Gelman et al. (1998), we do not very often see parents giving complex scientific explanations. But, consistent with the guidelines of developmentally appropriate practice and with Keil's (1998) arguments mentioned above, we would agree that school-like tutoring is not the best way to support young children's engagement in scientific thinking. Across groups of parents with very different educational and cultural backgrounds, we have generally seen a tendency for parents to respond to their children's curiosity in ways that are suggested by child development experts. In particular, they contextualize new concepts and experiences by relating them to familiar topics, and they follow their children's lead by taking their questions as an invitation to reflect on and discuss complex phenomena.

Finally, our data may also have some relevance for the design of informal science education programs. In the field of museum learning, constructivist theory has been very influential over the past several decades, leading to many hands-on interactive exhibits and to a philosophy that children are best left to explore exhibits on their own terms. Our findings support a slightly different approach to museum design, which is gaining popularity, and which is based on sociocultural theories such as Vygotsky's (1978; see also Schauble, Leinhardt, & Martin, 1998). In our work, parents' conversations with children about scientific topics seem to structure and guide children's interactions with exhibits in fruitful ways, suggesting that exhibits should be designed to increase the potential for interaction. As Crowley and Callanan (1998) argued, designing exhibits so that they foster parent-child interaction may increase the potential learning experiences for children in exhibits. Supporting parent-child involvement can be achieved in many ways. Even such mundane issues as whether there is a place for parents to sit near the exhibit can have impact on the likelihood that meaningful interactions will take place. Precise decisions about how to improve the quality of interactions await further research and debate. For example, many complex decisions go into the design of signs to accompany exhibits. Parents may need to know something about how an exhibit works before they are able to give clear explanations to children. Signs that are too didactic, however, may lead to stilted conversations. Solutions to such problems will vary depending on the philosophy of the design team and the goals of the particular exhibit.

Conclusions

Across several different projects, we are beginning to formulate a model of how explanatory conversations may impact children's learning. Parents are not often guiding children directly toward reflective, abstract understandings of science. However, by focusing on particular events of interest in the moment, they may be giving children fragments of information that allow them to build up coherent understanding of particular events. What is strikingly similar across the conversations we have studied is that parents' explanations are likely to be focused on the particular event on which children are focused. Rather than trying to teach children an abstract principle, parents are likely to be providing a narrative of a particular experience. In line with Keil's (1998) argument about explanatory satiation, we would argue that this focus on specificity may be the appropriate level of focus for preschool children. The child may be able to gradually accumulate these understandings to develop a broader understanding of a phenomenon.

In addition to guiding children's understanding of specific causal mechanisms, parents are also modeling for children various aspects of the process of discovery in science: showing them how to formulate questions, find answers, and test predictions. Further, parents' explanations demonstrate for children that there is value in knowing about causes for events.

Exploring these conversations is relevant to research and theory in several different areas in cognitive development and education. The "theory theory" approach in cognitive development focuses on children as little scientists, developing and revising theories of the world around them (Gopnik & Meltzoff, 1997; Wellman & Gelman, 1998). Studying children's conversations about science might help us to understand how children encounter evidence that leads them to change their theories over time. These conversations are also relevant to research in scientific reasoning. Although much of the research on science reasoning focuses on older children (e.g., Schauble, 1996), studying preschool children's thinking can tell us about the early development of such skills as hypothesis-testing and use of evidence. A third relevant research area is recent work on science education. As mentioned earlier, recent work in science instruction emphasizes the importance of social construction of scientific knowledge. Warren and Rosebery's (1996) work with Haitian immigrant students, for example, focuses on argumentation in the activity of doing science and shows that children's science learning can be more effective when taught in the context of collaboration (see also Brown, 1997; Greeno, 1998). By exploring the social contexts within which preschool children engage scientific ideas, we may be able to learn more about ways that this process of discovery can be extended and encouraged. Investigating whether and how these conversations vary across cultures will be very important in future research.

The results of our studies cannot, in themselves, tell us whether children learn new theories through conversation. A description of parents' explanations to children, however, is a starting place from which we can begin to consider the possibility that theory development is not purely an internal matter. There are hints in these data about the possible ways that the social context and the cultural background of families create different environments within which children are learning about theory-relevant phenomena. The challenging next step is to find ways to assess the importance of these conversations for children's developing scientific literacy.

Acknowledgements

This research was supported by the National Institute of Child Health and Human Development (HD26228) and by the University of California, Santa Cruz. The work was also supported in part under the Education Research and Development Program, PR/Award No. R306A60001, the Center for Research on Education, Diversity & Excellence (CREDE), as administered by the Office of Educational Research and Improvement (OERI), National Institute on the Education of At-Risk Students (NIEARS), U.S. Department of Education (USDOE). The contents, findings and opinions expressed here are those of the authors and do not necessarily represent the positions or policies of OERI, NIEARS, or the USDOE. We thank the staff of the San Jose Children's Discovery Museum and the families who have participated in these studies. Thanks are also due to Margarita Azmitia and the editors of the volume for helpful comments on a previous draft.

References

Bredekamp, S. (1987). *Developmentally appropriate practice in early childhood programs serving children from birth though age 8.* Washington, DC: National Association for the Education of Young Children.

Brown, A. L. (1997). Transforming schools into communities of thinking and learning about serious matters. *American Psychologist, 52,* 399-413.

Callanan, M. A., & Oakes, L. M. (1992). Preschoolers' questions and parents' explanations: Causal thinking in everyday activity. *Cognitive Development, 7,* 213-233.

Callanan, M. A., Pérez-Granados, D., Barajas, N., & Goldberg, J. (1999). "Why" questions in Mexican-descent children's conversations with parents. Manuscript under review.

Callanan, M. A., & Shrager, J., & Moore, J. (1995). Parent-child collaborative explanations: Methods of identification and analysis. *The Journal of the Learning Sciences, 4,* 105-129.

Carey, S. (1985). *Conceptual change in childhood.* Cambridge, MA: MIT Press.

Chi, M. T. H., Slotta, J. D., de Leeuw, N. (1994). From things to processes: A theory of conceptual change for learning science concepts. *Learning & Instruction, 4,* 27-43.

Chukovsky, K. (1963). *From two to five.* Berkeley, CA: University of California Press.

Crowley, K., & Callanan, M. A. (1998). Describing and supporting collaborative scientific thinking in parent-child interactions. *Journal of Museum Education* (Special issue on Understanding the Museum Experience: Theory and Practice, Scott Paris, Ed.), 23, 12-17.

Delgado-Gaitan, C. (1994). Socializing young children in Mexican-American families: An intergenerational perspective. In P. Greenfield & R. Cocking (Eds.), *Cross-cultural roots of minority child development* (pp. 55-86). Hillsdale, NJ: Lawrence Erlbaum Associates.

Dunbar, K. (1997). How scientists think: On-line creativity and conceptual change in science. In T. Ward, & S. Smith (Eds.), *Creative thought: An investigation of conceptual structures and processes* (pp. 461-493). Washington, DC: American Psychological Association.

Eisenberg, A. (1991). *Task effects on social class and ethnic variation in mother-child communication.* Paper presented at the Biennial Meeting of Society for Research in Child Development, Seattle, WA.

Elkind, D. (1986). Formal education and early childhood education: An essential difference. *Phi Delta Kappan, 67,* 631-636.

Gallas, K. (1995). *Talking their way into science: hearing children's questions and theories, responding with curricula.* NY: Teachers College Press.

Gelman, S., Coley, J., Rosengren, K., Hartman, E., & Pappas, A. (1998). Beyond labeling: The role of maternal input in the acquisition of richly structured categories. *Monographs of the Society for Research in Child Development.* Serial no. 253.

Goodnow, J. (1990). The socialization of cognition: What's involved? In J. W. Stigler, & R. A. Shweder, (Eds.)., *Cultural psychology: Essays on comparative human development* (pp. 259-286). New York: Cambridge University Press.

Gopnik, A. (1998). Explanation as orgasm. *Minds and Machines, 8,* 101-118.

Gopnik, A., & Meltzoff, A. (1997). *Words, thoughts, and theories.* MIT Press; Cambridge, MA.

Greeno, J. G. (1998). Middle school mathematics through applications. Project Group, USA. The situativity of knowing, learning, and research. *American Psychologist, 53,* 5-26.

Hart, C., Burts, D., & Charlesworth, R. (1997). *Integrated Curriculum and Developmentally Appropriate Practice: Birth to Age Eight.* Albany, NY: State University of New York Press.

Heath, S.B. (1986). Sociocultural contexts of language development. In Bilingual Educations Office (Ed.), *Beyond Language: Social and cultural factors in schooling language minority students,* (pp. 73-142). Los Angeles: Evaluation, Dissemination and Assessment Center.

Hirsh-Pasek, K., Hyson, M., & Rescorla, L. (1990). Academic environments in preschool: Do they pressure or challenge young children? *Early Education and Development, 1,* 401-423.

Jipson, J., & Callanan, M. A. (1999). Do crystals grow? Children's understanding of biological and physical change-of-state events. Manuscript under review.

Keil, F. C. (1998). Words, moms, and things: Language as a road map to reality. Commentary in Gelman, S., Coley, J., Rosengren, K., Hartman, E., & Pappas, A. (1998). Beyond labeling: The role of maternal input in the acquisition of richly structured categories. *Monographs of the Society for Research in Child Development.* Serial no. 253.

Klahr, D., Fay, A. L., Dunbar, K. (1993). Heuristics for scientific experimentation: A developmental study. *Cognitive Psychology, 25,* 111-146.

Kuhn, D. (1996). Is good thinking scientific thinking? In D. R. Olson & N. Torrance, (Eds.), *Modes of thought: Explorations in culture and cognition* (pp. 261-281). NY: Cambridge University Press.

Laosa, L. (1980). Maternal teaching strategies in Chicano and Anglo-American families: The influence of culture and education on maternal behavior. *Child Development*, 51, 759-765.

Lemke, J. L. (1990). *Talking Science: Language, Learning, and Values.* Norwood, NJ: Ablex Publishing Co.

Moll, L. C., & Gonzalez, N. (1994). Lessons from research with language-minority children. *Journal of Reading Behavior*, 26, 439-456

Piaget, J. (1974). *The language and thought of the child.* NY: Meridian.

Rogoff, B. (1990). *Apprenticeship in thinking.* NY: Oxford University Press.

Rogoff, B. (1998). Cognition as a collaborative process. In D. Kuhn & R. Siegler (Volume editors) *Cognition, Perception, and Language, Volume 2* (pp. 679-744), in W. Damon (Ed.), *Handbook of Child Psychology, Fifth edition.* NY: Wiley.

Rogoff, B., Mistry, J., Göncü, A. & Mosier, C. (1993). Guided participation in cultural activity by toddlers and caregivers. *Monographs of the Society for Research in Child Development, serial no. 236.*

Rosengren, K., Gelman, S., Kalish, C., & McCormick, M.(1991). As time goes by: Children's early understanding of growth in animals. *Child Development, 62,* 1302-1320.

Samarapungavan, A., Vosniadou, S., & Brewer, W. F. (1996). Mental models of the earth, sun, and moon: Indian children's cosmologies. *Cognitive Development,* 11, 491-521.

Schauble, L. (1996). The development of scientific reasoning in knowledge-rich contexts. *Developmental Psychology, 32,* 102-119.

Schauble, L. (1990). Belief revision in children: The role of prior knowledge and strategies for generating evidence. *Journal of Experimental Child Psychology, 49,* 31-57.

Schauble, L., Leinhardt, G., & Martin, L. (1998). A framework for organizing a cumulative research agenda in informal learning contexts. *Journal of Museum Education* (Special issue on Understanding the Visitor Experience: Theory and Practice, Scott Paris, Ed.), 22, 3-8.

Tharp, R. (1997). *From At-Risk to Excellence: Research, Theory, and Principles for Practice.* Center for Research on Education, Diversity and Excellence, Santa Cruz, CA.

Tharp, R., & Gallimore, R. (1988). *Rousing minds to life: Teaching, learning, and schooling in social context.* Cambridge: Cambridge University Press.

Tversky, A., & Kahneman, D. (1990). Judgment under uncertainty: Heuristics and biases. In P. K. Moser (Ed.), *Rationality in action: Contemporary approaches.* NY: Cambridge University Press.

Vosniadou, S., & Brewer, W. (1992). Mental models of the earth: A study of conceptual change in childhood. *Cognitive Psychology, 24,* 535-585.

Vygotsky, L. S. (1978). *Mind in society: The development of higher psychological processes.* Cambridge, MA: Harvard University Press.

Warren, B., & Rosebery, A. (1996). "This question is just too, too easy": Students' perspectives on accountability in science. In L. Schauble & R. Glaser (Eds.), *Innovations in learning: New environments for education*. Mahwah, NJ: Lawrence Erlbaum Associates.

Wellman, H. M., & Gelman, S. A. (1998). Knowledge acquisition in foundational domains. In D. Kuhn & R. Siegler (Volume editors) *Cognition, perception, and language, Volume 2*, in W. Damon (Ed.), *Handbook of child psychology*, 5th edition. New York: Wiley.

3

The Rhythms of Scientific Thinking: A Study of Collaboration in an Earthquake Microworld

Margarita Azmitia
University of California, Santa Cruz

Kevin Crowley
University of Pittsburgh

In this chapter we explore how people build new theories in the context of collaborative scientific thinking. As illustrated by many of the chapters in this volume, our default notion of "scientific thinking" has changed from that of the lone scientist or student toiling away on a magnum opus or in the laboratory, to that of people working as part of collaborative groups who negotiate goals for the task, co-construct knowledge, and benefit from the diverse prior knowledge that each collaborator brings to the table. In some ways, conceptualizing scientific thinking as fundamentally collaborative is not new. There are famous stories of how collaboration has played an important role in many scientific breakthroughs, from the discovery of the structure of DNA (Watson, 1968) to pioneering work in Artificial Intelligence (Simon, 1996). Furthermore, the goal of creating learning environments that support rich collaboration has also been at the heart of many innovations in science education.

Yet, psychologists who study scientific thinking from a cognitive perspective have only recently begun asking questions about how scientific understanding occurs within collaborative groups. One research direction has involved demonstrating that group work leads to greater conceptual change than individual activity. For example, Okada and Simon (1997) showed that pairs of undergraduate science majors were more successful than singletons in discovering scientific laws governing a computer microworld, while studies with children and adolescents suggest that working with a peer is more likely to promote mastery of a variety of scientific concepts than working alone (Kuhn & Phelps, 1979; 1982; Teasley, 1995). A second research direction has involved in-depth analyses of the group process to try to identify factors that facilitate or undermine shared scientific thinking. Coleman (1998), for example, investigated how expertise, gender, and social status influenced collaboration and learning, Forman and Larreamendy-Joerns (1995) assessed how the ongoing negotiation of problem solving goals related to successful and unsuccessful collaborations, and Azmitia and Montgomery (1993), Bianchini (1997), Dunbar (1997), and Suzuki (1994) studied the relation between role negotiation (i.e., each collaborator's responsibilities), features of dialogues (e.g., conflict and consensus, explanation, elaboration, synthesis, and analogy), and the processes and outcomes of collaborations.

In this chapter, we build on this research to describe the growth of scientific understanding as reflecting the rhythm of relatively individual and social moments of thought. The collaborative cognition of conversations and the individual insights from solitary reflection are both common characteristics that contribute to discovery and theory building in science. By referring to *relatively individual moments of thought,* we want to underscore the fact that scientists are never truly alone. They may be working by themselves in their laboratories, homes, or offices, but their thoughts are contextualized by those of others and by cultural tools and artifacts, such as the cannons of the scientific method and word processors (Cole, 1996; Wertsch, 1991). Conversely, even when members of a group sit across a table in face-to-face collaboration, it is only a *relatively social moment of thought.* Collaborators do not have complete access to the contents of each other's minds and must reveal their thoughts through talk or action to construct a shared understanding. Collaborators may also disengage temporarily from social interaction to either work out a new idea or to reduce frustration when collaborations do not proceed smoothly. Indeed, we have come to believe that, more often than not, collaborations, especially those that extend over time, are characterized by periods of engagement, disengagement, and re-engagement that may or may not be marked explicitly by the collaborators.

The structure of the chapter is as follows: We begin by selectively summarizing theoretical and empirical evidence for the interplay between relatively individual and social modes of thinking, discovery, and understanding. After reviewing the microgenetic methodology that allowed us to study this interplay, we describe the social mechanisms of change we investigated in our research. Then, we present research in which we studied the relation between relatively individual and social modes of scientific thinking while adult friends collaborated to build tall towers that could withstand the lateral forces of a simulated earthquake. We map the nature of the changes in their theories about the task and then discuss the relation between these changes and what transpired during their collaborations. Finally, to illustrate further the social context of theory building and change, we present two case studies, one of a pair who solved the problem successfully and one of a pair who did not.

Scientific Understanding as a Relatively Individual and Relatively Social Process

The view that discovery and theory change require a delicate interweaving of relatively individual and relatively social processes has been proposed by scholars studying a wide range of phenomena. Because of space limitations, we only consider two of these programs of research. We review work exploring the role of peer collaborations in the mastery of Piagetian concepts because Piaget's theory has played a central role in studies of conceptual development and scientific understanding, and because researchers in this tradition typically include individual and collaborative assessments in their research. Because the timing of the individual and collaborative sessions is controlled by the experimenter, however, this work cannot inform us about how individual and social processes are naturally interwoven in scientific thinking. Research that has documented the process of creative insight addresses this issue, and thus, we included it as our second example of the relatively individual and social rhythms of science.

In the late 1970s and early 1980s, the Social Genevans (e.g., Doise & Mugny, 1984; Perret-Clermont, 1980) devoted considerable attention to studying the cognitive consequences of peer collaborative problem solving. Their motivations were both theoretical and applied. Theoretically, they wanted to re-examine the claim that Piaget had made in his studies of moral development in the 1930s, that conflicts about ideas that occur during interactions between relative equals, i.e., peers, can provoke the cognitive disequilibrium that is a prerequisite for conceptual change. They reasoned that if they were able to demonstrate this empirically in the laboratory and develop procedures to evoke disequilibrium reliably, they would be able to apply their work to peer collaborative learning in the classroom. Perret-Clermont, in particular, was also interested in whether forming collaborative peer groups that included economically and socially-advantaged and disadvantaged children would reduce or eliminate differences in academic performance and conceptual understanding that are often evident in the cognitive performance of children of different socioeconomic backgrounds.

While these studies explored a variety of Piagetian concepts such as conservation, perspective taking, and isolation of variables, they generally shared the same experimental design: Participants were given an individual pretest, randomly assigned to either work alone (the control condition) or with partners (the experimental condition), and, finally, given an individual posttest. Researchers used changes in individuals' performance from the pretest to the posttest to infer conceptual change.

Because in our research we have been interested in the patterning of relatively social and relatively individual understanding over time, the studies that are especially relevant to us are those in which participants received an immediate and a delayed individual posttest following the collaborative session. These studies revealed that the cognitive gains that accrued from the collaboration often increased from the immediate to the delayed posttest. The researchers concluded that their findings supported Piaget's claim that the cognitive restructuring that follows disequilibration can take some time to materialize because intramental processes and knowledge need to be recalibrated. The recalibration process is captured by Piaget's definition of equilibration, Damon's percolation metaphor (personal communication, October, 1996), and Draper's discussion of fermentation (Laboratory of Comparative Human Cognition electronic discussion, 1989). Unfortunately, although these explanatory constructs and metaphors are provocative, there is little empirical documentation of how exactly they operate to produce conceptual change.

Although the specifics of equilibration, percolation, or fermentation remain fairly obscure, recent research has replicated and extended Perret-Clermont's, Doise's, and Mugny's early finding of the social-constructive nature of conceptual change. Howe, Tolmie, and Rogers (1992) and Tolmie, Howe, Mackenzie, and Greer (1993) used immediate and delayed posttests in their studies of how elementary schoolchildren's collaborations promoted or impeded their understanding of concepts such as buoyancy. Their results showed that not only was conceptual change greater in the delayed than the immediate posttests, but that individuals also produced ideas that were not discussed in the collaboration or stated in the immediate posttest. At first glance, the emergence of new ideas in the delayed posttest could be taken to support the view espoused by Piaget that individual restructuring and recalibration is more important for cognitive growth than what transpires in the collaborative context. However, when the researchers analyzed the collaborative sessions, they found that the individuals who generated new ideas and made the most gains in understanding from the immediate to the delayed posttest were members of groups in which partners had refined, extended, and challenged each others' ideas during collaboration. Members of groups in which individuals had merely stated their views, conflicts had gone unresolved, or partners had been unable to establish a shared frame of reference showed the least amount of progress and produced fewer new ideas from the immediate to the delayed posttests. Taken together, the results of these studies add to the growing literature (for a review, see Rogoff, 1998) that the substance of what transpires in the collaboration plays an important role in conceptual growth (or lack-thereof) and support our proposal that theory development accrues from both relatively individual and relatively social modes of reasoning.

In a more naturalistic situation, Csikszentmihalyi and Sawyer (1995) illustrated the dynamics of individual and social rhythms in their work on how creative insight—usually considered an intramental process—occurs within social contexts. Csikszentmihalyi and Sawyer interviewed 60 people nominated by their peers as especially creative in their fields (e.g., political and environmental activism, business, the arts, and a variety of academic disciplines). In their extensive retrospective interviews, these individuals recounted the process through which they produced their best work. Csikszentmihalyi and Sawyer's content analyses of nine of these interviews (an environmental activist, two physicists, a banker, a mathematician, an economist, a literary critic, an expert in ceramics, and a sculptor) suggested that creative insight was the result of a four-stage process. The first stage included a period of intense hard work and research; the second stage a period of idle time spent alone, often in activities unrelated to the creative activity (e.g., gardening, taking a walk); the third stage the moment of insight itself; and the fourth stage a return to hard work to bring the insight to fruition. Csikszentmihalyi and Sawyer's interviewees reported that during the periods of hard work that preceded and followed their insights, they frequently interacted with colleagues to propose and discuss ideas. Eventually, however, the social context saturated their thinking and they needed to engage in solitary reflection to make sense of the social discourse.

In considering why researchers who are interested in creativity (e.g., Martindale, 1990) have usually drawn on the intramental cognitivist tradition and disregarded the social and cultural context of scientific and artistic creativity (but see Harrington, 1990; John-Steiner, 1992), Csikszentmihalyi and Sawyer (1995) stated:

When we look at the complete "life span" of creative insight in our sub-jects' experience, the moment of insight appears as but one short flash in the complex, time-consuming, fundamentally social process. It is true that the individuals we interviewed generally report their insights as occurring in solitary moments: During a walk, while taking a shower, or while lying in bed just after waking. However, these reports usually are embedded within a more complex narrative, a story that describes the effort preceding and following the insight, and the overall sense of these complete narratives stresses the salience of social, interactional factors. It seems that the solitary nature of the moment of insight may have blinded us to the social dimension of the entire creative process. (p. 331)

Microgenesis and Scientific Reasoning

As noted earlier, while the work of the Social Genevans demonstrated the interplay between intramental (i.e., individual) and intermental (i.e., interpersonal) components of cognitive change, it only revealed products, not processes of change. Csikszentmihalyi and Sawyer's research does speak to this issue, but the phenomena of interest emerged over a fairly long period of time and under unpredictable, uncontrollable circum-stances; most researchers do not have the resources to carry out this research (but see Dunbar, 1995; 1997; this volume). An additional limita-tion of this work is that it is based solely on self-reports; these self-reports may omit or distort some of the processes of interest. In our view, the microgenetic methodology represents a reasonable compromise for observing the interplay between individual and social rhythms of scien-tific discovery and theory change.

The microgenetic methodology involves carrying out fine-grained analyses of changes in behaviors (e.g., dialogues, strategies) over the course of one or several sessions. Researchers assume that these changes reflect moment-to-moment learning and development in a particular problem-solving context and thus, index what may be occurring within the unobservable confines of people's minds (Klahr & MacWhinney, 1998; Rogoff, 1998). Microgenetic analyses do not require that participants achieve complete mastery of the task; all that is required is that some change, whether progression or regression, occur (Kuhn & Phelps, 1979). In many cases, one of the goals of these studies is to accelerate change by giving participants repeated opportunities to engage in the concepts, skills, or strategies under investigation to ensure that the researchers will be able to map the patterns of change (Kuhn, 1995; Siegler & Crowley,

1991).

Because of its potential to reveal learning and development, the microgenetic methodology has been employed by researchers from a wide variety of theoretical approaches to conceptual development. Working from a neo-Piagetian constructive orientation, for example, Kuhn, Amsel and O'Loughlin (1988) and Schauble (1996) explored how individual children, adolescents, and adults learned to coordinate scientific theory with evidence over the course of several sessions in which they attempted to isolate variables responsible for a variety of scientific phenomenon. Within the information processing approach, Siegler (1996) has employed this methodology to study how individual children acquired mathematical strategies over time. Finally, in contrast to scholars focusing on individual problem solving, researchers in the sociocultural tradition have focused their efforts on mapping microgenetic changes that occur in situations when pairs or groups work together on a variety of tasks such as classifying objects (Ellis & Rogoff, 1992), story book reading (Edwards & García, 1999), putting together puzzles (Wertsch, Minick, & Arns, 1984), or developing and testing causal hypotheses in the laboratory (Azmitia & Montgomery 1993) or the classroom (Greeno & Goldman, 1998).

Microgenetic studies of individual problem solving have shown that development is gradual and uneven, characterized by progressions and regressions in both strategy use and conceptual understanding. At any point in time, individuals apply multiple strategies to a problem and hold a variety of beliefs that may or may not be consistent with each other. Also, less adequate strategies and beliefs coexist with better ones (Kuhn, 1995; Siegler, 1996). Kuhn and Phelps (1982) found that one of the major impediments to learning was not the absence of sufficient knowledge or sophisticated strategies, but rather, the difficulties that people experienced in giving up inaccurate beliefs and inefficient but familiar problem solving strategies. Their findings challenged the prevalent view that theory development occurs primarily through the addition of information (for a more extensive discussion of this issue and about whether or not this methodology is informative concerning 'natural' change processes, see Kuhn, 1995). Having a partner (or partners) can remove or reduce resistance to relinquish ineffective strategies when individuals are exposed to alternative perspectives, are asked to clarify and justify their views, or are able to observe others' problem solving (Azmitia, 1996; Crowley & Siegler, 1999; Dunbar, 1995; Finholt & Olson, 1997; Hatano, 1994; Kobayashi, 1994; Latour & Woolgar, 1979). Thus, solving problems in a social context can accelerate change; while both singletons and teams eventually formulate correct hypotheses and solutions, teams often reach this goal sooner (Teasley, 1995; but see Okada & Simon, 1997).

Studies of dyadic or group problem solving have shown that positive change is more likely when collaborators have different but overlapping backgrounds and knowledge (Dunbar, 1995; Kobayashi, 1994) and are able to establish a joint frame of reference and shared goals (Rogoff, 1998; Teasley & Rochelle, 1993; Tharp & Gallimore, 1988). Developing this shared understanding, however, does not imply that reaching consensus is necessary or sufficient for theory change; dissension can also serve as a catalyst for progress either during or following the collaborative session (Azmitia & Montgomery, 1993; Matusov, 1996).

Finally, the nature of collaborators' dialogues plays an important role in microgenetic change. For example, *transactive dialogues*, which are conversations in which partners critique, refine, extend, and paraphrase each other's actions and ideas or create syntheses that integrate each other's perspectives, have been linked to shifts in both moral reasoning (Berkowitz & Gibbs, 1983; Kruger, 1992) and scientific understanding (Azmitia & Montgomery, 1993; Howe et al., 1992). These transactive dialogues may be the epitome of collaborative theory construction because in many cases, individuals walk away with a joint product for which they are no longer certain (and may not care) who gets credit for particular ideas (for a more extended discussion of this phenomenon, see Bos, 1934; John-Steiner, 1985). Proffering *explanations* during social discourse has also been associated with conceptual change in a variety of domains, including emotion (Cervantes & Callanan, 1998) and science (Okada & Simon, 1997; Teasley, 1995). This work on explanations converges with findings from research (e.g., Chi, de Leeuw, Chiu, & LaVancher, 1994; Crowley & Siegler, 1999) demonstrating the importance of self-explanations for problem solving. Finally, *analogies* that are used to provide explanations, design or refine experiments, and formulate hypotheses also play an important role in scientific discovery and theory change (Dunbar, 1995; 1997).

In our research, we explored collaborators' use of transacts, explanations, and analogies while they collaborated on a design task. We were interested in the functions of these utterances during the problem-solving process and in their association with hypothesis generation, theory change, and problem solving success.

A Microgenetic Study of Collaborative Scientific Understanding

We now turn to a study in which we used the microgenetic method to trace changes in individuals' and pairs' understanding in a task that draws on participants' knowledge of earthquakes. We observed changes in their theories about the task over a series of four individual and two collaborative sessions. The collaborative sessions were spaced one week apart and each collaborative session was preceded and followed by an individual session, yielding four relatively individual assessments. We considered the four individual assessments to be relatively individual windows into participants' understanding because the experimenter posed questions that required participants to reflect upon and externalize their theories about the task. We controlled the timing of the sessions, so we cannot speak to processes that occurred outside of our periods of observation and cannot claim that we were mapping the natural timeline of conceptual change in this task. However, by providing opportunities for collaboration and individual reflection, we implemented a gross manipulation of the flow of individual and collaborative moments that have been shown to characterize theory building and revision in previous work (e.g., Csikszentmihalyi & Sawyer, 1995; Dunbar, 1995; 1997).

Our collaborative sessions reflected the convention of organizing ongoing research around scheduled meetings where team members assemble with the explicit goal of working together on a problem. In his study of scientific discovery in real-world laboratories, Dunbar (1995; 1997; this volume) provided in-depth analyses of these structured activities. An additional way in which we tried to model real-world collaboration is that our participants were friends and had worked together on projects in the past, much like scientists who at the very least have a working relationship. We did not use the individual sessions in the traditional sense of pretests and posttest, i.e., as measures of task mastery. Rather, we used them to provide individuals with opportunities for reflection and to gather snapshots of their theories that allowed us to assess the functions of collaboration in theory development and change. We were especially interested in whether partners used the collaborative sessions to confirm ideas and hypotheses for which they had already gathered evidence (i.e., ideas that were already part of their theories) or whether they used these sessions to develop new ideas.

Twelve pairs of undergraduate friends participated in the study. We chose the domain of earthquakes because it is a standard unit in the elementary school and high school science curriculum and because we anticipated that their personal experiences with earthquakes would be part of our California participants' informal knowledge (all reported that they had experienced at least one earthquake).

In most laboratory studies of collaborative scientific reasoning, participants work on tasks in which they manipulate a small set of established parameters to isolate the ones responsible for the phenomenon. These tasks often also have either a single or at least an ideal solution. These features rarely characterize the open-ended problems of everyday scientific practices. In the "real world," before carrying out controlled tests of hypotheses, scientists have to identify the relevant variables and construct a language to talk about variables and outcomes. Even if they attain this goal, it may not be possible to design a controlled test to choose between competing theories and if controlled tests can be devised, feedback can be error-laden and there may be more than one satisfying solution to the problem.

The earthquake task is an open-ended task that shares many of these complexities. The earthquake machine is a device that shakes a platform back and forth to generate a simulated earthquake; our device is similar to earthquake machines used in demonstrations in university earth science courses and science museums. Participants use foam blocks to build towers that will withstand the simulated earthquake.

As is the case for everyday scientific problems, there are multiple strategies for designing towers that withstand the simulated earthquake. The problem is also of interest because it cannot be tackled efficiently with a systematic control of variables strategy (see Klahr, Chen, & Toth, this volume). Unlike steel or wood frames in real buildings, the block towers are compression structures. Blocks are held together by gravity and friction rather than bolts or nails. Thus, adjacent blocks do not necessarily respond as a single unit to the same lateral forces. The individual square blocks respond unpredictably because their shapes generate additional impacts each time they rock back and forth on their flat bases.

However, the difficulty of obtaining precise quantitative predictions does not mean that there is nothing to learn and measure in this task. The cathedrals of Europe are, in essence, nothing more than stacks of independent stone blocks held together by gravity and friction. Without the ability to make precise quantitative predictions, their architects were able to erect structures which have, for several hundred years, successfully resisted the toppling influence of winds, and, in some cases, earthquakes. What is responsible for the continued stability of these buildings is exactly what guided our participants' design of block buildings: Their theories about structural stability, we hypothesized, would be created through a mix of intuition, analogy to existing buildings, experiences building with blocks or stacking objects such as books, and structural experimentation.

The sessions were videotaped and transcribed. In each relatively individual session, we assessed participants' current theories by first giving them 12 foam blocks and asking them to build a tower that they thought would withstand the earthquake. After they built their tower, we asked them to explain its strengths and weaknesses. Finally, we showed them pictures of block towers others had built. For each picture, we asked participants to predict whether the tower would remain standing after being subjected to the simulated earthquake and to list its strengths or weaknesses. In the collaborative sessions, pairs were given 12 foam blocks and asked to build a six-story tower that would withstand the simulated earthquake. The side of a block was equivalent to one story. They were told they would have had 15 minutes and to build and test as many towers as they wished. When they were ready to test a tower, they pressed a button that caused the machine to produce a five second earthquake. If they succeeded before the end of the session, they called the experimenter to witness another test of their tower and were given four more blocks and a new goal (eight stories).

Building stable towers on the earthquake machine was not a trivial task for the undergraduates. Three pairs achieved the goal of building a stable six-story tower in the first session and two more achieved this goal in the second session; no pair was able to build an eight-story tower that withstood the five-second simulated earthquake, although one pair built an eight story tower that stood for four seconds. While the seven remaining pairs did not achieve success by our experimenter-imposed standards, they were all able to build stable five-story structures by the end of either the first or second collaborative session.

Theory Change

To assess changes in participants' individual theories, we tracked six structural features over the course of the two sessions. We identified participants' *implicit theories* by coding the features that appeared in the towers they built in the individual theory assessments and the collaborative sessions. We identified participants' *explicit theories* by coding what they told the experimenter about their towers in the individual sessions and what they talked about with their partner during collaboration. Three of the six features we coded were global properties of the whole structure:

1. *Expanded Base*: The base should be wider than the top.
2. *Symmetry*: The building should be symmetric in at least one dimension around the central axis.
3. *Two Dimensions (2D)*: The building does not need to expand more than one block perpendicular to the direction of motion.[1]

Three features characterized local building techniques within the structure:

4. *Cross Bracing*: Use of post-and-beam bracing (one block lying across the top of two others).
5. *Closed Gaps*: Blocks in the same story of the building should be touching each other rather than spaced apart.
6. *Stories-in-Line*: Blocks in subsequent stories should be flush rather than sticking out at different angles.

Changes in Implicit Theories

At the beginning of each of the four individual assessments, participants were asked to build a tower that they thought could withstand the earthquake. The three global features were coded as either present or absent. The three local features were coded as being present on few (zero to 33% present), some (34% to 66%), or many (67% to 100%) of the stories in the tower. Figure 1 shows changes in feature use for each participant across the four theory assessments.

Participants began the study (T1 column in Figure 1) by building towers that incorporated a range of features. The most common global feature was symmetry (92% of the towers), followed by expanded base (71%). In contrast, the other global feature, 2D, characterized only 10% of the first buildings. The most common local feature was stories-in-line, with 92% of the towers having many stories in line, 8% having some stories in line, and no towers having only a few. Closed gaps were also com-

---

1. In the "real world," earthquakes create lateral and perpendicular movements and thus, buildings need to be three dimensional. Because the earthquake machine only moved laterally, however, buildings only needed to extend along the direction of this lateral movement, in two dimensions.

mon (62% many, 21% some, 17% few) while cross-bracing was less common (37% many, 21% some, 42% few).

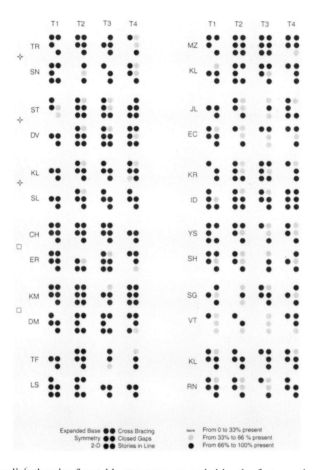

Figure 1. Implicit theories for stable structures, as coded by the features characterizing towers built in each of the four individual interviews (T1, T2, T3, T4). Each tower was coded for six target structural features, represented here on a 2 X 3 grid. As shown in the figure legend, the left column of each grid represents three global features (expanded base, symmetry, 2D) coded as being either present (black dot) or absent (blank). The right column of each grid represents three local features (cross bracing, closed gaps, stories in line) coded as being present on few (blank), some (gray dot), or most (black dot). Stars indicate the three pairs who successfully built six-story towers that could withstand the simulated earthquake in session one. Squares indicate the two additional pairs who achieved this goal for the first time in the second session.

By the last relatively individual theory assessment in the study (the T4 column in Figure 1), the overall level of the six features exhibited some changes. For the global features, symmetry dropped from characterizing almost all towers to only 67%. Expanded base held steady at 75% while 2D grew somewhat to 25%. For the local features, prevalence of closed gaps within a tower held more or less steady (66% many, 29% some, and 4% few), while stories-in-line decreased somewhat (83% many, 17% some, and zero few). The largest changes in local features occurred in use of cross-bracing. In the first theory assessment (T1) it had been most common to have few joints cross-braced. However, by the end of the study (T4) only 17% of towers had few cross-braces while 50% had many and 33% had some.

The overall patterns underestimate the amount of change that occurred in particular individuals' theories. In fact, an examination of the individual participant patterns in Figure 2 reveals that it was quite uncommon for participants to maintain the same features on subsequent assessments: 91% of all towers differed in at least one feature from the tower built by the same person in the previous individual assessment. On average, participants made changes in about two of the six features between successive towers in the individual assessment. Interestingly, this rate of change was about the same within each of the sessions and across the two sessions. Thus, both the collaborative activity and the week off between sessions appeared to induce change.

We had anticipated that, over time, the collaboration would bring partners' individual theories closer, but we observed the opposite. In T1 (before the first collaborative session) the overall overlap between partners' implicit theories was about as large (72% of features shared) as it would ever get. The overlap at T2 was similar (74%), but overlap was markedly lower in T3 (58%) and T4 (60%). Thus, over time partners' implicit theories drifted apart.

Changes in Explicit Theories

After participants built towers in the individual theory assessments, the experimenter asked them to talk about the features of the tower that would help it withstand the earthquake. We coded their talk for mentions of each of the six features; this talk indexed their explicit theories for the task (Figure 2).

The first thing to notice about Figure 2 is that participants never talked about all six features when analyzing their buildings. In the first individual assessment, they mentioned an average of only 1.7 of the six target features. There was a significant increase in the number of different features participants talked about across the sessions, with means of 2.2, 2.5, and 2.7 features in T2, T3, and T4, but they still talked, on average, about less than half of the six features.

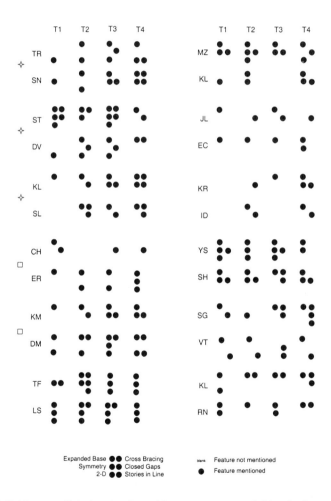

Figure 2. Subjects explicit theories for stable structures, as coded by the features of their towers that subjects talked about during each of the four individual interviews.

The most commonly-discussed global feature, and also the feature that was mentioned most often overall, was expanded base, which rose from 67% of the participants mentioning it in T1 to 92% in T4. Mentions of symmetry rose from 38% to 46%, but mentions of 2D support decreased from 29% in T1 to 25% in T4. All three local features showed increases over time: Spacing from 29% to 58%; cross-bracing from 4% to 33%; and stories-in-line from 4% to 17%.

Figure 2 shows that, as was true of individual participants' implicit theories, their explicit theories changed frequently between assessments, with 82% of theories changing by at least one feature. The mean rate of change was a little less than 1.5 features, which, because the average number of features in an explicit theory was about 2.5, amounts to more than half of the features changing from one individual assessment to the next. Again, similar to the case for implicit theories, changes in explicit theories were equally common within a session and between the sessions

In contrast to changes in implicit theories, which were as likely to involve feature addition as deletion, changes in explicit theories most often involved deleting old features. For four features (symmetry, two-dimensions, cross-braces, and closed gaps), 50% or more of the participants who included the feature in their theories on one assessment dropped it from their theories on a subsequent assessment. The feature that was most likely to be added and not deleted was expanded base; the only feature mentioned by everyone at least once and which was subsequently dropped by only 25% of participants. Stories-in-line was mentioned by just one participant before the fourth and final individual theory assessment, and she ended up dropping it from her final theory. The finding that participants were more likely to delete than add features is in contrast to Kuhn and Phelp's (1982) study, in which individuals resisted relinquishing old knowledge or strategies even when confronted by evidence of their inadequacy. However, our research differs from theirs in that the open-ended nature of the task did not lend itself well to systematic hypothesis testing and evaluation. Therefore, the frequent changes in tower features may reflect the trial-and-error approach adopted by many of our participants.

Similar to the case of implicit theories, partners' explicit theories were not more likely to become shared by the end of the study. We calculated the overlap in explicit theories by dividing the number of the six features that both partners had talked about in a given theory assessment by the total number of the six features mentioned by either partner. Overall, partners' explicit theories remained distinct across the study, rising only slightly from 35% shared on T1 to 47% on T4. Note that this overlap in explicit theories was always lower than had been the case for implicit theories.

The Social Context of Theory Change

All pairs began the first collaborative session by exploring the earthquake machine and sharing some of their beliefs about features. They also showed evidence of their mastery of the scientific practices that we teach in Western schools in several ways: While building their first few towers, they formulated hypotheses and tried to set up critical tests for them; they evaluated the results of these critical tests and used them to refine their hypotheses; and they discussed whether there was a correct (ideal) solution to the problem. However, in this particular task, such an approach is a hindrance because all the relevant variables are not known, the feedback is error-laden (in part because there is an element of luck in whether towers stand or fall), and there are numerous solution pathways. Moreover, time is limited, so building and testing as many towers as possible can lead to greater success than carrying out and evaluating a limited set of controlled tests. Over the course of their collaboration, all pairs came to realize this, and discontinued their critical tests of hypotheses. The three pairs who achieved the goal of six stories in the first session appear to have come to this realization earlier (i.e., by their second or third tower) than other pairs.

As discussed, prior research has revealed an association between constructing a shared understanding of the task and scientific discovery and theory change. Our preliminary analyses of participants' dialogues suggest that most partners were responding to and building on each other's ideas. Surprisingly, however, collaborators who succeeded in the task not only retained a significant number of unique ideas from their original individual theories, but failed to discuss these ideas with their partner. Because they built towers that contained these features, it may be that they were using the collaborative session, at least in part, to test and reflect upon their own ideas. Why they did not discuss their ideas with their friend is a question that deserves future study. Perhaps they reasoned that by using them in their buildings, they were communicating their views. Perhaps the knowledge remained an implicit part of their theories and they did not even know that they knew it.

We will assess the interplay between verbal and non-verbal communication of ideas in future analyses. In any case, our findings suggest that building an explicitly-shared theory was not necessary for making good progress on the task. This suggestion receives further support from our analysis of the discussions of our least successful pairs. After a series of unsuccessful towers, these pairs adopted a brainstorming strategy. Their lack of success on the task may have led them to discuss as many ideas as they could in an attempt to create a shared theory and succeed. It is possible that, given enough time, their discussion would have cohered into a narrower shared theory that would lead to success. However, a close examination of their discourse suggests that this brainstorming was not moving their theories forward. In particular, they seemed to be constrained by a problem of set (i.e., they returned to the same ideas time and time again even though they had already accumulated evidence that they did or did not work) and had trouble distinguishing between relevant and irrelevant information (i.e., their problem set was too large). These findings converge with those of other who have demonstrated that brainstorming can sometimes limit creativity and impede problem solving (for a review, see Lamm & Tromsdorff, 1973).

Thus far, we have contrasted the manipulation in which we forced individual and social modes of thinking to occur by asking pairs to work together or reflect relatively individually on the task. We now turn to a more naturalistic examination of individual and social processes, those which occurred during the collaborative session as partners disengaged and re-engaged in the collaboration. Our analysis of the interaction patterns of the twelve pairs who participated suggests that one function of disengagement was to modulate affect and frustration. The task is challenging, and partners often commented that they doubted whether it was possible. In 36% of the instances in which partners expressed frustration or reached an impasse, they disengaged from the collaboration and worked in parallel for some time. Another function of disengagement from the collaboration was for individuals to work on an idea that they would subsequently suggest to their partner or try on the earthquake machine. We had provided notepads and pencils to participants, and occasionally, one of them left his or her partner working on the machine and used the notepad to draw possible tower constructions or outline a building principle or feature of the machine. These solitary moments were relatively brief (seldom more than a minute), and partners soon returned to the collaboration to try the new idea or propose a compromise position, such as taking turns or testing both of their ideas to see which would be most successful. Thus, it appears that relatively individual rhythms can occur during collaboration when partners need to reduce negative affect, when they are engaged in a power or dominance struggle, or when they are trying to work out an idea of their own.

Social Mechanisms of Change

At present, we have completed the analyses of the collaborative dialogues of six pairs. The results of these analyses show that discussions in which partners used explanations and transacts (i.e., critiques, elaborations, clarifications, paraphrases, or syntheses of each other's ideas) sometimes led to feature addition in individual explicit theories, and deletion in the concurrent or subsequent towers the pairs built. However, these changes were not always carried over to the relatively individual theory assessments that followed collaboration. Interestingly, while feature deletion was more common than feature addition in the individual assessments, in the collaborative dialogues the opposite was true, feature addition was more likely than feature deletion. Thus, in this social, but not the individual, context, our findings supported Kuhn and Phelp's (1982) claim that one of the major impediments to learning involves giving up our old, inefficient ideas or strategies. Note, however, that this finding contradicts our earlier proposal that people may be more willing to relinquish ideas (in this case, delete features) during collaboration than during individual problem solving. Even though, as we proposed, their partners or the evidence pointed to the erroneous nature of their ideas, participants still resisted dropping features they believed in.

Although the finding that high level discussions can lead to theory change was consistent with our predictions and the results of previous research, it is important to note that the frequency of transacts and explanations was relatively low. It is possible that because the earthquake task is very visual (i.e., participants can share theories through building demonstrations), non-verbal interaction was as important as verbal exchanges in promoting theory change. We plan to explore this possibility after we analyze the dialogues of the remaining six pairs.

The six pairs we have analyzed also used analogies to bring their informal and formal knowledge to bear on the task. The most common analogies involved block-building (e.g., blocks, block-balancing games such as Jenga), relating the motion of the earthquake machine's platform to the movement of tectonic plates in real earthquakes, and comparing the movement of block towers on the machine to the movement of buildings during a real earthquake. Analogies were more frequent in the opening stages of collaboration, when partners were engaged in working to relate their extant informal and formal knowledge to the present task and develop a language to talk about the features of their towers and the machine. We also found that, like Dunbar's (1995; 1997) scientists, our participants used analogies to formulate hypotheses, design and evaluate experiments (i.e., test and evaluate tests of their block towers), and explain their findings.

An analogy that consistently led to theory change (i.e., the feature was deleted or added in participants' subsequent relatively individual theory assessments) involved partners' realizing that to withstand earthquakes in the real world, buildings need to be reinforced from all sides (three-dimensional support), although on the earthquake machine buildings only needed to be reinforced in the direction of the lateral movement of the building platform (2D support). For example, in their first collaborative session, ST shared with DV his view that to withstand the earthquake, the towers needed to be three-dimensional so they would be supported on all sides. DV countered that the machine moved laterally only in one direction, and thus, two-dimensional support was sufficient. This discussion may have been what led ST to delete this feature from his subsequent relatively individual theory assessments.

An analogy that did not consistently lead to individual theory change involved allusions to the ways in which cross-bracing supports buildings. In two of the pairs, individuals tried repeatedly to convince their partners about the importance of this feature. Even when they demonstrated how this feature strengthened a tower, their partners did not add the feature to their individual theories. Unlike Dunbar (1995), then, we did not find a simple relationship between analogy and theory change. Note, however, that Dunbar's study involved expert scientists working on problems over the course of a whole year. Our participants' domain knowledge and time was more limited, and these factors may have prevented them from taking full advantage of their partners' analogies. In one case, analogies actually hampered progress because partners generated a wealth of analogies and did not, like other pairs, discriminate between those that applied and those that did not apply to the task. Their plight is a nice illustration of Perkins' (1997) suggestion that to facilitate creativity and conceptual growth, analogy must be used selectively and judiciously. Finally, it is also possible that the analogies that our participants produced were not as sophisticated as those produced by Dunbar's expert scientists and thus, were less powerful agents of change.

Case Studies of Collaboration

We have presented some suggestive evidence that analogies, explanations, and transacts promoted theory change and problem solving success. However, the relationship between these sophisticated features of collaborative scientific discovery and problem solving success is not that simple, as the following two case studies of an unsuccessful and a successful pair illustrate. We selected these two pairs because they both began by trying to set up critical tests of hypotheses, they communicated their beliefs and tried to build a shared understanding of the task, they frequently used transacts, explanations, and analogies in their discussions, and they built and tested a similar number of towers in the first collaborative session. Note that by successful and unsuccessful we mean success in building a stable six-story tower. Both pairs were very successful in establishing a collaboration.

LS and TF, an Unsuccessful Pair

LS and TF began their first collaborative session by each stating and testing some of the features of their individual theories (expanded base and no spacing between the blocks, respectively). They also explored the machine's movement, placing blocks on the platform to determine the most stable location and discussing whether the orientation of the tower on the platform affected its stability. LS commented that she wished she could remember her physics so she could use physics principles to make the towers more stable. Most of LS's and TF's conversations and work during this session were devoted to the pros and cons of placing their towers in different locations on the earthquake platform and the best way to orient blocks on the different stories (these locations and orientations were also the focus their hypothesis testing). While LS did not state her belief that the stories needed to be lined up and TF did not state her view that symmetry was important, both built towers that contained these features, a finding that demonstrates once again the importance of non-verbal demonstrations for theory building, refinement, and testing in this task and in science in general.

Table 1. Explanations, analogies, transacts, and scientific methodology used by TF and LS in the first and second collaborative sessions.

LS and TF	Session 1	Session 2
Towers built and tested	10	29
Explanations of building features	7	5
Analogies	4	3
Transacts (critique, elaborate, synthesize)	5	3
Scientific Methodology		
Critical tests of hypotheses	4	2
% Tests evaluate and explain outcomes	30	34

As can be seen in Table 1, LS and TF explained why they believed particular features were building strengths or weaknesses, engaged in transactive dialogues in which they critiqued, clarified, and elaborated each other's reasoning, produced analogies (e.g., LS commenting on the movement of the machine as she watches their tower fall: "See, that's what earthquakes do, the first jolt isn't gonna do it, it's the last couple of seconds"), carried out critical tests of hypotheses (i.e., tested a tower with the feature and then a tower without the feature), and commented on the success and failure of their towers, although they only engaged in evaluative discussions of strengths and weaknesses of their towers after 30% of tests. During this first collaborative session, LS and TF also discussed features individually as well as holistically, i.e., how features interacted to produce stability or instability. Their discussions displayed the systematicity of the scientific method in that they kept track verbally of ideas they had tested to avoid repeating tests and their critical tests of hypotheses built on each other (e.g., after testing whether an expanded base was important, they tested whether an expanded base with spacing between the blocks was better than an expanded base without spacing between the blocks). Towards the end of the session, they considered whether the task was possible and acknowledged that there was an element of chance in whether towers stood or fell during the simulated earthquake.

Their second collaborative session was markedly different. They began with a brief discussion of towers that may work or fail on the earthquake machine and then decided to adopt a trial-and-error strategy to build and test more towers than they had in the first session (29 versus 10). This initial discussion was not related closely to the relatively individual theories they had espoused immediately prior to the second collaboration (i.e., the third relatively individual theory assessment). Rather, their discussion concerned the block-building they had carried out at home in preparation for this session and the pictures of towers they had seen in the preceding relatively individual theory assessment. Interestingly, after their first two towers failed, they redefined the goal of the task and spent the next eight minutes building and testing four or five story towers, alternating between systematic critical tests of hypotheses about features and haphazard trial-and-error construction. LS and TF may have redefined the goal of the task in an effort to regulate and manage the high levels of frustration they were experiencing because of their lack of success. They mentioned, for example, how confident they had been after consulting with their architect friend that they would be able to solve the task in this second session and how disappointed they were that his advice had not worked. Also, in the first session, they explicitly expressed their frustration with the task and with each other twice, but in one instance this emotional event did not produce a shift in their collaborative style and in the other it led to LS becoming an onlooker, still engaged but letting TF try out her idea. In contrast, in the second session their expression of negative affect doubled and in three of the four instances they led to parallel work and to them speculating that the task was really a social psychology experiment on participants' tolerance for frustration. For part of this segment, LS and TF were also off-task and engaged in social conversation, again perhaps as a way to reduce the negative affect produced by their multiple failure experiences.

During the last 4 minutes of the session, LS and TF returned to the goal of building a six-story tower, trying to test individual features of towers systematically. Because they did not mark their re-engagement in the task with an explicit comment, we do not know what led them to return to pursuing the task goal, especially because they continued to discuss whether the task was possible as they built and tested their towers. They did not make much progress, perhaps because the towers and features they tested had already proved unsuccessful in earlier trials.

It is possible that the lack of change in LS's and TF's individual theories from the third theory assessment (i.e., immediately preceding the second collaborative session) and the fourth theory assessment (i.e., immediately following this second collaborative session) was due to their realization that for most of the session, they had been trying to solve a problem (build a stable four or five story tower) that was not equivalent to the experimenter-imposed goal or to the haphazard nature of most of their building making it difficult for them to assess whether the evidence suggested a change in their views.

DV and ST, a Successful Pair

Like LS and TF, DV and ST began their first collaborative session by stating some of the features of their individual theories (DV, no spacing between blocks; and ST, expanded base). Interestingly, DV also brought up a feature that had not been in his initial theory, three-dimensional support. After ST pointed out that only two-dimensional support was needed because the earthquake machine did not move like real earthquakes (i.e., it only moved in one direction and did not have rippling waves), DV abandoned this idea. DV and ST also resembled LS and TF in that they devoted most of their work and discussion to working out a particular feature, in this case, determining whether the spacing between the blocks mattered for tower stability. Their first three towers represented critical tests of the hypothesis that spacing mattered (i.e., they built the first tower with spacing, the second one without spacing, and the third one with spacing). However, after the third tower they decided that because the features of the towers interacted, critical tests of individual features would be of little use. In contrast, while LS and TF questioned the utility of critical tests of individual features of towers, they still returned to the strategy in their second collaborative session.

Table 2. Explanations, analogies, transacts, and scientific methodology used by ST and DV in the first and second collaborative sessions.

DV and ST	Session 1	Session 2
Towers built and tested	14	11
Explanations of building features	6	6
Analogies	3	1
Transacts (critique, elaborate, synthesize)	4	6
Scientific Methodology		
Critical tests of hypotheses	2	1
% Tests evaluate and explain outcomes	42	18

An additional difference between DV and ST and LS and TF concerned their use of explanations, transacts, and analogies. LS's and TF's were interspersed relatively equally during the building and evaluation (i.e., after the test) phases of the session. DV's and ST's, in contrast, were concentrated more heavily during the evaluation phase. It is possible that their more in-depth approach to evaluation was responsible for their greater success in the task; by the end of the first session, DV and ST had built a successful six-story tower. Interestingly, given that the prevalent pattern was for pairs' theories to diverge over time, while DV and ST's initial theories differed, they converged following the collaboration, i.e., in the second relatively individual assessment. Their individual theories still were quite similar (they differed only in one feature) when they returned one week later and received the third relatively individual assessment.

DV and ST began their second collaborative session by reviewing the characteristics of the successful tower they had built in the previous session. They built and tested this tower successfully on their first try and were given four more blocks and the goal of building an eight-story tower that would withstand the simulated earthquake. After receiving this new goal, their discussion shifted from considering the merits of specific features to considering features as interrelated to each other and how these interrelationships might differ in six- versus eight-story towers. As they discussed these interrelations, they tinkered with their original six-story design to adapt it to a successful seven-story tower and subsequently, to an eight-story tower that withstood a 4-second earthquake. An additional change during this session was that their explanations and transacts were no longer concentrated heavily in the evaluation phase; rather, they were more frequent during the building segment. Perhaps this redistribution of transacts and explanations reflects their emphasis on tinkering and refining their design to meet their new goal. Once again, the theories they espoused in their fourth and final relatively individual assessment (i.e., after the second collaborative session) differed only in one feature. However, there were shifts in the strength with which they held particular beliefs. For example, relative to his third relatively individual assessment, ST became more convinced that cross-bracing and absence of spacing were important, and less convinced that an expanded base was necessary. DV's conviction that cross-bracing was important increased from the third to the fourth relatively individual theory assessment and he became more unsure about whether spacing between blocks was desirable. Taken together, these individual and collaborative patterns suggest that DV and ST devoted their first collaborative session to theory building and their second collaborative session to theory refinement.

In contrast to LS and TF, DV and ST did not question the feasibility of solving the task. They also did not explicitly express frustration in either session and their interaction style across trials was smoother, rarely deviating from collaboration. Their confidence in their ability to solve the task may have allowed them to have a smoother and less frustrating interaction, which, in turn, freed more resources to devote to the task. As proposed earlier, it is possible that their decision to abandon critical tests of hypotheses and their tendency to engage in regular post-mortem discussions may have helped them succeed.

Conclusions

Taken together, our findings add to previous research showing that in designing for science, we need to allow for both relatively social and relatively individual moments of work and reflection. In classrooms, laboratories, or research studies we often worry when collaborators disengage and individuals proceed to work on their own. Our preliminary data suggest that these moments are necessary for theory building and revision. However, it is important to distinguish these moments of solitary reflection or emotional regulation from situations that signal that the collaboration has fallen apart and cannot be repaired. Currently, we are continuing to analyze our collaborative sessions to address further the question of when and why people work together during scientific discovery and when they prefer to work alone. Our hope is to link these individual and social rhythms systematically to both affective processes and knowledge states. We are also continuing to try to discern why individuals did not communicate verbally all of the features of their theories. Thus far, we have ruled out the hypotheses that they communicated verbally about features that they were unsure about and its alternative, that they shared ideas they were highly confident about. While we are only in the beginning steps of this work, we hope that it will contribute to our description and explanation of the social context scientific reasoning and discovery.

We close by returning to our opening point that science is situated in historical, cultural, and social contexts. Whether we are examining scientific understanding at a particular time in history, the scientific practices of a culture, or the social discourse in a research group meeting or a classroom, it soon becomes evident that certain knowledge, problems, processes, and solutions are privileged over others. Through participation in scientific activities, children and adults master the valued practices of their communities (Goodnow, 1990; Hatano, 1994; Wertsch, 1997). Mastery of scientific practices can further individuals' cognitive development and provide opportunities for success in a variety occupations. However, these practices can also be constraining because they involve particular ways of conceptualizing reality and exploring causal phenomena (Wertsch, 1997). Shifts in scientific paradigms and perspectives occur when enough members of a community become so dissatisfied with the prevalent theories or methodologies that they seek alternatives (Kuhn, 1964). Often, these alternatives draw on different disciplines. An example of such shift is the current influx of ideas and methodologies from literary theory (e.g., Bakhtin, 1981) into the social and, to an extent, natural sciences that started in the late 1970s when many scholars rejected the positivist tradition.

Although alternatives to the positivist tradition have been created within professional communities, it is still the case that in Western schools, we socialize a way of thinking about and doing science that involves inductive and deductive reasoning and controlled experimentation and hypothesis testing. Whether it is working on a project for a science fair in elementary school and junior high school, carrying out laboratory assignments for physics, chemistry, or psychology courses in high school and college, or designing theses and dissertations, we teach students to follow appropriate procedures for building, testing, and revising their theories about particular domains. As we showed in this chapter, despite this socialization, adults can recognize when the scientific method will not be useful in solving a problem. When they leave the classroom and become professionals or engage in everyday science, people will encounter the ill-formed types of problems that we used in the present research. Thus, we suggest that identifying the nature of the problem—whether or not it is amenable to critical hypothesis testing and has a preferred or ideal solution pathway—should be an important part of training and designing for science.

Acknowledgements

The research reported in this chapter was funded by grants from the Committee on Research and the Social Sciences Division of the University of California, Santa Cruz to the first author. Feedback from Maureen Callanan, Chris Schunn, and Takeshi Okada improved the chapter greatly. Correspondence can be addressed to either author.

References

Azmitia, M. (1996). Peer interactive minds: Developmental, theoretical, and methodological issues. In P.B. Baltes & U. M. Staudinger (Eds.), *Interac-*

tive minds: Lifespan perspectives on the social foundations of cognition (pp. 133-162). New York: Cambridge University Press.

Azmitia, M., & Montgomery, R. (1993). Friendship, transactive dialogues, and the development of scientific reasoning. *Social Development, 3,* 202-221.

Bakhtin, M. (1981). *The dialogic imagination: Four essays by M. Bakhtin* (C. Emerson & M. Holquist, Eds.), Austin, TX: University of Texas Press.

Berkowitz, M. W., & Gibbs, J. C. (1983). Measuring the developmental features of moral discussion. *Merrill-Palmer Quarterly, 29,* 299-410.

Bianchini, J. A. (1997). Where knowledge construction, equity, and context intersect: Student learning of science in small groups. *Journal of Research in Science Teaching, 34,* 1039-1065.

Bos, M. C. (1934). Experimental study of productive collaboration. *Acta Psicologica, 3,* 315-426.

Cervantes, C. A., & Callanan, M. A. (1998). Labels and explanations in mother-child emotion talk: Age and gender differentiation. *Developmental Psychology, 34,* 88-98.

Chi, M. T. H., de Leeuw, N., Chiu, M-H., & LaVancher, C. (1994). Eliciting self-explanations improves understanding. *Cognitive Science, 18,* 439-477.

Cole, M. (1996). *Cultural psychology: The once and future discipline.* Cambridge, MA: Harvard University Press.

Coleman, E. B. (1998). Using explanatory knowledge during collaborative problem solving in science. *Journal of the Learning Sciences, 7,* 387-427.

Crowley, K., & Siegler, R. S. (1999). Explanation and generalization in young children's strategy learning. *Child Development, 70(20),* 304-316.

Csikszentmihalyi, M., & Sawyer, K. (1995). Creative insight: The social dimension of a solitary moment. In R. J. Sternberg & J. E. Davidson (Eds.), *The nature of insight* (pp. 329-264). Cambridge, MA: MIT Press.

Doise, W., & Mugny, G. (1984). *The social development of the intellect.* Oxford: Pergamon Press.

Dunbar, K. (1995). How scientists really reason: Scientific reasoning in real-world laboratories. In R. J. Sternberg & J. E. Davidson (Eds.), *The nature of insight* (pp. 265-396). Cambridge, MA: MIT Press.

Dunbar, K. (1997). Conceptual change in science. In T. B. Ward, S. M. Smith, J. Vaid (Eds.), *Creative thought: An investigation of conceptual structures and processes* (pp. 461-494). Washington, DC: American Psychological Association.

Edwards, P. A., & García, G. E. (1999). The implications of Vygotskian theory for the development of home-school programs: A focus on storybook reading. In P. Lloyd & C. Fernyhough (Eds.), *Lev Vygotsky: Critical assessments: Future directions, Vol. IV* (pp. 359-378). New York: Routledge.

Ellis, S., & Rogoff, B. (1992). The strategies and efficacy of child versus adult teachers. *Child Development, 53,* 730-735.

Finholt, T. A., & Olson, G. M. (1977). From laboratories to collaboratories: A new organizational form for scientific collaboration. *Psychological Science, 8,* 28-36.

Forman, E. A., & Larreamendy-Joerns, J. (1995). Learning in the context of peer collaboration: A pluralistic perspective on goals and expertise. *Cognition and Instruction, 13,* 549-565.

Goodnow, J. J. (1990). The socialization of cognition: What's involved? In J. Stigler, R. Shweder, & G. Herdt (Eds.). *Culture and human development* (pp. 259-286). Chicago: University of Chicago Press.

Greeno, J. G., & Goldman, S. V. (Eds.) (1998). *Thinking practices in mathematics and science learning.* Mahwah, NJ: Lawrence Erlbaum Associates.

Harrington, D. M. (1990). The ecology of human creativity: A psychological perspective. In M. A. Runco & R. S. Albert (Eds.), *Theories of creativity* (pp. 143-169). Newbury Park, CA: Sage.

Hatano, G. (1994). Introduction (Special issue on conceptual change: Japanese perspectives). *Human Development, 37,* 189-197.

Howe, C. J., Tolmie, A., & Rodgers, C. (1992). The acquisition of conceptual knowledge in science by primary school children: Group interaction and the understanding of motion down an incline. *British Journal of Developmental Psychology, 10,* 113-130.

John-Steiner, V. (1985). *Notebooks of the mind.* New York: Harper.

John-Steiner, V. (1992). Creative lives, creative tensions. *Creativity Research Journal, 5,* 99-108.

Klahr, D., & MacWhinney, B. (1998). Information processing. In D. Kuhn & R. S. Siegler (Eds.), W. Damon (Series Ed.), *Handbook of child psychology, Vol. 2., Cognition, perception, and language* (pp. 631-679). New York: Wiley.

Kobayashi, Y. (1994). Conceptual acquisition and change through social interaction. *Human Development, 37,* 233-241.

Kruger, A. C. (1992). The effect of peer and adult-child transactive discussions on moral reasoning. *Merrill-Palmer Quarterly 38,* 191-211.

Kuhn, D. (1995). Microgenetic study of change: What has it told us? *Psychological Science, 6,* 133-139.

Kuhn, D., Amsel, E., & O'Loughlin, M. (1988). *The development of scientific thinking skills.* NY: Academic Press.

Kuhn, D., & Phelps, E. (1979). A methodology for observing development of a formal reasoning strategy. *New Directions for Child Development, 5,* 45-58.

Kuhn, D., & Phelps, E. (1982). The development of problem solving strategies. In H. Reese (Ed.), *Advances in child development and behavior* (Vol. 17, pp. 1-44). New York: Academic Press.

Kuhn, T. (1964). *The structure of scientific revolutions.* Chicago: University of Chicago Press.

Lamm, H., & Tromsdorff, G. (1973). Group versus individual performance on tasks requiring ideational proficiency (brainstorming): A review. *European Journal of Social Psychology, 3*, 361-388.

Latour, B., & Woolgar, S. (1979). *Laboratory life: The social construction of scientific facts.* London: Sage.

Martindale, C. (1990). *The clockwork muse: The predictability of artistic change.* New York: Basic Books.

Matusov, E. (1996). Intersubjectivity without agreement. *Mind, Culture, and Activity: An International Journal, 3*, 25-45.

Okada, T., & Simon, H. A. (1997). Collaborative discovery in a scientific domain. *Cognitive Science, 21*, 109-146.

Perret-Clermont, A. N. (1980). *Social interaction and cognitive development in children.* London: Academic Press.

Perkins, D. N. (1997). Creativity's camel: The role of analogy in invention. In T. B. Ward, S. M. Smith, J. Vaid (Eds.), *Creative thought: An investigation of conceptual structures and processes* (pp. 523-538). Washington, DC: American Psychological Association.

Rogoff, B. (1998). Cognition as a collaborative process. In D. Kuhn & R. S. Siegler (Eds.), W. Damon (Series Ed.), *Handbook of child psychology, Vol. 2., Cognition, perception, and language* (pp. 679-744). New York: Wiley.

Schauble, L. (1996). The development of scientific reasoning in knowledge-rich contexts. *Developmental Psychology, 32*, 102-119.

Siegler, R. S. (1996). A grand theory of development. *Monographs of the Society for Research in Child Development, 61* (n1-2), 266-275.

Siegler, R. S., & Crowley, K. (1991). The microgenetic method: A direct means for studying cognitive development. *American Psychologist, 46*, 606-620.

Simon, H.A. (1996). *Models of my life* (reissue). Cambridge, MA: The MIT Press.Simonton, D. K. (1988). *Scientific genius: A psychology of science.* Cambridge, England: Cambridge University Press.

Suzuki, H. (1994). The centrality of analogy in knowledge acquisition in instructional contexts. *Human Development, 37*, 207-219.

Teasley, S. D. (1995). The role of talk in children's peer collaborations. *Developmental Psychology, 3*, 207-220.

Teasley, S. D., & Rochelle, J. (1993). The construction of shared knowledge in collaborative problem solving. In S. Lajoi & S. Derry (Eds.), *Computers as cognitive tools* (pp. 229-258). Hillsdale, NJ: Lawrence Erlbaum Associates.

Tharp, R. G., & Gallimore, R. (1988). *Rousing minds to life: Teaching, learning, and schooling in social context.* Cambridge: Cambridge University Press.

Tolmie, A., Howe, C., Mackenzie, M., & Greer, K. (1993). Task design as an influence on dialogue and learning: primary school group work with object flotation. *Social Development, 2*, 183-201.

Watson, J. D. (1968). *The double helix: A personal account of the discovery of the structure of DNA*. NY: Atheneum.

Wertsch, J. V. (1991). *Voices of the mind*. Cambridge: Cambridge University Press.

Wertsch, J. V. (1997). *Mind in action*. NY: Oxford University Press.

Wertsch, J. V., Minick, N., & Arns, F. (1984). The creation of context in joint problem solving. In B. Rogoff 7 J. Lave (Eds.), *Everyday cognition: Its development in social context* (pp. 151-171). Cambridge, MA: Harvard University Press.

4

Acquiring Expertise in Science: Explorations of What, When, and How

Christian D. Schunn
George Mason University

John R. Anderson
Carnegie Mellon University

Relatively little is known about the skills that practicing scientists actually use. This lack of knowledge makes the design of science curricula rather difficult. How can we train students to be scientists if we do not know what it means to be a scientist? In this chapter, we ask two central questions about the nature of expertise in science: 1) Are there general skills that scientists from different domains share?, and 2) If there are any general skills, are these skills just ones that any intelligent adult would have, or are they the result of training and practice in scientific activities? To answer these questions, we present a study of expert research psychologists working on a scientific discovery problem taken from psychology. Then we turn to a more practical question: 3) If there are general skills not possessed by average intelligent adults, are they being covered in undergraduate education? As a preliminary answer to this question, we present an evaluation of several research methods courses in psychology at one university.

Are There General Skills That Scientist From Different Domains Share?

Within cognitive psychology, there is some debate about the generality of expertise. On the one hand, there is discussion of general problem solving procedures and general characteristics of experts in a domain. For example, it has been argued that experts (at least in some domains) use forward reasoning whereas novices use backward reasoning (Larkin, 1980)—i.e., reasoning from goals to givens versus from givens to goals. On the other hand, the most prevalent view of expertise in cognitive psychology is one of domain-specific pattern recognition skills (Chase & Simon, 1973; Chi & Koeske, 1983; Ericsson & Charness, 1994; Gobet & Simon, 1996; Hayes, 1985; Johnson & Mervis, 1997; Larkin, 1980). For example, chess experts are thought to have learned tens or hundreds of thousands of patterns of chess positions. It is this pattern recognition expertise that is thought to underlie their superior performance in chess, rather than differences in general intelligence or sophisticated strategies. Consequently, their expertise is extremely domain specific. For example, while chess experts can play several games of chess simultaneously while blindfolded, their impressive memory for chess positions disappears when random positions are used that could not normally occur in a game (Chase & Simon, 1973).

Moreover, cognitive psychology is filled with examples of failure to transfer knowledge from one domain to another domain. When two domains have superficial differences, people tend to have a very difficult time spontaneously noticing underlying similarities between the domains (Duncker, 1945; Gentner & Toupin, 1986; Holyoak, 1985; Holyoak & Thagard, 1995; Ross, 1989).

Does this perspective of expertise apply to science as well? In particular, are expert scientists experts in only their narrow area of specialization, or is there a set of general skills shared by different kinds of scientists? Expertise in science shares many of the characteristics of expertise in other domains. For example, focused practice of an extended period (usually 10 years) is required before a scientist attains world-class expertise (Hayes, 1985). This 10-year-rule has been found in all other domains of expertise (Ericsson, Krampe, & Tesch-Römer, 1993). One might expect there to be a large amount of domain-specificity to this expertise. Moreover, one might expect that the higher the level of expertise, the more separation between different sciences. For example, with higher levels of training, a chemist might have increasingly less in common with a psychologist.

Yet, science has some properties that seem to make it different. While pattern recognition is also likely to be important in science, more conceptual and procedural components are also likely to be important. Thus, the research on less complex tasks like chess may not generalize to science. Moreover, some research on transfer has found that experts can be more able to transfer knowledge from their domain of expertise than are novices, at least in simple problem solving contexts (Novick, 1988).

Models of science education also rest on certain assumptions about the nature of expertise in science. On the one hand, there is discussion of the scientific method, as if there is some central aspect that all or most sciences share. On the other hand, fairly early on in a student's high school education, science is taught separately by discipline. For example, there are physics, biology, and chemistry classes, and physics, biology, and chemistry labs, rather than general science classes or general science labs. Underlying this design is an assumption that relatively little can be taught in a generic fashion about science. Thus, we have these opposing views of science as very general and science as very specific.

In sum, it is possible that scientists do not share skills across the different scientific domains. It is also possible that, even if they share skills, they will not be able to apply those skills in a domain outside their narrow specialization. This chapter reports a study that examines this issue and finds that scientists do share skills in common and can transfer their skills to other scientific domains.

If There Are Any General Skills, Are These Skills Just Ones That Any Intelligent Adult Would Have?

In the cognitive and developmental psychology literature, there is a long tradition of viewing individuals (children or adults) as intuitive scientists (Klahr & Dunbar, 1988; Kuhn, 1989; Piaget, 1952). Under this view, people are thought to naturally explore their world, developing and testing hypotheses by conducting simple experiments. For example, the infant learns about gravity and cause and effect by systematically dropping objects from a high chair. Or a chef learns about what factors produce a good cake by trying different ingredients or different cooking methods. Thus, it is quite likely that scientists from different domains do share some general scientific reasoning skills because they share problem solving weak methods (e.g., hill-climbing and means-ends analysis) and some basic scientific reasoning skills with all (or most) humans.

However, there is also a long tradition in the cognitive psychology literature of describing in intricate details the logical reasoning errors that humans tend to make. The average university undergraduate has been found to make basic reasoning errors in syllogistic reasoning (Johnson-Laird, 1972), conditional reasoning (Wason, 1968), probabilistic reasoning (Cheng & Holyoak, 1985), and scientific reasoning (Kuhn, 1989; Wason, 1960). It is typically assumed (although not always found (Mahoney, 1979)) that well-trained scientists would not make these kinds of reasoning errors.

Assuming scientists are better reasoners than the average university undergraduate, this difference in reasoning ability is not necessarily a result of scientific training and practice. In addition to having had much training and experience in scientific reasoning, scientists also tend to have higher general intelligence levels, even before their training began. This difference is not to say that science requires high levels of intelligence. In fact, there is some controversy about whether intelligence measures can predict whether a scientist will be successful (Sternberg & Williams, 1997). However, there is a simple observation that, in selecting individuals for science training, IQ surrogates like the SATs and the GREs are used quite heavily. This reason alone is sufficient to produce higher levels of general intelligence in scientists compared to the general population.

In sum, even if scientists share abilities in common with one another, these commonalities may not be a consequence of training and experience in science, nor are they necessarily specific to science. This chapter reports a study that examines exactly this issue and finds that scientists do share abilities that are specific to science and are not attributable to general reasoning ability differences.

If There Are General Skills Not Possessed By Average, Intelligent Adults, Are They Being Covered in Undergraduate Education?

Given evidence for general skills that scientists share amongst one another, the question arises: Where did they get those skills? One obvious alternative is that these skills are acquired as a result of thousands of hours of practice conducting and interpreting experiments. Another alternative is that many of these skills are acquired in formal education at either the undergraduate or graduate level. Since the issue is domain-general skills, one might expect that they should be included in existing courses on research methodology. It would certainly be efficient to focus on domain-general skills which students are likely to use independent of which particular scientific domain they end up pursuing.

There are several reasons, however, why existing research methods courses might not cover these domain-general skills. First, there may be an overemphasis on domain-specific information. For example, many psychology departments have separate courses called cognitive research methods, social research methods, tests and measurements, developmental research methods, etc. Similarly, chemistry departments have labs in physical chemistry, organic chemistry, etc. Even when a department has a more general research methods class, it is still tied to a particular research domain (e.g., psychology vs. physics. vs. chemistry vs. biology). Thus, it is possible that these domain-specific research methods courses would neglect the domain-general research skills.

Another possibility is that existing research methods courses might cover domain-general skills, but not the ones actually used by scientists. Research methods curricula are typically developed from armchair, self-reflective analyses of the skills used in scientific settings rather than detailed, systematic observation of practicing scientists. Research on expertise has shown that experts are often unaware of the components of their expertise. Many skills begin as conscious, declarative knowledge, and then, with enough practice, they become effortless, unconscious, procedural skills (Anderson, 1983, 1993; Anderson, Fincham, & Douglass, 1997).

This chapter reports an evaluation of several research methods courses at one research-oriented psychology department. The study examined 1) whether the domain-general skills are taught in such courses, and 2) whether the skills are acquired by the students in such courses. The study found that many of the skills were not covered explicitly in the courses. Moreover, while there was some improvement on some of the skills, even the most basic and central skills showed only modest improvements.

The Studies

Overview

The studies reported here are really a case study of expertise in and teaching of research psychology. However, the list of skills examined is not logically tied to psychology, and we suspect they will generalize to many other sciences. For example, the ability to read tables of data is a skill that one would expect to generalize to many other sciences. The first study examines whether psychologists from different subdomains of psychology share skills in common, as evidenced by their performance on an experimental design and outcome interpretation task. This first study was reported in great detail in Schunn and Anderson (1999). The second study examines whether undergraduate psychology majors show improvement in those very skills identified in the first study using the same task as was given to the experts. Because these two studies examine performance on the same skills in the same tasks at four points along an expertise continuum, we will present the studies as one large study with four groups.

The Subjects

Most expert/novice studies confound two different types of expertise: Expertise in the tasks being studied (skills) and expertise in content domain (knowledge). In this particular study, the general task is designing and interpreting experiments, and the specific content domain is the cognitive psychology of memory. To isolate domain-general skills, we have two kinds of experts. The first group consists of cognitive psychologists who study memory. Thus, they are experts in both the content area and the general task. For convenience, we will call these the Domain Experts. The second group consists of social and developmental psychologists who do not study memory. Thus, they are experts only in the task but not in the content area. We will call these the Task Experts. A non-psychologist might expect that there is little different between cognitive and developmental or social psychologists. However, they are quite different domains in terms of the journals in which they publish, the primary conferences they attend, the theories they use, and the methodologies they use.

The third group is undergraduate psychology majors in their second year of study. None of them have yet taken a research methods course, and thus they are experts in neither the task nor the domain. We will call these the Pre-RM group (pre-research methods). The fourth group is undergraduate psychology majors in their third and fourth year of study immediately after having taken a research methods class in psychology. We will call these the Post-RM group.

There were four Domain Experts. They were highly productive research faculty at a well-established, top-tier, research university. All had conducted many studies and written many journal articles in the area of the cognitive psychology of memory. There were six Task Experts. They were also highly productive research faculty and were taken from the same department as the Domain Experts. None of the Task Experts had worked in the domain of memory (cognitive or otherwise). The two groups of experts were equivalent in terms of the number of years since Ph.D. and in the number of publications overall (approximately 65) and in the last year.

There were twenty-two students in the Pre-RM group. All were psychology sophomores at the same university as the experts. None had previously taken a research methods course. The students were recruited from five different lower level psychology classes to ensure a breadth of student interests. There were forty-one students in the Post-RM group. They were recruited from five different psychology research methods courses: two developmental research methods, two social research methods, and one cognitive research methods. All students were paid $8 for their participation in the study. There was no relationship between volunteering for the study and grade received in the course.

In cross-sectional designs, one must always worry about selection artifacts. A somewhat atypical feature of the undergraduate psychology curriculum at this particular university made this particular cross-sections design cleaner than most. At this university, psychology majors are required to take two research methods courses (from the three available) in order to graduate. However, the number of offered classes and the maximum enrollment size in these classes is severely limited and thus only seniors and a few juniors are able to enroll. Consequently, none of the sophomores could have taken a research methods class, but all of these sophomores must eventually take several research methods classes before graduating. Therefore, we need not worry about the Pre-RM being systematically different from the Post-RM groups in orientation towards research (vs. clinical psychology) or in area preferences (cognitive vs. social vs. abnormal) or in general intelligence.

The Task

The task given to the faculty and students was designed to be representative of experimentation and analysis in psychology, but to also have certain extra properties. In particular, it was important to have the task be sufficiently realistic and complex that experts in the area would not know the answer and yet would feel that the question was answerable. If the experts could simply retrieve the answer from memory, then it is unlikely that we would see evidence of the strategies they use in their own scientific research, which, by definition, involves a solution that cannot be simply retrieved from memory. However, it was equally important to have the terminology and issues be understandable to individuals outside of that area of expertise. If the other groups misunderstood the issues and terms, their problem solving behavior would be different from that of the Domain Experts for very uninteresting reasons.

The task that met these criteria was as follows. People were given a description of a simple and pervasive phenomenon from the cognitive psychology memory: the spacing effect. The spacing effect is simply the advantage of studying that is spaced out in time over studying that is lumped all together. For example, on a later test, students who study for one hour straight typically remember less than students that study three different times for 20 minutes. Even though the total amount of study time is the same, the group with more spaced out study episodes remembers more at a later test. This effect is very simple to describe to people who are not cognitive psychologists. However, even cognitive psychologists do not yet know why the spacing effect occurs. The task given to all the subjects was to design an experiment to determine the cause of the spacing effect.

To make the task more similar to the one faced by the experts in the area (who already had many theories for the cause of the spacing effect), everyone was given a description of two different theories for the spacing effect. These two theories are the most common ones proposed by experts in the area. The first theory, called the shifting context theory, assumes that memories are associated with the context under study and that context gradually shifts with time. Under this theory, the spacing effect occurs because spaced practice produces associations to more divergent contexts, which in turn are more likely to overlap with the test context. The second theory, called the frequency regularity theory, states that the mind estimates how long memories will be needed based on regularities in the environment and, in particular, adjusts forgetting rates according to the spacing between items. Under this theory, items learned with short intervening spaces decay more rapidly (because they are not expected to be needed again after long delays) whereas items learned with long intervening spaces decay more slowly (because they are expected to be needed again at long delays).

Everyone was given much longer, more concrete descriptions of the two theories, and the study did not continue until they felt that they understood the spacing effect and the two theories. The specific goal given to the subjects was to determine the cause of the spacing effect. They were told that the answer could be that one, both, or neither theory was correct (as is the typical case in science).

The Simulated Psychology Lab

The most straightforward way to proceed would be to give everyone a pencil and paper and have them design an experiment or series of experiments that would test between the theories for the spacing effect. This technique would make the problem realistically open-ended. Any kind of experiment could be proposed. However, it would not be possible for the subjects to see the results of their proposed experiments. In this way, the task is very much unlike real science. Scientists very rarely answer any questions with only one experiment, and certainly never the first experiment that gets designed. Instead, scientists design an experiment, run it, and construct a new experiment based on the problems revealed by the outcomes of the first experiment. Much of their expertise lies in being able to interpret the outcome of one experiment and use the information to design a better experiment. Additionally, scientific discoveries involve designing good experiments *and* correctly interpreting their outcomes. Using a pencil and paper task, we could not examine the skills that scientists possess for interpreting the results of their experiments.

To achieve these goals, a computer environment, called the Simulated Psychology Lab (SPL), was developed. The SPL environment simplifies the experimental design process by presenting the individual with a large but limited number of experiments that can be designed. The advantage of SPL is that it allows people to see the results of the experiments that they designed. Thus, we can observe how scientists iterate through the cycle of experiment design and outcome interpretation.

The hypothetical experiments that one could create within SPL were simple list learning experiments. The hypothetical subjects would get a list of items to study for a later test. The list could be studied several times under a variety of contexts. The later test could occur in a variety of contexts at various different times. There were six variables that could be manipulated within this basic scenario. Two variables were highly relevant to the theories under test: *spacing* between study repetitions (from one minute to 20 days), and *source context* (whether it was the same context for each study repetition). Three variables were moderately relevant: *test context* (whether it was the same context as during study), *delay* (the time between the last study episode and the test, from one minute to 20 days), and *test task* (whether the test was free recall, recognition, or stem completion). Finally, there was one irrelevant variable: *repetitions* (the number of times each word is studied; two, three, four, or five times).

Participants selected variable settings using a simple mouse-controlled interface. For each of the six variables, they could select whether to manipulate that variable (or hold it constant) and what particular values to pick (for each condition or for the constant value). When a variable was manipulated, two or three different levels could be used. Participants could only vary up to four variables simultaneously in any given experiment. With the six variables, there were almost 400,000 unique experiment settings that could be generated.

To provide a concrete example, a participant might have selected to conduct the following experiment: Vary study spacing (five minutes versus 20 minutes), test delay (five minutes, 20 minutes, or two hours), and source context (same versus different rooms), and hold constant repetitions (three), test task (free recall), and test context (different room). In this sample experiment, there are 12 different conditions (2 x 3 x 2).

The participants were given outcomes in a table format with all cells being shown at once. Tables rather than graphs were used because tables were thought to be easier for undergraduates to understand and manipulate. Before being given the table, participants had to select on which dimension each manipulated variable would be plotted (i.e., rows, columns, across tables vertically, or across tables horizontally).

The table of results included a display of the variables held constant and their values (see Figure 1).

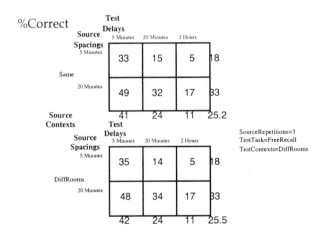

Figure 1. The interface used for displaying the outcomes of experiments.

To facilitate comparison across rows, columns, and tables, the row, column, and table means were also provided. Figure 1 also illustrates the key results in this task: the effects of spacing and delay, and their interaction (the drop-off with increasing delay is faster at smaller spacings), and the lack of an effect of source context.

In order to lead the participants to treat the outcomes of their experiments as real data (with noise levels and other properties of real data), the participants were told that the computer had access to a large database of experiments and would simply present the results of those experiments on the screen. However, in reality, a mathematical model was used to produce the results of each experiment. The model was selected to be roughly consistent with existing results from research on memory and the spacing effect. The model also incorporated random noise at a typical level for these kinds of experiments (i.e., between -2% and +2% added to each cell).

Participants worked at the task—iterating through the process of experiment design, choosing a table structure, and viewing outcomes—until they felt that they had found out what the cause of the spacing effect was or 40 minutes had elapsed. The primary data gathered in this experiment were keystroke data as the participants generated experiments, choose the table structures, and interpreted experiments. However, the participants were also asked to give a think-aloud verbal protocol throughout the task (Ericsson & Simon, 1993). Moreover, at the end of the task, participants were asked to verbally report their conclusions about the spacing effect—i.e., whether the shifting context theory, the frequency regularity theory, both theories, or neither theory explained the spacing effect. The participants were also asked to give conclusions about the effects of each of the six variables.

Terminology

To avoid confusion between this overall study and the experiments that the participants designed and analyzed, the following conventions will be used. The participants designed *experiments*; they took part in this *study*. The participants viewed their results in the form of tables; we will present analyses of their aggregate behavior in this study in the form of graphs.

Skills Examined

Finding the general skills used by scientists is a very open-ended research goal. What particular skills should be investigated? To generate a list of general skills, we constructed a computational model of scientific discovery behavior in the SPL domain (Schunn & Anderson, 1998). The model uses the ACT-R production system framework (Anderson, 1993; Anderson & Lebiere, 1998), which captures skills as if-then rules (in contrast to Minstrell's Facets, this volume). The model is capable of designing appropriate experiments to test the two theories for the spacing effect and analyzing the data to examine whether the data is consistent with each theory. From this model, we extracted twelve skills that 1) did not appear to be specific to the particular domain, and 2) could be examined with the behavioral data provided by our participants. To keep the current story brief, we will focus on six representative skills in this chapter (see Table 1; see Schunn and Anderson (1999) for the full list of 12 skills). There are three skills associated with designing experiments and three skills associated with interpreting outcomes.

Table 1. List of skills examined by skill type, along with English form of the skills in the computational model that implements them.

Skill	Detailed Description of the Skill
Experiment design	
Design experiments to test theories	If given theories to test, then set goal to test some aspect of theory
Keep experiments simple	If variable is not relevant to hypotheses under test, then hold variable constant
Keep settings constant across experiments	If not varying a variable, then pick the value used in the previous experiment
Interpret outcomes	
Encode interactions	If effect of variable X is significantly different at different , levels of Y then conclude there is an interaction
Ignore small noise levels in data	If an effect or interaction is very small , then ignore it
Relate data to theories under test	If finished encoding the results of an experiment, then relate results to theories under test

Table 1 also lists a description, in English, of exactly what the skill entailed in the computational model. The skills included in this list are basic skills that are applicable in a broad range of scientific settings. Thus, one could argue that they are especially important targets for science education. While some of the skills may seem quite obvious and simple to the reader, we shall see that they were not so obvious and simple to the undergraduates in the study. The following sections describe the results for each of these skills, grouped by type of skill (experiment design versus interpret outcomes).

Group Comparisons

To answer the main questions raised in this chapter, there are three key comparisons between the four groups (that will be made repeatedly on the range of skills just described). If the domain and Task Experts perform equally well on a given skill, then this is evidence that 1) this skill is domain general (at least across different areas of psychology); and 2) that expert scientists can apply their expertise to problems in other content domains. If the Task Experts do not perform equally well on a given skill, then this would suggest that either the given skill is not domain-general (i.e., not used by experts in multiple domains) or that expert scientists are limited in their ability to apply their skill expertise outside of their domain of expertise.

Comparing the two expert groups with the Pre-RM group establishes whether skills shared among the scientists are also shared with non-scientists. If the Pre-RM group also performs well on a given skill, then this argues that the skill is common to most adults (or at least those found in university settings). If the Pre-RM group performs much more poorly on a given skill, then this suggests that the skill is not common to most adults and is the result of formal training and/or extensive practice in science.

Of course, there are always other possible explanations for differences between the Pre-RM group and the experts. For example, the groups also differ in age, personality types, overall intelligence levels, etc. The difference that seems most plausibly related to performance differences in this domain is an overall intelligence difference. To address this issue, the undergraduates were also asked about their SAT scores, which ranged in this sample from levels close to the average population to levels very close to those of the faculty's. We then analyzed whether SAT scores predicted performance differences within the undergraduate groups. If SAT scores do not predict performance differences on any of the skills, then overall intelligence differences is not likely to be the cause of performance differences between the undergraduates and the experts.

Finally, comparing the Pre-RM group with the Post-RM group examines whether the existing research methods courses teach the students any of the general skills that they were missing. The instructors were shown a list of the skills examined and were asked whether these skills were covered in their course, and (whether or not it was explicitly covered) how likely it was that the students would possess those skills at the end of the course. Thus, we can examine whether these skills were explicitly covered in the research methods courses and how that related to whether the students had acquired the skills.

Stylistic Notes

There are two things to note about the format of the results section. First, we will not present inferential statistics in the text. All the appropriate inferential statistics were computed and only the statistically significant ($p<0.05$) results are discussed as differences. Second, since there is a natural set of three pairwise comparisons between the four groups (Domain Experts versus Task Experts, experts versus Pre-RM undergraduates, and Pre-RM versus Post-RM undergraduates), the groups are always presented in the order Domain Experts, Task Experts, Pre-RM, and Post-RM to facilitate these comparisons.

Results

Overall Results

Before examining the performance of the different groups on each of the skills, we will mention the overall performance levels of each group. First, there is the performance on the overall goal of the discovery task: To determine which theory of the two theories (frequency regularity and shifting context) provides a good explanation for the spacing effect. The memory model built into the interface was strongly inconsistent with the shifting context theory and generally consistent with the frequency regularity theory.[1] We coded the participants' final conclusions to examine whether the participants were able to discover and correctly interpret these results. One point was given for accepting a theory, zero points for no conclusion, and -1 for rejecting the theory. Figure 2 presents the means for each group on each theory. Somewhat surprisingly, the undergraduates were more likely than the experts to accept the frequency regularity theory. This occurred because there were several results that were inconsistent with the frequency regularity theory, and the experts were more likely to notice these inconsistencies. For the shifting context theory, the Domain Experts all discovered that this theory was incorrect, whereas far fewer of the other participants were able to come to this conclusion.

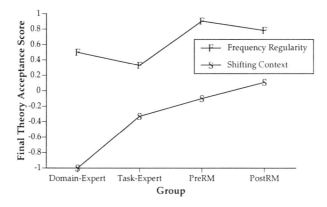

Figure 2. Mean acceptance score for each group for each of the two theories.

Turning to time-on-task, the three groups spent approximately an equal amount of time to complete the task (36.0, 38.0, 31.2, and 34.2 minutes for the Domain Experts, Task Experts, Pre-RM and Post-RM undergraduates respectively). However, Domain Experts conducted fewer experiments (2.8) than did the Task Experts (4.8) who in turn conducted about as many experiments as the undergraduates (5.5 and 5.8 respectively). As we shall see below, this occurred because the Domain Experts conducted a small number of complex experiments, whereas the other groups conducted a larger number of simple experiments.

---

1. There was no effect of source context, which is strongly inconsistent with the shifting context theory, and generally consistent with the frequency regularity theory. However, a strong form of the frequency regularity theory implies that there should be a matching effect between delay and spacing such that performance is best when delays exactly match study spacing—this was not to be found in the data.

Experiment Design Skill 1: Design Experiments to Test Theories

Not all experiments done by scientists test hypotheses (see Okada and Shimokido, this volume). However, when there are theories to test, the details of the theories should be taken into account when designing the experiment. Although this would seem obvious to the reader, as we shall see, this was not so obvious to the students. Using the verbal protocols, we classified the participants according to whether or not they mentioned either of the two theories (frequency regularity and shifting context) during the course of designing experiments, either during the first experiment or during any experiment. Note that this is a very lax criterion for measuring use of theories in experiment design—the theory need only be mentioned in passing. Below is an example of what one participant said before designing her first experiment:

> Alright. The first thing that I think about these two theories, as I understand this, what is it, frequency regularity theory, it doesn't say anything about context at all. It says the thing that matters is whether you have, um, close or far intervals. So. One way to attack the problem is to show that there is a context effect.

This (Domain Expert) participant not only mentioned one of the theories but also mentioned how it influenced her design. In this coding scheme, only the mention of the theory was necessary. Here is an example of what a participant not mentioning the theories would say (also before the design of the first experiment):

> Ok. Click on repetitions... I'm going to set it. Number of different repetitions. I'll have them do all the same number of repetitions at one. And I'll set the repetitions to... four... Ok... Now, there's spacings. Number of different spacings ... uh. I'll set that at…two…and... Do the first one ... in minutes for ... fifteen. And the second one, in hours.

As we can see, this participant is simply selecting options within the interface, apparently without thinking about the theories under test.

As one would expect, all of the Domain Experts and Task Experts mentioned the theories, starting with the very first experiment (see Figure 3). However, fewer than half of the Pre-RM undergraduates mentioned the theories during *any* of the experiments. Thus, they appeared not to understand the experimentation should be guided by theories at hand. Taking the research methods courses did appear to help: The proportion of undergraduates mentioning the theories in the design of the first experiment almost doubled from Pre-RM to Post-RM. However, there remained a fairly substantial proportion of Post-RM undergraduates who did not ever mention either of the two theories during the design of their experiments.

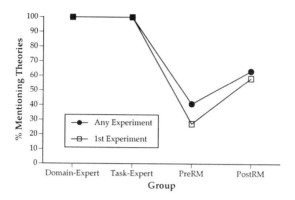

Figure 3. The percentage of participants in each group who mention the theories during experiment design in the first experiment or in any experiment.

Were these mentionings of the theories correlated with using the theories to guide experiment design? It is possible that the undergraduates used the theories but did not name them directly. To examine this issue, the variables manipulated in the undergraduates' first experiment were analyzed as a function of whether or not they mentioned the theories (see Figure 4). These two groups of undergraduates ran rather different first experiments.

The undergraduates that mentioned the theories focused on the source context, spacing, and delay variables—the variables that are most obviously relevant to the theories. By contrast, the undergraduates not mentioning the theories primarily varied repetitions, the upper-leftmost variable in the interface.

Moreover, relative ordering of variable use in this group is highly suggestive of a left-to-right, top-to-bottom strategy, which is much more consistent with simply varying variables without regard to their relevance to the theories.

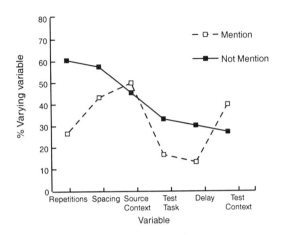

Figure 4. Proportion of undergraduates varying each of the variables in the first experiment as a function of whether or not they mentioned the theories in their first experiment.

Figure 5 presents the corresponding variable use in the first experiment for the domain and Task Experts, who all mentioned the theories in their first experiment. While the experts focused on different variables than the undergraduates, perhaps reflecting different views of what variables were relevant to the theories, the experts did prefer spacing and source context (the variables of obvious relevance) and avoided repetitions, the variable of least apparent relevance of the theories.

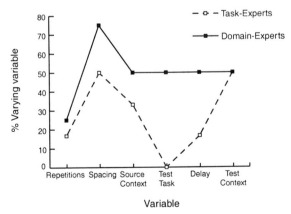

Figure 5. Proportion of domain and Task Experts varying each of the variables in the first experiment.

Experiment Design Skill 2: Keep Experiments Simple (When Necessary)

One general principle of experiment design is to keep experiments simple, especially as a first approach. One rough measure of the complexity of an experiment in this context is the number of cells in an experiment. For example, the experiment in Figure 1 has 12 cells (2 x 3 x 2). Figure 6 presents the mean experiment complexity for participants in the various groups, defined as the mean number of cells in the design of each experiment.

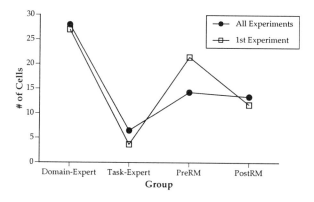

Figure 6. Mean number of factorial design cells per experiment in the first experiment and across all experiments.

The Domain Experts designed more complex experiments than did the Task Experts, and the Pre-RM undergraduates designed more complex experiments than did the Task Experts.[2] These differences are reflected, both in the number of variables that the participants manipulated (Task Experts manipulated two or fewer variables, the other groups manipulated two or more variables), and in the number of levels per manipulated dimension (Task Experts typically included only two levels in their manipulations, the other groups two or three levels equally often). Moreover, 40% of the Pre-RM undergraduates attempted to design experiments with more than four factors, whereas none of the Task Experts attempted such complex designs. Thus, it appears that Domain Experts

---

2. Readers outside of cognitive psychology may be shocked by the size of the experiments generated by the Domain Experts. However, in this area of cognitive psychology, with many short-duration trials, it is not uncommon to have designs with 20+ cells.

do not need to keep experiments simple, and that the Pre-RM undergraduates do not know that they should keep experiments simple. There was a small influence of the research methods courses on the undergraduates: They appeared less likely to start with very complex experiments and they were less likely to try to design an experiment with more than four factors (27%). However, there was no impact on the mean complexity across later experiments.

Experiment Design Skill 3:Keep General Settings Constant Across Experiments

In the current context, it is not possible to examine the traditional experiment design issue of avoiding confounds (see Klahr, Chen, and Erdosne-Toth, this volume) because the SPL interface forces participants to use full factorial designs—it is impossible to design a confounded experiment. However, it is possible to study a related general heuristic of experimental design: use the same constant values across experiments (Schauble, 1990; Tschirgi, 1980). By continuing to use the same constant values, it makes comparisons across experiments easier and it capitalizes on the success of previous experiments. To illustrate this issue, consider the following example sequence of experiments. Suppose that a participant decides in the first experiment to manipulate only the repetitions variable, holding the other variables constant. This manipulation and the constant values chosen for the other five variables are listed as Experiment 1 in Table 2. Suppose that the participant finds little effect of repetitions but wants to see whether a stronger manipulation of repetitions would have a more noticeable effect (e.g., two versus five repetitions). What values should be selected for the other variables? In particular, should the participant use the same constant values again (as in Experiment 2 of Table 2), or should the participant select new constant values (as in Experiment 2' of Table 2)? The general wisdom, as we shall see, is to keep most if not all the values the same.

Violations of this heuristic were counted by examining the situations in which a variable was not manipulated in consecutive experiments and then determining whether the same constant value was used in both experiments (e.g., hold spacing constant at 10 minutes across multiple experiments).

Table 2. Example experiments illustrating the coding of feature changes from experiment to experiment. Experiment 2 changes zero features from Experiment 1. Experiment 2' changes five features from Experiment 1.

Variable	Experiment 1	Experiment 2	Experiment 2'
Repetitions	2 vs. 3	2 vs. 5	2 vs. 5
Spacing	10 minutes	10 minutes	2 days
Source context	Same room	Same room	Different room
Test task	Recall	Recall	Recognition
Delay	1 day	1 day	20 minutes
Test context	Same room	Same room	Different mood

Since there are occasionally good reasons for changing one or two constant values (e.g., to examine whether the result generalizes to a different task or population, or to address floor or ceiling effect problems), we focused on the frequency of extreme changes: Changing more than two constant values from one experiment to the next. Figure 7 presents the percentage of participants in each group ever changing more than two constant values.

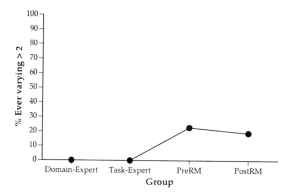

Figure 7. The percentage of participants in each group varying more two values (for variables held constant) from one experiment to the next.

Experts appear to be sensitive to this heuristic and never changed such a large number of values. By contrast, a sizeable minority of undergraduates did undergo such extreme changes. Moreover, this estimate of the number of heuristic violators is likely to be a large underestimate: Many of the undergraduates conducted complex experiments that by definition reduces the number of constant variables that could be changed.

Thus far, we have seen clear evidence of domain-general skills of experimental design: Skills that the experts share among one another and are not possessed by untrained undergraduates. There is also some evidence for some learning of these general skills in an undergraduate research methods course. Now we shall turn to the case of outcome interpretation skills.

Outcome Interpretation Skill 1: Encode Interaction Outcomes

A very basic interpretation skill is the ability to correctly encode main effects and interactions from a table of data. However, most of the variables in this task had main effects that one would have expected. For example, more repetitions produced better recall, longer delays produced worse recall, etc. Thus, examining performance on main effects is not likely to produce insight into the participants' abilities. By contrast, the interactions in this task were less obvious. There were two, two-way interactions. First, there was a quantitative spacing x delay interaction, such that the spacing effect was larger at longer delays. Second, there was an effect/no-effect spacing x test task interaction, such that there was no spacing effect with stem completion. Participants' final hypotheses were coded for correctness on these two interactions, and only those participants who had conducted the relevant experiments were included in this analysis. Overall, the Domain Experts and the Task Experts were equally able to correctly encode these interactions (see the upper curve in Figure 8). By contrast, the undergraduates were half as likely to encode the interactions, and this ability did not improve with a research methods course.

Outcome Interpretation Skill 2: Ignore Small Noise Levels in Data

In addition to being able to encode interactions when they exist, there is also the skill of noting non-interactions (i.e., not being deceived by small levels of noise). To see whether the groups differed in their ability to note non-interactions, the participant's final conclusions were coded for descriptions of non-existent interactions. The Domain Experts and Task Experts almost never made such errors (see the lower curve of Figure 8). The Pre-RM also rarely made such errors.

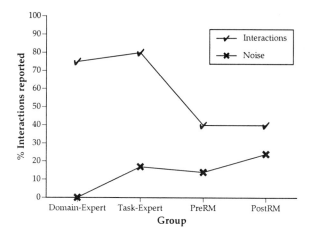

Figure 8. The percentage of participants in each group making correct conclusions about each interaction given opportunity to observe the interaction (Interactions) and percentage of participants making extraneous interaction conclusions (Noise).

However, the presence of any errors shows that undergraduates were willing to pay attention to and report interactions. Thus, the difference in the ability to report interactions is not likely to be due to an unwillingness to discuss interactions. Interestingly, there was a slight increase in the number of false interactions reported following the research methods course.

Outcome Interpretation Skill 3: Relate Results to Theories

After encoding the basic results of each experiment, the participants should have attempted to relate the experimental evidence to the theories under test. To investigate potential differences across groups in this skill, we coded for the presence of conclusions made about the two theories while interpreting outcomes (during the first experiment or during any experiment). The Domain Experts and Task Experts all mentioned the theories at some point, and usually mentioned a theory during the interpretation of the first experiment. By contrast, only half of the Pre-RM undergraduates ever made any mention of the theories, and they mentioned theories much less often in interpreting the outcome of the first experiment (see Figure 9). Thus, it appears that many of the undergraduates did not use the theories in designing or interpreting the experiments. As with mentioning theories in the design of experiments, there was a slight improvement with a research methods course in the mentioning of theories during outcome interpretation.

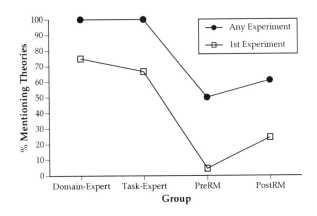

Figure 9. Percentage of participants in each group who mention the theories during outcome interpretation (during the first experiment or during any experiment).

One interpretation of the lack of mention of the theories is that the undergraduates did not understand the theories and thus did not mention them. There is data from the students' final conclusions that addresses these issues. After conducting all their experiments, the participants were asked about their conclusions for each theory. If the students did not understand the theories, then they would be unlikely to provide any conclusions regarding the theories. However, over 90% of the undergraduates made conclusions about the correctness of each theory. Of these, most provided some empirical justification to support their claims (e.g., the shifting context theory is correct because there is a context effect). Yet many of these comments about the relationship between the theories and the evidence appeared to be constructed only when asked. That is, when first asked about conclusions, the students tended not to comment on the theories but instead comment on the effects of the various variables (e.g., there is an effect of spacing and delay, but not of source context). When subsequently asked about the theories, the students made comments like: "Oh, the theories. What were they again? Let me think about that." Providing further support that the undergraduates understood the theories, approximately 10% of the undergraduates who made conclusions about the theories provided no empirical justifications for their claims—instead they simply referred to their own personal experiences and beliefs (e.g., the shifting context theory is correct because that is what works for me). Thus, not only did the undergraduates understand the theories well enough to make conclusions regarding them, but they also understood them so well to apply them to their own lives. Of course, in this context, it was not particularly appropriate to rely exclusively on personal experience and belief as a justification. This is further evidence that some of the undergraduates did not understand the basic role of experimentation in theory testing.

General Discussion

The chapter began with three questions. The results from the studies provide partial answers to these questions. First, it appears that there are general skills shared by different kinds of scientists, or at least different kinds of psychologists. On all of the dimensions, the Domain Experts and Task Experts performed quite well and equally well. Thus, this study has identified a core set of experiment design and outcome interpretation skills that psychologists share, independent of their research styles, training background, and research domain.

Second, these core skills are not ones already possessed by all intelligent adults. The experts performed significantly better than the undergraduates. Moreover, when the undergraduates were split by their SATs,[3] there were no performance differences on these dimensions. Thus, at least within these ranges of intelligence and for these skills, overall intelligence appears not to play a role. What is surprising from these results is that so many of the undergraduates were missing such fundamental skills. These were bright students at a strong private university and presumably had already been exposed to many science content courses. Yet, they appeared to be unclear on the important and basic relationship between theory and experimental data.

The implication for science education from these results are clear. We have identified important skills that can be applied across a wide range of domains and are not yet possessed by untrained adults. Therefore, we

---

3. The undergraduates were divided using a median split of 1240 combined math plus verbal. The mean combined scores of the two groups were 1152 and 1340. Thus, there was a fairly large difference in scores between the two groups, and the higher group had scores more than adequate for entry into graduate school in psychology.

have a clear target for instruction. What is not so clear is how to teach these skills.

Third, and relevant to this last point, it appears that current undergraduate research methods classes in psychology address only some of these skills. On only half of the six skills were there signs of improvement as a result of taking a research methods course. Moreover, on all six dimensions, there was still room for improvement—there were still significant differences between the Post-RM and expert groups for all six skills. This lack of improvement cannot be attributed to one bad instructor or one bad curriculum. The Post-RM group included students from five different classes, taught by five different instructors, teaching, in some cases, very different curricula.

There are several interpretations of the mediocre improvement of the Post-RM group. For example, it is possible that the students had been taught the relevant skills but did not see the relationship between their class material and the SPL task. In the psychological literature on analogical reasoning, this might be called a failure to spontaneously notice the deep similarity between the two domains. At the end of the SPL task, the students were asked whether their psychology course had helped them do the task, and if so, what aspects. Three-quarters of the Post-RM students thought their course had helped, whereas only half of the Pre-RM students thought their course had helped. When the Post-RM students thought the courses had helped, the two most common aspects that students mentioned were various aspects of designing the experiment (being systematic, avoiding confounds) and various aspects of interpreting the outcomes (organizing the tables, reading the tables for main effects and interactions). The Pre-RM group mentioned design aspects 25% of the time and never mentioned interpretation aspects. Many of them felt their course had helped but could not name a particular way in which it had helped. The Post-RM group mentioned design aspects 50% of the time and interpretation aspects 33% of the time. Thus, many of the Post-RM group were more likely to see a connection to their research methods class and could be more articulate about that connection.

Of particular interest are the Post-RM students that did not feel that their research methods course had helped them. Why did they feel that the course that should be so directly relevant to the current task had not helped? A few said that they already knew how to do this kind of task before taking the research methods. However, most said that the current task was too different from what was covered in the course.

This pattern of responses suggests that noticing the relationship between their research methods course and the SPL task may be part of the problem, but it is not likely to be the primary reason for their poor performance on the SPL task. This raises the question: What material was covered in the courses? Perhaps the skills examined in this study were not the ones covered in those courses. To address this issue, the instructors were shown a list of the skills examined, and were asked to rate the skills on two dimensions: 1) Were these skills covered in their course, and 2) whether or not a skill was explicitly covered, how likely it was that the students would possess those skills at the end of the course?

Looking at the correlations among instructors' responses, there were great similarities in what was covered, but essentially no agreement in what the students should be able to do. This lack of agreement about what students could do was true for both the items that the instructors felt they covered and for the ones they felt they did not cover. The instructors used a scale of zero (never) to four (often) for the taught question and zero (none of the students) to four (all of the students) for the "should possess" question. The mean ratings for each skill are indicated in Table 3. As can be seen in the table, the instructors felt that five of the six skills were taught in their class, and that at least some of their students should possess each of the six skills.

Table 3 also indicates that improvement on each skill as a result of taking these research methods classes. An effect size measure was used—it divides the difference in group means by the standard deviation in group performance (i.e., an effect size of 1 is a one standard deviation improvement).[4] As noted earlier, only three of the six skills showed significant improvements. The one skill that the instructors unanimously agreed was not covered (keep settings constant across experiments) was among the skills that showed no improvement. Thus, we have an explanation for the lack of improvement on one of the skills (and we have evidence that studies of the current type can provide new insights into what skills should be included in research methods courses). However, the other two skills that showed no improvement were rated as covered—in fact, one of the skills (encode interactions) had the highest ratings on the taught dimension. Thus, some of the skills showed no improvements despite (apparently) being covered in the courses.

---

4. For the skills in which two measures had been gathered (first experiment/all experiments), the first experiment measure was used because it seemed to most cleanly represent transfer from the course rather than learning that occurred during the study.

Table 3. For each of the six skills examined, the improvement from Pre-RM and Post-RM groups (difference in group means divided by group standard deviation), and the mean instructor ratings on whether the skills were taught and whether the students should possess those skills.

Skill	Improve (Effect Size)	Taught (0-4)	Should possess (0-4)
Design experiments to test theories	0.62	2.5	2.5
Keep experiments simple	0.51	2.5	2.3
Keep settings constant across experiments	0.09	0.0	2.0
Encode interactions	0	3.8	3.3
Ignore small noise levels in data	0	2.5	2.5
Relate data to theories under test	0.52	3.5	3.3

In sum, the courses produced at best small improvement on these core skills, and the variability in improvements can only be partially explained by what was explicitly not covered in the courses. What can be done to improve the situation? It may be that these skills, while basic and simple to describe, are not so simple to learn. This could be because they have many, many component skills. For example, encoding interactions in tables may have many component skills relating to the many types of interactions one may find. In support of this interpretation, the computational model that we developed required a surprisingly large set of If-Then rules to search a table and encode interactions. We are investigating this interpretation further using eye-tracking studies of how experts and undergraduates scan tables of data.

Another reason for why the skills could be difficult to learn is that they involve deep misconceptions rather than simple lack of knowledge. For example, understanding the basic relationship between theory and evidence may involve a deep misconception. Kuhn (1989; 1991) has argued that many children and adults have confusion between theory and evidence—that they treat the two as the same. The work by Lehrer, Schauble, and Petrosino (this volume) suggests that many students do not understand the larger context in which experiments fit. The current findings are consistent with those views.

There is another line of research suggesting that many teenagers have an epistemological stance in which all beliefs are viewed as equally valid—every belief is just someone's opinion. It is often only with extended undergraduate and graduate school experience that many individuals appear to acquire the more sophisticated view that while nothing can be known with 100% certainty, some views are more credible that others given the current evidence (Kitchener & King, 1981; Kitchener, King, Wood, & Davison, 1989). One could see how an individual with the perspective that all beliefs are equally valid could find the task of designing experiments (i.e., collecting data) to select among theories as a fundamentally confusing, if not wrong-minded, activity (similar to a claim currently made by deconstructivists).

Designing for Science: The Simulated Psychology Lab

A more optimistic interpretation of our results is that, while current instruction has produced little improvement on these skills, alternative forms of instruction might produce more consistent and strong improvements. We propose that the Simulated Psychology Lab might contain the seeds of such an alternative form. In this chapter, we have presented thus far two uses of the SPL task. First, we presented it as a research tool for understanding what skills experts use in designing and interpreting experiments. This has advantages for instruction in that it can help identify which skills need to be covered (e.g., keep settings constant across experiments).

Second, SPL can be used as an assessment tool for understanding what undergraduates learn or do not learn in research methods and other psychology classes. The essay and multiple choice exams that courses typically use are not likely to be good tests of the complex procedural skills required in experimental design and outcome interpretation. The project-based assessment that research methods courses also use has its own problems, too. The students are typically scaffolded through the design and interpretation process to such a heavy extent that it is often unclear what was the student's skill and what was the teacher's skill. By contrast, SPL offers a way to test the complex skills involved in experimental design and outcome interpretation.

The third and new use of SPL that we propose is one of a teaching tool. With the use of computer projection screens that are now readily available in university settings, the instructor can bring the SPL task into the classroom and use it as a teaching tool. As a group activity, experiments can be designed and outcomes can be interpreted. The students can quickly see the experiment design cycle at an appropriately detailed level.

Misconceptions can be addressed and correct behavior can be modeled by the instructor. On the experiment design end, the advantage of SPL is that the consequences of various design decisions can be quickly and concretely explored. For example, the rapid growth of the number of cells in a factorial design becomes quickly clear. On the outcome interpretation end, the SPL task can be used to show how the results of one experiment can be used to inform the design of the next experiment. For example, floor or ceiling effects can be used to calibrate the difficulty of test items in an experiment (and they make clear the importance of pilot experiments!).

SPL is written in an educationally-targeted programming environment, called cT (Sherwood & Sherwood, 1988), that is cross-platform (i.e., Mac, PC, unix). The SPL program is freely available for distribution from the first author. The interface was designed such that it could be generalized to other scientific domains. For example, by changing the names of the variables to be manipulated and by specifying the equations determining outcomes, the SPL task can be used in other domains such as social psychology, physics, sociology, etc. The only requirement is that factorial experimental designs be appropriate for the domain. Looking to the future, we are currently developing an HTML variant that allows more flexibility in both the range of experiments that can be designed and the kinds of outcome analyses that can be conducted (e.g., graphs, inferential statistics, etc.).

Acknowledgements

This work was supported by grant N00014-96-1-0491 to the second author from the Office of Naval Research. The authors would like to thank Kevin Crowley and Takeshi Okada for comments provided on earlier versions of the manuscript. Correspondence regarding this chapter may be addressed to the first author at Department of Psychology, MSN 3F5, George Mason University, Fairfax, Virginia 22030-4444. Electronic mail may be sent to schunn@gmu.edu.

References

Anderson, J. R. (1983). *The architecture of cognition.* Cambridge, MA: Harvard University Press.
Anderson, J. R. (1993). *Rules of the mind.* Hillsdale, NJ: Lawrence Erlbaum Associates.

Anderson, J. R., Fincham, J., & Douglass, S. (1997). The role of examples and rules in the acquisition of a cognitive skill. *Journal of Experimental Psychology: Learning, Memory, & Cognition, 23(4), 932-945.*

Anderson, J. R., & Lebiere, C. (1998). *Atomic components of thought.* Mahwah, NJ: Lawrence Erlbaum Associates.

Chase, W. G., & Simon, H. A. (1973). The mind's eye in chess. In W. G. Chase (Ed.), *Visual information processing.* New York: Academic Press.

Cheng, P. W., & Holyoak, K. J. (1985). Pragmatic reasoning schemas. *Cognitive Psychology, 17,* 391-416.

Chi, M. T. H., & Koeske, R. D. (1983). Network representation of a child's dinosaur knowledge. *Developmental Psychology, 19,* 29-39.

Duncker, K. (1945). On problem solving. *Psychological Monographs, 58.*

Ericsson, K. A., & Charness, N. (1994). Expert performance: Its structure and acquisition. *American Psychologist, 49(8), 725-747.*

Ericsson, K. A., & Simon, H. A. (1993). *Protocol analysis: Verbal reports as data (Rev. Ed.).* Cambridge, MA: MIT Press.

Ericsson, K. A., Krampe, R. T., & Tesch-Römer, C. (1993). The role of deliberate practice in the acquisition of expert performance. *Psychological Review, 100,* 363-406.

Gentner, D., & Toupin, C. (1986). Systematicity and surface similarity in the development of analogy. *Cognitive Science, 10,* 277-300.

Gobet, F., & Simon, H. A. (1996). Recall of random and distorted chess positions: Implications for the theory of expertise. *Memory & Cognition, 24(4),* 493-503.

Hayes, J. R. (1985). Three problems in teaching general skills. In S. Chipman, J. W. Segal, & R. Glaser (Eds.), *Thinking and learning skills, Vol. 2* (pp. 391-406). Hillsdale, NJ: Lawrence Erlbaum Associates.

Holyoak, K. J. (1985). The pragmatics of analogical transfer. In G. H. Bower (Ed.), *The psychology of learning and motivation (Vol. 19).* New York: Academic Press.

Holyoak, K. J., & Thagard, P. (1995). *Mental leaps: Analogy in creative thought.* Cambridge, MA: MIT Press.

Johnson, K. E., & Mervis, C. B. (1997). Effects of varying levels of expertise on the basic level of categorization. *Journal of Experimental Psychology: General, 126(3), 248-277.*

Johnson-Laird, P. N. (1972). *Psychology of reasoning: Structure and content.* Cambridge, MA: Harvard University Press.

Kitchener, K. S., & King, P. M. (1981). Reflective judgment: Concepts of justification and their relationship to age and education. *Journal of Applied Developmental Psychology, 2(2),* 89-116.

Kitchener, K. S., King, P. M., Wood, P. K., & Davison, M. L. (1989). Sequentiality and consistency in the development of reflective judgment: A six-year longitudinal study. *Journal of Applied Developmental Psychology, 10*(1), 73-95.

Klahr, D., & Dunbar, K. (1988). Dual space search during scientific reasoning. *Cognitive Science, 12,* 1-48.

Kuhn, D. (1989). Children and adults as intuitive scientists. *Psychological Review, 96(4),* 674-689.

Kuhn, D. (1991). *The skills of argument.* Cambridge, MA: Cambridge Press.

Larkin, J. H. (1980). Skilled problem solving in physics: A hierarchical planning model. *Journal of Structural Learning, 6,* 271-297.

Mahoney, M. J. (1979). Psychology of the scientist: An evaluative review. *Social Studies of Science, 9,* 349-375.

Novick, L. R. (1988). Analogical transfer, problem similarity, and expertise. *Journal of Experimental Psychology: Learning, Memory, & Cognition, 14*(3), 510-520.

Piaget, J. (1952). *The origins of intelligence in children.* New York: International University Press.

Ross, B. H. (1989). Distinguishing types of superficial similarities: Different effects on the access and use of earlier problems. *Journal of Experimental Psychology: Learning, Memory, & Cognition, 15,* 456-468.

Schauble, L. (1990). Belief revision in children: The role of prior knowledge and strategies for generating evidence. *Journal of Experimental Child Psychology, 49,* 31-57.

Schunn, C. D., & Anderson, J. R. (1998). Scientific discovery. In J. R. Anderson & C. Lebiere (Eds.), *Atomic Components of Thought.* Mahwah, NJ: Lawrence Erlbaum Associates.

Schunn, C. D., & Anderson, J. R. (1999). The generality/specificity of expertise in scientific reasoning. *Cognitive Science, 23*(3), *337-370.*

Sherwood, B. A., & Sherwood, J. N. (1988). *The cT language.* Champaign, IL: Stipes Publishing.

Sternberg, R. J., & Williams, W. M. (1997). Does the Graduate Record Examination predict meaningful success in the graduate training of psychology? A case study. *American Psychologist, 52*(6), *630-641.*

Tschirgi, J. E. (1980). Sensible reasoning: A hypothesis about hypotheses. *Child Development, 51,* 1-10.

Wason, P. C. (1960). On the failure to eliminate hypotheses in a conceptual task. *Quarterly Journal of Experimental Psychology, 12,* 129-140.

Wason, P. C. (1968). Reason about a rule. *Quarterly Journal of Experimental Psychology, 20,* 273-281.

5

What Scientific Thinking Reveals About the Nature of Cognition

Kevin Dunbar
McGill University

The mental processes underlying scientific thinking and discovery have been investigated by cognitive psychologists, educators, and creativity researchers for over half a century. Despite this wide interest in scientific thinking, the field has been regarded as an intriguing offshoot of cognitive psychology that provides scientific cover stories for theories of analogy, concept acquisition, problem solving, and cognitive development rather than revealing something new about the nature of cognition. In this chapter, I will provide a summary of recent research that we have conducted on scientific thinking and I will argue that this research provides a new perspective on the ways that basic cognitive processes function. Thus, scientific thinking allows us to understand complex cognition and generate new models of basic cognitive processes that have eluded researchers using arbitrary and simple stimuli that are commonly used in psychology experiments. Rather than being an offshoot of mainstream cognitive theories, I will propose that scientific thinking is a paradigmatic example of cognition that reveals the key features of many basic cognitive processes. Recent research on the nature of scientific thinking has implications not only for theories of cognition, but also for both the content and practice of science education.

Part I: The In Vivo/In Vitro Approach to Cognition

One important issue for understanding scientific thinking is to determine an appropriate strategy for discovering the types of reasoning processes that people use when they reason scientifically. The traditional cognitive approach has been for researchers to introspect on what is important in science, such as concept formation, and then design a task that can be used to investigate this process (e.g., Bruner, Goodnow, & Austin, 1956). Using this approach, researchers interested in scientific thinking have investigated many different issues, such as the forming of concepts, analogical reasoning, and problem solving (for reviews see Dunbar, 1999a; 1999b; Klahr & Simon, 1999). While this approach has been very successful, and we now have many excellent models of these types of cognitive processes, the results of basic research on scientific thinking are somewhat puzzling: Much cognitive research and research on scientific thinking has demonstrated that human beings are prone to making many different types of reasoning errors and possess numerous biases. For example, people tend to consider only one hypothesis at a time, only use analogies that are superficially similar to the problem that they are currently working on, and ignore important information when reasoning causally (Feist & Gorman, 1998; Tweney & Chitwood, 1995; Tweney, Doherty, & Mynatt, 1982). Sadly, informing subjects of these biases does little to improve performance, and even teaching subjects strategies for overcoming them does little to ameliorate these biases either. In fact, even a brief perusal of an introductory cognitive psychology book reveals that much research on human thinking and reasoning shows that thinking is so error-prone that it would appear unlikely that scientists would make any discoveries at all!

How should we interpret these findings? One answer that is frequently offered is that people in cognitive experiments are often novices and that the errors that they make are due to their lack of expertise. Research on expertise has indeed shown that there are many important differences between experts and novices and that these differences in knowledge representation and problem solving strategies are very important (Ericsson & Smith, 1991). Thus, it may be the case that for any type of successful thinking and reasoning to occur people must have expertise in the domain. In standard psychological experiments, subjects are usually non-experts in the tasks given to them. The subjects are often given arbitrary stimuli, no knowledge of a domain, and an arbitrary task to perform. In these contexts, it may not be possible for subjects to use the standard cognitive machinery that they use in their normal lives. Thus, research in cognition may have found out about two extreme cases: knowledge-rich—with experts—and knowledge-lean situations—with novices. The majority of people are probably not in either of these two camps, most of what we reason about, such as why my car will not start, or why my pasta takes so long to boil is dependent upon some knowledge—definitely not that of an expert, but not arbitrary. This is a well recognized issue in cognitive research and many researchers have formulated different approaches towards generating cognitive theories that are more "ecologically valid." (Bartlett, 1932; Brunswik, 1943; Cole, 1996; Gibson, 1979; Neisser, 1976). More recently, many researchers have argued that factors of the context in which experiments are conducted are very different in cognitive experiments and naturalistic situations. These researchers have argued that it is important to investigate cognition in natural situations, as results from cognitive experiments are inherently misleading (Lave & Wegener, 1991; Suchman, 1987). Advocates of this approach thus stress the contexts within which reasoning occurs and have recommended that we turn to naturalistic settings and situations to understand human cognition. Furthermore, many advocates of the situated approach have argued that cognitive researchers have ignored the most important aspects of what determines cognition—the environment. Thus, many of the advocates of the situated approach have argued that the experimental approach is bankrupt (see Seifert, 1999 for a summary of the situated approach).

While the situated cognition approach tackles some important problems with traditional cognitive experiments, and very clearly brings into focus many of the problems with the traditional approach, do we need to throw out experimentation entirely? This is an important issue for all educators and cognitive researchers and is particularly poignant for science educators as a large component of what is taught in science classes is through experimentation. In my lab we have developed another approach to understanding human cognition that we argue preserves the best features of the situated and experimental approaches: Rather than using only experiments, or observing only naturalistic situations, it is possible to use both approaches to understanding the same phenomena. An analogy for this can be found in the research practices of current day biologists. In much biological research, scientists conduct both *"in vivo"* and *"in vitro"* research. For example, in HIV research, the researchers investigate parts of the virus in a petri dish, outside of a host organism. This is their *in vitro* research. The same researchers also investigate the virus *in vivo* when it infects a host organism. Using both the *in vivo* and *in vitro* approaches the scientists build a more complete model of the way that the virus functions. Both approaches compliment each other and have profound effects on the research conducted. *In vitro* and *in vivo* approaches can be also used in cognitive research in general and scientific thinking in particular.

What we have been doing in my laboratory for the past decade is to pursue an *in vivo/in vitro* approach to scientific thinking and reasoning.

We have observed and analyzed scientists as they think and reason "live" at laboratory meetings. This is the *in vivo* cognition component of the research. We have then gone back into the cognitive laboratory and conducted experiments on the cognitive processes that we have identified *in vivo*. This is the *in vitro* component of the research. Using this two-pronged approach, we have found that *in vivo* scientists make far less of the reasoning errors that have been identified in the psychological laboratory, and use new reasoning strategies that had not previously been identified. When we have gone back into the psychological laboratory we have been able replicate what the scientists do. We have also been able to discover some of the reasons why previous researchers have not seen these cognitive processes used in more traditional experiments. Furthermore, by comparing expert scientists with non-expert subjects in our laboratory, we also investigate how important expertise is to some of the reasoning strategies that the scientists use. In this chapter, I will show how we have used this approach to understand aspects of analogical reasoning and causal reasoning. I will then draw some general conclusions on what this approach reveals about the nature of cognition and how these findings can be applied in educational settings.

The *In Vivo/In Vitro* Method

A key feature of the *in vivo/in vitro* method is that we can investigate a question in a naturalistic situation and then go back into the psychological laboratory and conduct controlled experiments on what has been identified in the naturalistic settings. Here, by observing naturalistic settings, new issues, topics, and ideas can be identified which have not been the focus of traditional experimental approach. Thus, the *in vivo* research can introduce new issues into a field and has the potential to radically shift the types of questions and theories that a field holds. By going from naturalistic settings with a multitude of factors interacting back into the cognitive laboratory, it is possible to avoid the problem of extrapolating from an artificial experimental task that has little to do with what naturally occurs in cognition. Thus, by using the *in vivo* approach it is possible to increase the likelihood that important real-world cognitive phenomena are investigated (see Cole, 1996 for a discussion of similar issues in relation to education).

The most important feature of the *in vivo* method (Dunbar, 1993; 1995; 1997a; 1999c) is that cognition is observed in its naturalistic context. Rather than isolating one small component of cognition, cognition is investigated in a naturally occurring situation; what this means is that the whole gamut of psychological processes are observed. The first step in conducting this type of research is to identify a naturally occurring situation where the topic of interest would occur. In my case, I was seeking to understand the ways that scientists think, reason, and make discoveries. I picked a field in which many discoveries are being made—molecular biology. Many of the brightest and most creative minds in science are attracted to this field, and molecular biology has now taken over the biological and medical sciences as the major way of theorizing and as a set of methodologies. As a consequence, the field of molecular biology is undergoing an immense period of scientific discovery and breakthroughs, making it an ideal domain within which to investigate the scientific discovery process. Having identified molecular biology as a scientific domain, I then identified leading laboratories in the United States that I could investigate. My goal was to investigate the thinking and reasoning strategies that leading scientists use while conducting their research. I consulted with a number of leading scientists, including one Nobel Prize winner, and also conducted an extensive search of the literature. I identified six laboratories at major U. S. universities, headed by scientists with an international reputation. Each scientist had conducted path-breaking research that changed theory, methods, and approaches in their fields. Each scientist was concerned with discovering new biological mechanisms that give fundamental insights into biology. Once I had selected the six labs, I then asked the scientists for permission to investigate them. All of the laboratory directors agreed to participate in the study. I then conducted extensive interviews with the scientists on what their theories and methods were, their current research projects, and what their managerial styles and discovery heuristics were. This interview made it possible for me to select four labs for further investigation.

My initial *in vivo* work thus focused on four labs in the United States. Subsequently we have used the same method for investigating laboratories in Canada and Italy. We have also investigated labs with many women scientists, labs that are all male, and a leading lab that had only women scientists. Thus, we are using the *in vivo* method to explore cognitive, social, cultural, and gender issues in science.

Having identified molecular biology as the domain to investigate, and having selected four labs to investigate, I had to determine what was the best way to investigate scientific discovery in these labs. The first few months were spent visiting the labs every day, chatting with the scientists and gaining their trust. At this point I was searching for the most naturalistic way of observing the scientific mind at work. What I discovered was that a place where scientists displayed a wide range of reasoning abilities was at the weekly lab meeting. All of the labs have weekly lab meetings that involve the professor who runs the lab, post-doctoral fellows, graduate students, and technicians. The usual lab meeting consists of a scientist presenting her or his latest research. Members of the lab ask questions about the research, propose new experiments, hypotheses and interpretations, often forcing the presenting scientist to reconceptualize his or her ideas. At some meetings totally new concepts are generated and modified by members of the laboratory. Often the senior scientist who runs the laboratory plays a crucial role in the development of new ideas and concepts at the meeting. The scientists' reasoning at lab meetings is often spontaneous and the "live" interactions concern some of the most creative moments in science.

The finding that lab meetings are a key place in which scientific thinking and reasoning takes place is important because the reasoning that occurs at these meetings occurs through presentations and spontaneous interactions. Because the scientists are talking out loud there is an external record of thinking and reasoning. The scientists externalize much of their thinking through interactions with other scientists in the lab. Thus by recording laboratory meetings it is possible to gain access to "live" thinking and reasoning without influencing the way that the scientists think, as might be the case with asking an individual scientist to give a verbal protocol. While it is certainly the case that scientific thinking and reasoning occurs outside the laboratory meeting, what I found is that the laboratory meeting provides a representative cross-section of the cognitive processes that occur in working alone, dyadic interactions, and hallway conversations. I found that the laboratory meetings provide a much more accurate picture of the conceptual life of a laboratory than interviews, lab books, or papers. In fact I found that the scientists were often unable to remember the steps in the development of a particular concept. The laboratory meetings provided a far more veridical and complete record of the evolution of ideas than other sources of information. Having collected data from interviews and lab meetings, I used the laboratory meetings as the core source of data and the interviews and papers as supplemental sources of information.

The particular method that I used to collect data revolved around the discovery that the laboratory meetings are central to the conceptual life of a laboratory. I designed a pre-present-post design for uncovering the effects of laboratory meetings on the scientists' theories and methods: Prior to a lab meeting I interviewed the scientist to find out what their hypotheses were, what they thought the data meant, and what they were going to do next. Then I recorded the lab meeting (videotape or audiotape). After the lab meeting I interviewed the scientist to determine whether the lab meeting had an effect on their knowledge. I also interviewed the senior scientist on their conceptualization of the research project. This was a cyclical process in which I observed the scientist present work a number of times. In addition to recording laboratory meetings, I conducted interviews with members of the laboratory, was given copies of grant proposals, drafts of papers, attended lectures by the senior scientists, and attended many impromptu meetings. Thus I collected data on all aspects of scientific research with the central focus being the laboratory meetings.[1]

A Typical Lab Meeting

A typical lab meeting consists of the director of the lab, two to four postdoctoral researchers, three to six graduate students, and two or three technicians (though we do have data from a lab with 22 postdocs!). Often the lab meetings have two components. In one component, the scientists discuss the day-to-day chores of the labs such as ordering reagents, who didn't clean up, and who should do what job to keep the lab running smoothly. This component of a lab meeting lasts approximately ten to fifteen minutes. Then the scientists spend the rest of the meeting discussing research. The most common style is for one of the scientists to present a set of findings. Often they are asked questions about what a finding is, are challenged about their interpretation of the results, and the theoretical interpretation of the results is often discussed. Much of the time the scientists have unexpected findings, ambiguous results, and uninterpretable data. Discussion of these issues are at the core of the lab meetings and can

---

1. While the scientists did request anonymity, it is important to note that all the scientists allowed free access to their laboratories, to interview anyone in the laboratory, attend any meeting, read and keep copies of their grant proposals (including the pink sheets), attend their talks and lectures, and read drafts of their papers. Thus, there was complete access to the day-to-day activities of laboratories. In addition, the laboratories were so cooperative that they frequently phoned me to attend impromptu meetings and discussions within the laboratory, or they would call me to come over when they felt that interesting events were occurring in the lab. Because of the request for anonymity, I have changed any identifying details from the excerpts of lab meetings presented here.

result in major new theories and discoveries. A number of discoveries occurred "live" at these meetings. What is important for cognitive researchers is that the discussions at these meeting are spontaneous, and that the whole range of cognitive and scientific reasoning strategies that scientists use in their day-to-day research can be observed. Another type of lab meeting that we have observed is where more than one lab member will speak. These types of meetings are often very problem oriented— where the members of the lab help solve conceptual, methodological, or analytic problems in a research project.

To provide a flavor of a lab meeting, I will now discuss a meeting where a postdoc presented her latest experiments on a parasite. The lab meeting lasted 90 minutes. The postdoc presented, and four other post-docs, two graduate students, a technician, and the professor who runs the lab were also present. The lab meeting was audiotaped and I had interviewed the presenting postdoc the day before the meeting. This lab meeting is typical in the sense that no earth-shattering event occurred at the meeting. While there were a few meetings where major conceptual changes occurred, these types of meetings are not representative. The excerpts here are representative and show a scientist formulating hypotheses, drawing analogies, having difficulty interpreting data, and designing further experiments. This is the standard approach of most scientific labs. She was conducting research on the ways that the parasite enters the host. Her goal was to identify the genes that are responsible for the parasite entering the host. At the lab meeting she discussed five different research projects. For each project she gave a statement of her goals, briefly mentions the method, and gives the results. Other members of the lab frequently asked questions, gave suggestions, and reasoned about her findings.

The postdoc initially formed hypotheses by making an analogy with malaria and by unpacking the analogy until she has both a specific hypothesis and a specific method for investigating the hypothesis that she mapped over from other peoples' research on malaria. She initially gave background for her experiment. She identified the mitochondria as an important component of the invasion process:

> "The Mitochondria, vary very much in sizes in nuclear membranes. It has not been well characterized in Para…and uh nobody really knows a lot about it. But ah, in malaria I tested. It has been extensively studied. And Uh their genome is unexpectedly complex. You have not only a, a, nucleus, uh information, but has two um, organular genomes. This is a linear one, 8Kb molecules, which contain two protected genes that are

usually found in mitochondrial genomes (she is pointing to a gel). So that people believe that this is a mitochondrial genome. And beside that there is a 40kb molecule which is circular, which contain a very big, uh, cruciform structure… This cruciform structure was in a chloroplast genome. This is one evidence to think that maybe, this come, this is a plastid genome… But this 40Kb molecule, it would be interesting to look for it (in Para). But this 40Kb molecule, it would be interesting to look for it… The problem about malaria is that its very AT rich. So you can't really do some uh analysis, analysis of homology with chloroplast uh genome, because of this very AT rich uh business. That would not be the case for Para and could give a better answer for some of the putative homology."

The postdoc initially attempts to purify her sample. She then conducts experiments probing for a gene. She has the problem of not getting clear data, and tries a number of different ways of cleaning up her experiment:

"I was thinking that it would be better instead of using P50 to use one of the probes from malaria that would be a real positive control because here what I'm supposed to see is some difference between the rap1 and the p50 because the P50s, and if I have a signal for a 40Kb molecule, it would be a positive."

The Director then interjects. "What about using Danny's rap1 or rap2 as a probe. The ones that have these mitochondrial sequences in them?"

Other members of the lab then provide different suggestions for control conditions and the post-doc then moves on to the next project:

"I was just doing some routine tests of infection with Para and uh cos cells and with the yield of Para. And I repeat it, and I dilute them, to be sure that the cos cells will be in really good shape, proliferating, as you know. And all the time I was infecting and I couldn't get really nice lysis. And so I said this is really strange. I mean uh this was just a qualitative experiment. And then I thought that maybe I should quantify the invasion in cos cells. Uh, so this is one of the things that I observed. First of all, uh, the growth. Para enters the cos cells. But they do not form this very typical rosette… But still, I mean the problem for me is that there is some controversy how the Para are synthesized. Either they are growing, growing, and the cell explodes, or they, there is lysis and toxin working to lyse the cells… But it seems to me that the cos cells are resistant to Para. I would say extremely resistant… It's really strange"

She replicated the results, tried using different conditions, but discovered that the cell is not being infected. After seeing a series of findings like this she concluded that it is impossible to infect these types of cells and switches to using a different type of cell. She then described four more lines of experiments. Clearly, the transcripts provide a rich database of different types of cognitive operations that have important implications for both our understanding of the ways that scientists work and how scientists should be educated. The next step was to code these transcripts.

Transcription and coding of the data are a very time consuming process. Transcription of a one-hour audio/videotape generally takes about eight hours: the tapes contain many novel scientific terms, and the speakers are not always clear in their enunciation. All coding is conducted by coding the transcriptions into a computerized database. Multiple coders are used, and independent coders conduct reliability checks. The basic unit of analysis is the statement. A statement is essentially equivalent to a clause or sentence. Statements are the basic unit of analysis as they contain a verb phrase, which in turn contains the core mental operation (proposition or idea) that the presenter is employing at the time. Thus, we treat statements at a meeting in the same way that statements are treated in standard protocol analyses (cf. Ericsson & Simon, 1993): We use the statement to build a representation of scientists' mental operations. One of the reasons that we are able to have a coding scheme of this power and flexibility is because of the MacSHAPA coding and database software that we use (Sanderson, Scott, Johnston, Mainzer, Watanabe, & James, 1993). Using this coding scheme we code a number of important dimensions of on-line scientific thinking and on-line interactions at laboratory meetings. The three main dimensions that we code are the scientists' representation of their research, group interactions, and the scientists' cognitive operations.

Using this coding scheme we have investigated the roles of analogy, experimental design, group reasoning, induction by generalization, and unexpected findings in science. For example, in analyzing the lab meeting mentioned above, we coded each condition in the experiment (experimental or control), type of result (expected, or unexpected) and how the data from the experiment were treated (replicated, extended, abandoned, dismissed). In her first project there were seven different conditions, ten in her second project, eight in the third, eight in the fourth, and four in the fifth. Overall, there were 21 unexpected and 16 predicted findings. We also coded the types of social interactions (such as suggestion, elaboration, challenge, etc.), and whether certain types of social interactions are related to certain types of cognitive operations. We coded the types of causal chains that she made. Finally, we coded the use of analogy, particularly looking at the triggering conditions for specific types of analogy use. She used 12 analogies, generalized over sets of findings eight times, and gave 12 causal explanations for sets of findings and predicted results in future experiments. The results of the initial analyses can be seen in a number of publications (Dunbar 1995; 1997a; 1999a), however this data analysis is still an ongoing process! Rather than reiterating the results of these findings, I will use these results as a vehicle for arguing that by investigating scientific thinking we discover more about the nature of cognition. Furthermore I will argue that by using the *in vivo/in vitro* approach we discover new aspects of cognition that have not been seen using the traditional cognitive approaches.

Part II: In Vivo/In Vitro Analyses of Analogy and Causal Reasoning

Analogical Reasoning

One of the most recent major discoveries in science, that of three planets circling around the star Upsilon Andromedae, 44 light-years away, was based on analogy. Scientists have frequently postulated that there must be another solar system similar to ours and have spent decades searching for this analogous system. On April 15, 1999 scientists announced the discovery of an analogous solar system and immediately began mapping features of our solar system onto the newly discovered solar system. This type of thinking by analogy is frequent in science and in all aspects of human thinking. Because of its importance, cognitive researchers have spent over twenty years delineating how people make analogies and have identified some of the specific cognitive processes that make it possible to draw analogies (see Gentner, Holyoak, & Kokinov, in press for a summary of recent work on analogy). Hundreds of experiments on analogy have been conducted and numerous different models of analogical reasoning have been proposed.

Researchers on analogy distinguish between two main components of an analogy—the source and the target. The source is the concept that the person is familiar with. In the case of the solar system analogy above, our solar system is the source. The target is the other concept that features of the source are mapped onto. In the case of the solar system analogy, the target is the new solar system in Andromedae Upsilon. What is interesting about this work on analogy is that one of the most consistent findings in the literature is that unless people are given hints or extensive training, they will not see the relationship between a source and a target unless the source and target share superficial features. When the source and target share only deeper structural or relational features and have no superficial similarities, subjects miss the analogical similarity and have great difficulty in solving analogically similar problems. Many different experiments and different experimental approaches have demonstrated a reliance on superficial features in using analogies (Forbus, Gentner, & Law 1996; Holyoak & Thagard, 1997b). However, when we look at the use of analogy outside the experimental context, what we find is that people often use analogies where the source and target share only deep structural features. This is paradoxical, and I have referred to this difference as the "analogical paradox" (Dunbar, in press).

We have used the *in vivo/in vitro* approach to understanding the analogical paradox. Our *in vivo* research on the use of analogy in science has shown that scientists frequently use analogy (Dunbar 1993; 1995; 1997b; 1999c). We found that scientists use anywhere from three to 15 analogies in a one hour laboratory meeting (see Dunbar, 1999a). What we also found is that the majority of analogies that scientists use are from the domain that they are working in. Thus molecular biologists and immunologists use analogies from the biological or immunological domains and not from domains such as economics, astrophysics, or personal finances. For example, in the meeting discussed in the previous section, one of the postdocs at the meeting drew an analogy between the experiments that she has conducted and the experiments that the presenter conducted. She noted that she had conducted a similar experiment at the same temperature as the presenter, and had also obtained strange results. She then said that she had changed the temperature and the experiment then worked. Thus she mapped over the feature of temperature from her experiment (the source) onto the presenter's experiment (the target). Both source and the target are highly similar here. At first glance, these findings are consistent with the results of the experimental research— many of the analogies that the scientists used had superficial features in common between the source and the target. However, the picture of analogy is slightly more complicated than this. What I found was that when scientists were using analogy to fix experimental problems, the sources and targets did indeed share superficial features.

When scientists switched goals from fixing experiments to formulating an hypothesis analogy use also changed. I found that the distance between the source and the target increased and that the superficial features in common between the source and target also decreased. In this situation, the scientists used structural and relational features to make an analogy between a source and a target. For example, when a postdoc in one of the labs initially obtains an unexpected finding, he makes analogies to other experiments in the lab. However, when he obtains a series of unexpected findings he draws an analogy to another type of bacterium B subtlis:

> "B subtlis may have a del B fusion protein which may mean that it can both make and degrade at the same time, in the same protein. Certainly something that would be consistent with this data. If the data repeats, it would be that maybe GN156 is a mutant in both or something that controls both and that if you were increasing the activity because we are increasing the amount of clexon and that cell can't even degrade it. So that's when we seeing this huge increase. And that's one possible explanation. Um there's no evidence. I have no real data for this, um it might be something to, to sort of keep in mind."

Over 25% of the analogies that the scientists proposed were based on relational features like this rather than superficial features. Furthermore, the few analogies that the scientists used that were from non-biological domains were used to explain a concept or idea to another person. Thus I hypothesized that when scientists are attempting to explain an idea to others, they may use sources that are from very different domains (Blanchette & Dunbar, 1997; submitted; Dunbar, 1993; 1995; 1997; 1999). Christian Schunn has recently collected data consistent with this hypothesis and found that psychologists are more likely to use more distant analogies in colloquia than at their weekly laboratory meetings (Saner & Schunn, 1999). Overall, what these data show is that while scientists use many analogies that share superficial features between the source and the target, they can and do produce analogies that are based on deeper structural or relational sets of features. Analogy use appears to be flexible and change with the goals of the analogizer. This result provides new information on analogy use that is somewhat inconsistent with the idea that people are *a priori* biased to use superficial features when making analogies.

Is scientists' ability to produce analogies based on structural features a product of expertise? The hypothesis here might be that as expertise in a domain increases, knowledge of underlying structural relations also increases. This means that experts can seek other sources that have similar underlying structures and hence produce analogies that have few superficial features in common between the source and the target. While, expertise is certainly an important part of the story, we were concerned that there might be more than expertise involved in scientists' use of analogy. Thus, switching to an *in vitro* approach to analogy, Isabelle Blanchette and I went back into the psychological laboratory and conducted more experiments on analogical reasoning (Blanchette & Dunbar 1998; in press). Our main concern was that, in most experiments on analogy, subjects are given the source and the targets. Often the subjects must select a source from a number of sources provided by the experimenter. Generally, subjects choose sources based on superficial features. When we looked at scientists and at other naturalistic situations such as politicians using analogies, we saw one key difference between psychology experiments and naturalistic settings: In the naturalistic settings the scientists and politicians generated their own analogies. If subjects in a psychology experiment were also asked to generate their own analogies, would they use superficial features, or structural features? If the standard view on analogy is correct, then people who are not experts in a domain are *a priori* constrained to using superficial features, then we should not see the use of deep structural features. In fact we found the opposite. Over 80% of the analogies produced by subjects were based on deep structural features and not on superficial features (see Blanchette & Dunbar, in press). When we changed the task to one of choosing an analogy rather than generating an analogy, we obtained the standard results that previous researchers have found. We found that if subjects were asked to choose between analogies that were based on either superficial or structural features, the subjects choose sources that were based on superficial features 80% of the time.

What the combined results of our research using the *in vivo/in vitro* methodology suggests is that analogy is a more complex process than had previously been imagined. People can, and do, use analogies based on structural or relational features, but that the task used with people must be appropriate. This finding has important implications for educational research. As the previous experimental work on analogy implied, unless a person was an expert in a domain, he or she would rely on superficial features when using analogy. If this was the case, then using analogy to make someone more expert in a domain will be an uphill battle as people would be caught in a vicious circle (if you need to be an expert to use analogy, how can analogy be used to make you an expert?). However, our research indicates that if subjects generate their own analogies, they can find important structural features and relations in a concept. Some recent work on the use of analogy in educational settings is consistent with our findings. For example, Wolfe, Duncan, and Cummins (1999) found that generating analogies to the concept of geologic time allows students to discover underlying structural features of the concept. The results of our work on analogical reasoning indicate that scientific thinking can be used as a vehicle to understand important cognitive processes such as analogy. By investigating analogy use both *in vivo* and *in vitro* it is possible to discover fundamental components of this cognitive process.

Causal Reasoning

Scientists must constantly reason about causes and effects. They must design experiments where a particular manipulation is expected to cause a particular effect. Often they the must discover a cause for a particular effect when they obtain an unexpected result. One of the problems with science is that experiments do not always turn out the way that we expect. Sometimes data is obtained that is due to error; other times, scientists interpret data erroneously—mistakenly assuming that a particular cause generated a certain effect. How do scientists in particular, and how does science in general, deal with these types of errors? Put another way, much of dealing with error is a way of deciding what is the cause of a particular effect. Dealing with error is therefore a type of causal reasoning that scientists must constantly grapple with.

Before tackling causal reasoning in science let us consider what cognitive research has demonstrated about causal reasoning. Much research on causal reasoning over the past forty years has demonstrated that people have a variety of biases when attempting to discover the cause of a particular effect. For example, in research where people have been presented with scenarios with a cause being present or absent and an effect occurring or not occurring, it has been demonstrated repeatedly that people focus on the joint presence of the cause and the effect and do not consider situations where the effect does not occur and the cause is present (Ahn & Bailenson, 1996; Cheng 1999; Einhorn & Hogarth 1986). For example, when subjects are given scenarios such as: eight out of ten people who have the CLA gene get cancer, and that six out ten people who do not have the CLA gene get cancer, people will ignore the six out of ten and assume that the CLA gene does cause cancer (this is a stripped down version of this type of task, but shows that people are ignoring relevant information). In other words, people ignore much relevant information when evaluating whether a potential cause really is relevant. Subjects also seem to favor simplicity over complexity, with unicausal explanations being favored over multicausal explanations. While it is plausible to argue that people have biases for preferring simple explanations (see Spellman, 1996) and have to attend to small amounts of information, when deciding on a cause, it may be the case that as with analogical reasoning, these types of causal reasoning biases are not as prevalent or as in-built as the research literature would lead us to believe. Thus, using the same approach that we used with analogical reasoning, we will first of all investigate causal reasoning by scientists *in vivo* and then further investigate causal reasoning by subjects in our lab using an *in vitro* approach.

When scientists suspect that a particular result might be due to error they attempt to isolate the cause of the error. Furthermore, when designing experiments, scientists anticipate potential types of errors and build specific types of controls into their experiments that help them determine whether an unusual result is due to error or some other process. In this section, I will first of all describe our findings on scientists reactions to results that are potentially due to error, then I will describe the ways that scientists design experiments and how the threat of error is constantly evaluated by scientists.

Is it Due to Error? Dealing With the Unexpected

Here, I will focus on scientists' use of unexpected findings at these meetings (see also Dunbar, 1999c). What we have found is that when both scientists and subjects in psychology experiments obtain an unexpected finding their first reaction is to blame it on some sort of error or mistake in the experiment. This is not an isolated phenomenon. Unexpected findings are very important in science. When I looked at the types of findings that the scientists made, I found that over 50% of the findings were unexpected and that these scientists had evolved a number of important strategies for dealing with such findings. The scientists initially attribute the unexpected findings to some sort of methodological error. For example, one postdoc said, "So it may be something funny like that. Or it may be something funny about, you know, the cytoscale and Northern under cos cells." Once they have obtained an unexpected result, the scientists either replicate the experiment, change aspects of the experiment, or change the experimental protocol entirely. Thus, causal reasoning strategy number one for an unexpected finding is to "blame the method."

What is interesting about the "blame the method" is that this strategy has a number of interesting sub-components that are highly regular. The first sub-component of "blame the method" is one of looking at the unexpected findings and comparing them to those obtained in their control conditions. They use a "check controls" strategy. By comparing their unexpected results to their controls they can determine whether the result was due to some sort of error, or was due to the discovery of some new type of process. Another aspect of this reaction to unexpected findings is that the director of the laboratory has seen many of the straightforward errors before and will draw analogies to other experiments conducted in the lab. Thus, another strategy that scientists use in dealing with potential error is to point out the similarity of a particular experimental result to a result that has previously been obtained. This is the "find similar result" strategy. The analogy to a previous example often contains a solution. If the type of error has been encountered before, the scientists have probably used a method to solve the problem that can also be used to overcome the current error. This use of analogies to similar situations is highly frequent. Scientists' initial reactions to an unexpected finding is that it is due to error. Only after repeated examples of similar unexpected findings will the scientists start to propose new theories and hypotheses.

Stepping back to the issue of causal reasoning, we can see that a key component of the scientists' causal reasoning is that they make comparisons to controls. Unlike subjects in psychology experiments, the scientists are attending to many different results and making comparisons between different conditions. While we have no statistical data on differences between expert and novice scientists, it appears that the expert scientists tend to pay more attention to the control conditions than the novice scientists and often ask the novice scientists to include more controls in their experiments. Thus, the use of these controls may be a function of expertise.

Given that controls are an important aspect of the scientists' reasoning about unexpected results, Lisa Baker and I decided to investigate the use of controls in the design of experiments (Baker & Dunbar, 1996; in press). Scientists design experiments that have both experimental conditions and control conditions. The experimental conditions usually consist of a manipulation of the variable that the scientist is interested in. For example if a scientist thinks that a particular protein is responsible for a cell having a particular function, the scientist might add this protein to cells and to see if the cells gain this function. However, the scientists also have numerous control conditions in their experiments. One type of control that they use is "known standard controls" (Baker & Dunbar, 1996). These "known standard controls" consist of conditions that have previously been used and validated and are standardized. These known controls are important for comparisons. If an unexpected finding is obtained in the experimental condition, the scientists can compare the unexpected result with a known control. If the known controls are also giving an unexpected result, then there is a problem with the method, and it is not some new exciting finding. What these controls do is to ensure that the technique really works and can allow the scientist to conclude that they are conducting the experiment in an appropriate manner. Another type of control is a "baseline control" in which something is taken away from the experiment or not added to an experiment. When we analyzed the types of experiments that scientists conducted we found that "known standard controls" were particularly important in controlling for error. When scientists were designing experiments and worrying about error they frequently included different types of "known standard controls."

Following our initial analyses we decided to further probe the use of control conditions and the relationship of controls to error (Baker & Dunbar, in press). We analyzed the design of experiments at four meetings in two Canadian immunology labs. We coded the goal that the scientist had (testing an hypothesis, or anticipating error) and we also coded the type of control conditions used ("baseline control" or "known standard control"). As can be seen from Table 1, what we found was that most "baseline controls" were proposed when testing an hypothesis, and most "known standard controls" were used when ruling out potential errors in the use of the techniques. This result is interesting as it shows that the use of controls, particularly "known standard controls" is one way that scientists attempt to determine whether errors have occurred in their experiments. One important point to note is that these controls are put into the experiment before the experiment is conducted. The scientists are attempting to minimize error before they conduct an experiment. In other words, the scientists are making sure that they have the right information present when reasoning causally about their results.

Table 1. Control conditions and their goals used by immunologists *in vivo* at four lab meetings. Reprinted from Baker and Dunbar (in press).

	TYPE OF CONTROL	
Goal	Baseline	Known Standard
Test Hypothesis	7	4
Possible Error	2	7

Table 2. Control conditions and their goals used by immunology and developmental biology students *in vitro* (N=60). Reprinted from Baker and Dunbar (in press).

	TYPE OF CONTROL	
Goal	Baseline	Known Standard
Test Hypothesis	31	4
Possible Error	5	28

Having found that scientists spend much of their time both anticipating and dealing with error, we decided to go back into the cognitive laboratory and conduct our own *in vitro* experiments on the ways that scientists deal with error (Baker & Dunbar, in press). In one experiment, we asked immunology and molecular biology students to design experiments that would test a hypothesis regarding a particular gene function. Once the students had designed their experiments we told them that the professor who wanted the experiment done was afraid that there was an error in the experiment. That is, initially we gave the students the goal of testing a hypothesis and then we switched the students to the goal of worrying about the possibility of error in their experiments. Would the science students, like the scientists, use "baseline controls" when testing an hypothesis and "known standard controls" when anticipating error? As can be seen from Table 2, the answer is yes. We found that both immunology and developmental biology students used "baseline controls" when testing hypotheses and "known standard controls" when anticipating error. These results indicate that using "known standard controls" is a strategy that scientists use for anticipating error and interpreting results.

Given that we had seen the use of the "known standard controls" strategy by scientists and science students, we next turned to the issue of, "How general is this strategy?" That is, is this a general reasoning strategy, or something that only domain experts would know? Put another way, would non-science students also use this strategy? We gave non-science students simplified versions of the same problems that we gave to the science students. What we found was quite different from what we saw with the science students. The non-science students did not use "known controls" on the science problems. Thus, the strategy of using "known controls" appears to be one that scientists have acquired as a result of their training. However, they did use baseline controls. These results indicate that one important thing that scientists know is the appropriate type of control to use in experiments. Scientists know that "known controls" are appropriate for finding errors in their experiments and "baseline controls" are appropriate for testing hypotheses. Most psychological treatments of control conditions, and most educational curricula dealing with experimental design, do not distinguish between these two types of controls. One possible reason for this is that in most simple experiments, known controls are not necessary. We have hypotheisized that in the complex experiments that molecular biologists and immunologists conduct, there are many different steps in the experiment, and many places in which an experiment can provide erroneous results. To check these steps it is necessary to use many different types of "known controls." The implications for education are that if the goal is to train students to conduct complicated experimental work, it is necessary to also educate the students to use both "baseline controls" and "known controls."

What does this research reveal about causal reasoning in science? Clearly causal reasoning is a very complex process and we have investigated only a very small aspect of this process. However, what we have found is that both subjects in our *in vitro* experiments and scientists in our *in vivo* work are highly aware of the use of controls, particularly baseline controls. Unlike the subjects in many causal reasoning experiments, both scientists and subjects can and do consider situations other than the joint presence of a cause and an effect. What is also clear from this work is that expertise also has an effect on causal reasoning. On the one hand, baseline controls are the types of controls that both expert scientists and novices are aware of. It may even be the case that children are also aware of these types of controls (e.g., Sodian, Zaitchik, & Carey, 1988). On the other hand, known controls appear to be the result of training in a particular domain.

The results of the research reported here indicate that a number of new strategies that scientists use that have not been previously tackled in the education of scientists. For example, while there has been much work on experimental design, the tasks that subjects have been given to design have been modeled after the traditional psychology experiment, such as seeing if people can design factorial experiments. Thus, typically, we have asked people to design experiments that are similar to the ones that we conduct in our own cognitive experiments. While this has been a good approach that has important theoretical and educational implications, we must be constantly aware that we are training future scientists in many different disciplines, and that these disciplines often use methods and experiments in ways that are radically different from the classic psychology experiment. For example, many biology and immunology experiments have 12 to 15 conditions in them, with four or five control conditions. Students learn to use these different types of controls by the classic apprenticeship method, rather than by being formally taught these methods. Clearly control conditions are an area that could be much widened and could be incorporated into the scientific education curriculum.

One possible interpretation of these types of results is that as the data on causal reasoning were collected from molecular biology laboratories, the results are only applicable to these types of sciences. However, a look at recent research in psychology indicates that psychologists also use baseline controls and known standard controls in their experiments. These types of conditions are now present in PET and fMRI investigations of brain function. Scientists using these technologies frequently use all these different types of controls. Given that many sciences are becoming increasingly more complex, I expect the use of different types of controls will be an important part of future curricula.

Part IV: Conclusion

What can we learn about cognition by looking at scientific thinking? First, we must consider what we know from standard research on cognition. Much progress has been made over the last twenty years in our understanding of both analogical and causal reasoning. Many important and detailed models of these cognitive processes have been made. However, research has often painted a bleak picture of the human capacity to think and reason. By comparing the results of *in vivo* and *in vitro* investigations of these cognitive processes, we can now ask the question of how representative of human cognitive capacities these studies are and also begin to articulate some reasons for the somewhat different results that have been obtained. Most models of analogical and causal reasoning have been constructed based upon experiments that use very simple and arbitrary stimuli. Furthermore, the domains that the subjects must reason about are usually novel and unknown. By conducting experiments using these types of stimuli it is possible to discover important features of cognition, but when stimuli are made more realistic, less arbitrary, and subjects can use some of their day to day knowledge, then additional, and different reasoning strategies are used and some of the cognitive biases identified in previous research begin to disappear. We have seen these other reasoning strategies in both non-experimental contexts and in experimental contexts. Thus, by using a knowledge-rich domain such as science, it is possible to discover new basic facts about cognition. It may also be the case that the types of reasoning that we see in these knowledge-rich domains are more representative of the basic cognitive abilities of human beings than the stripped down tasks used in much cognitive research.

One possible interpretation of the research reported in this chapter is that while conducting research using *in vivo/in vitro* methods may uncover aspects of cognition that have not been observed using the more traditional methods, the traditional framework will remain intact. The implication is that by tying *in vivo* research to theories and models of traditional cognitive research we are merely forcing *in vivo* findings into a pre-existing closed framework that will vitiate the *in vivo* research of any of its real power. While this is a potential limitation of some applications of the *in vivo/in vitro* method, current and future applications of the method point to at least three possible outcomes of the use of it. These three types of outcomes of the method are the three forms of conceptual change most frequently mentioned in the literature on science itself (Carey, 1992; Chi, 1992). First, the findings of some *in vivo/in vitro* investigations may be consistent with what has been found using traditional cognitive research. Here, the results of the research confirm what is already known. Second, *in vivo/in vitro* research may extend traditional cognitive findings into new areas and domains. New concepts, models and theories will be added to the extant cognitive framework. Third, the *in vivo/in vitro* method has the potential—because it is an open system not under the control of the researcher—to radically restructure our understanding of cognition (see also Cole, 1996). The important point here is that the *in vivo* component of the research is not under the control of the experimenter. This allows many different factors to play a role—factors that traditional experimental work seeks to exclude. However, by using the *in vivo* method, new factors are introduced into the *in vitro* research that can change the nature of *in vitro* research itself.

Implications of the *In Vivo/In Vitro* Findings for Science Education

Research on scientific thinking, reasoning, and discovery is of paramount importance to science education. Recent work on science education (e.g., Bransford, Brown, & Cocking 1999; a forthcoming special issue of the journal *Applied Developmental Psychology* on cognitive approaches to education) shows that the field is in a great period of transition. One of the key components of contemporary teaching of scientists, particularly at science education beyond the undergraduate degree, has been the apprenticeship method. Students work with their advisor and learn the methods and theories by participating in research projects in a lab. Using this method of training, some students become excellent researchers and rise to the top of their fields. Unfortunately, many students fall by the wayside, and are unable to learn this way. Clearly, there are many reasons that students do not make it through the system. One of the reasons is that the apprenticeship method is *ad hoc*. What the research that we have conducted shows is that there are definite strategies that scientists use. These strategies such as "blame the method," followed by "check the controls," and "find similar results" could easily be taught to students in both undergraduate and graduate curricula. Another place where *in vivo/in vitro* research can be applied is in the area of experimental design. The use of baseline and "known standard" controls is essential to the design of complex experiments in many disciplines and is a key component of reasoning about all experimental findings. Finally, other findings on the types of social interactions that are conducive to scientific discovery (Dunbar, in press b) could also be incorporated into the scientific curriculum. The results of *in vivo* research on scientific thinking have the potential to radically change the undergraduate science curriculum and make the training of graduate students and postdocs less *ad hoc* and more principled.

Acknowledgements

I thank the Facoltà di Psicologia at the Università San Raffaele in Milan for providing the facilities for writing this chapter. In particular Professor Massimo Piattelli-Palmarini for the invitation to Milan. I would also like to thank the editors of this volume for their astute comments on an earlier version of this chapter. Finally, I thank the scientists who have graciously allowed us to investigate them, and the numerous colleagues and students for assistance on this complex project. Research reported in this paper was funded by The Natural Science and Engineering council of Canada, SSHRC, The Spencer Foundation, and the U.S. Office of Naval Research.

References

Ahn, W., & Bailenson, J. (1996). Causal attribution as a search for underlying mechanisms: An explanation of the conjunction fallacy and the discounting principle. *Cognitive Psychology, 31*, 82-123.

Baker, L. M., & Dunbar, K. (in press). Experimental design heuristics for scientific discovery: The use of "baseline" and "known standard controls." *International Journal of Computer Studies.*

Baker, L. M., & Dunbar, K. (1996). Constraints on the experimental design process in real-world science. In *Proceedings of the eighteenth annual meeting of Cognitive Science Society.* Mahwah, NJ: Lawrence Erlbaum Associates.

Bartlett, F. C. (1932). *Remembering.* Cambridge, UK: Cambridge University Press.

Blanchette, I., & Dunbar, K. (in press). How analogies are generated: The roles of structural and superficial similarity. *Memory & Cognition.*

Bransford, J. D., Brown, A. L., & Cocking, R. (1999). *How people learn: Brain, mind, experience, and school.* Washington, DC: National Academy Press.

Bruner, J. S., Goodnow, J. J., & Austin, G.A. (1956). *A study of thinking.* New York: Wiley.

Brunswik, E. (1943). Organismic achievement and environmental probability. *Psychological Review, 50*, 255-272.

Carey, S. (1992). Conceptual change within and across ontological categories: Examples from learning and discovery in science. In R. N. Giere (Ed.), *Minnesota studies in the philosophy of science: Vol. 15: Cognitive models of science.* Minneapolis, MN: University of Minnesota Press.

Cheng, P. (1999). Causal reasoning. In R.A. Wilson & F. Keil (Eds.), *The MIT encyclopedia of the cognitive sciences.* Cambridge, MA: MIT Press.

Chi, M. T. H. (1992). Conceptual change within and across ontological categories: Examples from learning and discovery in science. In R. N. Giere

(Ed.), *Minnesota studies in the philosophy of science: Vol. 15: Cognitive models of science.* Minneapolis: University of Minnesota Press.

Cole, M. (1996). *Cultural psychology: A once and future discipline.* Cambridge, MA: Harvard University Press.

Cole, M. (1999). Ecological validity. In R.A. Wilson & F. Keil (Eds.), *The MIT encyclopedia of the cognitive sciences.* Cambridge, MA: MIT Press.

Dunbar, K. (in press). The analogical paradox: Why analogy is so easy in naturalistic settings, yet so difficult in the psychology laboratory. In D. Gentner, K. Holyoak, & B. Kokinov (Eds.), *Analogy: Perspectives from cognitive science.* Cambridge, MA: MIT press.

Dunbar, K. (1999a). Science. In M. Runco & S. Pritzker (Eds.), *The encyclopedia of creativity.* San Diego, CA: Academic Press.

Dunbar, K. (1999b). Cognitive development and scientific thinking. In R.A. Wilson & F. Keil (Eds.), *The MIT encyclopedia of the cognitive sciences.* Cambridge, MA: MIT Press.

Dunbar, K. (1997a). "On-line" inductive reasoning in scientific laboratories: What it reveals about the nature of induction and scientific discovery. *Proceedings of the Nineteenth Annual Meeting of the Cognitive Science Society.* Mahwah, NJ: Lawrence Erlbaum Associates.

Dunbar, K. (1999c). The scientist *in vivo*: How scientists think and reason in the laboratory. To appear in Magnani, L., Nersessian, N., & Thagard, P. (Eds.), *Model-based reasoning in scientific discovery.* New York: Plenum Press

Dunbar, K. (1997b). How scientists think: Online creativity and conceptual change in science. In T.B. Ward, S.M. Smith, & S.Vaid (Eds.), *Conceptual structures and processes: Emergence, discovery and change.* Washington, DC: APA Press.

Dunbar, K. (1995). How scientists really reason: Scientific reasoning in real-world laboratories. In R. J. Sterberg & J. E. Davidson (Eds.) *The Nature of Insight.* Cambridge, MA: MIT Press.

Dunbar, K. (1993, March). In vivo *cognition: Knowledge representation and change in real-world scientific laboratories.* Paper presented at the Society for Research in Child Development. New Orleans, LA.

Einhorn, H. J., & Hogarth, R. M. (1986). Judging probable cause. *Psychological Bulletin, 99,* 3-19.

Ericsson, K. A., & Simon, H. A. (1993*). Protocol analysis: Verbal reports as data.* Cambridge, MA: MIT Press (Revised Edition).

Ericsson, K. A., & Smith, J. (1991). *Toward a general theory of expertise: Prospects and limits.* Cambridge, UK: Cambridge University Press.

Feist, S., & Gorman, M. (1998). The psychology of science: Review and integration of a nascent discipline. *Review of General Psychology, 2(1),* 3-47.

Forbus, K., Gentner, D., & Law, K. (1995). MAC/FAC: A model of similarity-based retrieval. *Cognitive Science, 19,* 141-205.

Holyoak, K. J., & Thagard, P. (1997). The analogical mind. *American Psychologist, 52,* 35-44.

Gibson, J. J. (1979). *The ecological approach to visual perception.* Boston, MA: Houghton-Mifflin.

Klahr, D., & Simon, H. A. (1999). Studies of scientific discovery: Complementary approaches and convergent findings. *Psychological Bulletin, 125(5),* 524-543.

Lave, J., & Wenger, E. (1991*). Situated learning: Legitimate peripheral participation.* Cambridge, UK: Cambridge University Press.

Neisser, U. (1976). *Cognition and reality: Principles and implications of cognitive psychology.* San Francisco, CA: W.H. Freeman.

Sanderson, P. M., Scott, J. J. P., Johnston, T., Mainzer, J., Watanabe, L. M., & James, J. M. (1993). MacSHAPA and the enterprise of exploratory sequential data analysis. Unpublished manuscript.

Saner, L., & Schunn, C. D.(1999). Analogies out of the blue: When history seems to retell itself. *Proceedings of the Twenty-First Annual Conference of the Cognitive Science Society.* Mahwah, NJ: Lawrence Erlbaum Associates.

Seifert, C. (1999). Situated cognition and learning. In R. A. Wilson, and F. C. Keil (Eds.). *The MIT encyclopedia of the cognitive sciences.* Cambridge, MA: MIT Press (pp. 767-769).

Sodian, B., Zaitchik, D., & Carey, S. (1991). Young children's differentiation of hypothetical beliefs from evidence. *Child Development, 62,* 753-766.

Spellman, B. A. (1996). Acting as intuitive scientists: Contingency judgments are made while controlling for alternative potential causes. *Psychological Science, 7(6),* 337-342.

Suchman, L. (1987). *Plans and situated actions: The problem of human-machine communication.* Cambridge, UK: Cambridge University Press.

Tweney, R. D., & Chitwood, S. T. (1995). Scientific reasoning. In S. E. Newstead & J. S. B. T. Evans (Eds.), *Perspectives on thinking and reasoning: Essays in honour of Peter Wason.* Hillsdale, NJ: Lawrence Erlbaum Associates.

Tweney, R. D., Doherty, M. E., & Mynatt, C. R. (Eds.) (1982). *On scientific thinking.* New York: Columbia University Press.

Wolfe, C. R., Duncan, S. C., & Cummins R. H. (1999). The effects of generating analogies on the mental representation of geologic time. Manuscript submitted for publication.

6
Scientific Thinking: A Cognitive-Historical Approach

Ryan D. Tweney
Bowling Green State University

Science looms large in our daily life. Its products surround us, and much of our political and social policy is—at least nominally—justified by appeals to the work of experts in the processes of science. Few will disagree that we must understand the workings of science, certainly to better understand how to optimize its role in our lives, but also because we still fear the possibility of "Frankenstein" excesses. It is therefore important to ask: Can we "design" science to better meet personal, educational, social, cultural, and political goals? The chapters in this book present a compelling case that the answer is yes. In the present chapter, I argue that, to fully understand the workings of science, we must incorporate a historical perspective into a cognitive account of scientific thinking.

Science, of course, is located within historical time. It manifests a constantly changing set of conceptualizations and a constantly changing set of methods for the attainment of new conceptualizations. *History* in the loose sense is simply a record of such changes. Further, perhaps more than in other cultural domains, the producers and consumers of science are necessarily committed to understanding that science has a "past," if only to differentiate the past results from the present-day evolving state of knowledge. In general, the history of science and the study of science by cognitive scientists have not been linked. However, I want to argue for a stronger sense of the term history. In my view, history constitutes a living cognitive presence, a part of the "now" of science. In the present paper, I attempt a reconciliation between the two domains, by arguing that cognitive scientific accounts of science must incorporate historical perspectives, if they are to be complete.

I begin by sketching some aspects of research in the history of science, and follow this with some recent work on the cognitive science of science. The review serves as an introduction to a proposed model of science that emphasizes a multi-leveled approach to its understanding. I then provide a few examples of how this approach works, and close the paper by considering some of the implications of the perspective for the design of science in the future.

Historical Approaches to the Understanding of Science

For historians of science, a traditional goal has been to understand the way in which scientific conceptualizations change over historical time: How Ptolemaic astronomy was replaced by Copernican astronomy, alchemy by modern chemistry, classical mechanics by quantum mechanics, and so on. Much of this effort has centered on understanding scientific "revolutions," those epochal transformations in our view of the universe (signified by the names of Copernicus, Newton, Einstein, and so on) that resulted in what we now think of as the scientific worldview. In 1962, Thomas Kuhn's seminal work, *The Structure of Scientific Revolutions*, gave a new direction to such work. Kuhn convinced most historians that it was important to begin accounting for the role of the non-logical (or even irrational) factors that impelled scientists to adopt a new "paradigm." As a result, Kuhn is frequently seen as marking the beginning of the rejection of logical positivist models of scientific change, views that emphasized the importance of logical and formal aspects of science (Bechtel, 1988). Freed from merely recounting the "logical inevitability" of scientific conclusions, historians began to incorporate the findings and approaches of social scientists within historical inquiry as such (e.g., see the papers in Thackray, 1995). The attention of historians began to shift, as a result, from the finished products of science to its processes—to laboratory work, to the influences of cultural background on scientific ideas, and to the social interests and influences of its practitioners.

To make his argument, Kuhn had emphasized both sociological principles and psychological principles (mostly drawn from Gestalt psychology) to account for changes in belief about scientific constructs. Ironically, however, while the sociological factors seem to have impelled much subsequent research, the psychological aspects of science, until very recently, have been the subject of much less effort. My claim is that Kuhn was right—that we must recognize that there are deep connections between cognitive approaches and historical approaches.

In a simplistic sense, history is merely a record of what happened, a chronicle of the particularities of events. As such, it is the antithesis of what a scientific or social scientific approach is usually concerned with, namely, the elucidation of general laws that hold true across particular events. History, in the eyes of most cognitive scientists, is thus seen as part of the humanities, not of the sciences or social sciences, and has no more to do with the scientific understanding of cognition than does, say, literary criticism. For example, in a recent paper, Klahr and Simon (in press) argued that historical accounts of scientific activity, while possessing enormous face validity and great potential for discovering "new" aspects of cognition, are necessarily limited in the degree of rigor that can be brought to their analysis, and that they thereby suffer, in comparison to "real-time" direct observations of scientific activity. In making the present argument, I hope to show, first, that historical analyses are capable of the same kind of rigor as well-accepted cognitive analyses, and, second, that the relation between historical and cognitive accounts is more than a matter of which is better on one or another dimension of comparison. Instead, I believe both are necessary parts of a full account, and that the relative strengths and weaknesses of each complements the other. To begin, consider what the "data" of history actually are.

The Data of History

Scientific thinking by its very nature is predisposed to leave "traces" or "records" of itself. Scientists take notes, keep diaries, write papers, and thus externalize much of the representational product of their thought. In a number of cases (as with some diaries or laboratory notebooks), the time course of such records is well preserved, leaving a record of the change in representations over time, as well as of many of the activities that accompany such changes; conducting experiments, interpreting evidence, and so forth. Clearly, such data are a rich resource for historians, and the same is true for cognitive scientists as well.

Most historians have relied upon the public records of scientists—papers, books, conference proceedings, and the like, whereas diaries and correspondence, among traditional historians of science, have mostly been used by biographers. At times, however, the evidence left by individual scientists has been rich enough that historians have been able to reconstruct the movements of thought of an entire scientific community. Thus, Rudwick (1985) was able to use the correspondence, diaries, and papers of the British geological community during the 1830s and 1840s to reconstruct the emergence of the concept of the "Devonian Era," a controversial construct that had a stormy birth. Rudwick was able to show that differential social interests and differential powers of persuasion could be used to account for the details of the formulation and dissemination of the new concept, and he was able to summarize the results in a series of clever diagrammatic charts (one of which is shown in Figure 1).

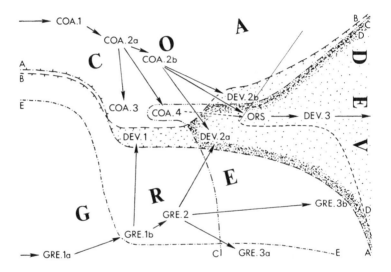

Figure 1. The progress of the controversy over interpretation of the older rock strata found in Devonshire. Time is on the horizontal axis (from roughly 1834 to 1842); the vertical axis represents "theoretical distance," that is, Rudwick's judgment of the changing plausibility of each of the alternative constructions. Subsequent (more complex) diagrams specify more closely the positions of the 40 or so scientists whose views were influential during the period. The major abbreviations are COA, referring to "Coal Measures," GRE, "Greywacke," and DEV, "Devonian," and refer to the major theoretical interpretations of the nature of the strata. Arrows indicate lines of interpretive development. From Rudwick, 1985, p. 408. Copyright 1985 by the University of Chicago.

The figure has several characteristics that are important to my argument. In particular, note that it is organized across time (on the horizontal axis), but that there is also a vertical dimension, corresponding to the relative strength of various theoretical views. In effect, the vertical dimension gives a kind of "population density" across time for each of the major views. Thus, "DEV," the idea that there is a separable "Devonian Era," only appears in the middle of the graph (about 1838), but has become the most popular idea by the end of the period.

If we think of Rudwick's graph as a "map" of the cognitive progress of the Devonian construct, we can see that it has social and cognitive aspects as well; the Devonian idea was (a) held by individuals and (b) shared by individuals within groups. Much of the text of Rudwick's book, then, constitutes a narrative "fleshing out" of these cognitive and social relations.

While Rudwick's analysis was not explicitly based upon cognitive scientific concerns, it is clear that much of the data used by him could be construed as cognitive in nature, and could be applied to the analysis of "real-time" science, not just to historical records. For example, Kevin Dunbar, a cognitive scientist, is currently engaged in analyzing data obtained by an *in vivo* study of four molecular biology laboratories (Dunbar, 1995). His primary database consists of video recordings of weekly lab meetings across the course of a year. Such data would permit an analysis similar to that conducted by Rudwick; it is not hard to imagine one part of Dunbar's analysis ultimately resulting in a diagram like Figure 1. In effect, the methods of the historical analyst could be surprisingly similar to those of the cognitive scientist.

Sometimes it is possible to use the records of an individual scientist to reconstruct the course of thought within one individual. For example, records of the results of experiments can sometimes be traced through a diary, along with evidence of the changing beliefs of a single scientist about the interpretation of the experiments. It is thus possible to trace at least some scientific episodes in rich detail through time, with an evidentiary base that includes both the flow of thought and the reciprocal flow of external events (the outcomes of experiments, for example, or the appearance of a relevant new publication in the literature). Scientists' diary records are a primary source of data for such analyses. Of course, such records are widely variable in content and completeness, even given that not all scientists keep (or preserve) diaries, and even those that do sometimes fail to maintain chronological consistency. Fortunately, there are excellent examples of scientists who have kept meticulous notebooks, characterized by an amazing degree of completeness, chronological consistency, and span. One of these is of central concern to the present chapter.

Michael Faraday

Of those whose extensive records are an invaluable source, Faraday (1791-1867) was exemplary in the completeness and span of his notebooks, and he has therefore served as "database" for a number of cognitively-oriented scholars, including myself.

Among Faraday's discoveries, the most famous is the discovery, in 1831, of electromagnetic induction, the finding that electrical currents can be generated in a conductor which is near a changing magnetic field. The practical importance of the discovery (which led to the invention of the dynamo) was immense, but it also had important implications for the later research of Faraday and others on the nature of electricity and magnetism. Thus, in the 1840s, Faraday became the first to recognize the important distinction between paramagnetic and diamagnetic substances, and the first to find an effect of magnetism on light, by demonstrating the rotation of the plane of polarization of a polarized beam passed through a magnetic field. In chemistry, he was the first to liquefy gases, the first to prepare colloidal solutions, and the discoverer of benzene. And his theoretical views on fields, which at the time were out of step with those of most of his contemporaries, inspired James Clerk Maxwell, who codified and extended Faraday's findings in the form of "Maxwell's Equations." During his time, Faraday became widely known among a British public that was beginning to pay attention to the progress of science. Indeed, in his lectures at the Royal Institution of Great Britain, Faraday set new standards for the "demonstration lecture," a popular lecture combined with tabletop demonstrations of unparalleled clarity. For example, his *Chemical History of a Candle* (Faraday, 1861), based on lectures given to a "juvenile audience," is even today a readable introduction to the chemistry and physics of combustion, and is filled with easily replicable experiments that are no less fascinating for their simplicity. (Williams, 1965, is the standard biography of Faraday.)

Faraday left a richer documentary legacy of thought than exists for perhaps any other scientific figure in history. His daily laboratory notebooks, diaries, and commonplace books are a rich source for the historian. "The" Diary, transcribed and published by Martin (Faraday, 1932-36), is a set of bound volumes recording Faraday's most important laboratory activity after 1820, but also including miscellaneous observations, theoretical developments, speculations, etc. Almost all of the entries except those in the first part (from September 1820 to September 15, 1832) are numbered sequentially from 1 (August 25, 1832) to 16,041

(March 6, 1860). As a rough guess, the diary contains records of about 30,000 experiments, both successful and unsuccessful (Tweney, 1991b). Early in his career, Faraday also kept a variety of "idea books," records of speculations, possible experiments, theoretical musings, and the like. Organized by topic, with frequent blank spaces of various size, the most important one, the "Chemical notes, hints, suggestions, and objects of pursuit" (Faraday, 1822) contains a variety of speculative ideas, and was used by Faraday over at least a decade. It includes a number of remarkable premonitions of his later discoveries, and is a valuable source for revealing just how long he thought about certain topics. Once the diary proper was developed into a sequential, numbered record (1831 and after), idea books became scarcer and, when they do survive, are shorter, more narrow in focus, and unbound (see Tweney, 1991a and 1991b, for an account of the retrieval schemes used by Faraday to "navigate" this immense record).

Some recent analyses of Faraday's diary records have a surprisingly cognitive flavor, even when carried out by those not working within the traditional cognitive approaches. For example, David Gooding used diagrammatic means to represent the results of an analysis of a portion of Faraday's diary (Figure 2).

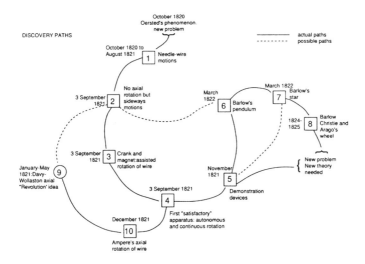

Figure 2. The numbers indicate the chronological order of discovery. From Gooding, 1990, p. 154. With kind permission from Kluwer Academic Publishers.

Figure 2 shows a representation given by Gooding (1990) of the actual and possible discovery paths that led to Faraday's discovery, in 1821, that an electrified needle could be made to rotate in a magnetic field.The figure bears a "family resemblance" to Rudwick's (Figure 1) in that each is based upon the interpretation of the "movement" of ideas. While Gooding's does incorporate some "community" interactions (as the references to Barlow, Wollaston, and Ampére indicate), the bulk of the figure is based on his reconstruction of the discovery process from Faraday's diary.

Gooding's work shows how history and cognitive science can "coexist" in a single study. In a later section of this paper, I will show how Faraday's records can be used in an explicitly "cognitive-historical" fashion. For now, note that Kulkarni and Simon (1988) were able to use Holmes's (1980) reconstruction of the biochemist Krebs's discovery of the ornithine cycle as the basis for a computational model that was remarkably similar in its behavior to the behaviors recorded in Krebs's diary. And, in a similar effort, Kulkarni (1988) was able to capture some of the highlights of Faraday's discovery of electromagnetic induction, following an analysis by Tweney & Hoffner (1987) of a portion of Faraday's diary. Duncan and Tweney (1999) are currently using neural network models to simulate some of Rudwick's (1985) descriptions of the Devonian controversy. Finally, Gooding and his colleagues (Addis, Gooding, & Townsend, 1993; Gooding & Addis, in press) used a reconstruction of Faraday's Diary (Figure 2) as the basis for a computer simulation of the discovery path, and similar efforts have been carried out by Gorman (1992), using the patent sketches and notebooks of Alexander Graham Bell.

Cognitive Approaches to the Understanding of Science

In a famous passage, Simon (1996/1969) argued that the task of understanding problem solving could be illuminated by a useful analogy. He first considered the path made by an ant as it winds its way across a sandy beach, asking how we can understand and explain the geometric complexity of the twists and turns of the ant's trajectory. The real complexity is not in the ant, however; it is to be found in the environment within which its relatively simple "homing" device is operating. Simon concluded that:

> An ant, viewed as a behaving system, is quite simple. The apparent complexity of its behavior over time is largely a reflection of the complexity of the environment in which it finds itself. (Simon, 1969/1996, p. 52).

Similarly, Simon argued, the path of problem solving (as revealed in a think-aloud protocol, say) was only seemingly complex; it too was based on the workings of relatively simple and lawful processes in a complex symbolic environment:

> Human beings, viewed as behaving systems, are quite simple. The apparent complexity of our behavior over time is largely a reflection of the complexity of the environment in which we find ourselves. (Simon, 1969/1996, p. 53)

One of Simon's major insights was to recognize that the complexity of problem solving is itself what we need to understand. Rather than trying to simplify the process in laboratory conditions, thereby isolating one or another "factors" that are causally linked to the problem solving activity, Simon instead sought a way to characterize the complexity of real-world problem solving. In particular, he took seriously the conscious, often verbalizeable, steps that people take when trying to solve a difficult problem. The record of such steps is, in effect, a map of their attempt to traverse a problem "space," just as the geometric path of an ant is the record of an attempt to traverse a physical space.

Simon's approach was brilliantly successful. Since the 1960s, it has been clear that scientific accounts of complex cognition are possible, particularly in domains which can be "reflected" by an ongoing think-aloud protocol. If circumstances are such that a protocol gives even a partial record of the successive fixations of attention (or of the successive contents of working memory), there is now broad consensus that rigorous accounts can be given of the specific path used by a problem solver to search a problem space (Ericsson & Simon, 1993; Newell & Simon, 1972). Even where a specific path cannot be reconstructed, such protocols can still serve as important constraints on the representations used by a problem solver. Thus, as just one example, James Voss was able to capture much of the underlying structure of informal thought, as experts and novices in international affairs carried out a think-aloud "thought analysis" of Soviet Russian agricultural policy (Voss & Post, 1988). No specific problem space could be constructed for these problems, but the protocols still permitted extensive characterization of the heuristics used to explore the issue.

Think-aloud protocols in some sense resemble the diary records of an individual like Faraday; both a diary and a protocol contain a chronological record of the course of thought in an individual, and each can therefore be used as the basis for a cognitive account. However, diary records differ from protocols in that the contents reflect an "editing" process. Even in the case of a meticulous diarist like Faraday, the record is clearly only partial, reflecting, at best, the highlights of thought, rather than the more nearly complete account of a think-aloud protocol. It is, at best, the difference between a "grain size" of minutes or hours, rather than seconds. As I will show below, however, sometimes the diary records do permit a close-grained analysis, to nearly the same level of detail that can be found in tasks given in a psychology laboratory. In any case, the most detailed microstructure available to the historian of science comes close to the detail available to the cognitive scientist, and calls for similar analyses (Holmes, 1987), provided that we use an appropriate adjustment for the different levels that may be manifest in the records. Taking account of the need for these adjustments is, in fact, one of the goals of the theory presented later in this paper.

A Model of Problem Solving

Because problem space search is so fundamental to this chapter's goal, it is worth looking at in more detail. Newell and Simon (1972) relied upon a characterization of thought in which mental states were transformed into other mental states by specific operators, construed as symbolic rewrite rules. *States*, for Newell & Simon, were simply symbolic representations of the momentary contents of working memory. *Operators* were the minimal symbolic operations that change one state onto another. In the right kind of think-aloud protocol, the states and operators can be directly mapped to the utterances of the participant. For example, if someone is solving a difficult mental arithmetic problem (e.g., "Multiply 13 by 26") we can interpret each of the utterances of a protocol ("Let's see, three times six is 18, so remember eight, carry the one") as separate states ("18," for example, is one state, "three times six" is another) and operators ("Retrieve from long-term memory," "Store a sub-result," "carry a digit," and so on). In effect, the states and operators of a given problem-solving episode represent moves along the solution path, transformations of the successive numeric symbols representing the mental state of the solver at a given step. Such analyses are easiest with problems that have a formal character and can be specifically defined using a formal problem space, that is, a map of all possible moves from one state to another. Solving the problem can then be construed as finding a path from an initial state to a final state representing the solution to the problem.

This theory possesses broad generality as an account of human problem solving. Given a problem space, problem solving can be described as a search for a solution path, and the empirical program becomes one of characterizing the heuristics used by solvers, that is, of finding the overall strategies by which specific operators are clustered together to move from one part of a problem space to another. Across a wide range of problems, Newell and Simon were able to characterize a small number of general heuristics of great power; "hill-climbing search," "means-ends analysis," and so forth (see Mayer, 1992, for a concise introduction). To apply the theory to a new domain of problem solving, one needs only to identify domain-specific states and operators. These, together with domain-general heuristics (such as means-ends analysis) can then be applied directly to the record at hand. In fact, part of the success of the theory was based on the empirical finding that there were powerful domain-general heuristics that sufficed to account for many of the otherwise intractable characteristics of the data of problem solving.

In subsequent decades, variations of the same approach were widely adopted, for instance by Klahr and his associates (Klahr & Dunbar, 1988; Shrager & Klahr, 1986), who looked specifically at "science-like" problem solving. By asking college students to determine the functions of an unfamiliar device, Klahr and Dunbar showed that the observed behavior of their participants could be modeled by positing search through two related but independent problem spaces, a space of possible hypotheses and a space of possible experiments relevant to testing these hypotheses. Schunn has extended this even further, showing that no fewer than four problem spaces may be searched for certain scientific problems (Schunn & Anderson, 1998). Given its generality, Perkins (1992) argued that such accounts could be used to understand manifestations of "creative" problem solving, especially in educational contexts.

In addition to its specific theoretical and empirical claims, the notion of problem solving as problem space search was widely influential in stimulating use of two specific methodologies: Simulation as a test of a theory of human problem solving, and the use of think-aloud protocols as a principal source of data. A computer simulation can be seen as a sufficiency test for a theory of human thought. Insofar as a computer trace based upon theoretical considerations resembles the activity of a human participant, to that extent the theory is sufficient as an explanation of the human data. Such a test is obviously not adequate to show the necessity of a theory but can go a long way toward delimiting the class of possible theories.

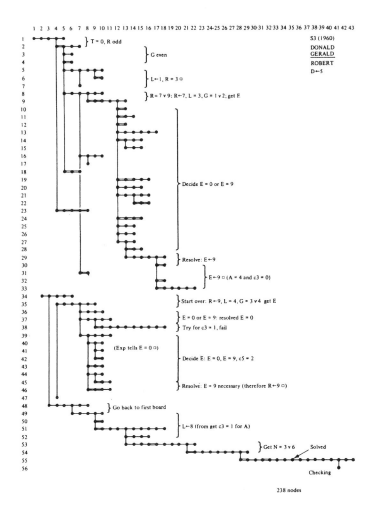

Figure 3. The Problem Behavior Graph of a single subject solving the cryptarithmetic problem shown at the top right. Each black dot (or node) represents a verbalized mental state. The nodes are linked by horizontal lines to represent operations that change one state into another. Vertical lines are "placeholders" that signal backups to an earlier state of the problem. Time moves rightwards and downwards. Halfway through the process, the subject abandoned his previous efforts and started over at the very beginning. From Newell & Simon, 1972, p. 181. Reprinted by permission of Prentice Hall, Upper Saddle River, New Jersey.

In some instances, it has been possible to use simulations together with other kinds of converging evidence. For example, Chase & Simon (1973) were able to validate their account of expert chess playing by constructing simulations, and matching the program trace to think-aloud protocols and eye-movement records of participants.

In addition to simulation, much of the research has relied upon think-aloud protocols in which a problem solver is asked to verbalize aloud during the course of thought. Under the right circumstances, such protocols can be mapped in a two-dimensional graphical representation, like that in Figure 3, known as a *Problem Behavior Graph* (see also the papers in Cross, Christiaans, & Dorst, 1996, for extensions of such representations). Such graphs can reveal the flow of thought, clearly capturing, for example, the nature, location, and extent of "blind alleys" along the way to solution. Figure 3 shows a "cryptarithmetic" problem, and the record of one subject trying to solve it. The problem requires one to search through a space of possible letter-number substitutions, such that the "alphabet" sum shown is a correct arithmetic sum. As a starting hint, the subject was told that D=5. The Problem Behavior Graph, constructed from the subject's think-aloud protocol, then records each move taken by the subject in navigating the problem space.

Note the similarity between Gooding's analysis of Faraday's diary (Figure 2) and this figure. Here is our first hint that methods of protocol analysis based on the problem space search approach may have something in common with historical analysis!

Is Science Just Problem Solving?

Simon and his students and colleagues extended the problem space search account to focus upon aspects of scientific thinking. Thus, Langley, Simon, Bradshaw, and Zytkow (1987) developed several AI routines, including BACON and STAHL, intended to simulate particular aspects of the course of scientific thought. BACON was able to induce mathematical function forms when given tables of numerical data, and was therefore primarily data-driven. STAHL, on the other hand, could identify the components of specific chemical reactions given only the results of specific experiments as data. To achieve this, STAHL incorporated a conjectural capacity, a kind of "generate-and-test" capability. Like BACON, STAHL began by being data-driven, but became increasingly hypothesis-driven as its analysis proceeded. Both programs were tested on historically reconstructed data. For example, BACON was given numerical data corresponding to some of Kepler's observations, and was able to correctly determine the algebraic equations of Kepler's Laws. In later efforts, Simon and his colleagues returned to think-aloud data. For example, Qin & Simon (1995) showed that visual representations in the form of diagrams could be incorporated within a similar account. They showed that a participant's comprehension of a difficult paper by Einstein could be described as a search for "simulations" or "mental models" in which diagrams and sketches served as heuristic guides to the properties of conjectured understandings. Multiple representations were crucial to their account, and subsequently Tabachneck-Schiff, Leonardo, and Simon (1997) described a computational model, CaMeRa, that can accommodate such representations, even across groups of people.

What cannot be easily accommodated within the problem space search account? Much problem solving is best understood as dependent upon retrieval of known relevant information and skills in ways that are not generally captured by a think aloud protocol. Thus, John Anderson (1990) noted that everyday problem solving differed from the kinds of tasks usually studied in the laboratory, in that, in the real world, there were rarely explicit rules that had to be followed to reach a goal. Instead, there are usually only probabilistic relations between particular "paths" and a solution, and there are often specific costs and benefits that favor particular heuristics over others (in spite of considerations of accuracy or correctness). In considering his own attempts to fix a broken clothesline, for example, Anderson's self-reflexive account suggested that there was no problem space! Instead, he was relying upon search over a set of external entities (clothesline, poles, etc.), depending heavily upon stimulus-cued operations. Under such circumstances, it is hard to define any but the vaguest "states and operators," making the entire approach, he suggested, open to question about its real utility outside certain carefully defined artificial situations.

Anderson's criticism is an important one for the understanding of scientific thinking. Much scientific thinking could, in fact, constitute a "clothesline problem," in that the search is not over a defined problem space but across a domain consisting of, say, apparatus, external texts (books, articles, tables, etc.), internal memory (reflecting the scientist's domain knowledge), and a symbol system that may need to be altered or created, rather than merely rearranged. In such cases, the problem space search account becomes increasingly metaphorical in character, and loses utility as an analytical tool. Fortunately, it is precisely these kinds of situations that lend themselves most readily to an approach based upon historical considerations.

Cognitive-Historical Analyses of Scientific Thinking

The resemblance between Figures 2 and 3 is not accidental. Both Gooding and Newell and Simon are trying to represent the relationships among symbolic entities. Gooding provides a map of the relationships among specific hypotheses and empirical observations, on the one hand, and "moves" (experiments, conjectures, and the like) on the other hand. Note that the temporal order of Faraday's actions are not explicitly coded in a graphic manner in Gooding's maps; instead, the numbering of states (an "extra-graphical" device) captures the order. Newell and Simon are more explicit about the temporal relationships among the states and operators, in that time always, without exception, moves rightward and downward (the downward moves represent "backups," that is, returns to an earlier state, following the participant's awareness that a blind alley has been reached). Further, their rules for identifying each element of the graph are more precisely defined, since Gooding's map is based in part upon historical interpretive analysis not directly visible in the graph; to construct such a map requires more inferences than to construct the Newell and Simon kind.

Some investigators have taken the construction of graphical representations that resemble problem behavior graphs as a specific goal of their historical research; this has been an important strategy among those who have explicitly adopted a historical-cognitive approach to the understanding of science. Thus, Gorman (1997) constructed graphs based on Alexander Graham Bell's working diagrams and patent sketches to illuminate the flow of thought during the invention of the telephone. Gorman's diagrams resemble the Problem Behavior Graphs of Newell and Simon even more than do the maps developed by Gooding, or the broad schematic representations used by Rudwick. In particular, he preserved the temporal ordering of Bell's moves through the "invention space." Similarly, by using a representation explicitly modeled on those of Newell and Simon, Tweney and Hoffner (1987) constructed a Problem Behavior Graph based upon a portion of Faraday's diary record for the autumn of 1831. In their analysis, specific experiments served as states and the implied operators were the manipulations and observations that transformed one state into another. The graphs were useful in showing that Faraday quickly abandoned unpromising or unsuccessful lines of research. In contrast to most problem-solving protocols, Faraday's Problem Behavior Graph was much less "branchy," that is, he appeared to be adroit in keeping exploration of blind alleys to a bare minimum. Tweney and Hoffner concluded that Faraday was using a "confirm early, disconfirm late" heuristic, that is, that he deliberately ignored results that did not fit his conjectures about the domain, dealing with them only after he had some assurance that his conjectures were at least viable (see Tweney, Doherty, & Mynatt, 1981). It is clear from such results that the problem space search account can be used to explore historical episodes of scientific thinking, whether the approach taken resembles Gooding's or Newell & Simon's. But how general is the notion? In particular, can it account for the concrete actions of everyday thought at the laboratory bench? Can it account for discovery processes in science, which, by definition, implicate new domains for which problem spaces cannot be delineated? Or for the emergence of a new representation to replace an old one?

Some have expressed the view that problem space search reaches its limits when confronted with such issues. Thus, Ippolito & Tweney (1995) and Kurz & Tweney (1998) argued that the absence of a specific problem space to search is a characteristic feature of new domains of scientific and mathematical inquiry. The challenge facing a scientist is to develop a representation from the vague and insubstantial elements of a problem whose very goal may not be part of the problem statement. How can problem space search be an aid to our analytic understanding of the scientist under such circumstances? Similarly, Nersessian (1992; 1993) argued that problem space search is too limited to accommodate the centrality of analogical reasoning in problem solving. Finally, Gooding (1989, p. 64) noted that accounts of experimental research are dependent upon practices, specific sensory-motor activities, in much the same way that Anderson's "clothesline problem" is dependent upon concrete—nonsymbolic!—objects. These practices of "laboratory life," though often tacit, must be accepted by a community of scientists if the results are to be taken as acceptable. Here also, we see the partial character of a problem space search account.

Whether or not we follow the specific claims made about the generality of problem space search, the existence of detailed thought records (like Faraday's diary) poses a direct challenge to cognitive science's understanding of science: Can we show that the apparent complexity of scientific thinking is in fact a product of what we believe we know about scientific cognition in general? To demonstrate that the answer is yes, I propose an overall framework that makes this possible.

Levels of Analysis for Scientific Thinking

The historical cognitive reconstruction of scientific episodes poses special challenges for analysis. Such episodes can be seen as possessing a "dynamics" of varying frequency characteristics, which emerge with varying degrees of clarity depending upon the level of analysis. Thus, the long-term organization of overall intentions constitutes a slow-moving aspect of scientific research—these are the "slow" (or "low frequency") dynamics in which change occurs over months or years. At the opposite extreme, the "fast" (or "high frequency") dynamics reflect operators that move one symbolic state to another—these change from second to second. Part of my intent is to accommodate this complexity of temporal organization, adding, in effect, a "temporal" metaphor to the usual spatial metaphor that underlies the idea of problem space search. Further, as I will show, the need to incorporate historically-conditioned dynamics imposes special requirements on the theory—which is why it cannot be identical to the existing problem space search models.

The core of the framework is a set of distinctions among various levels of analysis, each of which is intended to capture a given "frequency band" of the temporal dynamics. From the lowest frequency dynamics to the highest, the levels are as follows:

Level 1: Purposes: The overall goals of the research endeavor.

Level 2: Heuristics: Strategies that organize specific moves within the research.

Level 3: Scripts & Schemata: Organized procedural knowledge (scripts) and organized groups of related knowledge (schemata.)

Level 4: Goals & Subgoals: The goals of a research episode, and the specific subgoals that are invoked to reach the goals.

Level 5: States & Operators: in the Newell & Simon sense, i.e., mental states and the symbolic operators that change one state into another.

It is important to note that my use of terminology in the levels sometimes differs from existing cognitive theory (e.g. Newell's, 1990, SOAR model treats all of my levels as States and Operators, instantiable using production rules). In fact, almost all of them have been used in prior literature at just about all dynamic levels. However, by imposing limits on how the terms are used, it is easier to separate the different aspects of the phenomena under study. Note also that the levels constitute a partially decomposable hierarchy (Simon, 1969/1996), in which each level can be seen as "assembled" from elements in the level below.

As an example, suppose that we are examining Faraday's diary records and wish to analyze a series of experiments in which he explores the nature of the interaction between moving conductors and a nearby magnetic field. Here, we might find that a purpose (e.g., "Find the relation between electricity and magnetism") is implemented by a selection of problem-solving heuristics ("Try to generate currents in rotating copper plates from a magnetic field," "See if electromagnets are the same as bar magnets"), which in turn are implemented using scripts drawing upon schemas (in the example, this could include winding coils, constructing hand-crank and pulley arrangements for rotating the copper discs, and invoking his prior knowledge about the relative strengths of different kinds of magnets). Each episode of script or schematic utilization is then pursued through a series of goals and sub-goals, which can be represented as the transformation of mental states by operators that transform one state into another. For example, a particular script (e.g., "Wind a coil") can be decomposed into specific sub-goals ("Obtain wire," "Wind wire on core," etc.), which in turn can be decomposed into specific States and Operators (perceptual-motor entities in this instance).

The decomposition into levels is only *partially* hierarchical, in the sense that any given "assembly" is not wholly independent of the levels below it or above it—there is some "cross-talk" among levels. In fact, we can take, as a starting point for further analysis, what I will call "Simon's Conjecture," namely, that all cognitive activity in science, across all five levels, reflects search through a problem space, exactly the kind of processing seen so clearly in prior research on problem solving with more restricted problems. If this proves to be true, then we could characterize scientific problem solving as having a kind of "fractal" organization. At each level, "moves" are invoked to transform one "symbolic representation" into another, so that the overall appearance of the cognitive activity is self-similar across the partially hierarchical levels. As will be clear, I believe that Simon's conjecture is *not* entirely true—the full understanding of scientific thought requires other ways of organizing our analyses.

The proposed five-level framework is useful both analytically and synthetically. Thus, analytically, at any given level it leads us to ask how we might separate out the phenomena at this level into those of the level below. For example, discussion of the changing purposes of a scientist can be turned into empirical questions about the heuristics used to achieve those purposes. Whether or not this can be done in a specific case depends, of course, on the quality and "grain" of the available data. If we have diary records, our chances are better. If we have think-aloud protocols (as we might in an *in vivo* study), then we may be able to carry out the analysis all the way down to the level of states and operators.

Synthetically, we can work the analysis process in reverse. Given an account of the goal and sub-goal structure of an episode, we can ask how it fits with the schematic knowledge and skills of the problem solver. Interestingly, when problem solving is studied in the laboratory, these higher levels (purposes and heuristics) are generally ignored. The higher levels are in effect held constant by placing participants in a context in which compliance with the social-psychological purposes and heuristics of the experimenter are taken for granted, and eliminated from analysis. Under such circumstances, we may get a good look at the lower level processing of the problem solver, but we cannot know how the higher level processes would manifest themselves in the real world. This alone suggests the need for both historical and *in vivo* studies of science. And the historical context is necessary because many of the purposes and heuristics of scientific thinking can change extremely slowly. Thus, Faraday was committed to certain theoretical endeavors for decades (elaborating his force-centered view of physics, for example), and he sometimes spent years pursuing a particular set of heuristics.

Scientific Cognition in Context

To show that the proposed theoretical approach can accommodate cultural and historical accounts, I present three examples, two drawn from work by my students and I on Michael Faraday, and one drawn from an account of how expert users created representations in differential calculus. In all three cases, it was not possible to formulate an adequate explanation without utilizing the cultural and historical context. That is, in all three cases, an account of the higher order processes was necessary, in order to make sense of what was happening at the lower levels. Thus, each can stand as an example of the limits of Simon's Conjecture, as well as of the importance of including historical context for a full cognitive account of scientific thinking.

Steps Toward Faraday's Field Theory

In 1831, Michael Faraday discovered the phenomenon for which he is most often remembered, the induction of electricity from moving magnetic fields. My terminology is anachronistic here; for Faraday, the notion of "field" was just beginning to be articulated in 1831; it would be 20 years before his "mature" concept was complete enough to publish (Nersessian, 1984, describes this evolution, and its place within the development of 19th and 20th century physics). In brief, Faraday's finished concept included the idea that magnetic and electric fields existed as non-material, vectorial, "lines of force" that spread throughout space. (Tweney, 1992b, provided an account that lists the emergence of these components.) The space around a magnet, for example, was filled with closed loops, the lines of force, which passed out of the magnet at one pole and reentered at the other. The 1831 experiments were important to his later theoretical ideas because they established, first, that electricity and magnetism were related and complementary forces, and because they showed (since the fields had to be moving) that the relationship of the two was a dynamic one.

Only the bare sketches of this theory existed in 1831, however. Duncan and Tweney (1997) selected an early series of Faraday's exploration of the induction of electricity from magnetism, focusing on the period from October, 1831 to March, 1832. Having shown that transient magnetic fields could induce transient electrical currents (in August), Faraday began in October to explore the effect of magnets on rotating metallic disks (partly to see if he could induce a steady electrical current, as well as a transient one). Confirming this point, he next explored the distribution of current flow within such disks, a problem that required him to substantially change his two-dimensional representation of the relation of magnetism and electricity to a *three*-dimensional representation in which motion was orthogonal to the magnetic and electric fields. This three-dimensional shift in turn was important to his later development of field theory (in the 1850s), since it implied that the lines of force filled all of space around a magnet. In the specific case at hand, there was a "spillover" effect in that attributes of the two-dimensional representation were carried over into the three-dimensional representation. The full significance of this shift is only apparent in the light of Faraday's later theoretical development. Note that Faraday's long-term purposes (Level 1), namely, to develop an integrated field theory and to determine the relation between electricity and magnetism, were instantiated via specific heuristics (Level 2, the experimental strategies used by Faraday), including especially his use of rotating copper discs. These heuristics interacted in a productive fashion with his developing representation of the field; in fact, the rotating copper discs can be seen as a kind of physical model of his nascent ideas about fields. It is no surprise, then, to find him working with spheres of metal later in the series (spheres being the three dimensional analog of discs), nor is it surprising to see him relate his laboratory phenomena to the interactions of the earth's magnetic field. In particular, at the end of 1831, he succeeded in generating electrical currents in a large loop of wire slowly rotating in his lab; that is, he succeeded in generating electricity from the earth's magnetic field.

Unless one "looks down the road" from 1831 to a much later formulation, it isn't possible to see why the "spillover" from two to three dimensions was significant. Without the posterior knowledge that it was the three-dimensionality of the solution that was the crucial shift here, we could not have seen the importance of the shift as it occurred in 1831. Thus, for this case, knowledge of the course of Faraday's investigations over a 20-year span is the key to an adequate cognitive account of his activity in 1831. There is no "backward causation" involved, of course. It is not the case that his later field theory *caused* his earlier shift from two to three dimensions! Rather, analytically, we could not have detected the significance of his move without the historical perspective. In a sense, this must have been true for Faraday himself, that is, the dimensional shift in 1831 must have reinforced his belief that explaining the phenomena would require a set of theoretical constructs that "filled all space." For Faraday, space was not empty, with material bodies acting on each other across a void. Until his discovery in 1831, however, it wasn't clear to him just how an alternative account could work (in fact, only in the 1850s did he feel comfortable in publishing such claims), but we can see, in retrospect, how exciting it must have been. In fact, the expectation is confirmed by the fact that, early in 1832, almost his last entry in the diary presented a sketch of a sphere representing the orthogonal relations of electricity. magnetism, and motion. The sphere was a kind of summary; after this point, Faraday almost immediately turned his major attention to problems in electrochemistry, rather than induction. But the sphere stands also as a kind of echo of what was to come, an icon, perhaps, of the larger issues that resided in the empirical generalities. In this sense, the shift to three dimensions opened the prospect of an explanatory spatial "plenum."

Acoustic Vibrations

Ippolito and Tweney (1995; see also Tweney, 1992a) examined Faraday's work on acoustics in 1831 (just prior to his August discovery of induction). Seemingly unrelated to the electromagnetic researches that followed, it has been suggested that Faraday's work on acoustics prepared the way for his later discovery (Williams, 1965). Be that as it may, this series of experiments is particularly striking because Faraday seems to be struggling to represent to himself how the appearances of vibrating fluid surfaces (as when the rim of a glass of water is rubbed) could be produced by the vibrations. The problem is that the surface of such fluids appears to have nearly stationary "ridges and valleys," but these should in fact be moving at a high rate, each ridge and valley being regenerated many times per second. Faraday actually, then, faced two problems—confirming the physical motion of the fluids and accounting for what otherwise could be seen as their "deceptive" appearances. He resolved the problem by invoking a cognitive theory of appearances (based on an earlier series of researches on movement illusions), and combining these with a series of geometric models of possible vibratory modes. Using both, he was able to create physical models of similar-appearing phenomena that were not vibrating, thus confirming his account.

Much of Faraday's experimentation in the series followed his close descriptions of the phenomena in their ordinary manifestations. The experiments themselves amount to taking very simple physical setups and making them move spatially again and again, as if he were "perceptually rehearsing" the phenomena. In fact, perceptual rehearsal is probably very close to the right term here. Faraday has to "see" in his mind's eye the phenomena at hand, and he then has to mentally modify the phenomena to carry out "tests" of his hypotheses. He then is able to construct apparatus that instantiates these hypotheses. We argued that Faraday thus manifested a progression from perceptual rehearsal through "inceptual rehearsal," in which selected aspects of his perceptual experiences were enhanced and "run" in stand-alone fashion (Ippolito & Tweney, 1995).

These inceptions formed the basis for the active construction of a mental model, which in turn, manifested in physical apparatus. In terms of the framework of levels that I am arguing for in this chapter, specific heuristics (Level 2: coordinate the vibration theory with the cognitive theory of deceptions) were instantiated via repeated use of scripts (Level 3: use perceptual rehearsal of known phenomena and modify these systematically), which in turn modified the heuristics, and so on; only then was physical instantiation (Levels 4 and 5) possible.

In this case, it is possible to see Faraday's perceptual and inceptual rehearsal (the Levels 2 and 3 processes) as manifestations of a "search," but it is not possible to specify anything like a problem space for this example. Instead, the processes that he is using are "recognition-like," in the sense that he is trying different configurations until one "looks like" the real phenomenon. Rather than the successive symbolic rewriting of a state, Faraday is using an inceptual process in a kind of isomorphic matching to a real process. It either fits or it doesn't fit, just as, when I look at a particular nine-digit number, it either is or is not my social security number. As in Anderson's clothesline problem, if we use a "state and operator" model as such, we gain no understanding of Faraday's discovery process in this series because the relevant symbols are outside the context in which problem spaces can be defined.

Historicity in Real-Time

So far, both of my examples have involved the use of historical material, and, in both, the historical context proved necessary to develop an appropriate cognitive model. However, the point extends beyond just historical material; the five-level framework is applicable to the understanding of real time cognition as well. In effect, with this third example, I present a case where an understanding of the historicity of cognition is essential, insofar as the historical development of a conceptual tool can be shown to open the way toward an understanding of how tool users function.

Kurz (1998) explored the way in which mathematicians and scientists used calculus as a representational medium to solve a physical rate-flow problem. Given the importance of mathematics in physical science, it is surprising how little research has been conducted on the issue of how scientists use mathematics in thinking about the subject of their investigation. And, when there have been exceptions (as in Langley, et al.'s analysis of Kepler, just described), relatively low-level mathematical formulations have been used. Yet most physicists will describe the use of differential equations as central to physical inquiry—an enormous number of problems amount to finding the proper differential equation to represent a rate problem, then seeking to integrate the differential equation to derive specific solutions for particular conditions. Once the equation is found, most such problems can be understood using the methods of problem space search; initial and goal states can be defined, a problem space specified, and the allowed mathematical moves translated into specific cognitive operators. But how do scientists get to this point? How do they construct the proper equation in the first place?

The principal participants in Kurz's study were a mathematician, a theoretical physicist, and a physical chemist. Each was given a rate flow problem in which a salt solution of a given concentration per liter was being added to a flask at the same rate that water was draining out of the flask. The problem was to find out how much salt was in the flask after 5 minutes. Participants were asked to think out loud while solving the problem. They could make notes and diagrams, and use a calculator, but no reference works were allowed. The problem is a simple one, and some version of it appears in many textbooks of differential equations. But the specifics had to be regenerated by each participant. All three solved the problem within 30 minutes or so, but not without substantial struggle, especially in the early stages. Their struggle centered on exactly how to use the relevant aspects of the calculus to represent this particular problem. All the participants realized that it was a calculus problem fairly early, but, interestingly, all three used a different way to reach the proper representation. None manifested an overt "problem-solving" strategy during this first phase, in that none explicitly searched a "problem space" in order to find a representation. Instead, each protocol had to be regarded as invoking specific heuristics which differed in the kind of "historicity" each manifested.

It is, of course, commonly known that different notations are available for users of the calculus. The most familiar is that invented by Leibniz, in which dy/dx stands for the derivative of y with respect to x. But variants of Isaac Newton's notation also are used, e.g., y' to represent the derivative of y with respect to x (x being understood here from the context), and there are other notations as well, e.g., $D_x y$ to represent the derivative of y with respect to x. But Kurz noted that underlying the notational differences, there are differences of conceptualization, a multiplicity of representations, each reflected in the long history of the calculus. For Newton, an absolute time flow was taken for granted, and "fluxions" were construed by analogy with moving points along a curve; it is a very physicalistic kind of calculus. For Leibniz, a ratio among infinitesimal entities, "differentials," was at the base of his calculus. What today is regarded by most introductory texts as "the" definition, namely, the limit of a ratio as some quantity goes to zero, emerged much later, out of the work of Cauchy (see Boyer, 1949, for an overview of this history).

Kurz found that understanding of the protocols of her participants was facilitated by looking at their search for a representation in these terms. Thus, for example, one protocol manifested a kind of "Leibnizian" strategy in which differential quantities were sought, whereas another manifested a "Newtonian" strategy in which an absolute time flow was taken for granted and something like "fluxions," roughly, "moving points on a curve" were sought. And, in the third case, a notion of functions and limits seemed to characterize the strategy. In each case, once the representation of the problem had been generated, the subsequent problem solving activity could be captured by a more traditional problem space search account, but the search for a representation in the first place reflected the adoption of one or another of these historically-rooted conceptualizations. There was no sense that the participants were able to use only one approach, of course; all three were very familiar with differential equations, and all three would easily recognize the approach taken by the other two. Instead, the calculus comes with its historicity wrapped up inside it, as it were. It provides its users with a variety of ways to approach a new application. We cannot say what led to the adoption of one or another approach in this case (there are only three participants!), but that is less important than the fact that knowledge of the historicity of the tool permits understanding of the tool user. In this example, the course of representational change was only capturable by using the rich historical context of the cultural artifact that constitutes modern calculus.

Kurz's study thus amounts to something like an "archeological" analysis (Foucault, 1966/1970) applied to a cognitive science context of explanation. Level 2, heuristics, of my framework was the focus of her study, and proved accessible by "digging" through the layers of the conceptual history of the calculus (Level 1, of course, was "held constant" here, and reflects the purposes of the investigator, the intentions of the participants to comply with her requests, and so on). Lower levels (3, 4, and 5) were recoverable from the protocols, as we would expect, but Kurz's study is unique in unraveling the properties of Level 2 in historical-cognitive fashion.

Historicity is the key to this last example; in fact, it is possible to regard the calculus much as an archeologist views a cultural tool, as an embodiment of cognition that we can use to interpret the actions of the participants. In a sense, of course, the same is true for all of science. Because scientific thinking depends upon the past actions of other scientific thinkers, in the form of methods, concepts, prior findings, and the like, it should be possible, in principle, to uncover the role of such "externalized agents" of cognition (Kurz, 1997) in any scientific episode. Just as Hutchins (1995) was able to describe "How a cockpit remembers its speeds," in reference to the externalized cognition of the system consisting of a pilot and an aircraft, so also is the system consisting of the calculus and a scientist able to solve rate problems. The fact that a cockpit is physically external to the pilot, whereas the calculus is internalized by the scientist, is incidental. In both cases, a complete account demands full analysis of the cultural tool in question. And in the case of the calculus, that cultural tool embeds its own history in a fashion that makes a cognitive-historical analysis possible.

What the Examples Tell Us

It is appropriate now to ask what the preceding three examples share that is potentially applicable to all three cases. One aspect stands out, in my estimation. In all three cases, representational change is the central characteristic of the narrative "story" told by the analysis. Thus, Faraday's field concept was seen at an early stage of its development, and it was captured as it underwent a fundamental change in dimensionality. The change was manifest primarily at Level 2, as a change in Faraday's strategic approaches to further experimentation and theory development. In the case of his work on acoustic vibrations, we saw that Faraday sought to build a representation "in the mind's eye" at what we regarded as primarily Level 3, that of scripts and schemata. Finally, in the last case, we again saw the emergence of representations at Level 2, as Kurz's calculus users exploited the multiple representational possibilities of the calculus and turned the result into lower level representations that could be worked with in a straightforward fashion. Clearly, the notion of representation is central, and cuts across the levels of my account. Furthermore, in all three cases, a historical-cognitive approach was necessary, in order to see the centrality of representational change.

It is also clear from the examples that the conduct of science is rooted in specific practices that underlie the activity of the scientist. That Faraday's thinking is closely tied to experimental practices is clear, of course, but notice that, in both cases, experimental practices are themselves tied to practices of thought (especially visualizing in two or three dimensions for the first case, and perceptually rehearsing movements in the second case). Such practices are a result of Faraday's socialization, both within the context of his times and in the context of the physical phenomena that he is observing. Each "kind" of context places constraints upon the allowable practices. Finally, as we saw from the calculus experts, practices need not be external behaviors, nor do the tools that are exercised in these practices need to be physical entities.

Implications and Applications of the Theory

The role of a general theory of scientific thinking for cognitive science generally can be appreciated by considering the recent claim that "ecological" theories will replace "cognitive" theories. Thus, Edward Reed (1997) has characterized the cognitive revolution as a failure, forcefully arguing that the ecological approach first manifested in the work of Gibson can better account for the phenomena of cognition. Reed objects, in particular, to the separation of representations from the action of the organism and from the environment. On his view, there is no distinction between thought and action, a distinction that only makes sense if the distinction between input and output is maintained:

> Cognition is a keeping-in-touch with the world around us, a keeping-in-touch that always includes both behavior and awareness, and which requires the utilization of ambient information. (Reed, 1997, p. 271).

On Reed's account, Anderson's clothesline problem should lead us to abandon representation as a central construct in cognitive science.

On my account, however, it would be disastrous to remove the notion of representation from any account of scientific thinking; a scientific construct is by its very nature a representation that is separable from the ambient information and the activity of the representing agent—otherwise it would have no value as a scientific construct! Reed no doubt would agree that characterizing how such representations are formed is at the heart of a theory of scientific cognition as such, and he presumably would not therefore object to, say, extensive studies of Faraday's diaries that trace the growth of his ideas through his manipulative interchanges with an experimental environment. But it would be wrong to assume that such interchange is the only characterization that is needed—Faraday does end up with a mental representation (of the field, say) and that mental representation is constructed precisely so that it can be independent of specific actors and specific ambient environments. In effect, concepts like that of the electromagnetic field, an atom, or heat, constitute "existence proofs" against Reed's assumption.

The present approach is consistent with some aspects of the "dynamical challenge" in cognitive science, which, according to Clark (1997), suggests that dynamic explanations may increasingly serve as "the spatially and temporally extended vehicles of specific representational contents" (Clark, 1997, p. 478). Of course, explaining scientific thinking depends heavily on accounting for the origin and development of scientific representations. In my account, the "vehicles" of such representation can equally be based upon sub-symbolic processes, as in Faraday's use of inceptions (Ippolito & Tweney, 1995) or on cultural entities, as in Kurz's (1997) account of the "historicity" of calculus. In each case, representations were accounted for by appeal to "vehicles" that themselves were not reducible to the simple states and operators of the classical sort. For Faraday, the perceptual and motor events recorded in his diary are "taken for granted" as vehicles of representation. For Kurz's calculus experts, the variety of historicized representations of change ("Leibnizian," "Newtonian," and so forth) are taken for granted as vehicles of representation.

Finally, note that the account leads to a general theoretical account of scientific thinking having broad applicability and generalizability. It builds upon the existing problem solving accounts of science, and accommodates the concerns raised by Anderson, in effect, by allowing entry for new kinds of interpretive processes (like those used by Rudwick and by Gooding, to construct Figures 1 and 2). Whereas the task of cognitive science was previously seen as different than the task of history, the present approach shows that they are complementary, and that there are cases where both are necessary for a complete account. In fact, the theory demands that we use methods derived from both the humanities (e.g., the history of science, culture studies) and the sciences (e.g., Newell & Simon's methods), and I suggest that any distinction between "soft" approaches and "hard" approaches is therefore illusory. Instead, both are necessary to account for the complexity of real world thinking in a socially- and culturally-conditioned domain. Such a blending of interpretive ("humanities-like") and scientific ("explanatory") accounts fits well with recent attempts to contextualize cognition (e.g., Greeno & Moore, 1993; Hutchins, 1995; see also Gruber, 1974).

The notion that different levels are needed to accommodate different explanatory goals is of course not new in cognitive science. As just one example, Anderson (1987) proposed that, at the "algorithmic" level of cognition (where protocol analysis is appropriate), explanation must center on the kinds of modifiable procedures used to carry out a computation, whereas at the "implementational" level of cognition, one is interested in relatively fixed and stable processes that do not generally change from one utilization to the next. A similar spirit underlies my account, all of which are at Anderson's algorithmic level. I depart from Anderson only in claiming that the contextual meaning of the scientist's activities sometimes forces a different approach—a cognitive-historical approach—to understanding the emergence, development, and utilization of scientific representations.

Designing for Science

What are the consequences for those whose goal is to "design" science? This is a very large question that can only be touched upon here. Let me approach this issue merely by stating three negative claims that result from my approach:

1) There is no science without representation.

2) There is no science without practices.

3) There is no science without historicity.

Each claim can be seen in the examples presented earlier. First, representational change is a central concern of all science, and it must be respected. Science is not *just* activity. Second, science is not *just* symbolic either! The practices of science (whether externalized or internalized) are central to the endeavor, a part of the cognition, and not always reducible to simple formulations. Third, science uses cultural tools that are themselves possessed of a history; at times this helps in analysis, but at all times it must be borne in mind, because at all times science is an activity carried out in social, cultural, and historical contexts that are deeply embedded in a real-time context. By acknowledging the need for such an "archeology" of knowledge, an archeology that is fully consistent with even the most molecular accounts of problem-solving activities, we open the way to resolving the merely apparent split between different approaches to the understanding of science. The cognitive sciences are concerned with untangling the complexity of an observed, phenomenological, world of intelligent agency; we should not hesitate to use whatever resources can help us toward that goal.

Acknowledgements

This paper has benefited from discussions with many individuals over an extended period of time, especially Sean Duncan, Mari Ippolito, and Elke Kurz. An early draft was much improved by the comments of Chris Schunn, Kevin Crowley, and Takeshi Okada.

References

Addis, T.R., Gooding, D. & Townsend, J. (1993). Knowledge acquisition with visual functional programming. In N. Aussenec, G. Boy, B. Gaines, M. Linster, J.-G. Ganascia, & Y. Kodratoff (Eds.), *Knowledge acquisition for knowledge-based systems: 7th European Knowledge Acquisition Workshop.* Berlin: Springer-Verlag.

Anderson, J. R. (1987). Methodologies for studying human knowledge. *Behavioral and Brain Sciences, 10,* 467-505.

Anderson, J. R. (1990). *The adaptive character of thought.* Hillsdale, NJ: Lawrence Erlbaum Associates.

Bechtel, W. (1988). *Philosophy of science: An overview for cognitive science.* Hillsdale, NJ: Lawrence Erlbaum Associates.

Boyer, C. B. (1949). *The history of the calculus and its conceptual development.* New York: Dover.

Chase, W. G., & Simon, H. A. (1973). The mind's eye in chess. In W.G. Chase (Ed.), *Visual information processing* . New York: Academic Press.

Clark, A. (1997). The dynamical challenge. *Cognitive Science, 21,* 461-481.

Cross, N., Christiaans, H., & Dorst, K. (Eds.) (1996). *Analysing design activity.* New York: John Wiley & Sons.

Dunbar, K. (1995). How scientists really reason: Scientific reasoning in real-world laboratories. In R. J. Sternberg & J. Davidson (Eds.), *Mechanisms of insight* (pp. 365-396). Cambridge, MA: MIT Press.

Duncan, S. C., & Tweney, R. D. (1997). The Problem-Behavior Map as cognitive-historical analysis: The example of Michael Faraday. *Proceedings of the Nineteenth Annual Conference of the Cognitive Science Society.* Hillsdale, NJ: Lawrence Erlbaum Associates.

Duncan, S. C., & Tweney, R. D. (1999). A framework for modeling representational change in scientific communities. *Proceedings of the Tweney-First Annual Conference of the Cognitive Science Society.* Hillsdale, NJ: Lawrence Erlbaum Associates.

Ericsson, K. A., & Simon, H. A. (1993*). Protocol analysis: Verbal reports as data.* Cambridge, MA: MIT Press (Revised Edition).

Faraday, M. (1822). *Faraday's 1822 "Chemical notes, hints, suggestions, and objects of pursuit."* Edited with an introduction and notes by R. D. Tweney & D. Gooding. London: The Science Museum & Peter Peregrinus, Ltd.

Faraday, M. (1932-36). *Faraday's diary.* (T. Martin, ed.) (7 volumes & Index vol.). London: Bell.

Faraday, M. (1861). *A course of six lectures on the chemical history of a candle.* London: Griffin, Bohn.

Foucault, M. (1970/1966). *The order of things: An archeology of the human sciences.* New York: Random House (Trans. from *Les mots et les choses,* 1966).

Gooding, D. (1989). History in the laboratory: Can we tell what really went on? In F.A.J.L. James (Ed.), *The development of the laboratory: Essays on the place of experiment in industrial civilization* (pp. 63-82). New York: American Institute of Physics.

Gooding, D. (1990). *Experiment and the making of meaning: Human agency in scientific observation and experiment.* Dordrecht: Kluwer Academic Publishers.

Gooding, D., & Addis, T. R. (in press). A simulation of model-based reasoning about disparate phenomena. In P. Thagard, N. Nersessian, & L. Magnani (Eds.), *Model based reasoning in scientific discovery.* Dordrecht: Plenum.

Gorman, M. E. (1992). *Simulating science: Heuristics, mental models, and technoscientific thinking.* Bloomington, IN: Indiana University Press.

Gorman, M. E. (1997). Mind in the world: Cognition and practice in the invention of the telephone. *Social Studies of Science, 27,* 583-624.

Greeno, J. G., & Moore, J. L. (1993). Situativity and symbols: Response to Vera and Simon. *Cognitive Science, 17,* 49-59.

Gruber, H. E. (1974). *Darwin on man.* New York: Dutton.

Holmes, F. L. (1980). Hans Krebs and the discovery of the ornithine cycle. *Federation Proceedings, 39,* 216-225.

Holmes, F. L. (1987). Scientific writing and scientific discovery. *Isis, 78,* 220-235.

Hutchins, E. (1995). How a cockpit remembers its speeds. *Cognitive Science, 19,* 265-288.

Ippolito, M. F., & Tweney, R. D. (1995). The inception of insight. In R.J. Sternberg & J.E. Davidson (Eds.), *The nature of insight.* (pp. 433-462). Cambridge, MA: The MIT Press.

Klahr, D., & Dunbar, K. (1988). Dual space search during scientific reasoning. *Cognitive Science, 12,* 1-48.

Klahr, D. , & Simon, H. A. (in press). Studies of scientific discovery: Complementary approaches and convergent findings. *Psychological Bulletin.*

Kuhn, T. (1962). *The structure of scientific revolutions.* Chicago: University of Chicago Press.

Kulkarni, D. (1988). *The processes of scientific discovery: The strategy of experimentation.* Unpublished dissertation, Carnegie Mellon University.

Kulkarni, D., & Simon, H. A. (1988). The processes of scientific discovery: The strategy of experimentation. *Cognitive Science, 12,* 139-176.

Kurz, E. M. (1997). *Representational practices of differential calculus.* Ph.D. dissertation, Bowling Green State University

Kurz, E. M. (1998). Representation, agency, and disciplinarity: Calculus experts at work. In M.A. Gernsbacher & S.J. Derry (Eds.), *Proceedings of the twentieth annual conference of the Cognitive Science Society* (pp. 585-590). Mahwah, NJ: Lawrence Erlbaum Associates.

Kurz, E. M., & Tweney, R. D. (1998). The practice of mathematics and science: From calculus to the clothesline problem. In M. Oaksford & N. Chater (Eds.), *Rational models of cognition,* (pp. 415-438). Oxford: Oxford University Press.

Langley, P. W., Simon, H. A., Bradshaw, G. L., & Zytkow, J. M. (1987). *Scientific discovery: Computational explorations of the discovery process.* Cambridge, MA: MIT Press.

Mayer, R. E. (1992). *Thinking, problem solving, cognition.* Second Edition. New York: W.H. Freeman.

Nersessian, N. (1984). *Faraday to Einstein: Constructing meaning in scientific theories.* Dordrecht: Nijhoff.

Nersessian, N. (1992). How do scientists think? Capturing the dynamics of conceptual change in science. In R. N. Giere (Ed.), *Cognitive models of science* (Minnesota studies in the philosophy of science, Vol. XV, pp.3-44). Minneapolis: University of Minnesota Press.

Nersessian, N. (1993). Opening the black box: Cognitive science and history of science. *Osiris, 10,* 194-214.

Newell, A. (1990). *Unified theories of cognition.* Cambridge, MA: Harvard University Press.

Newell, A., & Simon, H. A. (1972). *Human problem solving.* Englewood Cliffs, NJ: Prentice-Hall.

Perkins, D. N. (1992). The topography of invention. In R.J. Weber & D.N. Perkins (Eds.), *Inventive minds: Creativity in technology* (pp. 238-250). New York: Oxford University press.

Qin, Y. & Simon, H. A. (1995). Imagery and mental models in problem solving. In J. Glasgow, B. Chandrasekaran, & N.H. Narayanan (Eds.), *Diagrammatic reasoning: Cognitive and computational perspectives* (pp. 403-434). Menlo Park, CA: AAAI Press/MIT Press.

Reed, E. (1997). The cognitive revolution from an ecological point of view. In D.M. Johnson & C.E. Erneling (Eds.), *The future of the cognitive revolution* (pp. 261-273). New York: Oxford University Press.

Rudwick, M. J. S. (1985). *The great Devonian controversy: The shaping of scientific knowledge among gentlemanly specialists.* Chicago: University of Chicago Press.

Schunn, C. D. & Anderson, J. R. (1998). Scientific discovery. In J. Anderson (Ed.), *The atomic components of thought.* Mahwah, NJ: Lawrence Erlbaum Associates.

Shrager, J., & Klahr, D. (1986). Instructionless learning about a complex device: The paradigm and observations. *International Journal of Man-Machine Studies, 25,* 153-189.

Simon, H. A. (1996). *The sciences of the artificial.* (3rd ed.). Cambridge: MIT Press. (First published 1969).

Tabachneck-Schiff, H. J. M., Leonardo, A. M., & Simon, H. A. (1997). CaMeRa: A computational model of multiple representations. *Cognitive Science, 21,* 305-350.

Thackray, A. (Ed.). (1995). Constructing knowledge in the history of science. (Special Issue of *Osiris, 10.*) Philadelphia: History of Science Society.

Tweney, R. D. (1991a). Faraday's 1822 "Chemical hints" notebook and the semantics of chemical discourse. *Bulletin for the History of Chemistry, 11* (Winter), 51-55.

Tweney, R. D. (1991b). Faraday's notebooks: The active organization of creative science. *Physics Education, 26,* 301-306.

Tweney, R. D. (1992a). Stopping Time: Faraday and the scientific creation of perceptual order. *Physis: Revista Internazionale di Storia Della Scienza, 29,* 149-164.

Tweney, R. D. (1992b). Inventing the field: Michael Faraday and the creative "engineering" of electromagnetic field theory. In R. J. Weber & D. N. Perkins (Eds.), *Inventive minds: Creativity in Technology* (pp. 31-47).Oxford: Oxford University Press.

Tweney, R. D., Doherty, M. E., & Mynatt, C. R. (Eds.). (1981). *On scientific thinking.* New York: Columbia University Press.

Tweney, R. D., & Hoffner, C. E. (1987). Understanding the microstructure of science: An example. In *Program of the Ninth Annual Conference of the Cognitive Science Society* (pp. 677-681). Hillsdale, NJ: Lawrence Erlbaum Associates.

Voss, J. F. , & Post, T. A. (1988). On the solving of ill-structured problems. In M.T. Chi, R. Glaser, & M.Farr (Eds.), *The nature of expertise.* Hillsdale, NJ: Lawrence Erlbaum Associates.

Williams, L. P. (1965). *Michael Faraday: A biography.* New York: Basic Books.

II

Building for
Scientific Thinking

7
Complexity, Emergence, and Synthetic Models in Science Education

David E. Penner
University of Wisconsin-Madison

"Emergence is above all a product of coupled, context-dependent interaction."

Holland (p. 12, 1998)

Learning to do science primarily involves the enculturation of students to ways of thinking that reflect the systematicity characteristic of scientific practice (diSessa, 1988). In their search for systematicity, scientists spend considerable time and effort building and testing models of the phenomenon under investigation (Giere, 1988; Hestenes, 1992). Recognition of the importance of modeling by practicing scientists has lead to considerable research on the use of modeling as a central activity in science education (e. g., Penner, Giles, Lehrer, Schauble, 1997; Ost, 1987; Stewart, Hafner, Johnson, & Finkel, 1992).

  Within the last two decades, researchers in disciplines from biology to economics to psychology and sociology have proposed a new form of modeling (e. g., Arthur, 1990; Deneubourg & Goss, 1989; Doran & Gilbert, 1994; Epstein & Axtell, 1996; Franks, 1989; Herman & Gardels, 1963; Thelen & Smith, 1994; Tinbergen, 1951; Wilson, 1971). Simply put, this approach shifts from a concentration on large-scale patterns themselves to the local interactions that underlie such patterns. That is, this form of modeling characterizes many phenomenon as the *emergent* result of interactions within complex systems. The following example, taken from

Resnick (1994), describes a biological phenomenon that nicely illustrates the emergent modeling approach.

> Slime-mold cells typically exist as independent single-cell amoebas.
> However, when food becomes scarce, cells cease reproduction and
> begin to aggregate in large clumps with tens of thousands of cells. This
> mass begins to migrate as a single unit in search of a more hospitable
> environment. Upon finding a suitable location, the mass differentiates
> into a stalk supporting a mass of spores. These spores detach and
> spread throughout the new environment.

Biologists have argued for a number of mechanisms to explain
slime mold behavior. For many years, the prevalent belief was that there
were different types of slime-mold cells. Some cells, "pacemaker" cells,
were responsible for organizing the aggregation: their actions caused
other cells to aggregate. However, biologists now believe that slime-
mold cells are homogenous; that is, there is no cell specialization.
Rather, clustering occurs as the result of local interactions amongst
identical cells in response to a chemical they produce, emit, and to
which they are attracted.

The growing importance of emergent models for understanding
phenomena suggests that science educators need to consider the role of
such models in developing students' scientific thinking. However, to
date, we understand very little about *how* people come to understand
emergence. The few studies that exist suggest that people have difficulty
characterizing phenomena as the result of emergent interactions; however, they provide little insight into how this form of thinking might
develop (e. g., Resnick, 1994, 1996). This chapter attempts to begin to
address this issue. The two studies described below document middle-
school students' developing understanding of how global behavior
might emerge through simple, local interactions. Both studies use a synthetic modeling approach to engage students in thinking about emergence. Before describing the studies, I will clarify what is meant by a
synthetic modeling approach to science.

Analytic *Versus* Synthetic

Epstein and Axtell (1996) have defined the term emergent to denote
"stable macroscopic patterns arising from the local interaction of
agents" (p. 35). This definition implies qualitative differences between
individual and group behavior. That is, the group is not just the sum of

individual behaviors. Understanding how simple rules, with or without some degree of chance, interacting in a given environment can give rise to macro level regularities is a principle goal in the study of complexity.

A central issue in investigating complexity is determining an appropriate methodology. Much of modern science is based on an analytic tradition. Dynamic situations are typically modeled using differential or partial differential equations in which behavior is fully specified (Doran & Gilbert, 1994). In such models, parameters may be changed, but the underlying, pre-specified, formal model remains constant.

A classic example of the analytic approach are predator-prey models based on differential equations. Interactions between the two classes of animals are specified by two equations. Each equation specifies the rate at which a variable, such as the population density, changes over time.

The level of interaction typical in most complex systems makes an analytic approach daunting—the resulting mathematical models are often intractable or brittle, since they typically depend upon assuming idealized conditions (Sober, 1991; Wilensky, 1996). More critically, analytic approaches treat populations as homogenous: every member of a given class is identical to every other member. This assumption of homogeneity is the result of equations that arise from statistical estimates based on aggregate data in which individual variation is lost (Epstein & Axtell, 1996; Ray, 1995). Consequently, the analytic approach is characterized by a focus on population-based properties, such as birth and death rates.

Emmeche (1994) has argued that simulating complex systems is the most effective means of determining their behavior. In such an approach, behavior arises through local interactions among spatially distributed groups of individuals with similar, but not identical, behaviors. That is, rules define interactions amongst individuals and between individuals and the environment. An example will help illustrate this point.

In a synthetic predator-prey model, individual predators have a rule that states that they die if their energy level falls below some arbitrary level. However, in this approach individuals are typically randomly assigned starting energies. Consequently, individuals, not populations, live or die depending upon their initial energy reserve and their ability to successfully find prey. One result of the synthetic approach is that although the general predator-prey pattern emerges every time the model is run, the constituent individuals are not necessarily the same.

That is, a predator that survives in one model run, might not survive in a different run.

The synthetic approach is neither an inductive nor a deductive science, but rather a generative or synthetic science of the possible (Emmeche, 1994; Resnick, 1994). The goal of such a science is to specify the initial micro-conditions that are sufficient to generate the macro-level behaviors of interest. Rather than attempting to arbitrarily bound and subsequently analyze a complex behavior, start with a set of behavioral primitives—rules—and synthesize a complex system with the same functionality as the natural system (Mataric, 1993; Steels, 1995). Juxtaposing the artificial and real systems provides a test of the proposed model. Thus, a synthetic, emergent modeling approach is easily modified to test the effects of varying system conditions.

Two Forms of Modeling

Resnick and Wilensky (1998) have suggested two approaches to exploring the behaviors of complex systems. Phenomenon-based modeling begins by designing strategies for individual parts of the system in order to achieve a specific goal for the system as a whole. The "wave" at a sporting event is a familiar example of phenomenon-based modeling. The goal in this situation is to generate a human wave around a stadium or arena. Although there are many different ways that this could be accomplished, for example, a central plan in which individuals are told the time at which they are to stand up and then sit down, there is a much simpler method. Analyzing the actions that produce the wave leads to the following rule: If the individual to one side is sitting down, then you should stand up and sit down.

In contrast, exploratory modeling begins with a set of rules that govern individual parts of the system. The focus, in this case, is on the system-wide patterns that consequently arise through individual interactions. For example, driving a car is constrained by numerous traffic rules, including the speed at which one should be driving. If one driver is driving even slightly slower than the drivers following, the result is typically a localized mass of cars—a traffic jam.

In the remainder of this chapter I will briefly present two studies that exemplify these two approaches to exploring complexity. The first study describes a middle-school class using a phenomenon-based approach to investigate the process by which termites might build their nests. The second study describes four middle-school students' explorations using a cellular automata—Conway's game of Life—in which simple rules govern cell interactions. Their goal was to investigate the resulting global patterns.

Phenomenon-Based Modeling

Termite nests are amazing constructions. Nests in East Africa can be up to 20 feet in height above ground, with tunnels and chambers as deep as 32 feet below ground. Such nests may contain up to 5,000,000 termites. Moreover, the nest is constructed such that an integral system of ventilation helps to regulate internal temperature and humidity. Outside air enters down-sloping shafts on the side of the nest; internal air is exhausted through shafts that exit at the crest of the nest. By varying the size of the outlets, termites can control the rate at which warm, moist air leaves the nest. The result is a constant nest temperature within plus or minus one degree fahrenheit.

It is difficult to view a termite nest without wondering how such simple creatures could create such sophisticated artifacts. Resnick (1994) has suggested that when faced with complex artifacts, people tend to assume some form of centralized control. That is, they tend to believe that there is a central organization that develops, plans, and coordinates the construction of the artifact. In the case of many human constructions, such as cars, houses, factories, this assumption of central control is appropriate. However, this is not the only means by which complex artifacts, or behaviors, can occur, as the slime mold example previously described illustrated. Although such complexity suggests centralized control, in actuality, the organization emerges from purely lower level interactions.

Study Goals

As mentioned already, although scientists are coming to consider many phenomena, such as the behavior of slime molds and termites, as fundamentally emergent in nature, it is not clear how non-scientists, including students, come to develop such an understanding. The study reported below was conducted to investigate this issue.

This study took place within the larger context of a sixth-grade unit on insects. In order to engage student interest, the teacher had placed a number of different books on insects out in the classroom. As part of a class discussion on social insects, the question arose from one student as to how insects, such as bees, wasps, ants and termites create their intricate nests. Prior to this point, I had had no plans to study student understanding of emergence during this unit. However, given the nature of the students' interest, I thought an adaptation of Resnick's (1994) termite task might allow them to better understand how complex structures can occur without centralized control. Consequently, the teacher and I developed an activity in which students would model and discuss a simplified form of nest building. Teacher-lead class discussions were driven by questions and comments raised by the students. Discussions were audiotaped for later analysis.

The goals of this study were twofold. First, I wanted to explore sixth-grade students' thoughts about the process by which termite nests were constructed. Second, I wanted to see the effects of involving the students in a simple phenomena-based exploration. In this case, not the actual building of a termite nest, but a much simpler task, that of modeling the creation of "wood chip" piles in an environment in which chips initially are randomly distributed. The protocol excerpts presented below highlight aspects of the class discussions that are illustrative of students' thoughts.

As mentioned, the activity was initially motivated by one student's interest in termite nest building. The following excerpt highlights the nature of the resulting class discussion.

Student 1: *I was looking in one of the books and I noticed that most of the social insects live in nests. And some of these nests are huge. Like the termite nests in Africa can be 20 feet tall! How do termites build something like that?*

Teacher: *Good question. Anybody have any ideas?*

Teacher: *Well, let's think about this. What do you think they have to do to build their nests?*

Student 2: *They have to get the materials together. Like they have to have the wood or the mud.*

Teacher: *OK, so they need to have materials. What else?*

Student 3:   *They're going to have to know what to do.*

Teacher: *What do you mean?*

Student 3:   *Well, it's like when you build a house. You have to follow plans. Otherwise nothing will probably go together right.*

Student 4:   *Yeah, with a house you have to design it first it. Then you follow the plans.*

Teacher: *So, how do you think this happens with the termite nest?*

Student 3:   *I don't know. Maybe the queen tells them what to do.*

Student 5:   *Yeah, the queen is in charge. One of the books says that there are different types of termites. Some are workers and some are soldiers. But there is only one queen.*

Teacher: *What do you think the queen does to get the nest built? Any guess?*

Student 5:   *I don't know. I guess she must tell them what to do somehow.*

Teacher: *Tell who?*

Student 5:   *I guess the workers.*

This discussion nicely illustrates Resnick's (1994) hypothesis that people rely on a centralized cause for producing complex organization. In this case, a quick hand count during the discussion revealed that 15 out of 20 of the students claimed that the termite queen must be the source of the design and, consequently, the organizer of the construction process; the remaining students were unsure how nest building occurred. The teacher's attempts to have students expand on how the queen might do this were unproductive. The gist of the students' comments suggests that they believed that the queen somehow communicated to different workers what work needed to be done. One student did add that insects used pheromones to communicate; however, she had little idea of what pheromones were, or how this process might occur.

The following day, the teacher returned to the subject of nest building. The following discussion illustrates her attempts to probe students' conceptions of decentralized ways in which order might occur.

Teacher: *Remember our discussion yesterday about termite nests? Most of you thought that the queen planned and directed the nest building. Well, I was thinking about this last night and was wondering if all organized things had to have a central planner. What do you think?*

Student 1:   *Sure, how else could this happen?*

Student 2:   *Yeah, obviously things like cars, or houses, or planes. You need someone to design these things, and tell others how to build them.*

Teacher: *What about when we talk about actions? Do group actions depend on someone telling the group what to do?*

Student 3:   *What do you mean?*

Teacher: *Well, when you see groups of people or animals doing something. Like when you go to watch a football game and people do the wave. Does that happen because someone is telling others what to do?*

Student 4:   *The people know what to do and just do it.*

Teacher: *I'm not sure what you mean.*

Student 4:   *You know. People know that they are supposed to stand up and then sit back down.*

Teacher: *Can they do it whenever they want to?*

Student 5:   *No, they have to do it in order.*

Teacher: *What do you mean?*

Student 5:   *Well, they can't just sit up whenever they feel like it. They have to do it just after the people next to them stand up and sit down.*

Teacher: *Does someone plan all of this out ahead of time and then tell people when they should stand up?*

Student 3:   *No, somebody just starts doing it. Or maybe a group of people start standing and sitting.*

Teacher: *Then what?*

Student 6:   *Well, usually it takes awhile, but then other people start joining in.*

Teacher: *So, why do they call it "The Wave?"*

Student 7: *Because when you look at the whole thing it looks like a wave going around the stadium.*

Teacher: *But all any one person is doing is standing up and then sitting down?*

Student 7: *Yeah.*

Teacher: *So, is anyone telling each person when to stand or sit?*

Student 8: *No, you just do it right after the person next to you does it.*

Teacher: *So, can you get order without a plan, or a leader?*

Student 9: *Kind of. But people still need to know what to do and when to do it.*

Teacher: *OK. But if they know what to do can they sometimes figure out when to do it without a supervisor.*

Student 9: *I guess so.*

This excerpt illustrates a number of important points. First, the students had difficulty conceiving how order could occur without a plan and an organizer. This included not only artifacts, but also behaviors. However, the teacher was able to present an example that they were all familiar with. Note that she did not tell them that this was a case of emerging order. Rather, she helped them to consider the process by which a wave occurs: An individual's behavior—standing up, then down—is triggered by environmental conditions—the actions of individuals to one side. People perceive the resulting pattern as an undulation flowing around the stadium, much like they perceive waves at the beach. By using a familiar experience, the teacher was able to begin to introduce the ideas of rule-based individual actions leading to qualitatively different global patterns. This is in line with the contention that a learner's prior knowledge is best thought of as a useful basis for future learning, rather than a source of misconceptions that need to be replaced (Smith, diSessa, & Roschelle, 1993).

The above discussion served to motivate the wood-chip gathering task. The teacher introduced the task by asking the students to think not about building a termite nest, but just gathering scattered wood chips into piles.

Teacher: *So, how might you go about making piles of chips?*

Student 4:   *You could have one person telling the others what to do. Like, you could tell everybody to pick up a piece and put it down wherever.*

Teacher: *OK, how about this. What if all you can do is move straight ahead, turn ninety degrees left, ninety degrees right, pick up a chip if you aren't already carrying one, and put down a chip if you run into someone else carrying one? Do you think that eventually we would get piles of chips?*

Student 2:   *I don't see how. Nobody is telling people where to put things down. They could put them down anywhere!*

Student 5:   *Yeah, won't people just keep picking up and putting down?*

Although the discussion continued a little longer, students showed no indication that they believed that such a simple system could introduce order into a scattered distribution of chips. At this point the teacher suggested that they try out her rules and "just see what happens!"

The following day the students helped the teacher move the classroom furniture to the sides of the room. They then proceeded to spread out 5 inch by 8 inch sheets of paper over the classroom floor. The teacher explained the rules they were going to follow. The 20 students were to spread themselves out in classroom, to close their eyes and turn to face any direction they wished (this was done to randomly orient the students). To begin the simulation, students were told to take one step straight ahead. If there was a piece of paper underfoot, pick it up (note that students could hold no more than one piece of paper at a time). At this point the teacher flipped a coin: heads, students turned ninety degrees to the right; tails, turn 90 degrees to the left. Students then took another step straight ahead. At this point students followed the applicable rule from the following set:

1. If they were holding a piece of paper and subsequently stepped on another piece, they put their paper down.

2. If they were holding a piece of paper and ran into another person holding a piece of paper, both students placed their papers on the floor on top of each other.

3. If a student did not currently have a piece of paper, but was now standing on one, he or she picked it up.

4. If a student had a piece of paper, but did not meet with another person also carrying a piece of paper, or stepped on another piece of paper, he or she did nothing.

The simulation continued for approximately the next 20 minutes with the teacher flipping the coin to indicate directional changes and students picking up and depositing pieces of paper.

At the end of the allotted time, the students regrouped to discuss changes in the distribution of papers. During the simulation, numerous students had spontaneously commented about the increasing order in the arrangement—small piles of papers had begun to appear almost from the start.

Teacher:	*So, what do you notice about the papers?*
Student 11:	*Most of them are in some sort of pile. There are only a few that seem to be by themselves.*
Student 2:	*Yeah, and most of the piles have a number of sheets of paper in them.*
Teacher:	*What do you think might have happened if we had kept going?*
Student 5:	*Probably would have gotten fewer piles, but with more papers in each one?*
Teacher:	*Do you think we might eventually get just one pile?*
Student 9:	*I guess you could, but it might take a long time.*
Teacher:	*Why?*
Student 9:	*Well, at first everyone was picking up papers—they were everywhere. But, as we kept playing I noticed that a lot of the time I didn't have a piece of paper. There was more open space on the floor.*
Student 1:	*Also, you can always take papers away from any pile*
Teacher:	*Good points. But my big question is, did we get order, piles of papers, without a leader telling us where to put things?*
Student 12:	*I'm not really sure. Aren't the rules just another way of telling us how to make piles?*

Teacher: *What if I hadn't told you that we were going to see if we could make piles? What if I had just spread out the papers, told you the rules and said let's see what happens? Would you still have gotten piles?*

Student 12: *Well, yeah.*

Teacher: *So, do you need to know ahead of time what the end will be for it to happen?*

Student 12: *I guess not. But what if the rules were different?*

Teacher: *What do you think?*

Student 10: *Maybe, I guess we could try it.*

Student 3: *Yeah, it probably doesn't matter how many steps you take. I think what matters is how you pick up and put down the papers. If you don't put down your paper with others, it might take a lot longer to get piles.*

Teacher: *Do you think you might still get piles?*

Student 3: *I don't know, but like [S12] said, we could try it and see.*

Teacher: *OK, so maybe having the right rules in place is important. Anything else that might be important?*

Teacher: *Well, maybe that's something that we can think about for the future; what else is needed besides just rules to get something done.*

This excerpt reveals considerable insight into students' beginning understanding of the links between behavior at one level and emerging order at another level. It also reveals the difficulty students had with accepting that you could have order without it being explicitly planned for. As Student 12 pointed out, the rules are a description of the process by which piles of papers are produced. His difficulty was in understanding that piles were an emergent phenomena. That is, that as a large group of independently acting individuals interacted in accordance with the rules, piles of papers began to appear. The difficulty students had in separating what they literally did—follow rules—from what was produced—piles of paper—highlights that engaging students in activities does not necessarily produce changes in thinking. With respect to the above simulation, the teacher engaged the students in an activity that showed how individuals following simple rules could produce emerging structure in an initial high entropy environment. However, as might be expected given the prevalence of the centralized mindset

(Resnick, 1994), this activity only set the stage for further exploring properties of emergent phenomena.

Summary

In general, students agreed that the simulation showed that very simple rules could lead to emerging order and complexity. Moreover, they agreed that this could happen without the need for some central source of control. However, it was also clear that many students had difficulty understanding *how* this happened. That is, they understood and followed the rules, but still did not clearly see the connection between their actions and the emerging order.

This difficulty reflects the problem of linking behavior at one level with outcomes at another level. This is a critical concept in understanding emerging order—there does not have to be an explicit plan for the goal state. The termite simulation readily lends itself to exploring critical issues underlying emergence. For example, having students follow the rules, but without papers on the floor, highlights the fact that rules alone do not produce order. Rather, rules in conjunction with the environment—a room filled with papers, in this case—are necessary for emergence. Similarly, varying the numbers of students involved can draw attention to the fact that interactions amongst individuals is a critical factor; fewer "termites" results in fewer interactions, which can have unpredictable effects on the creation of paper piles.

Phenomena-based approaches offer considerable leverage to studying emergence. Although exploratory computational media, such as StarLogo (Resnick, 1994), offer considerable power and versatility, they are by no means the only way to explore some fundamental issues underlying emergence. Resnick and Wilensky's (1998) StarPeople activities highlight numerous ways in which large groups of people can simulate emergent behavior. However, as the above study illustrates, helping learners understand the underlying concepts requires more than just immersion in the activity. As Smith et al. (1993) pointed out, activity based on personal experience (everyone has experience following rules) provides an anchor point for further inquiry.

People typically believe that complex behavior is the result of complex causes (Stewart, 1997). However, as the termite example illustrates, this is often not the case. As mentioned above, Resnick and Wilensky (1998) have described two approaches to studying complexity. The above study showed how a phenomena-based approach can be used to study emergence. The goal of the study described below was to investigate how a small group of middle-school students make sense of the relationship between simple rules and emergent complexity—a process which Resnick and Wilensky call *exploratory modeling.*

Exploratory Modeling

The mathematician J. H. Conway developed a game—Life—that provides a suitable environment for such an investigation. Life is a cellular automata, a self-contained universe in which "organisms" live or die according to a small set of rules (Gardner, 1970). Life is enacted on an infinite two-dimensional grid in which cells can assume two possible states: black (alive) or white (dead). In the approximately 30 years since Life was introduced, it has been extensively studied. The most far-reaching result of this period of exploration is the discovery that Life can be used to simulate a Turing machine; that is, it can become a universal computer (Berlekamp, Conway, & Guy, 1982). More in line with the purposes of this chapter, it has been demonstrated that Life has the potential for capturing aspects of the biological world (Gardner, 1983).

A Life game begins with the construction of a simple configuration of black counters (see Figure 1). This defines an organism. Note that, including the diagonals, each cell has eight neighboring cells. Three simple rules govern transformations between generations:

1. Survivals: Every black counter with either two or three neighboring counters survives for the next generation.

2. Deaths: Every black counter with four or more neighbors dies (i.e., is removed from the board) from overpopulation. Every black counter with one or fewer neighbors dies from isolation.

3. Births: Each empty cell (i. e., white cell) with exactly three adjacent black counters is a birth cell. A black counter is placed on the empty cell in the next generation.

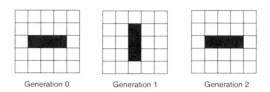

Generation 0   Generation 1   Generation 2

Figure 1. Example of a two-generation Life form.

Tracing Figure 1, we see that in Generation 0, the left-most and right-most cells each have a single neighbor.[1] Applying our transformation rules, we see that these cells will die off from isolation. The center counter has two "alive" neighbors and consequently will survive into the next generation. In addition, we see that in Generation 0, the cells immediately above and below the center counter each have three alive neighbors. Consequently, these two cells will give "birth" in the next generation. The net result is that in Generation 1, the automata has transformed from a horizontal arrangement of three cells into one of three vertical cells. Applying the transformation rules to the second generation reproduces the original horizontal arrangement. Continued application of the transformation rules shows that this particular automata oscillates between horizontal and vertical arrangements of three cells (a pattern referred to as a "blinker" in the Life community).

Life is a good environment for exploring complexity. The three rules completely describe the universe of any and all automata; however, a little experimentation shows it is difficult, if not impossible, to predict what will happen in most cases. For example, although a linear form of three cells forms a blinker, four linear cells never produces a blinker. Rather, a four-cell linear form becomes static in the second generation. Thus, one can see that Life supports the exploration of rules and emerging patterns.

This study was the first in a program of research on the development of reasoning about emergent phenomena. Given our relative lack of understanding of how children come to reason about emergence, the decision was made to concentrate on a small group of students over an extended period of time. This would allow me to more easily adapt sessions to follow up on previously raised questions and issues, as well as

1. Throughout this chapter the initial state is considered to be Generation 0.

track changes in their thinking. The classroom teacher was asked to identify four students interested in science who would be willing to meet in an after-school program. Under the general umbrella of how students come to understand the relationship between deterministic rules and emergent patterns, I looked at three specific questions:

1. How do children make sense of the patterns that develop? What types of regularities do they notice? How do they explain them?

2. Do children believe that there is anyway to predict future states from a given start state?

3. What effects do the children believe small changes in the initial state will have on future pattern development?

Over six sessions (each approximately 45-60 minutes in length), students investigated different aspects of the Life environment. Group discussions, which I led, at the beginning and conclusion of each session served to reinforce the goals of the investigations and document students' thinking about complexity. All interactions with the students were audiotaped for later analysis. To provide structure to the investigations, students were given the following tasks:

1. Trace the generations for all possible forms of three and four cell entities. This activity was carried out using notebooks of grid paper. Students shaded in squares to show the changes in form through generations. Guiding questions for the investigations were: (a) Is there a relationship between the number of starting cells and the number of possible starting arrays? (b) Is there a relationship between the initial form and the number of generations?

2. What happens to subsequent generations when looking at linear arrangements of cells? Start with three cells and then add one cell to the linear array in each new test. The guiding questions were: (a) What is the same/different about the patterns formed? What might underlie similarities or differences? (b) Is there a relationship between number of starting cells, number of generations, and final configurations? Can you predict what might happen for any given array?

The students were introduced to the Life environment as a "game that scientists use to study patterns in the world." Although a number of computer versions of Life are available, we initially used a 36 inch by 36 inch paper grid (one inch squares) and a set of black and white counters so that the students could learn the transformation rules.

The decision to not use a computer version of the game involved a number of tradeoffs. A computer version allows one to quickly and accurately run many experiments. Consequently, one can see many different patterns in a short period of time. However, the computational speed with which the rules are applied makes the transformation from one generation to the next almost impossible to follow. Moreover, there is a tendency for people to focus on producing an effect, rather than trying to understand how the rules lead to the effect.

My interest was in the students' understanding of the *how* the patterns were produced; consequently, I decided to initially have them enact Life by hand. This required them to keep the transformation rules in the foreground. One drawback was that the students were only able to explore a limited number of forms. However, since even four-cell forms produce complicated patterns, the decision to do things initially by hand was felt to be justified. Towards the end of the study when the students were exploring the effects of simple form changes, a computer version was utilized. At this point, students were now quite familiar with the transformation rules; moreover, the forms were becoming increasingly difficult to generate by hand. Using a computer version allowed students to focus on watching the pattern develop over time without worrying about making a mistake in applying the transformation rules.

The following presents and discusses a number of protocol segments that illustrate some aspects of the students' thinking about emergent systems.

Simple Forms

The initial Life activity was designed to focus students on possible links between the number of cells and the number of possible starting forms. Secondly, they investigated the possibility of a relationship between initial form and the number of generations an entity survives.

Students' comments suggest that they began the Life investigations believing that the environment was predictable. When asked how many generations any given form would live, they all stated unequivocal answers. For example, when asked how many generations an arrangement of three linear cells would last, responses ranged from "five" to "eight." However, probing revealed that the students could not explain how they arrived at their predictions.

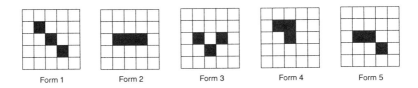

Form 1   Form 2   Form 3   Form 4   Form 5

Figure 2. Three-cell Life forms.

Through exploration, the students determined that there were five starting combinations of three-cell organisms (see Figure 2). In three of the forms (Forms 1, 3, and 5), the organism dies out following the first generation. Form 4 becomes static following the first generation. Form 2 oscillates between the initial linear array and the same array rotated 90 degrees. The discussion focused on the differences in final states.

Experimenter: *What did you notice about the different forms?*

Student 1: *Most of them disappear the second time.*

Experimenter: *The second time?*

Student 1: *Like when you use the rules twice, these three [points to the Forms 1, 3 and 5] disappear.*

Experimenter: *Why do you think that happens with those three? Is there anything the same about them?*

Student 2: *Well, in these two [points to Forms 2 and 4], the cells touch along the sides.*

Student 1: *But so does Form 5.*

Student 2: *Yeah, but in these [Forms 2 and 4] the middle one is surrounded on both sides. In Form 5, it's only on one side.*

As the excerpt reflects, the children were aware that initial configurations had important effects on the final outcome of the organism. In particular, they had noticed that in cases where cells shared vertices, not faces, the organism quickly died out. This led to an extended discussion regarding the orientation of individual cells.

Experimenter: *Why should how the cells touch make any difference?*

Student 3: *Well, like in this one [Form 1] nothing can be born.*

Experimenter: *Why not?*

Student 3: *None of the cells have more than two neighbors. So, nothing can be born.*

Student 2: *Yeah, when you have only diagonals [pointing to Form 1] you can never get new cells added. You need to have cells touching on the sides.*

Student 1: *No. Look at this one [Form 3]. They only touch at the corners and you get a new cell in the next generation.*

Experimenter: *So, how is Form 3 different from Form 1?*

Student 1: *This one [Form 3] has, like, a space . . . See, these two [points to Form 3] are on both sides of this space. But here [points to Form 1] there is no space.*

Experimenter: *Do you think it matters whether the cells touch on the faces or on the corners?*

Student 1: *Not really, as long as there are three neighbors. You need at least three cells that go around an empty space. That's all.*

Although the Life rules clearly specify the necessary conditions for the birth of a new cell, the above discussion reflects the children's initial difficulty in going from rules to phenomena. Only after exploration and discussion did the children realize relative orientation of cells is the critical factor. That is, it does not matter if the cells touch on faces or vertices. Thus, in looking at Form 3, the children realized that the initial form encloses an empty cell on three sides; this allows a new cell to be born in the following generation. Students quickly pointed out that this was true for all of the forms except Form 1.

Impact of Initial Conditions

Armed with some insight into how initial spatial orientation affects future development, the students were challenged to apply this knowledge to exploring four-cell entities. To highlight the effect of simply moving from three to four cells, students were asked to focus on two issues. First, they were asked to predict the number of Life forms they thought would be possible. The predictions ranged from an unqualified "lots" to more specific answers, such as "20 or maybe 30" or "10 to 15." However, when asked to justify their responses, none of the children were able to provide an explanation; as one child stated, "I'm just guessing." Following their investigation of four-cell forms, the children were asked if there was any way to predict the number of generations any give cellular configuration might proceed.

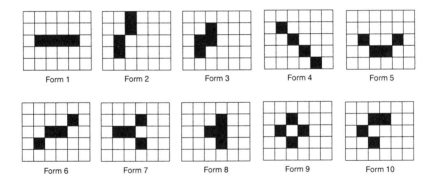

Figure 3. Four-cell Life forms.

Altogether, the students produced 10 unique four-cell organisms (see Figure 3). Six of the forms became static within three generations (Forms 1, 2, 3, 5, 6, and 9); a further two forms were quickly extinguished (Forms 4 and 10). Form 8 turns out to be a subset of Form 7. Forms 7 and 8 run 11 and 10 generations, respectively, before beginning a two-form oscillation. Following the development of the four-cell forms, the discussion again focused on possible relations between cell arrangements and the number of generations.

Experimenter: *So, do you think there is any relationship between how you arrange the cells and the number of generations?*

Student 1: *Well, they all go further.*

Experimenter: *What do you mean?*

Student 1: *When we did it with three [three cells] most of them only went one [one generation]. And here, four of them went more than one [one generation].*

Experimenter: *So, is there any way you can tell how far it is going to go?*

Student 3: *I don't think so.*

Experimenter: *Why not?*

Student 3: *. . . I don't know.*

Experimenter: *Well, remember when you looked at the three cells. What did you decide then?*

Student 3 *That the number of faces touching made a difference.*

Experimenter: *Anything else?*

Student 2: *No, remember, it's just how you set them up [how the cells are arranged] . . . You want to set them up so they surround cells. See, like in 2 [Form 2], there are only two places for a new cell to go; and in 4 [Form 4] there are no places for new cells.*

Student 3: *OK, but I still don't see how you can tell how far it's going to go. Look, number 1 [Form 1] can get four new ones [new cells], but it only goes twice [two generations]. In number 10 [Form 10] you only get 1 new one [new cell] and it goes the same number of times [two generations]. I don't think you can tell what's going to happen. You just have to see what happens.*

The above discussion highlights how students were able to use their experience with simpler Life forms to initially think about the relationship between cellular arrangement and the number of possible generations. Specifically, they showed that the number of possible birth cells in an initial arrangement does not predict the number of generations. This suggests that they are becoming aware that even simple situations rapidly become complex. As the one student stated, "You just have to see what happens."

Small Variations

Characteristic of complex systems is the fact that small changes can have significant effects. To explore this quality of complexity, students manipulated linear sequences of cells. Specifically, starting with a sequence of three cells, they used a computer version of Life to produce the generational forms, which they subsequently recorded. Using a computer version of the game allowed students to concentrate on observing the increasingly complicated patterns being generated.

The students extended the starting form by simply adding a single cell to one end of the string. In this fashion they explored the generational forms for linear arrays with lengths of three, four, five, six, seven, and eight cells (referred to below as Linear 1 through 6, respectively). Throughout, the focus was on similarities and differences in the patterns produced for each base form.

Differences

Students were quick to realize that modifying a form by adding a single cell had a number of effects. The two most obvious effects were the number of generations for each form, and whether the final generation oscillated, was static, or disappeared (see Table 1).

Table 1: Summary table for six linear forms.

Form	Number of Cells	Final State
1	3	Oscillate: Generations 0 & 1
2	4	Static: Generation 2
3	5	Oscillate: Generations 6 & 7
4	6	Extinct: Generation 11
5	7	Static: Generation 14
6	8	Static: Generation 48

The following excerpts highlight their thoughts about these differences.

Experimenter: *So, what do you notice about differences between the forms?*

Student 4: *They all go a different number of times.*

Student 1: *Yeah, like the first one [Linear 1] only one time, but this one [points to Linear 6] went 48 times.*

Experimenter: *How does it change?*

Student 2: *Well it gets longer each time. Like 1, 2, 7, 11, 14, and 48 [describing the number of generations for each form].*

Experimenter: *Does it change in a particular way?*

Student 2: *What do you mean?*

Experimenter: *Well, could you tell me how many generations there would be for a form with nine cells?… Anybody have any ideas?*

Student 1: *I don't see how you can tell.*

Student 3: *I don't either. I mean, it increases by one between number one and two [Linear 1 and 2]. Then it increases by five between number two and three [Linear 2 and 3]. But it only increases by four next [between Linear 3 and 4]; and only be three after that [between Linear 4 and 5]. Then it increases by . . . 34 [between Linear 5 and 6]!*

Experimenter: *So, do you see a pattern?*

Student 2: *No.*

Experimenter: *Is there anyway that you could determine how many generations a form with nine cells would go?*

Student 4: *I think you would just have to see what happens. Like, just go through them all until it stops.*

Experimenter: *Why would you have to do that?*

Student 4: *I don't see any pattern in how it changes. I don't think there is a pattern. So, you can't tell ahead of time what is going to happen.*

Experimenter: *Can the rules help you figure it out?*

Student 1: *I don't think so.*

Experimenter: *Why not?*

Student 1:   *They just tell you how to make the next one [the next gen-*
             eration]. They don't tell you anything about how many
             [generations] there will be. You'll just have to see what
             happens.

As the above highlights, students were aware that the increase in number of generations did not follow a simple pattern; in fact, by looking at the different forms, they became convinced that there was no principled way in which to know beforehand how many generations a form would have (i. e., the number of generations before the form either disappeared, became static, or began to oscillate). Moreover, they were reluctant to believe that simply knowing the transformation rules was sufficient for predicting the number of future generations. As the one student noted, the rules specify local changes—they are procedures, not explanations. That is, the rules tell you *how* to form the next generation, but they do not provide global information about what will happen to any given form.

Students also pointed out that the forms differed with respect to their final state. They noted that Linear 1 and 3 settled into two-generation oscillations. In contrast, Linear 2, 5, and 6 eventually became static, while Linear 4 ceased to exist. Discussion centered around why the forms have different final states.

Experimenter: *So, why do you think they're different?*

Student 1:   *Well, we kept adding a cell to each one.*

Experimenter: *Why would that make different things happen?… Well, do*
              you think there is anyway that you can predict what the
              final state of a string might be?

Student 3:   *Probably it will stop [become static].*

Experimenter: *Why?*

Student 3:   *Because most of them did that.*

Experimenter: *But can you know for sure without testing it?*

Student 2:   *No.*

Experimenter: *Why not?*

Student 2:   *Almost as many switch back and forth [oscillate].*

Experimenter: *So?*

Student 2: *I'm looking at them [the starting forms] and I can't see any-thing in common. At first I thought maybe an even number of cells. Because these three [Linear 2, 4, and 6] are all even. But two are static [Linear 2 and 6], but this one [Linear 4] disappears. Then I thought maybe it had something to do with prime numbers. Because this one [Linear 1] and this one [Linear 3] switch back and forth [oscillate]. But then this one [Linear 5] is prime and it just stops. So, I don't think you can tell.*

This excerpt reflects the students' attempts to make sense of the outcomes. Although they attempted to find some correlation between initial and final states, they concluded that there is no a priori means by which this is possible. That is, they again concluded that without explicitly running the simulation there was no way of knowing what would happen.

Similarities

Even though there is much about Life that appears unknowable, the students did find that there were some similarities that went across forms. The most obvious similarity was the gross form of the first generation.

Student 4: *The first ones [first generations] are all kind of the same.*

Experimenter: *How?*

Student 4: *They're all vertical columns. Like the first one [Linear 1] is three up and down. And the second one [Linear 2] is two columns of three.*

Student 1: *Yeah. Look at them. They all have columns of three.*

Experimenter: *How does it change?*

Student 2: *The first one had one column, the next one [Linear 2] had two columns, the next one [Linear 3] had three columns.*

Student 1: *It goes up one column each time.*

Experimenter: *So, how many columns would you get if you started with 100 in a row?...Well, is there anything you can think of by looking at the ones you have there?*

Student 2:   *I don't know.*

Student 3:   *If you have three [cells], you get one [column]; if you have four [cells], you get two [columns]; if you have five [cells], you get three [columns].*

Student 1:   *Oh, it is just two less than what you start with!*

Experimenter: *What do you mean?*

Student 1:   *Whatever you start with, you just take away two and that's the number of columns. So if you start with 100 [cells], you would have 98 columns next.*

This excerpt captures the students' first belief that there might be some regularities in the patterns. Even though they had begun the study believing that the Life environment was predictable, they had quickly come to see that very small changes had considerable effects—effects that they came to believe were unknowable in advance. However, they now began to believe that within global uncertainty you sometimes find local order.

Following this discussion, the children discovered that although the first three generations were similar across forms, in the fourth generation, forms began to diverge.

Student 3:   *See, in this one [Linear 3] and this one [Linear 5] when you get to four [fourth generation] they look like circles. But in this one [Linear 4] and this one [Linear 6] they look like broken circles.*

Experimenter: *Anything else?*

Student 1:   *Well, it looks like after that, after the fourth one [fourth generation] they all start looking different.*

Experimenter: *So, what can you tell about these?*

Student 2:   *I think that when it starts with an odd number, like this one [Linear 3] and this one [Linear 5] it goes to a circle in four [fourth generation]. But when it's even [number of starting cells], it goes to a split circle in four. Like this one [Linear 4] and this one [Linear 6].*

Experimenter: *Do you think that will always be true?*

Student 2: *Yeah.*

Experimenter: *How do you know?*

Student 2: *Because that's what happens here.*

This protocol segment further shows students' beliefs about regularities in the Life environment. In fact, the one student believed that he had found a general rule that determined what would happen in the fourth generation; a rule that would hold for all linear arrays.

Despite the discovery of some level of predictability, the students were convinced that you "can't know everything that will happen." They pointed out that they could not tell how many generations a given form would run; nor whether it would it disappear, oscillate, or become static. In fact, as one student pointed out, "Maybe some of them go on forever. You can't tell without trying them all." Moreover, they were skeptical that anyone could know in advance what would happen to any given form.

Summary

The Life environment provided students with the opportunity to explore how simple rules could produce large-scale patterns. Students' comments suggest that they began their investigations with little understanding of how local interactions can lead to global patterns. For example, students initially claimed that the Life environment was completely knowable in advance. As one child succinctly stated, "We know the rules." In his view, if you know the rules, you know how everything of importance.

As students explored the Life game their a priori perceptions of the limited nature of the environment changed dramatically. For example, they quickly saw that even a supposedly simple task such as predicting the number of generations that a linear combination of cells would live was impossible. That is, despite the deterministic nature of the domain, this question could not be answered without actually applying the rules. Moreover, as the protocol segments show, they believed that this was a fundamental fact of the Life environment—no one could know in advance how anything but the simplest forms would progress.

Overall, students gained some understanding of local rules, global patterns, and predictability. However, their passing comments suggest that it is one thing to consider artificial environments, such as Life, in terms of rules; it is a very different question to consider real-world interactions from such a perspective. For example, considering human behavior in terms of rules seems to ignore our conceptions of personal intentionality, something most people believe to be a fundamental quality of our species. Knowing how to structure tasks so that students learn to hold such firm beliefs in abeyance in order to test "what if" questions (e. g., How much of human behavior can be explained using an emergent systems approach?) is an issue that has only recently begun to get the attention it deserves (Smith et al., 1993).

General Discussion

Resnick (1994, 1996) has pointed out that helping people develop an understanding of the often emergent nature of complex systems is not a trivial task. However, given the growing importance of this methodology in real-world science, it seems important for science educators to consider how best to help students develop such understanding. A key goal of the research above is to begin to identify and detail peoples' understanding of complex systems as they work with emergent models. The results show that the students, to some degree, did come to better understand the link between low-level interactions and global patterns. For example, the termite activity, and resulting discussion, highlighted the key issue that order can occur without an explicit top-level plan in place. It is clear, however, that the students did not automatically consider the problem of linking behavior at one level with outcomes at another level. Undoubtedly, for students to automatically approach phenomena in this manner will require considerably more experience playing with, and thinking about, emergent systems than what was provided in the termite activity.

    This goal is complicated by the fact that many, if not most, students believe science to be a passive process of observing and recording events in order to discover facts (Carey, Evans, Honda, Jay, & Unger, 1989; Carey & Smith, 1995; Linn, Songer, & Lewis, 1991; Raghavan & Glaser, 1995; Tinker & Thornton, 1992). Moreover, this belief is fostered by a reliance on activities that focus on collecting data to "prove" well-established principles. Such data-driven approaches under-emphasize science as the building, testing and evaluation of explanatory models. In contrast, studies of professional scientists reveal a focus on the building and testing models (e.g., Giere, 1988; Hestenes, 1992). In these accounts, model building and testing are essential to the development of theory—models both channel observations, and drive the resulting interpretations (Doran & Gilbert, 1994; Hestenes, 1992). As Stewart (1997) has suggested, understanding the world depends upon becoming sensitive to patterns and to modeling the processes that give rise to patterns.

diSessa (1992) suggests that "a large part of science is a way of acting" (p. 28). The work reported attempted to follow this maxim by engaging students in the use of two forms of emergent models. However, Resnick (1996) argues that learners need to do more than just participate in activities that focus on emergent systems; rather they need to engage in the designing of such systems. That is, presenting students with "packaged" models, removes the need for them to explicitly consider the objects and relations that underlie the phenomenon under study.

One means of encouraging students to develop their own models is to utilize programmable mediums. Such interfaces not only encourage students to think about their thinking, but can be a means of introducing them to appropriate ways of acting that diSessa has claimed is central to scientific practice (diSessa, 1988; Papert, 1980). Programming environments, such as StarLogo (Resnick, 1994), require learners to externalize their intuitions—to focus on modeling, not just models (Tinker & Thornton, 1992). Once externalized, in the form of programs, these intuitions are accessible to personal reflection and public inspection.

Engaging learners in practices that promote understanding, such as developing programs that define behaviors as emerging from actions and interactions, opens up the knowing process. Such practices focus attention on the objects and interactions students believe are fundamental to understanding the phenomena under investigation. However, to date, only a few studies have begun to document people's thinking as they are engaged in building, not just using, emergent models (e. g., Resnick, 1994, 1996). More work of this type is necessary if science educators are to better facilitate students' understanding of emergence as powerful explanatory tool.

References

Arthur, W. B. (1990). Positive feedback in the economy. *Scientific American, 262(2).* 92-99.

Berlekamp, E. R., Conway, J. H., & Guy, R. K. (1982). *Winning ways for you mathematical plays. Vol. 2: Games in particular.* London: Academic Press.

Carey, S., Evans, R., Honda, M., Jay, E., & Unger, C. (1989). 'An experiment is when you try it and see if it works': A study of grade 7 students' understanding of the construction of scientific knowledge. *International Journal of Science Education, 11,* 514-529.

Carey, S., & Smith, C. (1995). On understanding the nature of scientific knowledge. In D. N. Perkins, J. L. Schwartz, M. M. West, & M. S. Wiske (Eds.), *Software goes to school: Teaching for understanding with new technologies* (pp. 39-55). New York: Oxford University Press.

Deneubourg, J. L., & Goss, S. (1989). Collective patterns and decision-making. *Ethology, Ecology, & Evolution, 1,* 295-311.

diSessa, A. (1988). Knowledge in pieces. In G. Forman & P. Pufall (Eds.), *Constructivism in the computer age* (pp. 49-70). Hillsdale, NJ: Lawrence Erlbaum Associates.

diSessa, A. (1992). Images of learning. In E. De Corte, M. C. Linn, H. Mandl, & L. Verschaffel (Eds.), *Computer-based learning environments and problem solving* (pp. 19-40). Berlin: Springer-Verlag.

Doran, J., & Gilbert, N. (1994). Simulating societies: An introduction. In N. Gilbert & J. Doran (Eds.), *Simulating societies: The computer simulation of social phenomena* (pp. 1-18). London: UCL Press.

Emmeche, C. (1994). *The garden in the machine: The emerging science of artificial life.* Princeton, NJ: Princeton University Press.

Epstein, J. M., & Axtell, R. (1996). *Growing artificial societies: Social science form the bottom up.* Washington, DC: Brookings Institution Press.

Franks, N. R. (1989). Army ants: A collective intelligence. *American Scientist, 77,* 139-145.

Gardner, M. (1970, October). Mathematical games. *Scientific American, 223(4),* 120-123.

Gardner, M. (1983). *Wheels, life, and other mathematical amusements.* New York: W. H. Freedman.

Giere, R. N. (1988). *Explaining science: A cognitive approach.* Chicago: The University of Chicago Press.

Herman, R., & Gardels, K. (1963). Vehicular traffic flow. *Scientific American, 209(6),* 36-43.

Hestenes, D. (1992). Modeling games in the Newtonian World. *American Journal of Physics, 60,* 440-454.

Holland, J. H. (1998). *Emergence: From chaos to order.* Reading, MA: Helix

Books.

Linn, M. C., Songer, N. B., & Lewis, E. L. (1991). Overview: Students' models and epistemologies of science. *Journal of Research in Science Teaching, 28*, 729-732.

Mataric, M. J. (1993). Designing emergent behaviors: From local interactions to collective intelligence. In J. A. Meyer, H. L. Raitblat, & S. W. Wilson (Eds.), *From animals to animats 2* (pp. 432-441). Cambridge, MA: MIT Press.

Ost, D. H. (1987). Models, modeling, and the teaching of science and mathematics. *School Science and Mathematics, 87*, 363-370.

Papert, S. (1980). *Mindstorms: Children, computers, and powerful ideas*. New York: Basic Books.

Penner, D. E., Giles, N. D., Lehrer, R., & Schauble, L. (1997). Building functional models: Designing an elbow. *Journal of Research in Science Teaching, 34*, 1-20.

Raghavan, K., & Glaser, R. (1995). Model-based analysis and reasoning in science: The MARS curriculum. *Science Education, 79*, 37-61.

Ray, T. S. (1995). An evolutionary approach to synthetic biology: Zen and the art of creating life. In C. G. Langton (Ed.), *Artificial life: An overview* (pp. 179-209). Cambridge, MA: MIT Press.

Resnick, M. (1994). *Turtles, termites, and traffic jams: Explorations in massively parallel microworlds*. Cambridge, MA: MIT Press.

Resnick, M. (1996). Beyond the centralized mindset. *Journal of the Learning Sciences, 5*, 1-22.

Resnick, M., & Wilensky, U. (1998). Diving into complexity: Developing probabilistic decentralized thinking through role-playing activities. *Journal of the Learning Sciences, 7*, 153-172.

Smith, J. P., diSessa, A. A., & Roschelle, J. (1993). Misconceptions reconceived: A constructivist analysis of knowledge in transition. *The Journal of the Learning Sciences, 3*, 115-163.

Sober, E. (1991). Learning from functionalism: Prospects for strong artificial life. In C. G. Langton, C. Taylor, J. D. Farmer, & S. Rasmussen (Eds.), *Artificial life II* (pp. 749-765). Redwood City, CA: Addison-Wesley.

Steels, L. (1995). Building agents out of autonomous behavior systems. In L. Steels & R. Brooks (Eds.), *The artificial life route to artificial intelligence: Building embodied, situated agents* (pp. 83-121). Hillsdale, NJ: Lawrence Erlbaum Associates.

Stewart, I. (1997). *The magical maze: Seeing the world through mathematical eyes*. New York: John Wiley & Sons.

Stewart, J., Hafner, R., Johnson, S., & Finkel, E. (1992). Science as model building: Computers and high-school genetics. *Educational Psychologist, 27*, 317-336.

Thelen, E., & Smith, L. B. (1994). *A dynamic systems approach to the development of cognition and action*. Cambridge, MA: MIT Press.

Tinbergen, N. (1951). *The study of instinct.* Oxford: Oxford University Press.
Tinker, R. R., & Thornton, R. K. (1992). Constructing student knowledge in science. In E. Scanlon & T. O'Shea (Eds.), *New directions in educational technology* (pp. 153-170). Berlin: Springer-Verlag.
Wilensky, U. (1996). Modeling rugby: Kick first, generalize later? *International Journal of Computers for Mathematical Learning, 1,* 125-131.
Wilson, E. O. (1971). *The insect societies.* Cambridge, MA: Harvard University Press.

8

From Cognition to Instruction to Cognition: A Case Study in Elementary School Science Instruction

David Klahr
Zhe Chen
Eva Erdosne Toth
Carnegie Mellon University

Developmental psychologists have produced a vast literature on how children's initial concepts emerge and change over the course of development. Within this conceptual change literature, one of the favorite topics is the development of scientific concepts such as heat, gravity, animacy, mechanics, and so on. In this chapter, we present a description of a different kind of conceptual change; one in which the focal concept has to do with the very nature of our enterprise—the translation of basic knowledge about scientific thinking into classroom lessons. Moreover, the entities who underwent this change are not the children in our studies, but rather us—the authors of this chapter.

Our change process fits the broad outlines of current views about the cause of conceptual change: a contradiction between expectations derived from existing concepts and the reality of phenomena in the world. The initial concept that underwent this change had several related parts. First, there was the idea that solid, well-controlled, cognitively-based research could provide a theoretical and empirical basis for understanding how best to teach children about important scientific concepts and procedures. Second, there was the idea that, with such knowledge in hand, one could make a fairly straightforward translation from the lab findings to classroom practice.

Our underlying metaphor was a kind of "scaling-up" model from basic science to engineering, or from the lab to the pilot plant to the production line. In our initial conceptualization (depicted in Figure 1) the convergence of cognitive theory and instructional topics yields some rigorous studies in the psychology lab, and the results of those investigations then are mapped directly into a cognitively-based curriculum unit. Even in this naïve model, the mapping is not trivial, and some of the more obvious differences between the lab and the classroom are indicated in the figure. (Of course, only in retrospect did we dub it the "Naïve Model.") Nevertheless—and this is the third important part of our initial concept—the flow of information and influence is primarily unidirectional and the influence of the real educational context shows up only in the choice of topic.

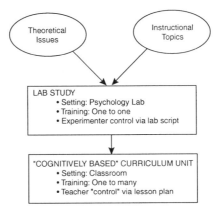

Figure 1. A naïve model of the relation between basic research and classroom instruction.

In this chapter, we chronicle our own conceptual change as we first applied and then revised this model in the process of creating a cognitively-based instructional intervention. Although others who have traversed the path from the psychology lab to the classroom have reported on the specific complexities and difficulties that they encountered along the way (e.g., Brown, 1992, 1997; Bransford, Sherwood, Vye, & Reiser, 1986; McGilly, 1994), it seemed to us that our instructional goals and processes were sufficiently well-focused and self-contained that we would not encounter any substantial barriers to a classroom implementation of an instructional procedure whose effectiveness had been demonstrated in the lab. As will become evident, we were mistaken, and we think that our story is sufficiently unique to warrant telling in the context of this volume devoted to the design of scientific and technical environments.

The chapter is organized as follows. First we describe the basic topic around which our instruction is constructed: The design of unconfounded experiments. Then we briefly address some theoretical issues surrounding the best way to teach the topic. Next, we provide an extensive description of the laboratory study that provided the basis for our intervention, followed by a description of how we made the lab-to-classroom transition, and how that process led to a substantial revision in our initial view of the relation between basic and applied research on the acquisition of scientific knowledge.

Before we embark, some terminological clarification might be helpful. Throughout this chapter we use *lab study* when referring to the type of one-on-one study that is typical of the research psychologist—exemplified by the first study to be described in this chapter. By *classroom study* we mean the kind of study described in the second part of the chapter, where a teacher introduces an experimental curriculum unit and we do several assessments of its effectiveness. The terminology can get confusing because our "lab" study, although carried out one-on-one with an experimenter and a child, was actually conducted (in a quiet room) in the school and our "classroom" study took place in the normal science lab in the school. One additional complexity is that immediately before and after the classroom study, we assessed some children in a one-on-one "lab" fashion in order to compare their performance to the earlier (true) lab study and to calibrate the lab assessments with the classroom assessments.

Designing Unconfounded Experiments: The Control of Variables Strategy

There is widespread agreement among science educators that "Even at the earliest grade levels, students should learn what constitutes evidence and judge the merits or strength of the data and information that will be used to make explanations." (NSES, 1995). But evidence does not spring forth unbidden. Instead it must be actively sought or generated. Thus, the ability to create informative experiments and to derive valid inferences from the evidence they yield is one of the fundamental design skills underlying scientific thinking (Klahr, 2000).

A central component of this skill is the *control of variables strategy* (CVS). Procedurally, CVS is a method for creating experiments in which a single contrast is made between experimental conditions. The full strategy involves not only creating such contrasts, but also being able to distinguish between confounded and unconfounded experiments. The logical aspects of CVS include the ability to make appropriate inferences from the outcomes of unconfounded experiments as well as an understanding of the inherent indeterminacy of confounded experiments.

Can elementary school children acquire these concepts and the procedures associated with them? Both the educational and the psychological literature suggest that they do not. Ross's (1988) meta-analysis of over five dozen CVS training studies from the 1970s and 1980s indicates that a variety of training methods can generate improvement in CVS performance, but only a handful of the studies in his sample included young elementary school children (i.e., below grade 5). The results of those few studies, as well as more recent ones in that age range, present a decidedly mixed picture of the extent to which young elementary school children can understand and execute CVS (Bullock & Ziegler, 1999; Case, 1974; Kuhn, Garcia-Mila, Zohar and Andersen, 1995; Kuhn & Angelev, 1976 ; Schauble, 1996). Moreover, even when training studies show statistically significant differences between trained and untrained groups, the absolute levels of posttest performance are well below educationally desirable levels.[1] Indeed, to get ahead of our story a bit, our first study (Chen & Klahr, 1999) showed that even in schools with strong elementary science programs in which components of CVS were taught repeatedly during the early science curriculum, fourth graders could correctly construct unconfounded experiments on fewer than 50% of their attempts.

Theories of Instruction, Learning, and Transfer

Given that CVS is a fundamental scientific reasoning skill, and given that few elementary school children master it even after several years of "good" science instruction, it is important to know whether there are effective ways to teach it and whether age and instructional method interact with respect to learning and transfer. One of the most controversial issues in instruction is whether or not discovery learning is more effective than traditional didactic methods (here called simply "direct instruction"). Part of the controversy derives from a lack of definitional consensus, so we need to clarify our use of the terms. Although the details will become apparent when we describe our studies, it is important to note at the outset that we do not associate one with "active" and the other with "passive" learning.

---

1. Ross found a mean effect size of .73 across all of the studies in his sample.

In *both* the "direct" and the "discovery" learning situations to be described in this chapter, students were actively engaged in the design and manipulation of experimental apparatus, and they were challenged with a series of probe questions. The main distinction between the situations is that in direct instruction, the instructor told the students how to do CVS and why it worked, whereas in other situations there was no such direct "telling."

Even with these distinctions, the relative efficacy of discovery learning versus direct instruction depends on many factors, one of which is the content of the learning tasks. Discovery learning has been considered an effective approach for the acquisition of domain-specific knowledge. Its advocates argue that children who are actively engaged in acquiring new knowledge are more likely to be successful in retaining and applying it than those who passively receive direct instruction (e.g., Jacoby, 1978; McDaniel & Schlager, 1990). Although discovery learning might be effective when problem outcomes provide informative feedback (e.g., Siegler, 1976), direct instruction may be appropriate in those cases where it is unlikely that a multi-step strategy would be discovered spontaneously. For example, Klahr and Carver (1988) found that a brief period of direct instruction in how to debug computer programs was more effective than hundreds of hours of discovery learning. With respect to CVS, unguided experimental designs typically do not provide informative feedback concerning their quality. This lack of feedback might render the discovery of procedures such as CVS particularly difficult for early elementary school children.

Background: A Laboratory Training Study

It is clear that the issue of the relative effectiveness of direct instruction versus discovery learning is extremely complex (and, unfortunately, somewhat politicized). Rather than examine the issue in the "messy" context of an ongoing classroom, we decided to begin by studying it in the relatively controlled confines of a laboratory study. Thus, we compared the relative effectiveness of different instructional methods for teaching CVS in a situation where children had extensive and repeated opportunities to use CVS while designing, running, and evaluating their own experiments. Eighty-seven second, third and fourth graders from two private schools in an urban area were randomly assigned to one of the three different instructional methods:

1. *Explicit training* was provided in the *training/probe* condition. It included an explanation of the rationale behind controlling variables as well as examples of how to make unconfounded comparisons. Children in this condition also received probe questions surrounding each comparison that they made. Before the experiment was executed, children were asked to explain and justify the design. After the experiment was executed, children were asked if they could "tell for sure" whether the variable they were testing made a difference and also why they were sure or not sure. This instruction was provided following the Exploration phase (see Procedure section below) in which children had designed a few experiments and pondered probe questions about those experiments.

2. *Implicit training* was provided in the *no-training/probe* condition. Here, children did not receive direct instruction, but they did receive probe questions before and after each of their experiments.

3. *Discovery learning* opportunities were provided in the *no-training/no-probe* condition. Children received neither training nor probes but they did receive the same number of opportunities as children in the other conditions to construct unconfounded experiments.

Materials, Procedure, and Measures Used in the Laboratory Study

We used three different domains in which children had to design unconfounded experiments: (a) springs, in which the goal was to determine the factors that affected spring elongation; (b) sinking, in which children had to assess the factors that determined how fast various objects sank in water; and (c) ramps, to be described below. The underlying CVS logic in all three domains was identical. In each, there were four variables that could assume either of two values. In each domain, children were asked to focus on a single outcome that could be affected by any of the four variables. For example, in the springs domain, the outcome was how far the spring stretched as a function of its length, width, wire size, and weight size. Each child worked with one of the three domains on his or her first day in the study (Exploration and Assessment phases) and then with two other domains on the second day (Transfer 1 and Transfer 2). Domain order was counter-balanced as was the order of focal variables within each task. Here we will describe only the ramps domain, because that was the one used in the classroom intervention described in the next section. (See Chen & Klahr, 1999, for a detailed description of all three domains.)

Ramps Task

In the ramps domain, children had to make comparisons to determine how different variables affected the distance that objects rolled after leaving a downhill ramp (Figure 2). Materials were two wooden ramps, each with an adjustable downhill side and a slightly uphill, stepped surface on the other side.

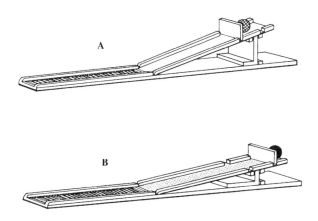

Figure 2. The Ramps Domain. On each of the two ramps, children can vary the angle of the ramp, the surface of the ramp, the length of the ramp, and the type of ball. The confounded experiment depicted here contrasts (a) the golf ball on the steep, smooth, short ramp with (b) the rubber ball on a shallow, rough, long ramp. [See Appendix for additional information.]

Children could set the steepness of the downhill ramps (steep and low) using wooden blocks that fit under the ramps in two orientations. Children could control the surface of the ramps (rough or smooth) by placing inserts on the downhill ramps either carpet side up or smooth wood side up. They could also control the length of the downhill ramp by placing gates at either of two positions different distances from the top of the ramp (long or short run). Finally, children could choose from two kinds of balls, squash balls and golf balls. To set up a comparison, participants constructed two ramps, setting the steepness, surface, and length of run for each and then placing one ball behind the gate on each ramp. To execute a comparison, participants removed the gates and observed as the balls rolled down the ramps and then up the steps and came to a stop. The outcome measured was how far the balls traveled up the stepped side of the ramp. Figure 2 depicts a comparison from the ramps domain. It is a completely confounded comparison because all four of the variables differ between Ramp A and Ramp B.

Procedure

Part I consisted of four phases: Exploration, Assessment, Transfer 1 and Transfer 2. In each phase, children were asked to construct an experimental contrast from which they could make a valid inference about the causal status of some dimension of the domain. For example, in the springs domain, the possible causal variables were spring length, width, wire size, and weight size. (See Chen & Klahr, 1999, for details.) The Exploration phase established an initial baseline of children's ability to design unconfounded experiments in the first domain (e.g., springs). For the Training/ Probe condition, the instructional session immediately followed the Exploration phase. Then followed the Assessment phase in which children were asked to design experiments on a different dimension but in the same domain (Thus, if, in the Exploration phase, the experiments focused on spring *length* then the Assessment phase would focus on spring *width*). Transfer 1 and Transfer 2 took place few days after Exploration and Assessment. Children returned to the lab and were asked to design unconfounded experiments in the other two domains (e.g., in the current example, they would do experiments with ramps and with sinking objects).

Part II was a paper and pencil, experiment evaluation posttest, given 7 months after the individual interviews. This consisted of a set of pairwise experimental comparisons in a variety of domains. The child's task was to examine the experimental set-up and decide whether it was a "good" or a "bad" experiment. (This type of assessment was used extensively in the classroom study, and it will be described in more detail later.)

Results of the Laboratory Training Study

Measures

Three measures used in the lab study that were also used in the classroom study were:[2] (a) *CVS score*: a simple performance measure based on children's use of CVS in designing tests; (b) *robust use of CVS*: a more stringent measure based on both performance and verbal justifications (in responses to probes) about why children designed their experiments as they did; (c) *domain knowledge*: based on children's responses to questions about the effects of different causal variables in the domain.

Use of CVS

Children's use of CVS was indexed by their selection of valid comparisons. An example of a valid design to test the effect of the wire diameter is that the pair differs only in the focal variable (e.g., wire diameter) while all other variables (coil width, length, and weight) are kept constant. Invalid designs included (1) non-contrastive comparisons in which the focal variable was not varied and one or more other variables were varied, and (2) confounded comparisons in which the focal variable as well as one or more other variables were varied. Each valid comparison was given a score of one. All other types of design were given a score of zero. Because children made four comparisons in each phase, the CVS scores for each phase could range from zero to four.

Robust Use of CVS

Children's responses to the probe questions "Why did you set up the comparison this way?" and "Can you tell for sure from this comparison?" were classified into four categories:

1. Explanations that included mention of CVS (e.g., "You just need to make the surface different, but put the gates in the

---

2. A fourth measure—*strategy similarity awareness*—was based on children's responses to questions about the similarity across tasks. This is described in Chen & Klahr (1999).

same places, set the ramps the same height, and use the same kind of balls").

2. Explanations that included controlling some but not all of the other relevant variables (e.g., "Cause they're both metal but one was round and one was square").

3. Explanations that mentioned a comparison within the focal variable (e.g., "Cause I had to make the surfaces different").

4. Explanations that were irrelevant to CVS.

Note that when children explained their designs and interpreted their test outcomes they did not simply repeat the terminology learned during training. CVS mention during the assessment phase (immediately following training, and in the same task domain) required a different focal variable than was used during training, and correct CVS mention during Transfer 1 and Transfer 2 had to go far beyond simple repetition of terminology, and had to make the correct mapping between the underlying logic of CVS and the new variables in the new task domain.

Children received a robust CVS score of one only for those trials for which they produced an unconfounded design *and* provided an explanation or interpretation that mentioned the control of all other variables (i.e., a response fitting category 1, above). Other trials received a score of zero. Again, because children made four designs in each phase, the range of robust use scores was zero to four.

Domain Knowledge

Knowledge about each domain was assessed by asking children how they thought each variable would affect the outcome both before and after they designed and implemented their tests. Children's correct prediction/judgment of each variable was given a score of one, and for incorrect prediction/judgment, a score of zero was assigned.

Initial Performance in Using CVS

Children's initial performance was measured by the proportion of unconfounded comparisons they produced during the Exploration phase. We found significant grade differences in this initial performance: 26%, 34%, and 48% in second, third, and fourth grade, respectively.[3] Note that, even for second graders, these scores are significantly above chance.[4] Thus, although repeated exposure to science classes in each grade does lead to improvement in children's ability to design unconfounded experiments, their overall performance is far below ceiling, leaving a lot of room for improvement.

Acquisition and Transfer of CVS

The three training conditions differed substantially in their effects. As indicated in Figure 3, the frequency of CVS use in the Training-Probe condition increased immediately following training, and remained at a relatively high level.

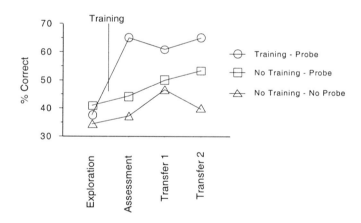

Figure 3. Percentage of trials with correct use of CVS by phase and condition (lab study).

3. Statistical detail has been surpressed throughout this chapter. Most of the effects reported as "significant" have p values less than .01, although a few are only .05, while "marginally significant" values are between .05 and .10. For more detail see Chen & Klahr (1999) and Toth, Klahr, & Chen (under review).

4. The chance probability of producing an unconfounded comparison is .083. See Chen & Klahr (1999) for a detailed explanation.

In contrast, for the No-Training conditions, the increase was slow (for No Training-Probe) and unsustained (For No Training-No Probe). Statistical analysis revealed that, when averaged over all three grade levels, the only significant gains occurred in the Training-Probe condition. A more detailed analysis, in which we looked at each grade level separately, revealed that only the third and fourth graders in the Training-Probe condition showed significant gains after training that were maintained into the transfer phases. For second graders in the Training-Probe condition, transfer performance was not significantly higher than the initial exploration performance (Figure 4).

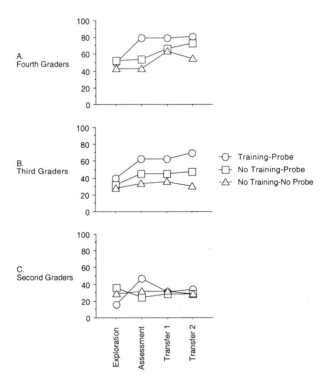

Figure 4. Percentage of correct CVS usage by phase, grade and condition (lab study).

In order to assess transfer in *individual* students, we defined a "good experimenter" as a child who produced at least seven out of eight unconfounded comparisons during Transfer 1 and Transfer 2, and then we computed the proportion of children who became "good experimenters" between Exploration and Transfer. There were substantial effects of condition: 44% of the children in the Training-Probe condition, 22% in the No Training-Probe condition, and 13% in the No Training-No Probe condition became good experimenters.

Relations Between the Use of CVS and Domain Knowledge

An important issue concerning the function of training in CVS is whether children's domain-specific knowledge—i.e., their understanding of the effects of the variables associated with springs, ramps, and sinking—improved as a result of training. Because our primary goal was to examine elementary school children's ability to learn and transfer CVS, neither the training nor the probe questions were directed toward, or contingent upon, the children's understanding of the *content* of the tasks. However, any change in children's beliefs about the causal mechanisms in the three tasks is of obvious interest because the ultimate goal of good experimental design is to learn about the world. We found that only those children who were directly trained to design informative (i.e., unconfounded) comparisons showed an increase in their domain knowledge (see Figure 5).

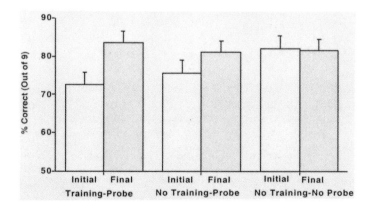

Figure 5. Initial and final domain knowledge for each condition (lab study).

Posttest Performance

The posttest was designed to see whether children were able to transfer the learned strategy to remote problems after a long (7 month) delay. Posttest data were collected only in School A and therefore only third and fourth graders were included. Recall that in School A all children who participated in the hands-on interviews were trained in CVS, either early in the procedure or at the end of the hands-on study. All children who participated in the hands-on interview are now considered the experimental group, while their classmates who did not participate make up the control group.

Far transfer was indexed by the number of correct responses to the 15 posttest problems. A correct response was given a score of one, and an incorrect response, a score of zero. We found that fourth-graders—but not third- graders—in the experimental condition outperformed those in the control condition (see Figure 6).

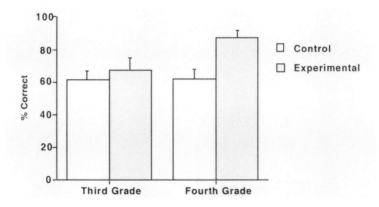

Figure 6. Percentage of correct posttest answers by grade and condition (lab study).

Another measure of remote transfer involved the percentage of "good reasoners" in the experimental and control condition. Children who made 13 or more correct judgments out of a total of 15 problems were considered good reasoners. Forty percent of the third and 79% of the fourth graders in the Experimental group were categorized as good reasoners, compared to 22% of the third and 15% of the fourth graders in the Control group. This difference was significant only for the fourth graders.

Main Findings From the Laboratory Study

To summarize the key results from our laboratory study: (a) absent direct instruction, children did not discover CVS on their own, even when they had repeated opportunities to work with hands-on materials, (b) brief direct instruction on CVS, combined with active participation in experimental setups and execution, was sufficient to promote substantial gains in CVS performance and (c) these gains transferred to both near and (for fourth-graders) far domains. These results gave us confidence that we were ready to move to the classroom and we began planning to recruit a few elementary school science teachers to let us implement the instructional method that had worked so well in the lab in their classrooms. Thus began the second phase of our project.

Moving From the Lab to the Classroom

At this point, it occurred to us that we really knew very little about what elementary school science teachers did in their classrooms when teaching experimentation procedures and concepts. Beyond some cursory informal observations in a couple of classes and a few meetings with teachers (necessary to get their cooperation to run the lab study) we had paid little attention to what was happening "on the ground," and therefore we had no way of knowing how well our instruction materials, scripts, and assessments would translate into the classroom context. The first signs that our initial model of the lab-to-classroom process was less than adequate began to appear.

We decided to remedy our ignorance through a six-step process. The first and most important step was to add to the two developmental psychologists on the research team (the first two authors) a person who had been trained as both a classroom science teacher and an educational researcher (the third author). The other five steps included (a) teacher networking, (b) survey of curricula, (c) classroom observations of current practices, (d) the development of a lesson plan, and (e) assessment of the effects of classroom instruction on children's ability to use CVS in designing and evaluating experiments. Steps a, b, and c were informal but focused, while steps d and e were very carefully crafted.

At the outset, we established a small network of experienced elementary school science teachers, all of whom were already including some aspects of CVS instruction in their current curricula. We met with these teachers in informal workshops in which we described our lab study and they told us about the content and methodology of their current CVS curricula as well as their beliefs about children's thinking and learning processes. After informal discussions with the teachers about these issues, we visited their classrooms to conduct classroom observations, in order to get first-hand exposure to the way in which teachers' theories and objectives for teaching CVS actually materialized during classroom instruction.

During this process, it became clear that even though our lab study demonstrated that participation in a brief session of direct instruction about CVS produced substantial and long-lasting learning in fourth graders, the type of one-on-one instruction and assessment used in a typical psychology experiment requiring strict adherence to a carefully crafted script would be impractical for everyday classroom use. Furthermore, we became increasingly aware that our lab study had a relatively narrow focus when compared to the multiple goals and pragmatic constraints that classroom teachers usually have when teaching about experimental design. Thus we formulated the goal of translating, adapting, and enriching this procedure so that it could be used as a lesson plan for a classroom unit—i.e., to engineer a classroom learning environment (Brown, 1992; Collins, 1992). In addition, because we wanted to study the effectiveness of this translation process, we recognized the need to include a variety of assessment procedures—assessments that would serve the dual purpose of enhancing students' learning while informing us about the relative effectiveness of our instruction.

With this as background, we began to craft a lesson plan based on our initial laboratory script. In designing the lesson plan and its associated assessments, we addressed the following questions: (a) Can fourth graders learn and transfer CVS when exposed to direct classroom instruction combined with hands-on experimentation? (b) Does the classroom introduce any new issues or difficulties in learning CVS? (c) Will instruction that is focused on the design and justification of students' own experiments increase their ability to evaluate experiments designed by others? (d) What is the relation between student's experimentation skills and the acquisition of domain knowledge?

Table 1. Comparison of pragmatics and instructional methods in laboratory and classroom study

	LABORATORY STUDY	CLASSROOM STUDY
INSTRUCTION		
Instructional objective	Mastery of CVS	Mastery of CVS
Instructional strategy	Didactic instruction of one student. Active construction, execution, and evaluation of experiments by solo student.	Didactic instruction – group of students. Active construction, execution, and evaluation of experiments by group (unequal participation possible).
Materials	Ramps or springs or sinking	Only ramps during classroom work. (Springs and sinking during individual pre- and post-test interviews.).
Cognitive mechanism targeted	Analogical transfer	Analogical transfer Representational transfer with interpretive use of experimenter-provided representation.
PRAGMATIC CONSTRAINTS		
Timing	Two 45-minute sessions, during or after school	Four 45-minute science classes
Teacher	Outside experimenter	Regular science teacher
Student grouping	Individual students	Entire classroom, organized into five groups of three to four students
Teacher - student ratio	One to one	One to 20
Record keeping	By experimenter, not available for students	By students in experimenter-designed data sheets
ASSESSMENT		
	Domain knowledge test	Domain knowledge test
	Experimenter's written record of comparisons made by students during individual interviews.	Experimenter's written record of comparisons made by students during individual interviews.
	Videotaped record of student's answers to questions about comparisons during individual interviews with subset of subjects.	Videotaped record of student's answers to questions about comparisons during individual interviews with subset of subjects.
		Students' written records of comparisons made and responses given during classroom work.
		Paper-and-pencil pre- and post-tests for all students in participating classes.

Throughout this process, we conceptualized our task in terms of differences and similarities between lab and classroom with respect to instructional objectives and pragmatic constraints, and types of assessments. These are summarized in Table 1. For a minimalist but still effective intervention we maintained both the instructional objective (teaching CVS) and the proven instructional strategy (direct instruction interspersed with hands-on experimentation) from the earlier laboratory study. In addition, we attempted, insofar as possible, to interpret any suggested modification in terms of our theoretical orientation that the mechanism of transfer from one domain to another was analogical processing. Within these constraints, there were several important differences between the laboratory script and the classroom lesson.

Pragmatic differences were extensive. Because the teacher could not keep track of the experimental set-ups of all of the groups, we transferred this responsibility to the students. They were instructed in how to record, for each of their experiments, the way that they had set up their pair of ramps. We provided students with worksheets that they completed after each experiment. The worksheets included a pre-formatted table representation to record ramp setups (see Appendix). The methods for filling out this table and the rest of the questions on the worksheet were discussed before experimentation. Thus, although students had to record the way in which they set up each pair of ramps, they did not have the additional responsibility of devising an external representation for the physical setup. However, they did have to negotiate the mapping between physical and tabular representations, and they received detailed instruction on how to do this. During the classroom work, only the ramps domain was used. (The sinking and springs domains were used in the individual interviews before and after the classroom work. See Method section.) Instead of a single student working with an experimenter, students in the classroom worked in groups of three to five people per pair of ramps. They made *joint* decisions about how to set up the pair of ramps, but then proceeded to *individually* record both their setup and the experimental outcome in their laboratory worksheets. (This will be explained in more detail below.)

Assessment methods in the classroom were derived from assessments developed for the laboratory study. In both environments, students were tested for their domain knowledge prior to and after instruction. In the laboratory work, this happened in a dialog format between experimenter and the individual student, while in the classroom, each student filled out a paper and pencil forced-choice test. Students' ability to construct correct experiments was measured in both situations from the experimental comparisons they made with the set of two ramps. (As noted, in the laboratory these results were recorded by the interviewer, whereas in the classroom, students recorded their ramps setups on the laboratory worksheets). In the classroom study, a paper and pencil experiment evaluation test—similar to the far transfer test used in the lab study—was given before and after instruction.

A Revised Model of the Relation between Lab-based Research and Classroom Instruction

Before describing the classroom study, we return to the tale of our own conceptual change. During the process of designing this study, it became clear to us that our initial model was in need of substantial revision. First, we had assumed that we could go directly from a lab study to a curriculum unit. However, our extensive interactions with teachers and their classrooms taught us that an intermediate process—to be described in this section—was necessary: One in which we did a reasonably well-controlled and carefully instrumented pilot study that preserved the essential aspects of the lab study while adapting to a host of classroom pragmatics. Second, because we wanted to be able to make comparisons between lab and classroom learning processes, we needed to formulate a portfolio of assessment procedures that combined lab techniques and "ordinary" classroom tests. Finally, we had to adapt our approach to the style, predilections, and expert knowledge of the teacher involved in our classroom study. The revised conceptual model is shown in Figure 7.

The most important changes depicted there are that the ultimate goal of producing a "stand alone" curriculum unit has been reconceputalized as something that should follow classroom studies, rather than being directly derivable from lab studies. And the important influences of classroom pragmatics, curriculum constraints, and teacher behaviors have now been indicated explicitly. Finally, the revised model now acknowledges the bi-directionality of basic and applied research, as the classroom studies now have—albeit somewhat tentatively at this point—arrows indicating a flow from the classroom studies back to both theoretical issues and instructional topics. (We will describe these new issues and topics later in the chapter). These influences began to arise as, in the course of the lab-to-classroom transition, we realized that we were often making decisions on the basis of hunches about yet-to-be investigated issues.

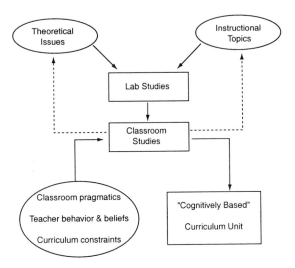

Figure 7. Not so naïve model.

Method

Research Design for Classroom Study

The research design for the classroom study included a set of nested pre-instruction and post-instruction measures (see Figure 8). The "inner" set of evaluations—depicted inside the solid box in Figure 8—used several assessment methods, including an in-class paper and pencil test for evaluating experiments that was identical in form to the remote posttest used in the lab study. The full set of assessments was designed to measure students' hands-on experimentation performance as well as their ability to evaluate experiments designed by others. These evaluations were administered by the teacher to all students, in class, immdiately before and after the instructional sessions. The "outer" set of individual one-on-one interviews used the same scoring procedures used in Part I of the lab study. For

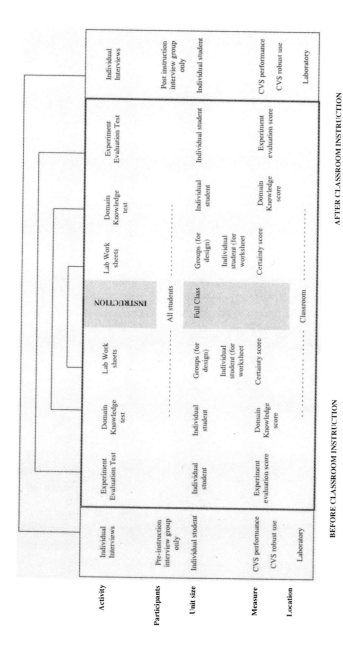

Figure 8. Schedule of various assessments before and after classroom instruction. All activities inside the solid-bordered box took place in the classroom.

half of the individual interviews, the pretest domain was springs and the posttest domain was sinking objects, and for the other half, the order was reversed.

Participants

Seventy-seven students from four fourth-grade classrooms in two demographically similar private elementary schools in southwestern Pennsylvania participated. Neither school had participated in the earlier lab study. One school was a school for girls while the other enrolled both boys and girls. Thus our subjects included 50 female and 27 male fourth grade students. Schools were selected from among the set of schools represented in our small teacher network on the basis of several pragmatic factors, including permission of school authorities, teacher interest, and available time, and the fit between the CVS topic and the normal progression of topics through the fourth-grade science curriculum. From these four classrooms, we recruited volunteers for pre- and post-instruction interviews. Of the 77 students participating in the study, 43 students volunteered to be individually interviewed. We interviewed 31 female and 12 male students. The mean age of the interviewed students was 10 years.

Procedure

Individual Interviews

The initial and final assessments were based on individual interviews that were essentially identical to those used throughout the lab study. The pragmatics of conducting research in schools shaped the design of this "outer" evaluation, because we could only conduct the individual interviews with "volunteers" for whom we had received parental permission.[5] Because we wanted to avoid any potential reactivity between the individual assessments and students' response to the classroom instruction, we included only half of the "permission" students on the individual lab pre-

---

5. This permission is required by our Institutional Review Board for all experimental work, but not for classroom interventions that do not depart substantially from normal classroom instruction. (This constraint is just one more example of the complexity of applied work.)

test and the other half on the individual lab posttest. Twenty-one of the 43 volunteer students were randomly assigned to the pre-instructional_interview group and were individually interviewed before the classroom activities began. The rest were assigned to the post-instructional interview group and were individually interviewed after the classroom activities had been completed. The assumption was that in each case, these students were representative of the full classroom and that there would be no reactivity. Subsequent analyses supported both assumptions.

These individual pre- and post-instructional interviews—conducted out of the classroom in a separate room—included students' hands-on design of valid experiments as well as verbal justifications for their experiments and the conclusions they drew from them. The experimenter followed the same script used in the lab study. Students were asked to design and conduct nine experiments: three with each of three variables. The experiments were student-designed comparisons of two experimental set-ups to decide whether a selected variable makes a difference in the outcome. After designing these experiments, students were asked to justify their experiments. They were also asked to indicate how certain they were about the role of the focal variable from the outcome of the experiment composed. They were asked: "Can you tell for sure from this comparison whether ___ makes a difference? Why are you sure/not sure?" The entire session was recorded on videotape.

Classroom Activities and Assessments

Experiment Evaluation Assessment

At the start of the first day of the classroom work, all students individually completed a paper and pencil experiment evaluation test on which they judged pre-constructed experiments to be good or bad. Students were presented with ten-page test booklets on which each page displayed a pair of airplanes representing an experimental comparison to test a given variable. For each airplane, there were three variables considered: length of wings, shape of body, and size of tailfin. Figure 9 depicts one of the types of comparisons that were used. Four different types of experiments were presented:

1. Unconfounded comparisons—correct, controlled comparisons in which the focal variable was different between the two planes, while all other variables were controlled (they were the same).

2. Singly confounded comparisons, in which one variable in addition to the focal variable was changed while other variables were kept the same between the two pictures. (Figure 9 depicts this type of item).

3. Multiply confounded comparisons, in which more than two variables on the airplanes were different between the two pictures.

4. Non-contrastive comparisons, in which only one variable was different between comparisons but this variable was not the focal variable being measured.

Students were asked to evaluate these comparisons—i.e., to judge whether each picture pair showed a valid experiment to test the focal variable—by circling the word "bad" or "good." (Only Type 1 comparisons are "good" tests; all others are "bad"). These assessments took place before and after classroom instruction (See Figure 8).

Classroom Instruction

Classroom instruction began with a short demonstration of the different ways the ramps can be set up and an explanation of how to map these ramp setups into the pre-formatted tables on the students' individual laboratory worksheets (to be described below). Following the demonstration, there was a short (5 minute) domain knowledge test, to assess students' prior beliefs about the role of different variables on the ramps. The next phase of classroom work comprised three parts: (a) exploratory experiments conducted in small groups, (b) direct instruction, for the whole classroom, (c) application experiments conducted in small groups.[6]

---

6. Assignment of students to groups was determined by the teacher's judgment of the ability of the different students to work together.

The engineers wanted to compare two planes to figure out whether the <u>length of the wings</u> makes a difference in how fast a model plane flies. Picture A shows one plane they built, and picture B shows the other plane they built.

- They built plane A with a thick body, and they built plane B with a narrow body.
- They built plane A with long wings, and they built plane B with short wings.
- They built plane A with a big tail, and they built plane B with a big tail.

Look at these two pictures carefully. If you think these two pictures show a good way to test if the <u>length of the wings</u> makes a difference, circle the words "Good Test" below. If you think it is a bad way, circle "Bad Test".

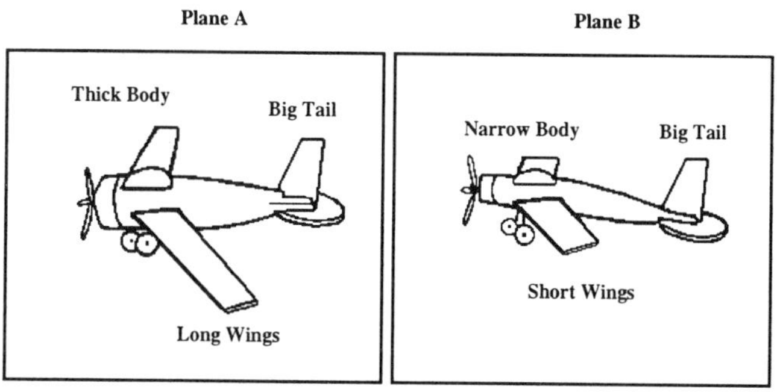

Plane A   **Plane B**

Good Test

Bad Test

Figure 9. Sample page from experiment evaluation assessment booklet used in classroom study (airplanes test). This example has a single confound because variation in body type is confounded with variation in the focal variable (wing length).

Exploratory Experiments

Students were asked to conduct four different experiments—two to test each of two different variables. The students decided how to set up their ramps to make a good comparison to test whether this focal variable makes a difference in how far a ball will roll down the ramp. Students were required to individually record their experimental setups and data into pre-formatted worksheets. These worksheets had two sections. The first section asked students to map their ramps setup into a table representation and the second section included questions about the outcome of each experiment and about whether the students were sure or unsure from this experiment about the effect of the focal variables influence on the experimental outcome.

For example, they were asked: Does the X (the focal variable) of the ramp make a difference? Circle your answer *Yes / No*. Think about this carefully, can you tell for sure from this comparison whether X (the current, focal variable) of the ramp makes a difference? Circle your answer *Yes /No*. The students were not asked to provide a rationale for their answer. These four experiments conducted in the first stage of classroom work were later analyzed for students pre-instruction knowledge of CVS.

The process whereby these worksheets were designed illustrates some of the complexities of the lab-to-classroom transition. Our initial conception was very simple: because we could not simultaneously observe what each group was doing, we needed some way to keep track of their experimental setups. Having each student record them seemed like the most obvious way to do this. In our collaboration with teachers prior to the classroom study, we considered several forms for this worksheet, and finally converged on the one illustrated in the Appendix. Although it seems fairly straightforward, we have no rigorous basis for claiming that it is optimal, or ideally suited for all students or all CVS instruction. At present, this form simply represents an educated guess of the kind that permeates many transitions between basic research and applied contexts. We will return to this issue at the end of the chapter.

Another important difference that emerged in the design of this form—and the classroom process in general—has to do with experimental error. In the course of rolling real balls down real ramps, a variety of errors can occur (even in unconfounded experimental designs). For example, the ball might bump into the side of the ramp, the experimenter (or student) might unintentionally accelerate or impede one of the balls, etc. In the lab study, any such anomalous experiments were simply corrected by the experimenter, with a minor comment (e.g., "Oops, lets run that one again"). In this way the experimenter could maintain control over the "good" and "bad" executions of each experiment and dismiss any effects of random error. However, in the classroom context, when groups of students are running experiments, this is not possible. Indeed, it is not even desirable because students' conceptions of error and their understanding of the distinction between a design error (i.e., a confounded experiment) and other types of error (random error and measurement error) are very important. Thus, the issue of how students understand error, absent from our lab study, arose for the first time as we moved to the classroom. As we shall explain later, it became one of the issues on our list of questions that flowed from the classroom study back to a future lab study. But this discussion of error is based on hindsight. At the time we designed the worksheet, we encapsulated the entire issue into a simple question about students' certainty about the conclusion they could draw from their experiments.

Direct Instruction

The second stage included about 20 minutes of direct instruction to the entire class on how to create valid experiments. The students' regular science teacher followed these 6 steps (see Toth, Klahr, & Chen, under review, for details):

1. *Motivate the necessity of unconfounded experiments* by providing an example of a "bad experiment" and explain to students the indeterminate nature of any result from such an experiment. After setting up a multiply confounded comparison, the teacher asked students whether it was a good or bad test. She provided opportunity for several conflicting explanations and she usually asked students to justify their responses.

2. *Resolve students' opposing points of view by modeling correct thinking.* After several conflicting opinions were voiced, the teacher revealed that, in fact, this was not a good comparison and she explained why.

3. *Test understanding* with another "bad" comparison. Next, the teacher tested the students' understanding with another "bad" comparison and asked a similar set of questions.

4. *Reinforce learning* by pointing out the error in the "bad" comparison.

5. *Summarize the rationale* for CVS. The teacher reinforced her teaching by providing a detailed account of the confounds in the "bad" test.

6. Finally, the teacher provided an overall *conceptual justification* for CVS with the following words:

Now you know that if you are going to see whether something about the ramps makes a difference in how far the balls roll you need to make two ramps that are different only in the one thing that you are testing. Only when you make those kinds of comparisons can you really tell for sure if that thing makes a difference.

Application

The third phase of the classroom work was created to allow students to apply their newly learned strategy during experimentation. The students' activity in this phase was very similar to what they did in phase one, with the exception that during the first application experiment, they tested the effect of a variable they had not tested previously. In the second application, they tested the same variable they tested in phase one.

Measures

We used measures, similar to those used in the lab study, designed to capture both the procedural and logical components of the control of variables strategy (CVS). They included:

1. *CVS performance score:* We measured student's *CVS performance* by scoring the experiments students conducted, i.e., the way they set up the pair of ramps in order to determine the effect of a focal variable. Each valid, (unconfounded) comparison was scored one, and all other, invalid comparisons (single confounded, multiply confounded, non-contrastive) were scored zero.

2. *Robust CVS use score.* Recall that, during individual interviews, students were asked to give reasons for their experiments. A score of one was assigned to each experiment on which a student gave a CVS-based rationale at least once in response to the two probe questions for that experiment. *Robust CVS use* was scored by measuring *both* CVS performance and the rationale the student provided for the experiment. This yielded a score of one for each valid experiment accompanied by a correct rationale.

3. *Certainty measure:* Probe questions asked students whether they were certain about their conclusion about the role of the focal variable. This question was stated in both the individual interviews and in the classroom worksheets. The certainty score (not used in the lab study) is intended to capture some of the additional complexity of the type of knowledge students extract from classroom experiences.

4. *Experiment evaluation score:* Student's *experiment evaluation ability*, i.e., their ability to evaluate experimental designs created by others, was assessed with the pre- and post-instruction experiment evaluation tests (airplanes comparisons) described earlier. Correctly indicating whether a given experimental comparison was good or bad gained students a score of one and incorrect evaluations were scored zero. Based on responses to the four types of problems (unconfounded, one confound, many confounds, and non-contrastive), we were able to identify several distinct reasoning strategies.

5. *Domain knowledge score:* We determined domain knowledge by asking students to indicate which level of each variable had the greater effect on the outcome. Students were provided a choice of the two settings for each variable (i.e. high/low, long/short, etc.) and were asked to circle their answer. Correct predictions were scored as one and incorrect predictions as zero.

Results (Classroom Study)

First, we present the results on procedural knowledge, i.e., knowledge about CVS based on all instruments: individual interviews, classroom worksheets and pre/post experiment evaluation tests. Next, we describe students' domain knowledge—i.e., knowledge about which values of the variables make a ball roll farther—before and after classroom instruction. Finally, we report on changes in students' ability to discriminate between good and bad experiments created by others. For each measure, we provide pre- and post-instructional comparisons (corresponding to the pairs of connected columns in Figure 8).

Analysis of CVS Performance and Certainty Based on Individual Interviews

CVS performance scores on the individual interviews increased dramatically following instruction: from a mean score of 30% prior to instruction to a mean score of 96% after instruction. With respect to individual students, we defined a CVS "expert" as a student who correctly used CVS on at least eight of the nine trials in the individual interviews. Only one of the 21 children taking the individual pretest interviews was an expert, whereas 20 of the 22 children in the posttest individual interviews exhibited such near-perfect performance.

A similar analysis on robust use (designing an unconfounded experiment *and* providing a CVS rationale) revealed an increase in the mean score from 6.3% on the pretest to 78% on the posttest. Prior to instruction, none of the 21 students in the pre-instructional interview group were robust "experts" (i.e., robust use on more than eight of nine trials), whereas after instruction 12 of the 22 in the post instructional interview group were experts. Interestingly, of the 20 *CVS use* experts, only 12 were *robust CVS use* experts. That is, a substantial proportion of children who could *do* CVS were still unable to adequately *explain* it.

Analysis of the certainty scores from the pre- and post-instructional individual interviews revealed that even though instruction led to a large increase in the proportion of unconfounded experiments (from 30% to 96%), there was not a corresponding increase in students' certainty about what to conclude from such good experiments. More specifically, as shown in Table 2, prior to instruction, on the 30% of experiments that were unconfounded, students said they were unsure about the causal factor 27% of the time. After instruction, this proportion of unconfounded experiments about which students were uncertain remained curiously high: 16%. There could be two quite different reasons for this lack of certainty about how to interpret the outcome of what is formally an unconfounded (and therefore unambiguous) experiment. First, the experiment might have been fortuitously unconfounded, even though the student did not fully understand the logic of CVS. Second, there might have been some aspect of the execution of the experiment that led to uncertainty. (We will return to this issue—on the different types of error—later in the chapter.) Further analysis of students' explanations for their certainty or lack thereof will help us to resolve this issue.

Table 2. Proportion of good and bad experimental designs and students' certainty about the conclusions they can draw from them prior to instruction and following instruction (based on individual lab interviews).

			PRE-INSTRUCTION					POST-INSTRUCTION	
			Certain?					Certain?	
			Yes	No				Yes	No
EXPERIMENTAL	Good	.30	.73	.27	Good	.96	.84	.16
DESIGN	Bad	.70	.63	.37	Bad	.04	.43	.57

Analysis of CVS Performance and Certainty From Classroom Worksheets

The nested design used in this study allowed us to measure several of the same constructs in both the lab and the classroom (see Figure 8). In this section we describe the results of the "inner" pairs of pre/post measures. As noted earlier, during classroom activities students worked in small groups. While the students made their ramp setup decisions and built experimental comparisons together, they each individually filled out a laboratory worksheet. Mean *CVS performance scores* derived from these worksheets increased from 61% before instruction to 97% after instruction. However, here too, students remained uncertain about the effect of the focal variable on approximately 20% of these experiments.

Analysis of Domain Knowledge Test

Recall that at no point was there any direct instruction regarding the role of the causal variables in the ramps domain. Nevertheless, there was a significant pre- to post-instructional increase in domain knowledge. While 79% of the students provided correct answers to all three questions of on the domain knowledge test prior to CVS instruction, *all* students correctly answered all three domain knowledge questions after instruction. However, we cannot attribute this gain entirely to the CVS training, because the classroom study had no control group of students who had an equivalent amount of experience in setting up and running experiments but without the direct classroom instruction.

Analysis of Experiment Evaluation Scores

We found a similar increase in students' ability to evaluate experiments designed by others. The mean experiment evaluation (airplanes comparison) scores increased from 61% correct on the initial test to 97% correct on the final test. The percentage of students who were evaluation "experts"—i.e., who could correctly evaluate at least 9 of the 10 comparisons—increased from 28% prior to instruction to 75% after instruction. Thus, a brief period of direct instruction interspersed with hands-on experimentation significantly increased students' ability to evaluate the validity of experiments designed by others.

Discussion (Classroom Study)

The main goal of the classroom study was to determine whether an instructional procedure that produced substantial and long-lasting learning in the psychology lab could be transformed to an effective instructional unit for everyday classroom use. The laboratory instruction involved one-on-one direct instruction coupled with hands-on experimentation. The classroom teaching also used direct instruction, but now it was instruction directed at several teams of students conducting hands-on experimentation. As indicated by a series of independent, but converging measures, the classroom instruction was overwhelmingly successful, not only in terms of statistical significance, but more importantly, with respect to absolute levels of performance. Overall, students' ability to design and assess unconfounded experiments, which was never more than 50% prior to our interventions, now was close to perfect.[7] Students learned to do CVS, to explain CVS, and to distinguish between CVS and non-CVS experiments designed by others. Contrary to previous suggestions that early elementary school students are developmentally unable to conduct controlled experiments because it requires formal operational thinking, our results indicate that students' procedural and conceptual knowledge significantly increased after a short, succinct, direct-instruction session combined with hands-on experimentation.

To what can we attribute this success? Why was our simple procedure so effective, when, as indicated earlier, even fourth-graders who had been

7. See Toth, Klahr, & Chen (under review) for more detailed analysis of the classroom study.

exposed to high-quality science curriculums for several years could design unconfounded experiments on fewer than one-third of their initial attempts, and could correctly explain their designs on fewer than 10% of their attempts? In order to give a complete answer to this question, we would have to carefully examine these children's prior exposure to CVS instruction and activities. However, in lieu of such information, we can look at a few examples of "model" practice, and contrast our procedures with what we find there.

Our examination of dozens of texts and monographs about science teaching and learning suggests that, at best, CVS receives only a few paragraphs in a handful of books. And in the rare instances when it is taught, instruction is both brief and confusing. The following two examples illustrate these points.

Example 1: A Middle-School Science Text

Consider the excerpt shown in Table 3, taken from the opening chapter of a widely used middle-school science text. (Although students do not use texts extensively in K-4 science instruction, teachers get advice and suggestions from a variety of such books and other teacher oriented materials; e.g., the journal, *Science & Children*. The content of such articles tends to be similar to the illustrative example used here.)

Table 3. Example of a description of a control of variables strategy (from Harcourt Brace: HBJ Science - Nova Edition, pp. 36-37. Emphasis in original. Sentence numbers added).

1. A simple question occurs to you.
2. Will mold grow better in the light or the dark? This, you decide, calls for an investigation.
3. So you divide a slice of bread in half and place each in a jar.
4. You add ten drops of water to each jar and cap tightly.
5. You put one in a dark closet.
6. You keep the other one in the light.
7. In a few days, you make an observation.
8. You observe that the mold in the light is growing better than the mold in the dark.
9. From this observation, you infer that mold grows better in light.
10. You are sure of your answer.
11. After all, the evidence seems clear.
12. Yet, in truth, scientists know that light has no effect on the growth of mold.
13. Why, then, did the investigation make it seem as though mold grows better in the light?

14. Think a moment.
15. Because the amount of light varied, we say that light was a **variable**.
16. Since light was the only variable considered, you assumed that it was the light that affected the growth of the mold.
17. Was light the only variable you changed? Or could you have changed another variable without realizing it?
18. What about temperature? Suppose that the temperature of the mold in the light was higher.
19. Then it is possible that the higher temperature, not the light itself, caused the growth.
20. Whenever you do an investigation, there may be several possible variables.
21. If you wish to see the effects of changing one variable, such as the amount of light, then you must make sure all the other possible variables remain the same.
22. That is, you must **control** the other variables.
23. In this investigation, to control the variable temperature, you must keep the temperature the same for the mold in the light and the mold in the dark.
24. If you had done so, you would have discovered that the mold grew just as well in the dark closet.
25. However, even then you could not be sure of your conclusion.
26. The investigation must be repeated many times.
27. After all, what happens once can be an accident.
28. Scientists don't base their conclusions on one trial.
29. They repeat the investigation again and again and again.
30. The rest of this year you will be an apprentice.
31. You will be an investigator.
32. You may even decide one day to become a scientist.

At first glance, the example seems like a well-designed treatment of many of the issues involved in CVS. However, a careful examination reveals several potential difficulties. For example, sentence 2 already presumes that the student believes that amount of light is a reasonable factor to control. But to a student lacking any domain knowledge about the growth of mold, this might seem as plausible (or implausible) a factor as day of the week.

Sentence 4, while intending to provide a control for another possible causal variable (water), introduces an unnecessary quantification of that variable (i.e., why 10 drops each? why not 12 drops each? Is it the "10" that's important here, or the "each"?) and adds a procedure whose impact is not explicit (is "cap tightly" important?).

Sentences 5 and 6 introduce categorical variables, but without any explicit statement that the experiment will be run in terms of categorical variables, rather than continuous variables. (And this is in contrast to the unnecessarily specific quantification of the amount of water.)

Sentences 9 through 18 are intended to demonstrate that it is easy to forget potentially important variables. More specifically, the intent is to show the student that it is important to consider causal variables other than light, and that temperature is one such possibility. But this example is problematic because it confounds the domain-general notion of a CVS with the domain-specific knowledge that temperature might be a causal variable in this domain. Thus, as stated here, the example might convey the mistaken notion that the logic of the control of variables strategy is flawed in some way. Moreover, the example takes the student down a garden path to a pattern of evidence that is particularly difficult to interpret. Young children are easily misled when they are faced with a single piece of positive evidence, and several remaining sources of unknown evidence (Fay & Klahr, 1996; Piéraut-Le Bonniec, 1980). They tend to believe that the single instance renders the situation determinate, even though they will acknowledge that additional evidence might change that decision.

Sentence 25 suddenly introduces the notion of error variance, but it does so in a way that suggests that just when you think you are sure, you are really not sure. It is not surprising that students come away from such examples believing that their subjective opinions are as valid as the results of scientific investigations.

Finally, as brief as it is, the example represents the *only* explicit attempt in the entire book to teach the principles of good experimental design, the logic of rival hypothesis testing, and the distinctions between valid and invalid inferences or determinate and indeterminate situations.

In summary, the example attempts to cover too many things at once, and it confounds issues pertaining to the abstract logic of unconfounded experimentation and valid inference with other issues having to do with domain-specific knowledge and plausible hypotheses about causal variables.

Example 2: Mode Inquiry Unit from NSES

As noted above, the middle-school science text example is used only to illustrate the complexity and subtlety of the topic. More relevant to our point about the inadequacy of the material available to K-4 teachers who would like to teach CVS is the model inquiry unit—entitled "Earthworms" provided in chapter 3 of the NSES. The full unit carefully and sensitively elaborates a process whereby third-graders interested in creating a habitat for earthworms could learn about the earthworm life cycle, needs, structure and function. However, its treatment of CVS is extremely sparse:

> Two groups were investigating what kind of environment the earthworms liked best. Both were struggling with several variables at once—moisture, light, and temperature. Ms. F. planned to let groups struggle before suggesting that students focus on one variable at a time. She hoped they might come to this idea on their own. (NSES, pp. 34-35)

This brief treatment of CVS—consisting of only about 50 of the 1000 words in the Earthworms inquiry unit—provides virtually no guidance to the teacher on how to present the rationale of CVS, how to provide positive and negative instances, how to draw children's attention to the variables and the design of tests, and how to guide students in interpreting results from controlled or uncontrolled experiments.

Contrasts Between Examples and Our Procedure

These examples suggest several potentially important contrasts between our approach and what children had experienced earlier. First, it is clear that the detailed components of CVS are not adequately isolated and emphasized either directly, as decontextualized domain-general principles or indirectly, as contextualized skill in a specific domain. In contrast, our instruction avoided, insofar as possible, potential confusion between CVS logic errors and inadequate domain knowledge by making it very clear exactly what dimensions were under consideration at all times. It also used positive and negative examples of CVS designs, and it presented students with both a mechanistic procedure and a conceptual justification for why the procedure worked. We presented several examples of each, so that students could construct an internal representation of CVS that could be transferred, via analogical mapping, to new, but structurally similar situations.

Second, in contrast to the second example's suggestion that children "might come to this idea on their own," we made instruction highly explicit and direct. Prior to the results of our lab study, this focus on explicit instruction was based partly on our own intuitions and partly on the results of other studies of the power of detailed and direct instruction about complex procedures (e.g., Klahr & Carver, 1988). The results of our lab study further demonstrated, in the specific context of CVS, that children find it very difficult to discover CVS on their own. As we have argued several times, we believe that there is too much here for students to acquire on their own, via discovery, so we opted instead for explicit and direct instruction about each of these aspects of CVS.

Conclusion

During the classroom study, several interesting and unanticipated issues arose—issues that forced us to revise, once again, our model of the lab to classroom transition. In this section we first describe the issues, and then we conclude with some comments on the revised model.

Representation

Recall that the classroom study used a worksheet on which students recorded the way that they set up their ramps. At the time we prepared these worksheets, we were working under the usual kinds of scheduling deadlines that surround any attempt to intervene in an ongoing "live" classroom during the school year, and so we did not have the luxury of carefully considering just what was involved in asking students to carry out this "trivial" task. However, as psychologists, we are well aware that such mappings entail a complex set of procedures for establishing correspondences between the physical setup of the ramps and a set of marks on paper that represent that setup. Indeed, the ability to move between various equivalent representations for both apparatus and data is one of the commonly stated goals of science educators. Only with systematic study in a laboratory context on just this issue could we claim that the particular form that we used is the best way to capture students' representations of their experiments. Thus, the issue of the most effective type of representation for this and similar types of classroom exercises has become a topic not only on our research agenda for further laboratory studies, but it has become a potential instructional objective for subsequent classroom work by the teachers in our schools.

While the lab studies of representation remain at the planning stages, we have already begun to explore the representation issue in the classroom by introducing a very simple change in our procedure. Rather than providing each group with a pair of ramps, we provide only one ramp. This requires students to setup, execute, and record the effect of one combination of variables, and then follow with another setup, execution, and recording. We believe that this will challenge students to consider the important role of "inscriptions" (Lehrer, Schauble, & Petrosino, this volume) as permanent, inspectable representations of transient events, and that it will motivate them to more accurately record and better interpret such external representations and their role in science.

Certainty and Error

Recall that although our students increased substantially in their CVS knowledge, there remained a non-trivial proportion of valid experiments from which the students were unwilling to draw unambiguous conclusions. For about 15% of valid experiments after instruction, students remained uncertain about the effect of the unconfounded variable comparison that they had just witnessed. This occurred for both the interview and laboratory assessments. Since, in the ramps task, all variables selected influenced the outcome measure—i.e., the distance a ball rolled down a ramp—this finding was, at first, puzzling to us (but not to the teachers).

Further consideration led to the following conjecture. We believe that children found it difficult to distinguish between a logical error (such as a confounded experiment) and other types of error (such as random error in the execution of the experiment or measurement error), and that they were unsure about which of several replications of the same setup was the "true" result. Although these are important aspects of a rich understanding of experimentation, we did not include them in our highly focused instructional goals. Thus, two additional topic for both detailed lab research and further classroom instruction arose: (a) the distinction among various types of errors involved in scientific experimentation, and (b) a better understanding of how to extract a general conclusion from several replications of the same experiment.

Innocence Lost

At this point, our story concludes, but not our work. Our simple—and perhaps "labocentric" view of how basic research in psychology could contribute to improved classroom practice has gone from the Naïve Model (Figure 1) to the Not so Naïve Model (Figure 7) to a more realistic (and complex) appreciation of the multiple interactions among several sources. Rather than draw another such figure, we ask the reader to just envision a version of Figure 7 with arrows of influence abounding from every box to every oval. This is clearly a complex agenda, and it has become the topic of an emerging body of literature to which we hope this chapter makes a contribution (e.g., Brown, 1992; Campbell, 1999; Collins, 1992; Robinson, 1998; Strauss, 1998). We are pleased that along the way, we have, in fact, produced a big improvement in a small corner of the elementary school science curriculum. We are also aware that we have a long way to go before making any claims about fundamental changes in any aspect of instruction. But we believe that continued careful and rigorous research, combined with a continuing level of self-reflection on where we are at any point in the complex system that mediates interactions between laboratory research and classroom practice, will be productive in the long run.

Acknowledgements

Portions of the work described in this chapter were supported in part by grants from NICHHD (HD25211) and the James S. McDonnell Foundation (96-37). We thank Jen Schnakenberg, Sharon Roque, Anne Siegel, and Rose Russo for their assistance with data collection and preliminary analysis. This project could not have proceeded without the generous cooperation of the parents and administrators at The Ellis School, Winchester-Thurston School, Shadyside Academy, and Carlow College, as well as the active involvement of the master teachers who allowed us into their classrooms and their teaching practice: Linn Cline, Patricia Cooper, Cheryl Little, and Dr. Mary Wactlar. We thank the editors of this volume for their insightful and constructive suggestions on how to improve earlier drafts of this chapter. Finally, our thanks to the children at all of these schools who participated with enthusiasm and excitement.

References

Bransford, J. D., Sherwood, R. D., Vye, N. J., & Reiser, J. (1986). Teaching thinking and problem solving: Research foundations. *American Psychologist*, 41, 1078-1089.

Brown, A. L. (1992) Design experiments: Theoretical and methodological challenges in creating complex interventions in classroom settings. *The Journal of the Learning Sciences*, 2, 141-178.

Brown, A. L. (1997) Transforming schools into communities of thinking and learning about serious matters. *American Psychologist*, 52, 399-413.

Bullock, M., & Ziegler, A. (1999) Scientific reasoning: Developmental and individual differences. In F. E. Weinert & W. Schneider (Eds.) *Individual development from 3 to 12: Findings from the Munich Longitudinal Study*. Munich: Max Plank Institute for Psychological Research (pp. 38-54).

Campbell, J. P. (1999). From basic to applied research, and back again: The Army's Project A and related studies. Symposium, conference of the American Psychological Society, Washington DC.

Case, R. (1974) Structures and strictures: Some functional limitations on the course of cognitive growth. *Cognitive Psychology*, 6, 544-573.

Chen, Z., & Klahr, D. (1999). All other things being equal: Children's acquisition of the Control of Variables Strategy. *Child Development* 70(5), 1098 – 1120.

Collins, A. (1992). Toward a design science of education: In E. Scanlon & T. O'Shea (Eds.), *New directions in educational technology*, New York: Springer-Verlag.

Fay, A. L., & Klahr, D. (1996) Knowing about guessing and guessing about knowing: Preschoolers' understanding of indeterminacy. *Child Development*, 67, 689-716.

Jacoby, J. (1978). On interpreting the effects of repetition: Solving a problem versus remembering a solution. *Journal of verbal learning and verbal behavior*, 17, 649-667.

Klahr, D. (2000) *Exploring Science: The cognition and development of discovery processes*. Cambridge, MA: MIT Press

Klahr, D. & Carver, S. M. (1988). Cognitive objectives in a LOGO debugging curriculum: Instruction, learning, and transfer. *Cognitive Psychology*, 20, 362-404.

Kuhn, D., & Angelev, J. (1976). An experimental study of the development of formal operational thought. *Child Development*, 47, 697-706.

Kuhn, D., Garcia-Mila, M., Zohar, A., Andersen, C. (1995) Strategies of knowledge acquisition. *Monographs of the Society for Research in Child Development*, 50, 4, (Serial No. 245, pp. 1–128).

McDaniel, M. A., & Schlager, M. S. (1990). Discovery learning and transfer of problem-solving skills. *Cognition and Instruction*, 7, 129-159.

McGilly, K. (Ed.). (1994*) Classroom lessons: Integrating cognitive theory and classroom practice*. Cambridge, MA: The MIT Press.

National Science Education Standards (NSES) (1995). Washington, DC: National Academy Press

Piéraut-Le Bonniec, G. (1980). *The development of modal reasoning: The genesis of necessity and possibility notions*. New York: Academic Press.

Robinson, V. M. J. (1998) Methodology and the research-practice gap. *Educational Researcher*, 27(1), 17-26.

Ross, A. J. (1988). Controlling variables: A meta-analysis of training studies. *Review of Educational Research*, 58(4), 405-437.

Schauble, L., (1996). The development of scientific reasoning in knowledge-rich contexts. *Developmental Psychology*, 32, 102-109.

Siegler, R. S. (1976). Three aspects of cognitive development. *Cognitive Psychology*, 8, 481-520.

Strauss, S. (1998). Cognitive development and science education: Toward a middle level model. In I. Sigel & K. A. Renninger (Eds.), (W. Damon, Series Editor), *Handbook of child psychology, V4: Child psychology in practice*. 357-400. NY: Wiley.

Toth, E. E., Klahr, D., & Chen, Z. (under review) Bridging research and practice: A research-based classroom intervention for teaching experimentation skills to elementary school children.

Appendix: Sample Page from Experiment Recording Sheets Used in Classroom

Does the surface make a difference?

I. FIRST COMPARISON FOR SURFACE:

How your ramp was set up:
[Teacher reads the table aloud to students and instructs them on how to fill it out: circle answer corresponding to team's ramp setup.]

VARIABLES	RAMP A	RAMP B
Surface	Smooth or Rough	Smooth or Rough
Steeness	High or Low	High or Low
Length of run	Long or Short	Long or Short
Type of ball	Golf ball or Rubber ball	Golf ball or Rubber ball

What happened after you rolled the balls down:

1. On which ramp did the ball roll further most of the time? Circle your answer.

RAMP A   or   RAMP B

[Teacher tells students : "Think about why you set up the ramps the way you did."]

2. Does the surface of the ramp make a difference? Circle your answer.

YES   or   NO

3. Think about this carefully, can you tell for sure from this comparison whether the surface of the ramp makes a difference? Circle your and answer.

VERY SURE   or   NOT SO SURE

9

Reconsidering the Role of Experiment in Science Education

Richard Lehrer
Leona Schauble
University of Wisconsin, Madison

Anthony J. Petrosino
University of Texas, Austin

The idea of "experiment" plays a central role in both popular and philosophical views of scientific practice. Perhaps as a consequence, it also occupies center stage in framing expectations about student activity and reasoning in science classes. In this chapter we argue that researchers and educators should reconsider the implications of focusing too narrowly on experiment as the canonical form of scientific reasoning. For one thing, experimentation is by no means the only form of argument on which science rests. Rudolph and Stewart (1998), for example, point out that evolutionary biology relies primarily on historical reconstruction, which has a very different structure than experimentation. For another, studies in the philosophy and sociology of science suggest that experiment is a complex form of argument deeply embedded within domain-specific practices of modeling, representation, and material manipulation of the world (e.g., Pickering, 1995). Yet psychological studies often focus on experiment as a form of hypothetical deductive reasoning, ignoring the very practices that set the foundations for such reasoning.

Because we are primarily interested in the *development* of scientific reasoning, in this chapter we examine in detail what it takes for elementary school students to learn to participate in this form of argument. We suggest that three related aspects of science—namely, rhetoric, representation, and modeling—must be well established in the background context if experimentation is to be a meaningful activity for students, rather than a disembodied method. In that sense, we believe these three aspects of practice are more fundamental than experimentation, and we suggest that they are more promising themes for organizing science instruction and supporting the long-term development of students' scientific reasoning.

What is an Experiment?

Students' Understanding of Experimentation

Before introducing this analysis, we first review some findings from research conducted previously by two of this paper's authors (LS & AP). It is reasonably well established that pre-adolescent students have not necessarily mastered the strategies and heuristics for experimentation that adults typically use (Klahr, Fay, & Dunbar, 1993; Kuhn, Garcia-Mila, Zohar, & Andersen, 1995; Schauble, 1996). However, our review also will suggest that it is more than heuristics and strategies that students need to learn—much must be mastered to understand the very enterprise. Students do not necessarily understand an experiment as a way of modeling, manipulating, and investigating a range of situations that are similar in theoretically important ways.

For example, Schauble, Glaser, Duschl, Schulze, and John (1995) asked 21 sixth-grade students (four from each of five classrooms) to repeat an experiment from their standard sixth-grade curriculum while being questioned by an interviewer about the purposes and procedures. The experiment was designed to demonstrate the effects of weathering on different kinds of rock. Students were prompted through the process of weighing, shaking in water, and re-weighing samples of several kinds of rock, entering the resulting data in a table, and then interpreting it. The data table was labeled, "Before shaking," "After 100 shakes," "After 200 shakes," etc., up to 500 shakes. In their classrooms, all of the students had recently received instruction concerning erosion, in general, and weathering of rocks, in particular. Four of the students had even conducted the identical experiment as a science lab. However, when asked what the experiment was about, only one-third of the students were able to give a plausible explanation, in spite of the fact that these students had just completed a full school year studying a curriculum based on "hands-on experiments" and had also just studied a unit that focused on the very concepts featured in this activity. Moreover, when asked to propose a minor modification of the experiment to address a new question, the students gave a variety of responses showing that they were struggling unsuccessfully with the idea that an experiment serves to model phenomena in the world. One-fifth of them stated that they could think of no way of adjusting the experiment. They claimed instead that one would have to go out to a "real" stream and observe. Half of the students proposed a modification that revealed that all along, they had been mismapping between the represented situation and the experimental procedure.

The Schauble et al. (1995) study goes on to report how several sixth-grade classrooms spent 3 weeks designing and testing "boat hulls" made of aluminum foil to investigate features of the design that affect the boats' carrying capacity. After completing this unit, students were re-interviewed, and asked, "Did making boats out of foil tell us anything about how to design real boats?" Most of the students agreed that making boats from foil was relevant to the design of real boats. They justified this response by explaining that making a model and testing it can tell you what size or shape to make the boat. However, even after these 3 weeks of specially designed instruction, over one-third of the students still struggled with the idea of the experiment as a modeling enterprise. They argued that making foil boats "does not tell you how to make real boats." They explained that "real boats don't rip," "real boats have motors and steering," and "real boats are made out of wood or steel or fiberglass." To understand how an experiment models objects, processes, or events in the world, students must understand which objects and attributes map from the world to the experiment and which do not. Although adults often assume that this information is transparent to students, in practice, it often is not. Many students seem to confuse experiments—which adults "see" as representations of the world—with replications of the world.

"Experiment" Plus Scaffolding

One might legitimately object that there is no reason to expect students to understand experimentation as a modeling enterprise without carefully tuned forms of scaffolding and instruction. In fact, there is good evidence that with appropriate forms of assistance, students can acquire at least the surface features of this form of argument, and two-thirds of the students in the Schauble et al. study seemed to do so eventually.

An example of scaffolding that is particularly interesting is the work of Petrosino and his colleagues (Lamon, et al., 1996; Petrosino, 1995; 1998), who sought to emphasize experimentation in a curriculum unit based on a "Mission to Mars" that included a module in which students built and launched model rockets. In spite of the fact that the launchings drew attention from teachers, parents, and the local press, analysis of student responses following some early trials indicated that fifth/ sixth grade students learned neither content knowledge nor experimental strategies by simply making and launching rockets.

Therefore, over the course of an 8-week summer session, Petrosino worked with a teacher of low-achieving summer school students to generate forms of scaffolding that were intended explicitly to help students acquire an understanding of experimentation. The teacher, Jeff Darby, attempted to introduce apprenticeship forms of teaching by devoting considerable attention to socializing his students into the goals and practices of a scientific community. First, Petrosino and the teacher generated a clear goal for the work—i.e., submitting a design plan to the National Aeronautic and Space Administration for a rocket kit that could be used by other students (a variation of a format designed by Duschl & Gitomer, 1997). The "NASA Request for Design Plans" directed students to investigate three questions about the design of rockets and then to submit a design packet that included a sketch of the model rocket, a sketch of the rocket in flight, and a report of tests and results. These goals provoked questions that students could pursue (e.g., Do large rockets go higher than small rockets?), and thus served to shift students from simply launching and observing rockets toward experimenting with design features.

A second form of scaffolding was to attune students to the features of rockets that affect their launch height. At the beginning of the summer session, students failed even to notice differences in features like the shape of the nose cones. Accordingly, Petrosino presented contrasting cases (e.g., rockets with three fins vs. four fins) to emphasize differences between otherwise similar examples. These contrasts served to focus students' interest on dimensions that they had overlooked at the beginning of the session.

Over the weeks of the summer program, students began to consider how their launches might serve as data to inform rocket design. They began to focus on fins and the shape of nose cones as they tried to incorporate some rudimentary understanding of aerodynamics into their explanation of the outcomes. Students recorded sources of variation in the data (e.g., temperature and weather conditions at launch) and discussed features that might be experimentally manipulated in future launches. Trial launches were conducted by groups of three students each (seven groups in all), and the groups then collated data from the class into tables for interpretation. Petrosino and the collaborating teacher supplemented these activities with lessons about aerodynamics and Newton's laws of motion to address students' questions about rocket flight and to supply information that students could use in preparing their final reports.

Repeated cycles of feedback and revision supplied yet another source of assistance. Students investigated various configurations of design features (nose cone shape, fin placement, weight, fuselage decoration, among others) and were supported in their reflection about their observations. To break down the relative isolation of the classroom (Barron, et al., 1998), Petrosino facilitated student participation in online internet discussions with other model rocket enthusiasts. Conversations with members of the internet usergroup rec.models.rockets helped students diagnose the "bugs" in their rocket designs. Over time, students began to appropriate the structure and content of the launch reports that they read on the Internet, leading to rounds of review and revision of the reports that the students themselves would submit on the site.

Toward the end of the 8-week session, the teacher posted descriptions of two of his "trials" on the school's local area network and asked for feedback from students. The posting was intended to serve as an assessment probe; that is, the teacher posed an ill-designed experiment to see if students would notice the "mistakes."

I went out to test my three-finned and four-finned rockets yesterday. I put the three-finned rocket (which was a 3-foot-tall, pointed-nose rocket with a B4-2 engine) on the launch pad. I walked off about 30 feet and launched it and measured the height with an altimeter. Then I went to fire my four-finned rocket (it was a 2-foot-high rocket with a pointed nose and a B6-4 engine). It had started to rain, so I had to hurry. I didn't really check how far away I was, but I launched the rocket and measured its height with the altimeter. By my test, I found that four-finned rockets do go higher. If you think I did it right, let me know. If not, please tell me what was wrong with it.

When asked to describe their first trials at the beginning of the 8-week session, students had talked exclusively about the outcomes—that is, they "guessed" how high the rockets went but did not mention differences among the rocket designs. Moreover, their claims about launch height were admittedly mere speculations that showed no concern for precision of measure. In contrast, responses to the teacher's posting at the end of the summer session suggest that students made considerable progress toward mastering the idea of a fair test, at least with respect to the variables to which they had been attuned:

> CT: The first thing you did wrong was that you used the wrong type of engine. Then you had different size rockets. You didn't go 150 meters away from the object. You launched a rocket in the rain, and since you didn't get the accurate measure, you got the wrong results.

> ID: On a three-finned rocket, you used a B4-2 engine, and on the four-finned rocket you used a B6-4 engine. When you did that, it threw your whole experiment off, big time. You also only went 30 meters away, when you were supposed to go 150 meters. You also used a 2-foot-high, four-finned rocket and used a 3-foot-high, three-finned rocket. You need to use the same height rocket for good results. When you fired the four-finned rocket it rained, and you didn't measure how far away you were, which means that your experiment is way off. You need to do your experiment in good weather.

Responses like these suggested that cycles of student inquiry and experimentation with the design of model rockets afforded increased opportunities to reflect upon the qualities of effective experiment and precise measurement. Hence, our review to this point is consistent with the way that most research interprets preadolescents' scientific thinking (e.g., Klahr, Fay, & Dunbar, 1993; Koslowski, 1996; Schauble, 1990). That is, it suggests that students sometimes misinterpret the goals and strategies of experimentation. However, with practice and good scaffolding, they appear to acquire its kernel. That is, they understand that features can be manipulated to learn about the relationships between attributes and outcomes, they come to prefer "fair tests" that control extraneous variation, and they progressively attune to those features that in fact, are reliably associated with the dependent variable or variables.

These advances are indeed impressive when viewed over the several-week time periods that are typical of these studies. However, widening the lens to capture a longer perspective on a student's educational history (e.g., over the elementary grades, from first grade through fifth) produces a somewhat different view. There are additional conceptual challenges that students must surmount that these briefer interventions overlook. Our observations in classrooms and our reading in the history and philosophy of science suggest that to make sense, experimentation must be firmly embedded in a context of rhetoric, representation, and modeling practice. When these aspects are stripped away, students tend to construct a distorted and denuded sense of the enterprise.

Most research (e.g., Kuhn et al., 1995) portrays experimentation primarily as a psychological phenomenon involving the coordination of information about the world, or data (captured with one's perceptual apparatus) with theory (described as conceptual structures, or systems of mental representation). This view undoubtedly illuminates some aspects of experimentation. However, in our opinion, argument, representation, and modeling comprise a more fruitful focus for science instruction than experiment, which makes sense only when it is erected on the foundation of these three aspects of reasoning. We next justify our claim that each of these ideas is foundational.

Argument

Bazerman (1988) explains, "Experimental reports tell a special kind of story, of an event created so that it might be told. The story creates pictures of the immediate laboratory world in which the experiment takes place, of the happenings of the experiment, and of the larger, structured world of which the experimental events are exemplary" (p. 59). In this passage, Bazerman emphasizes the concept of an experiment as a model, that is, as an example or stand-in for an entire class of events. By manipulating variables in the experiment, one explores the class of situations that the experiment models. Yet, an important aspect of experiment involves justifying the experiment as a legitimate model of the events in question. For this reason, experimentation is always embedded in a context of argument or rhetoric about the model-appropriateness of the materials, procedures, instruments, objects, and manipulations that are employed.

Although Bazerman (1988) is concerned primarily with recounting the history of the experimental report as a genre, his summary of the genre's evolution reveals that "experiment" did not exist apart from the rhetorical practices within which it developed. For example, he notes that until 1800, experimental articles accounted for very small percentages of the pages of scientific journals. Until that time, most articles and pages were devoted to mere reports of observations of natural events. Moreover, the earliest definitions of "experiment" did not include the idea of manipulating nature for purposes of investigation, but instead entailed simply putting in place appropriate conditions so that interesting phenomena would reveal themselves. Therefore, early experiments were not about the testing of hypotheses that could adjudicate between two or more proposed views, but about providing "a clear window to a self-revealing nature" (p. 67). Only gradually, over the course of history, did experimental articles in journals become increasingly investigative. These changes occurred as science became increasingly argumentative—that is, as scientists encountered the need to reply to readers who did not share their knowledge of the experimental apparatus, their assumptions about the way the experiment worked (or failed to), or their theoretical interpretations of the outcomes. Bazerman attributes the origins of this rhetorical force of experiment to Newton, who responded to critics by creating an aura of inevitable discovery through textual manipulation of the sequence of his thoughts and experiments about optics, and later, mechanics. In Bazerman's words, Newton's rhetoric created a "logical and empirical juggernaut" (p. 121).

As we will describe later, our observations of young school students suggest that they, too, must construct the understanding that one can go beyond simply observing things that naturally occur, to posing questions that can be answered by the systematic manipulation of a modeled world (e.g., Driver, Leach, Millar, & Scott, 1996). Ideally, classrooms should be populated by many kinds of argument—including, but not limited to experimentation. Routine exposure to and practice of different forms of disciplinary argument are likely to help students appreciate contrasts among their implications and entailments, and thus become better able to participate in the rhetorical forms and practices that are typically left implicit within the disciplines. For example, we have observed third-graders struggle with and eventually come to appreciate the differences between mathematical argument (in which an observed relationship between length and side of geometrically similar rectangles could be captured exactly by a "rule") and scientific argument (in which an observed relationship between volume and weight of objects made of bronze or Styrofoam or plastic approximated a mathematical "rule," but only imperfectly).

Representation

Latour and others (1990; Lynch, 1990) note that scientists construct their arguments not with the unprocessed "stuff" of the observed world, but with various forms of inscription (Hacking, 1992, prefers the more ambiguous term "mark"). *Inscriptions*, a term that we use to include drawings, maps, diagrams, text, recordings from instruments, mathematical formalisms of various kinds, and even physical models, serve to preserve, compose, and make public parts of the world so that they can be subjected to argument, they can be progressively built up and elaborated upon, and their history can be captured and preserved. Inscriptions do not merely copy the world; they select and enhance aspects of it, making visible new features and relations that cannot be seen by observing the objects and events themselves. For example, a road map selects and enhances aspects such as distance relationships and scale that are not visible to an individual at "ground level," while leaving out other features that are not important to the purposes of the inscription—such as trees, power lines, and buildings.

Of course, coming to understand the conventions and power of inscriptions is a long-term accomplishment, probably life-long, because new representational forms are continually being developed. Before one can look *through* an inscription to view previously unnoticed relations in the world, one must be thoroughly familiar with the syntax and conventions of the form. Without careful and sustained instructional attention, inscriptions, notations, and representations are as likely to be a source of confusion as of clarity. Research suggests that students often misinterpret the syntax and conventions in various forms of inscription like drawing, graphing, diagrams, mathematical formalisms, and maps (Braine, Schauble, Kugelmass, & Winter, 1993; diSessa, Hammer, Sherin, & Kolpakowski, 1991; Ferguson & Hegarty, 1995; Hegarty & Just

1993; Leinhardt, Zaslavsky, & Stein, 1990; Liben & Downs, 1989, 1993). Therefore, an important path that one must traverse toward understanding and participating in scientific forms of argumentation is the development of what diSessa, et al. (1991) call "representational competence." Cultivating a taste for and an understanding of a wide variety of inscriptional forms is a promising focus for science instruction. This objective is facilitated when students are given repeated opportunities to invent a wide variety of inscriptions, revise them in response to feedback from various audiences, and in this way, develop critical standards for their inscriptions' clarity, communicative properties, and potential for supporting argument (e.g., Lehrer & Schauble, in press; Lehrer, Jacobson, Kemeny, & Strom, 1999).

Naturally, it makes sense to regard argument and inscriptions as important mechanisms for developing students' scientific reasoning only if these resources are regularly recruited for supporting scientific practices. When students use inscriptions to support arguments about the world, they are engaged in the enterprise of modeling.

Modeling Practice

Regardless of their domain or specialization, scientists' work involves building and refining models (Giere, 1992; Stewart & Golubitsky, 1992). Experimentation is one means of constructing or refining a model (although not the only means). Moreover, experiments themselves are a form of model, for an experiment "stands for" a class of related events in the world. Yet in science instruction, experimentation is often presented as method, not model. That is, it is introduced as a set of strategies or rules for achieving valid knowledge. However, as Pickering (1995) points out, the results of scientific practice can never be guaranteed; the modeling enterprise is fundamentally open-ended in that no "scientific method" or algorithm can guarantee any particular outcome. Plans and goals initially drive the modeling enterprise, but they, too, are open to revision, because the world often fails to behave in expected ways. When scientists develop instruments, machines, and experiments, they do not really know how they will work (in the case of instruments and machines) or come out (experiments). Therefore, in scientific practice, goals and plans are constantly subject to adjustment in response to feedback. Pickering (1995) refers to this continual process of accommodation or "tuning" to properties of the world as "the mangle of practice." Science is more than reasoning or philosophy; it involves acting in a material world. For this reason, epistemic rules do not guarantee success; nor can they predict with certainty how knowledge will unfold in time.

> A given model does not prescribe the form of its own extension. ... The choice of any particular model opens up an indefinite space of modelling vectors, of different goals (p. 56). How concepts are to be extended is not determined within those concepts, but in relation to other concepts and material performances, which again contain no blueprint for their own existence (p. 93).

Because of the open-endedness of modeling, the construction of scientific knowledge is historically contingent and temporally emergent (Tweney, this volume). Consider, for example, lines of force, readily observed in the spread of iron filings and magnet, and therefore often considered as self-evident in school science. Gooding (1989) describes a 30-year history in which the construct of the idea "line of force" emerged from a progressive history of inscription, material, and retrospectively understood critical experiment. Yet science instruction often obscures histories like these and ignores contingencies among materials and representations. Instead, students replicate experiments whose outcome is known or engage in "inquiry" activities in which the questions, procedures, and results are severely constrained, even given. These forms of instruction tend to distort students' views of the epistemology of science, because they encourage students to focus unduly on a presumed correct "method" for designing and interpreting experiments—removed from a context of understanding how questions develop and change, how attributes are constructed and measures are devised, and how these aspects of inquiry are under continual evolution as the modeling enterprise unfolds in time (for a fuller discussion of these issues, see Driver et al., 1996).

Rhetoric, Representation, and Modeling in Instruction

We have argued that experiment, although ostensibly about method, encompasses a larger network of shared understandings, especially those related to rhetoric, representation, and modeling practices. Learning to experiment does not inevitably lead to these understandings, so pedagogy must be designed to foster them. In this section, we describe elementary-grade classrooms where experiments are embedded in a chain of inquiry. We work with teachers and students in the district's schools in a collaborative effort to develop a modeling approach to mathematics and science (Lehrer & Schauble, in press). Because entire elementary schools are involved in this work, we have the opportunity to study the long-term development of student thinking. It is this long-term (e.g., 5 years or more) perspective that motivates our re-examination of casting the development of scientific reasoning within a framework of experimentation.

In the participating classrooms, experiments do emerge, but as particular kinds of explanation within forms of contingencies among representational redescription, modeling, and argument. We summarize two cases to illustrate some of the spadework that we believe should precede experiment, as well as some of the necessary attention to mathematics and material as a language for framing and interpreting the outcomes of experiments.

Is it Alive? Experiments in the First Grade

Ms. Putz is a first-grade teacher who attends to children's inquiry (see Lehrer, Carpenter, Schauble, & Putz, in press, for greater detail about this case). At the beginning of the school year, she asked children to bring apples to the classroom as part of her fall "theme." An important step for children is to come to regard an object as a collection of attributes (Lehrer & Romberg, 1996), and as these children described attributes of their apples (size, shape, color), one student commented that apples *change* color. Ms. Putz asked how one might account for this change, and a few children suggested that the sun might be the cause. Ms. Putz countered by asking children if they could think of a way to find out more about how the sun affects apples. She followed up the next day by asking children how they might "test" their conjectures. By modeling questioning and by revoicing children's questions in a way that ensured they would be heard by all, Ms. Putz established a relation of inquiry to the natural world. By asserting the need for a test, she embarked children on a gentle slope of valuing forms of argument other than simple assertion.

Upon further discussion, the children decided that apples change color as they ripen, and moreover, that it would be more feasible to conduct their "test" with tomatoes (which ripen quickly) than with apples (which ripen slowly, if at all, once they are picked). Notice how, with this step, children accomplished a shift from focusing on color change in apples in particular, to the more general phenomenon of ripening. Attempting to discover more about the role of the sun, a group of children decided to place one tomato on a window sill and another in the "dark." Although all the students accepted placement on the windowsill as an acceptable operationalization of "light," many children were uncertain about what would count as "dark." They argued about its meaning but eventually settled upon a placing a tomato under an opaque cover. Although this procedure was extremely simple, it involved the important transition of anchoring observation to a particular form of material agency, in the sense described by Pickering (1995). Having settled on dark and light, another child objected, "But the sun is hot, not just light. Does heat matter?" Several children found this objection compelling, and someone pointed out that although the windowsill was light, it was also cold. The ensuing discussion eventually resulted in an expanded space of comparison: light and cool (the windowsill), light and warm (a well-lit location away from the sill), dark and warm (the covered tomato), and dark and cold (inside the refrigerator).

Observing and Inscribing

Having arranged for conditions of observation (what scientists might call an apparatus), Ms. Putz encouraged children to "draw and show what changes." Even though recording change was anchored in an everyday practice (drawing), the need to show change provoked discussion about what changes should be represented and how they could best be displayed. These considerations signal the beginnings of a shift from regarding nature as a mere object of perception to a focusing on nature as represented. As we have claimed, inscriptions reflect choices about what is and is not worth paying attention to for particular purposes. Eventually, children agreed upon ways of using coloring and shading in their drawings to represent progressive discoloration and transitions in turgidity ("squishiness"). Over several weeks, the drawings served as records of change in these features and as a basis for comparing conditions. "Fixing" experience renders it public and permanent, and therefore, a potential source for further exploration (Latour, 1990; Olson, 1994). By reviewing the patterns in their drawings over time and inspecting changes in the tomatoes in each location, children concluded that light and warmth each made a difference. In fact, the difference was so notable that children began to use a new word to summarize the combination of discoloration, discharge, and (newly emerging) smell: rot. They decided to move the tomatoes outside for continued observation.

Rot

The onset of cold weather introduced another theme, pumpkins. In characteristic early elementary school style, the children did pumpkin math, pumpkin food, and pumpkin art. After carving their pumpkins, children noticed the telltale signs of pumpkin rot, leading to spirited discussion about whether tomato rot and pumpkin rot were similar or different. Because the weather was becoming unfavorable for outdoor observation, Ms. Putz suggested that they might want to continue their investigations of decay with compost columns (one-liter soda bottles filled with decomposing materials—the purpose of a compost column is to facilitate observation of changes in decomposing material). This proposal, of course, assumes that there is something common among various cases of the process of rot, whether it is rotting tomatoes, pumpkins, or other material. The move to constructing compost columns was therefore a move to developing a more general model of rot. Of course, it was not immediately apparent to all the first-graders what a compost column was good for. Children eventually agreed that columns could be considered models if they could be made to "look like" the piles of tomatoes they had placed outdoors. Accordingly, as they constructed the compost columns, they included moldy tomatoes, dirt, leaves, gum wrappers, and a piece of Styrofoam, all to mimic the outdoor piles. This initial insistence upon preserving literal similarity between the model and the modeled phenomenon is something that we (and others, e.g.,

Grosslight, Unger, Jay, & Smith, 1991) frequently observe in young students' initial attempts at modeling phenomena.

Ms. Putz asked which factors might influence rot. Drawing upon their previous experience with tomatoes, the children decided to put one column in "the warm" and another in "the cold." Additional compost columns were constructed with pumpkin (to compare to the tomato), and all were watered to mimic the effects of rain.

Seeing the World Through Inscription

As children inspected their compost columns to make drawings of change, they noticed something new and unexpected: fruit flies. The children wondered where they might have come from. In short order, complaints were being received from other teachers about the appearance of fruit flies in their classrooms. The first-graders sent envoys to each classroom in the school to count the number of flies observed. (The counting itself was an interesting exercise in the need to achieve agreement about an apparently self-evident procedure.) At the suggestion of their teacher, students represented their observations on a map of the school, replicated in Figure 1.

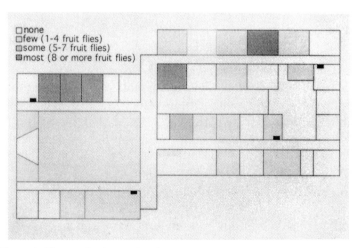

Figure 1. First-graders' map showing distributions of fruit flies in the elementary school.

How to represent the fruit fly counts was a further occasion for consideration of the qualities that children wanted to display. Eventually, they settled on ranges of counts, with higher ranges represented as green regions (the darkest shading on our replica). As the class reviewed their map together, Ms. Putz asked: "Why are there three green classrooms in a row?" One child replied: "That's easy, because they are next to our classroom, and our classroom has a lot of fruit flies." This invocation of propinquity as an explanation received widespread approval from the class. "Then why," asked Ms. Putz, "are some of these classrooms in a different hallway green?" This question sparked further review of the map to consider what children knew about some of the infested locations (like the cafeteria). Eventually, children concluded that food and water might differentiate classrooms with higher counts from those with lower counts, and they revisited classrooms to see whether their conjectures were sustained. They predicted that when the food ran out (a manipulation they arranged in some of the rooms), so, too, would the fruit flies. Subsequent observations confirmed these predictions. Importantly, if they had not created the map, children would never have been surprised by the far-ranging spread of fruit flies into distant classrooms and never would have investigated the availability of food and water resources as an explanation.

Is It Alive?

Children were puzzled about mold, which began to appear in the compost columns. Although most of the students confidently argued that mold was not alive, it continued to increase in all of the columns. Students initially attributed the increase to "a lot of dead things," suggesting that dead things (Styrofoam, dirt, "dead" pumpkin) were spawning other dead things (e.g., mold). (Of course, by this point, Ms. Putz had guided this investigation beyond its original emphasis on "ripening" to touch on broader and more central scientific themes, including properties of living things, such as growth and decay. Therefore, she knew she could afford to defer confronting these conceptions about "dead things," conceptions that were about to be challenged in the course of the children's ongoing investigation, as we will see in a moment.) Children noticed, however, that although all the columns contained "dead things," the increase of mold was greatest in the warm columns. Searching for explanations for these different rates of increase, the children used magnifying glasses and microscopes to observe the mold more carefully. They viewed a "Magic School Bus" video about fungi, which oriented them toward important attributes to observe. Children's drawings of the mold began to reflect vegetative structures, like "stems." These vegetative structures suggested to many of the children that the increase in mold might be due to growth, not some unspecified abiotic process. Entertaining the possibility that mold might be alive led to the reasonable extension that perhaps warmth was a factor in its growth. Ms. Putz spurred further consideration by asking children: "How is mold able to live in our compost columns?" Children suggested: "Because it has food (leaf litter, tomato, pumpkin), and we have water in the columns. It would die if we stopped putting water in." These suggestions again expanded the extension of the concept "alive" and suggested a practical test of conjectures (stop watering the columns). Students went on to develop conjectures about the potential roles of mold and fruit flies in eating the food sources—thus accounting for the observed steady decreases in volume of material in the columns over time—and wondered whether the fruit flies were dying and "going into" the soil. They also noticed that some food sources decomposed more rapidly than others, to which Ms. Putz again prompted further investigation by asking, "Why?"

In this evolution of the activity of young children, we observe the seeds of practices that may later blossom into more recognizable forms of scientific practice. Children began by posing a question, and each act of investigation afforded the opportunity for revision of old questions and generation of new ones. Representational redescription of the world played an important role in selecting and fixing attributes, and relational qualities of displays like maps triggered new cycles of investigation. Comparative study was motivated by questions and the search for explanation. The utility of comparison, in turn, raised the stakes for considering and defining an apparatus. That is, children had to decide on the material circumstances of "dark," and they constructed and manipulated a model (the compost columns) to bring it into alignment with their understanding of the world. The chain of inquiry, representation, and material was sustained throughout the school year, resulting in examination of important ideas in biology, like "alive" and "change."

How Does it Grow? Experiments in the Third Grade

With slightly older children, one can develop a more extensive repertoire of representation, especially mathematics as a language for modeling (Lehrer & Schauble, in press). Third-grade students designed and conducted a series of studies about growth (Lehrer, Schauble, Carpenter, & Penner, in press). During the course of these studies, mathematical descriptions became central ingredients in the development of children's models for describing and explaining the growth of plants. The prolonged duration of the third-graders' explorations of plant growth (these investigations lasted over several weeks) allows us to sketch the periodicity and mutual constitution of inscriptions and conceptions in the context of the classroom.

The teacher, Carmen Curtis, is unusual in that she promotes geometry and spatial reasoning in her teaching of third-grade mathematics (Curtis & Lehrer, in press; Lehrer, et al., 1998). As we will explain, this enriched repertoire of mathematics served as an important resource for modeling the phenomenon of growth. We describe transitions in children's reasoning in the context of two successive life cycles of Wisconsin "Fast Plants,™" a species of fast-developing *brassica* (a form of cabbage) that undergo a complete life cycle within 35–40 days. During the first cycle, children inquired about and observed the growth of plants. In the second, they conducted an experiment to test the effects of changing levels of fertilizer.

The First Cycle of Inquiry

Initially, children posed questions that centered primarily on endpoints of growth, like, "How tall can Fast Plants be?" Only a few children generated questions that focused on the form of the growth, such as, "How fast do plants grow?" The classroom teacher solicited predictions about the form of growth. These children had had extensive previous experience with coordinate plots, the first important mathematical resource that supported their reasoning during this unit. Most students predicted that height would be linearly related to time. When each student was asked to draw a "prediction graph" showing the growth they expected to observe, many drew graphs that expressed constant growth.

Each child then observed the growth of one plant, recording the height of the plant every few days as it grew from seed to seedling. Height proved to be as problematic as "dark" was for the first graders, although children eventually established a measurement convention (height would be measured in millimeters from the soil base to the tip of the highest leaf). The students also made use of a variety of other inscriptional forms, including drawings (top and side views) and photocopies of pressed plants that preserved most aspects of the morphological transitions in growth over time. These records were used later to construct bivariate plots of height and time (essentially, piecewise linear segments from one point of time to another). All but one of the 23 bivariate plots (one of the plants suffered an early death) showed a nonlinear, "S-shaped" form. This form did not confirm their initial expectation of constant growth and so merited further investigation. Children reasoned about both the appearance ("It goes up slow, then it goes up really fast, then it goes up slow again") and the possible biological functions of this form of growth ("Like, when you just plant your Fast Plant, it will start growing up slowly, but then it takes space to have the flowers. It needs to grow pretty big, so it takes a big jump and then it starts to slow down a little.") Superimposing the bivariate plots of different plants on the same axes facilitated comparison of the growth rates of different plants by comparing the "steepness" of the plots. Students began to appreciate the variability of the growth of these plants as they noted that the piecewise linear segments describing identical intervals were not the same.

Ms. Curtis helped children shift their attention from cases to models by asking children to draw representations of a "typical" plant—a line that captured the pattern of growth without replicating any particular case. In response to this request, students drew graph-like representations that captured the characteristic "S" form of the curves. Then children began to wonder about the S form itself. Was it characteristic of anything other than height? How about "width?" Moreover, they began to speculate about the potential role of factors like light or fertilizer. Would these factors help plants grow bigger or faster? These speculations led to a second round of study, in which experimentation was used as a tool for investigation.

The Second Cycle of Inquiry

The second cycle of inquiry was marked by expanded consideration of attributes of growth ("height" was now joined by "width" and "volume") and also comparative components of growth (e.g., roots vs. shoots). Working from this larger space of attributes and relations, the class decided to focus on what effect "food" might have on plants. They designed an experiment contrasting "regular amounts" (6 pellets) and "a lot" (18 pellets) of fertilizer. Children's speculations about the effects of fertilizer included: "Maybe high-fertilizer plants will have more buds or pods," "Maybe high fertilizer means more seeds in the pods," and "Maybe high fertilizer means the plants get wider or get wider more quickly." Some children were skeptical about fertilizer: "There will be no difference between pots with 6 pellets and pots with 18 pellets. They'll be about the same." The experiment was viewed as a means of testing these and related conjectures; the class agreed that they could not otherwise reasonably decide among the alternatives.

Although the experiment focused attention on comparison, these comparisons were embedded in new ways of inscribing and describing growth. Children's expanded sense of attributes led to investigation of new relationships, like that between "height" and "width." One child noted that "... perhaps right before it takes the big jump up, maybe right before the growth spurt, the height equals the width." Another child agreed, and many in the class observed that the growth was more "rectangular" after the growth spurt, meaning that the height far exceeded width at that point in the life cycle. Other children investigated relationships between elapsed time and changes in the canopy of the plants, representing the canopy as the volume of either a cylinder or a rectangular prism. Recalling their earlier classroom work with similar rectangles and cylinders, children initially conjectured that biological growth might be like mathematical growth (the constant proportion of similarity), so that the volume would grow as the cube of the length. This model was eventually disconfirmed by their observations, although it demonstrates yet again the ways in which observations were guided by models (geometric similarity) and material (the paper models of ideal prisms or cylinders that children made to test their conjectures).

Students employed the logic of comparison, if not experiment, to contrast the growth of roots and shoots of the plants. We provided a glass root chamber so children could observe and measure the growth of the roots. Although the chamber facilitated observation, children had to define the notion of "depth," just as they had to decide upon conventions for measuring height, width, and volume. Children debated how best to measure the depth of the meandering path of root growth and made decisions about which strands of the roots would be used as indicators of depth. The contrast between root and shoot growth proved especially intriguing, because the bivariate plots of height and depth over time suggested that although the rates of change in each of the intervals investigated by the children were different, the overall "shape" of the plots was similar (i.e., logistic). Although this comparison was not experimental, it nevertheless is suggestive of how representation (attributes, their measures, graphs) and material (the root chamber, the apparatus involved in growing the plants) are fundamental for grounding inquiry about the natural world.

When children considered the results of their fertilizer experiment, these, too, provided challenges for representing and reasoning about contrast. Children plotted the heights of the 6 pellet plants (represented as circles) and the 18 pellet plants (represented as squares) by arranging them along an axis of values where each case was represented (like a frequency plot). Children noted that the distributions of the plants grown in the two different conditions completely overlapped. They concluded that one of their favorite hypotheses, (more food=more height) could not be true. Similar conclusions were reached when they considered the number of seeds generated by the plants, although, once again, what to count and how to count were not trivial considerations. However, when comparing the distributions of 6- and 18-pellets on plant width, children noticed considerably less overlap in their displays. One child began to talk about relative degree of overlap (Lehrer et al., in press, p. 353):

Kyle: *They look like they're like in two different groups 'cause most of the 6 pellets are right here (gesturing toward one end of the line of values) and most of the 18 are more in the higher area (gesturing toward the opposite end of the line), so I think 18 pellets maybe are wider than the 6 pellets.*

Another student sought to quantify the degree of overlap as a ratio:

> Peter: *Because only four of the twelve, only 1/3 of the 18-pellet plants are*
> *less (wide) than the widest 6-pellet plants …*
> Teacher: *So you would feel pretty safe in saying to the second-grade class…?*
> Peter: *But we're not quite sure, because we only did it once, but I think*
> *it's pretty safe to say…well, we can't be exact… like 2/3, and we*
> *only did one round, but we could say that 1/2 or more of the high-*
> *fertilizer plants will be wider than the 6 pellets.*

In this last passage, Peter displays some beginning intuitions about sampling, suggesting that the class has only conducted a single experiment, and without some notion of the possible range of ratios, any single ratio is suspect. He offers the ratio of one half as a safe lower bound. Note that interpreting the results of the experiment depended upon the class's representation for visualizing overlapping distributions, their sense of ratio as a good means for characterizing the degree of overlap between distributions, and for some (like Peter), their intuitions about relationships between samples and population.

Recall that children's first questions about plant growth tended to focus on endpoints, like height. To answer questions about endpoints, children observed growing plants for over a month in their classroom. Nevertheless, even these simple observations involved layers of representation and material. Plants had to come to be seen as bundles of attributes like height, width, and volume. Attributes needed to be measured in ways that could be shared, so claims could find appropriate warrants. Classroom norms included justification based on common standards, so that it was considered unacceptable to simply go around the room stating claims but producing no evidence, or alternatively, producing evidence that only one person could understand. Representational redescription of change over time produced emergent phenomena, like the S-shaped (logistic) character of growth. Consideration of the form of growth was accompanied by increased attention to the implications of this form for varying rates of growth. The first cycle of inquiry served as grounding for a second cycle, in which the logic of experiment was used to resolve competing claims about the role of factors like "food" in the growth of plants.

What we find important, however, is that experimentation was conducted within a larger framework of inquiry. Observation was heavily dependent on material means (e.g., root chambers) and on decisions about the selection, definition, and measure of new attributes, like "width." Interpretation of the results of the experiment demanded the invention and use of data displays for visualizing distributions and the employment of mathematical logic (e.g., ratio) to make the degree of overlap between distributions publicly visible and hence, sharable.

Conclusion

In both of the cases we described, students eventually appealed to experiment as one component in an ongoing argument for settling disputes about matters of fact in the material world. The first-graders constructed an experiment to disentangle the effects of light and heat on "rot," and the third-graders investigated effects of varying the amount of fertilizer on various dependent variables of plant growth. However, in neither case was activity initially driven by the idea of designing an experiment. Instead, experimentation emerged only in the context of a wider program of inquiry that in each case involved selecting, defining, measuring, and representing attributes and their relations. Also, in neither case was experiment regarded as a particularly privileged source of knowledge about the phenomena in question. Experiments appeared to be neither culminating nor unusually definitive in children's exploration of phenomena. Instead, the experiments remained embedded in a much more encompassing classroom effort that revolved around inquiry and argument, including the development of conjectures and their support. For example, students' initial proposal that "the sun" affects ripening was eventually differentiated into attributes of both "light" and "heat," not out of a methodological concern for the control of variables, but because students disagreed about the respective contributions of these variables to the ripening of fruits and vegetables. As inscriptions of various sorts were recruited for these arguments and as the representations increasingly "lifted away" from the world, the inscriptions themselves, rather than the phenomena, became accepted both as evidence and as the inspiration for new questions.

As in the history of science (Kline, 1980), the pressure of argument and counter argument pushed children toward developing inscriptions that became increasingly mathematical. The first-graders struggled initially to find ways to represent change, and then eventually, to show changing *proportions* of material in the tomatoes and compost columns. Similarly, although over a longer period, the third-graders' inscriptions shifted from their initial near-copies of the plants (e.g., drawings and pressed plant silhouettes, which preserved shape, height, and width—but not color, volume, or weight) to two-dimensional graphs, to three-dimensional paper models of cylinders and prisms, and finally to mathematical relationships of rate and geometrical similarity. In neither of these cases was experimentation introduced as an ahistorical method; to the contrary, the careful co-development of a history of representation and understanding was fundamental. This history served as the essential foundation upon which children could construct the very idea of experiment.

Hence, by the time they developed their "instrumentation" for studying color change in tomatoes, the first-graders had already accepted the idea that change in this particular fruit could serve as a model for studying the general phenomenon of ripening. Similarly, settling on conventions for "light," "dark," "warm," and "cool" was central to constructing that model. Conduct of the experiment gave rise, in turn, to new questions that the experiment itself was not designed to answer: What is the relationship between ripening and rot? What features (e.g., constituents like pumpkin, apple, and tomato, and contextual factors, like heat, light, and water) affect the process of rot? What are the connections between growth (e.g., of mold, fruit flies) and decay? In that way, experiments were regarded not as favored methods for attaining valid answers to questions that were well-formulated in advance, but as one contribution to an ongoing, open-ended process of inquiry and modeling.

Research suggests that it is feasible to teach students the syntax of experimentation, for example, how to design informative experiments or how to interpret patterns of evidence demonstrating covariation or lack of covariation between potential causes and outcomes. Current debate concerns whether students should acquire this knowledge through direct instruction (e.g., Chen & Klahr, in press; Klahr, Chen, & Toth, this volume) or through practice and guided discovery (Kuhn et al., 1995). Our concern is a broader one—namely, that focusing on the syntactical aspects of experiment is an insufficient target for sustaining either effective instruction or an adequate account of the development of scientific reasoning. Such a focus renders invisible the need to construct a common history of rhetoric, representation, and modeling practice that can serve as a taken-for-granted assumptive structure on which experimentation rests. It is this history, we suggest, that imbues the dry bones of experimentation with meaning and significance—for school students, but also for practicing scientists.

Acknowledgements

This research was supported by the Cognitive Studies for Educational Practice Program of the James S. McDonnell Foundation and by a grant from the U.S. Department of Educational Research and Improvement, to the National Center for Improving Student Learning and Achievement in Mathematics and Science (R305A60007-98). The opinions expressed herein do not necessarily reflect the position, policy, or endorsement of the supporting agencies.

The authors gratefully acknowledge the contributions of Carmen Curtis, Angela Putz, Jeff Darby, and their students, as well as those of our staff, students, and other teacher collaborators.

References

Barron, B. J., Schwartz, D. L., Vye, N. J., Moore, A., Petrosino, A. J., Zech, L., Bransford, J. D., and CTGV (1998). Doing with understanding: Lessons from research and project based learning. *Journal of the Learning Sciences, 7*(3&4), 271-312.

Bazerman, C. (1988). *Shaping written knowledge. The genre and activity of the experimental article in science.* Madison: University of Wisconsin Press.

Braine, L. G., Schauble, L., Kugelmass, S., Winter, A. (1993). Representation of depth by children: Spatial strategies and alteral biases. *Developmental Psychology, 29*(3), 466-479.

Chen, Z., & Klahr, D. (in press). All other things being equal: Children's acquisition of the control of variables strategy. *Child Development.*

Curtis, C., & Lehrer, R. (in press). Why are some solids perfect? Conjectures and experiments by third graders. *Teaching Children Mathematics.*

diSessa, A. A., Hammer, D., Sherin, B., & Kolpakowski, T. (1991). Inventing graphing: Children's meta-representational expertise. *Journal of Mathematical Behavior, 10*(2), 117-160.

Driver, R., Leach, J., Millar, R., & Scott, P. (1996). *Young people's images of science.* Buckingham, UK: Open University Press.

Duschl, R. A. , & Gitomer, D. H. (1997). Strategies and challenges to changing the focus of assessment and instruction in science classrooms. *Educational Assessment.* 4 (1), 37-73.

Ferguson, E. L., & Hegarty, M. (1995). Learning with real machines or diagrams: Applications of knowledge to real-world problems. *Cognition and Instruction, 13,* 129-160.

Giere, R. N. (1992). *Cognitive models of science.* Minneapolis: University of Minnesota Press.

Gooding, D. (1989). 'Magnetic curves' and the magnetic field: Experimentation and representation in the history of a theory. In D. Gooding, T. Pinch, & S. Schaffer (Eds.), *The uses of experiment.* (pp. 183-223). Cambridge: Cambridge University Press.

Grosslight, L., Unger, C., Jay, E., & Smith, C. (1991). Understanding models and their use in science: Conceptions of middle and high school students and experts. *Journal of Research in Science Teaching, 28,* 799-822.

Hacking, I. (1992). The self-vindication of the laboratory sciences. In A. Pickering (Ed.), *Science as practice and culture* (pp. 29-64). Chicago, IL: University of Chicago Press.

Hegarty, M., & Just, M. A. (1993). Constructing mental models of machines from text and diagrams. *Journal of Memory and Language, 32,* 717-742.

Klahr, D., Fay, A. L., , & Dunbar, K. (1993). Heuristics for scientific experimentation: A developmental study. *Cognitive Psychology, 25,* 111-146.

Kline, M. (1980). *Mathematics: The loss of certainty.* Oxford: Oxford University Press.

Koslowski, B. (1996). *Theory and evidence: The development of scientific reasoning.* Cambridge, MA: The MIT Press.

Kuhn, D., Garcia-Mila, M., Zohar, A., & Andersen, C. (1995). Strategies of knowledge acquisition. *Society for Research in Child Development Monographs, 60* (4, Serial no. 245).

Lamon, M., Secules, T., Petrosino, A. J., Hackett, R., Bransford, J. D., & Goldman, S. R. (1996). Schools for thought: Overview of the international project and lessons learned from one of the sites. In L. Schauble & R. Glaser (Eds.), *Innovations in learning: New environments for education* (pp. 243-288). Mahwah, NJ: Lawrence ErlbaumAssociates.

Latour, B. (1990). Drawing things together. In M. Lynch & S. Woolgar (Eds.), *Representation in scientific practice* (pp. 19-68). Cambridge, MA: MIT Press.

Lehrer, R., Carpenter, S., & Schauble, L. & Putz, A. (in press). Designing classrooms that support inquiry. In R. Minstrell and E. Van Zee (Eds.). *Teaching in the Inquiry-Based Science Classroom.* Reston, VA: American Association for the Advancement of Science.

Lehrer, R., Jacobson, C., Thoyre, G., Kemeny, V., Strom, D., Horvath, J., Gance, S., & Koehler, M. (1998). Developing understanding of geometry and space in the primary grades. In R. Lehrer & D. Chazan (Eds.), *Designing learning environments for developing understanding of geometry and space* (pp. 169-200). Mahwah, NJ: Lawrence Erlbaum Associates.

Lehrer, R., Jacobson, C., Kemeny, V., & Strom, D. (1999). Building on children's intuitions to develop mathematical understanding of space. In E. Fennema & T. A. Romberg (Eds.), *Mathematics classrooms that promote understanding* (pp. 63-87). Mahwah, NJ: Lawrence Erlbaum Associates.

Lehrer, R., & Romberg, T. A. (1996). Exploring children's data modeling. *Cognition and Instruction, 14,* 69-108.

Lehrer, R. & Schauble, L. (in press). The development of model-based reasoning. In R. Glaser (Ed.), *Advances in instructional psychology, Vol. 5.* Mahwah, NJ: Lawrence Erlbaum Associates.

Lehrer, R., Schauble, L., Carpenter, S., & Penner, D. (in press). The inter-related development of inscriptions and conceptual understanding. In P. Cobb, E. Yackel, & K.McClain (Eds.), *Symbolizing and communicating in mathematics classrooms: Perspectives on discourse, tools, and instructional design.* Mahwah, NJ: Erlbaum.

Leinhardt, G., Zaslavsky, O., & Stein, M. K. (1990). Functions, graphs, and graphing: Tasks, learning, and teaching. *Review of Educational Research, 60,* 1-64.

Liben, L., & Downs, R. (1989). Understanding maps as symbols: The development of map concepts in children. In H. Reese (Ed.), *Advances in child development* (pp. 145-201). New York: Academic Press.

Liben, L., & Downs, R. (1993). Understanding person-space-map relations: Cartographic and developmental perspectives. *Developmental Psychology, 29,* 739-752.

Lynch, M. (1990). The externalized retina: Selection and mathematization in the visual documentation of objects in the life sciences. In M. Lynch & S. Woolgar (Eds.), *Representation in scientific practice* (pp. 153-186). Cambridge, MA: The MIT Press.

Olson, D. R. (1994). *The world on paper.* Cambridge: Cambridge University Press.

Petrosino, A. J. (1995) *Mission to Mars: An integrated curriculum*. Tech. Rep. SFT-1, Nashville, TN: Vanderbilt University, Learning Technology Center.

Petrosino, A. J. (1998). *At-risk children's use of reflection and revision in hands-on experimental activities.* Dissertation Abstracts International-A, 59(03). (UMI AAT 9827617).

Pickering, A. (1995). *The mangle of practice: Time, agency, and science*. Chicago: University of Chicago Press.

Rudolph, J. L., & Stewart, J. (1998). Evolution and the nature of science: On the historical discord and its implications for education. *Journal of Research in Science Teaching, 35*, 1069-1089.

Schauble, L. (1990). Belief revision in children: The role of prior knowledge and strategies for generating evidence. *Journal of Experimental Child Psychology, 49*, 31-57.

Schauble, L. (1996). The development of scientific reasoning in knowledge-rich contexts. *Developmental Psychology. 32*, 102-119.

Schauble, L., Glaser, R., Duschl, R., Shulze, S., & John, J. (1995). Students' understanding of the objectives and procedures of experimentation in the science classroom. *Journal of the Learning Sciences, 4*, 131-166.

Stewart, I., & Golubitsky, M. (1992). *Fearful symmetry: Is God a geometer?* London, England: Penguin Books.

10

Developing Reflective Inquiry Practices: A Case Study of Software, the Teacher, and Students

Ben Loh, Brian J. Reiser, Josh Radinsky, Daniel C. Edelson,
Louis M. Gomez, and Sue Marshall
Northwestern University

A group of students has decided to investigate Pluto's erratic orbit around the Sun. Their goal is to set up computer simulations with different configurations of planets orbiting the sun to determine which planet has an effect on Pluto's orbit (e.g., a simulation with only Pluto and the Sun; a second simulation with Pluto, Neptune, and the Sun, etc.). They gather some information about Pluto, the Sun, and other planets, such as mass, distance from the sun, length of an orbit, etc., and plan on using these values to set up the simulation. They have been working with the teacher to develop this basic research methodology, and everyone, including the teacher, is satisfied with the viability of this approach.

But when the students begin to set up the simulation using the simulation environment Interactive Physics, they begin to encounter problems. There is a significant mismatch between the information they gathered and the variables they can change in the simulation. The students are overwhelmed by the number of variables and do not know which to try and which are irrelevant. Should they change the gravitational constant, orbital velocity, xy coordinates, initial velocities, mass, or diameter? Moreover, the units of measure of the information they gathered are different from the units of measure used by the simulation (e.g. the data they collected was in kilometers per year, whereas the simulation required meters per second), adding another level of complexity.

As the students try different values, it soon becomes clear that it is a challenge to simply get any object to orbit another object, let alone set up a simulation that reflects the dynamics of our solar system. As they try to figure this out, the students set a variable and then run the simulation to see if it worked. But because some of the values were wrong, or some variables were overlooked, planets would fly into the Sun, or shoot off into space. So the students change a second variable, and run the simulation again. When that also does not work, they tweak the simulation, and try another value. Since nothing works, the students feel that they never find any of the "right" answers or relevant results, so they do not write anything down.

At the end of the class, when the teacher comes around to check their progress, she finds a struggling group of students who are somewhat able to articulate what they are doing but have no record of their work over the course of the period. The students have clearly been working throughout the period, but is their struggling a sign of progress or haphazard thrashing? How can the students learn from what they have explored so far to decide on the next steps of the investigation?

This example illustrates the kinds of challenges that arise when students do inquiry in science classrooms. Opening up laboratory work to student-generated questions and methodology means that students are not always going to "succeed" in their projects. The challenges presented by this example represent a progression of opportunities for learning and some partial success, rather than a project that failed completely. Students need to learn inquiry skills that help them to systematically pursue a solution to their question and to better manage their process of inquiry. To be successful in inquiry, they need to develop new habits and new conceptual frameworks that redefine the pursuit of science as a process of constructing new knowledge rather than a search for simple answers.

Seeking to understand the skills, the requisite dispositions, and the mechanisms for helping students develop into *reflective inquirers* is the goal of the Supportive Inquiry Based Learning Environment project (SIBLE). We are conducting iterative design research on the challenges faced by students as they work in information-rich environments and how their development of investigation skills can be facilitated through interactions with a software support tool and the classroom teacher. We developed a software support tool, called the *Progress Portfolio*, as an integral part of this research process. Our research is concerned with how to craft not just the software to foster reflective inquiry, but the whole learning environment, including the interactions among students, teachers, and materials.

In this chapter, we describe our initial foray into this process of supporting reflective inquiry in the context of a high school physics class. We describe the first iteration of our software design, and through a case study, explore how these tools can be integrated into the practices of an existing curriculum project. Our goal is to understand what it looks like when students are conducting these complex data-rich investigations, what kinds of supports are needed to foster reflective inquiry, and the shifts in thinking that students need to make as they learn this different mode of work.

The Need for Reflective Inquiry

Current science standards mandate that students learn the process of inquiry in scientific domains (AAAS, 1993; NRC, 1996). The goal is for student learning of scientific content to be grounded in an understanding of the processes of scientific investigation and their application to real problems. Despite this goal, much of science is still taught as a process of memorizing facts and conducting scripted confirmatory laboratory exercises (O'Sullivan, Reese, & Mazzeo, 1997). An inquiry approach to learning science needs to center around scientific process, not scientific facts (NRC, 1996; O'Sullivan et al., 1997). Students should be engaged in active inquiry, asking questions, gathering data, analyzing data, drawing conclusions, and communicating results (Linn, Songer, & Eylon, 1996).

These goals require a major shift in science curricula and teaching. Doing inquiry, especially open-ended inquiry, remains a challenge for both students and teachers. Students are rarely given the opportunity to pursue and manage their own research questions. Instead, they are often given tasks to do without a corresponding understanding of the purpose and goal of the task. They are given step-by-step instructions on how to reach that goal, relieving them of the need to thoughtfully engage with the content. This approach leads to students working without a clear understanding of how their investigation is situated within the practices and understanding of science. They develop skills, habits, and expectations about the nature of schoolwork that can hinder their success in conducting inquiry (Schauble, 1990). Students often develop an objectivist orientation towards science, viewing the process of science as seeking facts rather than the construction of knowledge (Tobin, Tippins, & Hook,

1995). They become accustomed to a non-reflective, action-oriented mode of work (Schauble, Glaser, Duschl, Schulze, & John, 1995).

Recent developments in educational technology hold promise in providing rich environments in which students can pursue and manage their own investigations. These classes of investigation tools include data visualization software (e.g., WorldWatcher, Northwestern University; EarthView Explorer, Columbia University), simulation environments (e.g., GenScope, BBN; Interactive Physics, Knowledge Revolution), modeling tools (e.g., ModelIt, University of Michigan), web-based information sources, and digital libraries of text, images, and video. These software tools enable students to query or generate their own data sets, to construct visualizations representing complex phenomena, and to set up and run their own simulations.

These software tools, in turn, open up new avenues for science activities in the classroom. While there are a myriad of ways to make science learning more constructivist in nature, these investigation tools afford a style of project-based work that takes advantage of the richness and complexity of data to provide authentic science opportunities (Soloway, Krajcik, Blumenfeld, & Marx, 1996). They afford student projects that make use of large amounts of data, providing students with a wide range of opportunities to pursue their own questions and construct their own explanations. They also afford extended projects in which students have the opportunity to learn how to manage and coordinate data collection and interpretation activities.

In addition to creating opportunities for inquiry, the introduction of information-rich computer environments can create new challenges for students. Students can become overwhelmed by the wealth of information and have trouble managing and making sense of it. They become mired in the activities of the investigation process, generating data, tweaking simulation variables, and exploring new hyperlinks, losing sight of their questions and purpose. The process through which students generated, analyzed, interpreted, and drew conclusions from data can be easily lost as students often can not remember what they did and fail to document their procedures. This problem is compounded with work in a digital medium, where the interim steps in the investigative process can be transient. While work with pencil and paper can leave a trail of artifacts, work in a digital medium often consists of little more than a series of mouse clicks. This lack of a concrete representation of the inquiry process can make it a challenge for students and teachers to review and discuss the process of the students' investigations. If students are to learn scientific process, they must have the means to reflect on and learn from their own investigative process.

Reflection, the act of stepping back from one's activity to view actions, objects, system states, or emerging understandings from a different perspective, is widely cited as an essential component of learning. *Learning* is itself a reflective process wherein students integrate new knowledge through a process of accommodation, in other words, reflecting on and transforming prior conceptions to account for new information (Perkins, 1998; Pintrich, Marx, & Boyle, 1993). In order to improve upon their own investigation and learning processes, students need to think metacognitively, to reflect on their work (Glynn & Duit, 1995). They need to be self-monitoring, to engage in strategic planning, reflect on strategies used, and evaluate the outcomes of using these strategies (Collins & Brown, 1988; Davis, 1996; Schauble, Glaser, Raghavan, & Reiner, 1991; Schoenfeld, 1987). Students also need to maintain goal orientation in inquiry, being mindful of the goals and subgoals that constitute scientific discovery and reflecting on these goals in the context of an investigation (Schauble, Raghavan, & Glaser, 1993; Shute & Glaser, 1990).

As is the case with investigation environments, technology can offer some compelling solutions for supporting reflection. Existing software support for developing these reflective skills falls mainly into two categories: self-contained, content-embedded investigation environments with built-in reflective supports (Schauble et al., 1993; Shute & Glaser, 1990; Tabak & Reiser, 1997; Tabak, Smith, Sandoval, & Reiser, 1996); and domain-general communicative structures designed to promote reflection (Edelson & O'Neill, 1994; Scardamalia, Bereiter, McLean, Swallow, & Woodruff, 1989; Suthers, Weiner, Connelly, & Paolucci, 1995). Content-embedded investigation environments have the advantage of being able to directly scaffold student thinking in domain-specific ways. For example, in the Biology Guided Inquiry-Based Learning environment, the software is designed to provide content-specific prompts that scaffold students as they construct explanations of evolutionary processes (Tabak et al., 1996). The disadvantage of this approach is that the scaffolding is limited to one particular project or one particular domain. In contrast, domain-general software supports provide more flexibility by being able to support different projects in different domains. For this latter class of tools, scaffolding is usually targeted at a generic inquiry level. For example, the Collaboratory Notebook (Edelson & O'Neill, 1994) scaffolds student discussions by helping them articulate the logical structure of a discussion, labeling their contributions to the discussion as "conjectures," "questions," and other rhetorical devices.

Both classes of software support provide students with some form of trace or record of their inquiry actions, allowing students to observe their own problem solving behavior after they have reached a solution, and perhaps comparing it with other solutions. For example Schauble, Raghaven, and Glaser's (1993) Discovery and Reflection Notation system provides software artifacts that show students a visual representation of the steps they took in their investigation, which can be used by students to reflect on their work and plan their next steps. Similarly, Collins and Brown (1988) describe the utility of computer artifacts in reifying the learner's actions so that they can become objects for reflection.

Our work builds upon this research to develop an understanding of reflective inquiry and inform the design of software and curriculum to promote this style of work. We are interested in a particular curricular context: investigations in which students work with large amounts of data, develop their own research questions, and need to manage a long-term project. We want to understand how to help students to create a trace or record of their investigations in the context of data-rich environments, and how to build domain-general supports that are useful across different kinds of data-rich investigations. At the same time, we want to understand how prompting—both content-specific and generalized prompting— might be tailored to help students focus on important issues in their investigations. We also want to understand how to facilitate the process of learning these reflective skills: Not just supporting student work, but understanding how to create opportunities for learning conversations between students and teachers. In addition, we want to understand how to support the activity of teachers in these contexts. Specifically, we want to understand how to provide teachers with a way to periodically assess student progress on long-term projects, to establish milestones, and to see what students are doing and thinking. In short, we are seeking ways of promoting reflective inquiry through the coordinated efforts of teachers, software, and curricular activities.

Three Components of Reflective Inquiry

Reflective inquiry is a style of inquiry that encompasses both effective inquiry strategies (e.g., systematically collecting and interpreting data) and reflective activities (e.g., monitoring, periodically evaluating progress, and revising plans). It focuses student attention on both the results of investigations and the inquiry process itself. Students need to be reflective inquirers in order to successfully complete their projects, gain a deeper understanding of the domain content, gain a better understanding of the scientific process, and improve their science skills.

Reflective inquiry can be characterized as three primary sets of activities. We will briefly outline the components, and develop the ideas more fully as we work through the examples in the rest of the chapter. The three basic activities are:

1. *Creating a record of progress:* A reflective inquirer needs to carefully record the activities of an investigation, ranging from gathering background information, to how an experiment is set up, to the results of particular experiments, and interpretation of the results. This record also needs to be carefully organized and managed.

2. *Monitoring progress:* In addition to creating a record of activities, a reflective inquirer also needs to monitor the progress being made in an investigation, reviewing and reflecting on where one has been, and revising investigation strategies to improve progress toward the goal.

3. *Communicating process and results to others:* Finally, an equally important aspect of reflective inquiry is being able to communicate one's process and results to others. While monitoring is a more obvious reflective activity, the act of communicating (as well as creating a record) can serve as a catalyst for reflective activities. To describe one's process and results, one must first step back from the activity itself and reflect on the salient or important aspects of the investigation.

Software Tools for Reflective Inquiry: The Progress Portfolio

We designed the Progress Portfolio to be a catalyst for these three reflective inquiry activities. Our basic approach to supporting reflective inquiry with the Progress Portfolio can be summarized by two design principles:

Tools for Creating Concrete Artifacts

First, our basic approach to promoting reflective inquiry revolves around the notion of creating concrete artifacts to anchor reflective processes. In order to reflect, one must have something to reflect on. We designed the tools of the Progress Portfolio to enable students to create artifacts that represent the evolving states of their investigation process. Our goal is for students to construct a record of their progress that can help them monitor their progress and communicate. These artifacts then serve as the objects of reflective conversations as students discuss their investigative process with fellow students and teachers. The artifacts also serve as objects of reflective actions, as students manipulate, organize, and construct narrative representations out of these artifacts using the tools.

Providing a Task Model

Second, we designed the tools of the Progress Portfolio to serve as an implicit task model for reflective inquiry. The tasks of creating a record, monitoring, and communicating are directly supported by our tools. Rather than asking students to create their own methods and representational forms for reflective inquiry, the Progress Portfolio provides tools and an implicit model for being reflective inquirers. The task model is "implicit" in that it suggests tasks, but relies on the students' initiative for action. Students use the Progress Portfolio as they conduct their investigations in other investigation environments. They use the investigation environment's tools for exploring content (e.g., Newtonian physics, urban planning), and simultaneously use the Progress Portfolio tools to create a record, monitor, and communicate about their work in the investigation environment. In this way, students are creating tangible representations of their ongoing work processes using a tool that guides them towards establishing the skills for these important scientific practices.

The Progress Portfolio Tools

As students conduct their investigations in other investigation environments (e.g., Interactive Physics), they use the Data Camera tool (see Figure 1) to create a record of their work. The Data Camera works by capturing a picture of their investigation environment screen. These screenshots are then saved onto pages in the Progress Portfolio. All data collected into the Progress Portfolio resides on individual pages, which can contain picture fields for the screenshots, text fields, and sticky notes (more on these later). As students work through their investigation, they create numerous pages that represent various states and intermediate products of their investigation. For example, a student might create a page that represents their investigation screen when they are first setting up an experiment, and a second page to document the results of the experiment. These pages then serve as concrete instantiations of important stages of the student's work process, providing a reminder of what the student did.

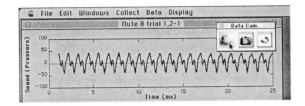

Figure 1. Data Camera tool. Clicking on the camera captures the screen of the investigation environment. Here the data camera is being used to capture a graph of a sound wave generated by a flute using Sound 3.01 software.

Capturing the screen using the Data Camera makes it easier for students to document many aspects their work. For investigation environments like Interactive Physics, documenting a simulation trial can be a tedious and visually intensive task. For instance, to properly document each trial, the students would have to record how many planets were present, the mass and distance/location of the planets, any changed parameters (e.g., gravitational constant, radians), and the results. Results of these simulation runs pose an especially difficult challenge as they are graphs of velocities and visual depictions of the orbital track of the planets. To record this kind of information using pencil and paper, students would have to sketch the resulting graphs and orbital tracks on a piece of paper.[1] The Progress Portfolio simplifies this process by making it easy to capture the screen and annotate variable values directly on the captured data.

---

1. Though some of this documentation could be done with a printer, not all classrooms have ready access to printing, nor the resources to allow each student to print out and keep track of multiple pages. The software allows comments to be integrated within the captured screen, and more effective access and organization than is possible with paper copies only.

In addition to holding screenshots, students can also annotate their pages with sticky notes and text fields. Sticky notes are like their physical counterparts (Post It™ notes), in that students can write short notes and then "stick" them onto a page. In addition, sticky notes have arrows that students can use to point out notable features on the screen, such as the peak of a graph. Students can use sticky notes to both record how they set up an experiment, and to help them remember how they interpreted the results of an experiment. Rather than simply taking a snapshot of their investigation work, sticky notes provide students with a way to attach metacomments about the images that they capture to help them remember what they were doing, or what they found interesting about the particular image they captured (see Figure 2).

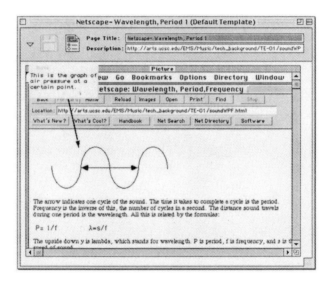

Figure 2. Students capture graphics and text from a web site onto a Progress Portfolio page and annotate it with a sticky note to help them remember why they captured it.

Text fields are similar to sticky notes in that they are intended to help students record their thoughts as they work. But they also have an advantage over sticky notes in that the teacher (or curriculum designer) can customize a text field with prompts to help students monitor and reflect on their progress. For example, text fields might be tailored to support generalized investigation strategies with prompts for "observations," "notes," and "next steps." Or, they might be more specifically tailored to a physics simulation, prompting students to record "What variables in the simulation did you change?," "What was the result?," and "Was this what you expected?" Prompted text fields help students develop reflective inquiry skills by reminding them to create a record of their progress (similar to the way a science notebook might be used), and prompting students to reflect. In addition to these process-oriented prompts, content-specific prompts could be created. For example, for a planetary motion investigation, the prompts could be tailored to help organize the conceptual space by focusing students on key variables that they need to change (e.g., masses, distances, and forces at work). Because these metacognitive prompts are customizable, teachers or curriculum designers can tailor them to help students reflect on specific aspects of their work (Davis, 1996). Moreover, using a common static page type across different activities or various phases of a student project (e.g., literature search, data collection, and presentation) can help reinforce skills, as students are repeatedly prompted to record observations, next steps, etc.

Pages themselves can be customized to promote monitoring and reflective activities by encouraging students to analyze and review the data they have collected in new ways. For example, one kind of customized page is a comparison page where students can place two or more captured images side by side in order to compare and contrast data (see Figure 3). Students can compare three graphs of sound waves created by different musical instruments and begin articulating hypotheses about what causes the instruments to sound different, and set new plans for collecting and analyzing data to confirm these hypotheses.

The Progress Portfolio also provides tools to help students organize and make sense of their documentation pages. Students can cluster thematically related pages together into folders to help them keep track of their pages and their investigation. For example, in exploring a simulation of planetary motion, students might put all of their experimental trials varying the distance between the Sun and the Earth together into one cluster, and their experiments with varying mass in another cluster. These clusters can help students monitor and reflect on how their data collection is progressing. As students collect more and more pages, keeping the pages together in a flat list can make it difficult to see what they have. Encouraging students to review their pages and develop an organizational structure can help them keep track of the data they have and see where data might be missing from their investigation.

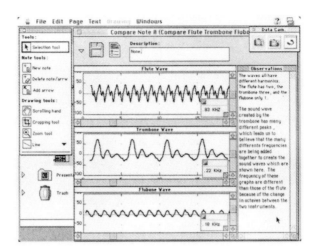

Figure 3. A Comparison Page. Students have constructed a comparison page in the Progress Portfolio using graphs to explore the similarities and differences of sound waves generated by three different musical instruments.

Communication is implicitly supported by many of these tools. Rather than mediating student communication, as other software, such as the Collaboratory Notebook does, the artifacts created in the Progress Portfolio afford reflective, face-to-face conversations. As students construct Progress Portfolio pages, they can discuss with each other what to document and how to document; what aspects of their investigation warrant documentation, keeping track of their plans and changes in the direction of their project. They can review their captured images as they plan their next steps. Teachers can engage students in conversations about what they are doing while looking through the students' work in the Progress Portfolio. In particular, the captured pages in the Progress Portfolio provide the teacher with a window into student conceptions of the task (e.g., what students capture and do not capture reflects their understanding of the value of different aspects of the inquiry process), student understanding of the science concepts (e.g., their written annotations can reveal their level of understanding), and the students' ability to interpret and analyze data (e.g. the teacher can review the original captured screens from the investigation to verify the students' interpretations of the events, rather than relying only on the students' interpretations of the data).

The Progress Portfolio also has presentation tools that more explicitly support communication. The presentation tools facilitate communication by giving students the ability to easily review their work and create a slide presentation to enhance an oral or written report. In the process of creating the presentation, students need to reflect on their investigative process; they review their captured pages to select the pages that best represent their investigation or help them to explain their process and their results. They create presentations by copying these pages into a presentation area, then reorder, revise, clean up, and add annotations to create presentation "slides." These presentation tools make it easy for students to go back and look at what they did. Their earlier efforts in creating documentation artifacts during their investigation take on new value as they re-purpose these artifacts for their presentation. Not only do their collected pages help them recreate their investigations, but they are also useful for illustrating their work. Teachers can also guide students to focus on specific aspects of their investigative process, encouraging students to reflect on the rationale for plans taken, the fate of different solution strategies, or how the students' ideas have evolved during the investigation. In creating and presenting the story of an investigation, reflection becomes a part of the work of doing the investigation, rather than an added-on activity serving no obvious purpose.

Taken as a whole, the tools of the Progress Portfolio promote reflective inquiry as students create and document artifacts that represent their investigative process, have reflective conversations around these artifacts, and are prompted to make sense of and present a story of their investigation. The Progress Portfolio provides a common repository for student work, a place where they can gather together all of their information for synthesis, analysis, and reflection. Student use of the Progress Portfolio can create learning opportunities as teachers review the trace of students' investigations and talk with students about their progress, point out mistakes, and suggest strategies for documenting. Students learn to engage in these reflective practices in action as they progress through their investigation, rather than just at the end of the investigation. Used together with an investigation tool, the Progress Portfolio promotes reflective inquiry by providing a concrete space for students to create a record, monitor, and communicate about their work.

The Focus of This Chapter: An Analysis of Steps Toward Reflective Practice

Designing software to promote reflective inquiry only addresses a small part of the challenge of promoting reflective inquiry. How software is used or not used in a classroom is determined by how teachers take advantage of the affordances of the software, and where students are in their understanding and skills. Successfully promoting reflective inquiry involves the careful coordination of teachers, students, and materials (including, in this case, software) (Ball & Cohen, 1996). Our goal with this chapter is a first pass at understanding the whole context of fostering reflective inquiry: supporting the three components of reflective inquiry (creating a record, monitoring, and communicating) not only with software, but also with teacher practices and classroom activities. This can be broken down into three basic questions:

1. *What kinds of challenges do students face?* What is difficult about working with complex investigations? What role does reflective inquiry play in their work? What shifts in their thinking are needed to move toward these practices?

2. *In what ways is the software effective in supporting reflective inquiry?* Does the task model embodied in the software match the needs of the classroom? How well do the tools support the activity tasks? What do students do with the software? How does the work that students do around the creation, documentation and use of investigative artifacts contribute to their success at being reflective inquirers?

3. *How do teachers make use of the software to promote reflective inquiry?* What kinds of guidance do teachers provide to students? How do teachers make use of the artifacts that students create in the software?

To explore these questions we conducted a pilot study with our first software prototype in a high school physics classroom. In this chapter, we highlight the role of reflective inquiry in the context of a long-term project that students in this classroom conducted. In particular, we describe the students' attempts at a reflective inquiry style of work: the ways in which students engaged in reflective inquiry, how the teacher worked to promote it, and the role the software played. In the rest of this chapter, we will first briefly describe the setting of this pilot study, then explore reflective inquiry through case studies, and finally conclude with some reflections on our design of software supports for reflective inquiry.

The Setting

This pilot study took place in two physics classes taught by Laura, a teacher in a suburban high school near a large midwestern metropolitan area. The classes were of mixed age groups, combining both high school juniors and seniors (ranging in age from 16 to 18 years old). The student population was mostly moderate income, middle-class students. One of the main activities in physics classes at Laura's school was a year-end long-term (6-week) physics project in which students conceived, set up, and ran their own experiments. These projects involved complex computer-based activities where students needed to coordinate and manage large amounts of data and background materials; in short, exactly the kind of project we designed the Progress Portfolio to support. In our initial conversations, Laura felt that bringing in the Progress Portfolio could enhance this technology-oriented project and that students would benefit from its documenting and reflection tools.

The End of the Year Physics Project

Laura and the other teachers in her department had designed the physics projects to address two primary goals. First, they wanted the students to have an opportunity to engage in doing "real" science, where students went through the whole cycle of inquiry, from doing background reading, to generating experimental questions, running the experiment, analyzing the results, and presenting and explaining their interpretations. The second goal was to give the students an opportunity to use computer technology in their investigations. The teachers provided the students with a range of software options, including physics simulation software, laser disc media, spreadsheets, and presentation software. All students were required to use the computer both as a data exploration and analysis tool, and as a tool to construct and present their findings. In the original curriculum, students were asked to create presentations using Apple's Hyper-Card, a word processor, or web pages.

The teachers guided the students through the task of conducting inquiry using two established formal structures. The whole project was decomposed into subtasks that were laid out for the students in sequence: literature search, topic identification, technology acquaintance, proposal of experiment, data collection, analysis and discussion of results, and presentation. The other formal structuring feature was setting expectations to help students get a sense for how they were going to be evaluated. First, the rubrics for grading were made public, identifying the dimensions that they were to be graded on, and guidelines for scoring each dimension. In addition, Laura demonstrated the grading process by going through a sample project and explaining how she used the rubrics to grade. Students also had opportunities to assess each other's work (peer assessments of rough drafts), in essence giving students practice at critiquing themselves. Finally, Laura assessed student progress at the end of each day, indicating satisfactory progress along six dimensions (measurements, use of class time, journal, project sustainment, teamwork, communication). Students received a rubber stamp on each item that they completed satisfactorily.

Although Laura provided a lot of guidance through the task model, rubrics, and day-to-day interactions, it was equally important to her that the students had an opportunity to struggle in their work, to define their own problems, and find their own solutions. This approach meant that there were times when her students floundered, but this too was seen as an opportunity for learning.

The Two Cases

Laura identified a number of student groups whom she thought would benefit from using the Progress Portfolio. The researchers then gave these students a short demonstration of the Progress Portfolio's capabilities. Two student groups from two separate classes volunteered to use it. One group was described by Laura as consisting of high achieving students (two seniors, two juniors; three males, one female), and the second group were average, or "B" students (two seniors, one junior; all male). These two student groups used the Progress Portfolio with their investigations while the rest of the class did similar projects without using the Progress Portfolio. While this was the most open-ended and longest-duration project in the school's physics curriculum, the students all had experience with similar, though smaller scale projects in other classes, and were relatively familiar with using computers in the classroom.

The students' first assignment was to pick a general domain of inquiry in physics from a set of materials and resources that the teacher provided (e.g., the physics of planetary motion, music and sound, sports, or automobile collisions). Our two groups selected music (high achievers) and planetary motion (average) students. After selecting their topic, they were required to conduct a literature search on their topic (using the school's library and the World Wide Web) to get some background knowledge and begin to narrow down the topic into an investigatable question. All groups were required to use technology to set up an experiment that investigated their questions. Music groups were provided with sound graphing software (Sound 3.01 from Tufts University), and planetary motion groups were provided with Newtonian physics simulation software (Interactive Physics by Knowledge Revolution).

We videotaped the student sessions with the Progress Portfolio and the final presentations for all groups. We also conducted exit interviews, and collected copies of the work they did in the Progress Portfolio throughout their investigations. At least one researcher was always present with the group, primarily providing support on how to use the software. The work in this chapter is based on analysis of videotapes, field notes, and computer artifacts.

Reflective Inquiry in Action

What are the challenges in incorporating a reflective style of inquiry into open-ended science projects? How does the teacher and the software help support reflective inquiry? In this section, we will highlight episodes from the investigations of the two student groups that illustrate the challenges of reflective inquiry and provide evidence of emerging inquiry habits and dispositions. We will discuss episodes in which the teacher or the software fostered reflective inquiry (with varying degrees of success). More importantly, we will see the students' progression of developing an understanding of the reflective inquiry skills and habits involved in creating a record of progress, monitoring, and communicating. We do not expect to see students master all aspects of reflective inquiry immediately. Rather, we will explore how students begin to shift towards reflective inquiry practices, and the challenges they face in this process.

Creating a Record of Progress

In order to be a reflective inquirer, students need to create a record of their thinking, ideas, and decisions, so that they can go back and reflect on, monitor, and communicate their progress. How are students able or not able to create a record of their work with the Progress Portfolio? When do they capture their work? What do these records look like? How can the software and the teacher push students toward better reflective inquiry documentation practices?

Successfully Setting up a Documentation Structure and Routine

Early in their project, one of the student groups demonstrated facility for creating a record by establishing a routine for their data collection activities. For their investigation, the music group had decided on the general task of comparing sound waves from three different instruments: a trombone, a flute, and an instrument they had created called the "flubone." They did not explicitly articulate their research question, but they did establish a general plan of comparing the sound waves generated by these three instruments. They systematically embarked on this task by creating a data table (which was one of the requirements specified by the project rubrics), using it to structure their work as they generated and collected sound waves from the various instruments. The data table was set up to record seven notes per instrument, with two samples of each note and information about how the note was generated (e.g., the fingering used on the instrument to create the note), and the measurements they made (e.g., the frequency, wavelength, and amplitude of each note). After some initial struggling with the sound software (e.g., how to record things, how to analyze, how to play a particular note, why graphs looked different), they quickly settled into a data collection routine.

The data collection routine itself was relatively complex, consisting of multiple steps, some of which were given to students, and some that they developed themselves as they worked (this will be discussed further in the Monitoring section). Collecting one piece of data entailed the following steps: (a) referring to the data table to determine which note needed to be captured; (b) playing the target note on an electronic keyboard to hear what the target note was; (c) figuring out the corresponding note on the instrument; (d) figuring out what sound level lent itself to a consistent graph in the Sound graphing software; (e) recording the note to create the graph; (f) using the Sound software to analyze the graph (to measure the frequency, wavelength, and amplitude); (g) capturing the graph in the Progress Portfolio; and finally (h) recording their measurements on sticky notes and the "observations" field. Figure 4 shows an example of their collected data in the Progress Portfolio. Over the course of approximately 4 class days, the students collected data on 21 separate pages.

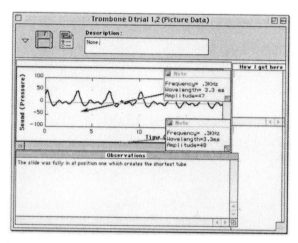

Figure 4. Students in the music group used the tools of the Progress Portfolio to document their data collection. They captured a screenshot of their sound wave, saved it on a Progress Portfolio page, and recorded their measurements using sticky notes and text fields.

Documenting Experimental Trials Only When They "Work"

The planet group, in contrast, experienced more challenges in their data collection activities. This group had decided to investigate Pluto's erratic orbit around the Sun. As described in the introduction to this chapter, their goal was to set up a number of simulations with different arrangements of planets orbiting the Sun to see which had an effect on Pluto's orbit. While both the music and the planet projects involved measuring and comparing, the music group's task consisted of a relatively simple process of analyzing sound graphs. In contrast, the planet group's data collection activity required that they first successfully set up and run a simulation of planetary motion.

The students encountered a lot of difficulty setting up their simulation, however. As we described earlier, setting up planetary motion simulations in Interactive Physics is a non-trivial task. The students were overwhelmed with too many variables to set and no clear notion of which variables were relevant, embarking on a haphazard trial-and-error approach to solving the problem.

There are a number of reflective inquiry issues that should be pointed out here. First, it is not necessarily the case that the students' trial-and-error approach is a bad thing. Indeed, it can be a useful approach to quickly zoom in on relevant variables. However, in order to learn from the trials, the students needed to keep track of what they tried. Students are not accustomed to documenting in this manner. They typically only see a need to write things down when they find the "right answer" or produce something that "works." And, like most people, they tend to overestimate their ability to remember things. This different style of work requires the students to make a conceptual shift in the way they think about what it means to document their work. In this mode of work, "failures" are as important as "successes," and progress towards a goal must be documented, even before the goal is achieved. Moreover, for classroom environments, these "failures" also hold value as a means of demonstrating progress toward a goal. Without such a record, it would be difficult for a teacher to assess how well students performed and in what ways the students had made progress.

Both Laura and the researchers wanted the students to document all of their efforts at getting the simulation to work, including correct and incorrect values and variables. Having this documentation could potentially help the students understand how the different variables do and do not affect the simulation, and eventually help them set up the simulation to test their original question.

The researchers and the teacher tried to instill this reflective inquiry habit in the students by a number of ways. The teacher monitored each group, reviewing and discussing their documentation work throughout the investigation, and reinforcing the affordances of the software by prompting them repeatedly to document their work. Whereas at the beginning of the period, the students did not really understand why or how to document, by the end of the period, through the coordination of the software affordances and teacher prompting, the students started to document their work.

The following example demonstrates this transition in thinking. In this example, the students in the planet group are in their second day of work with the simulation. All of their simulations are resulting in either no movement of the planets, or planets flying away out of their orbits. Over the course of the period, the teacher roved around the classroom helping various student groups, talking with the planet group four times, and each time, she encouraged them to document, getting more and more specific.

At the beginning of the period, the teacher tells the class what they are going to do for the day, and the groups go off to their computers and begin working. About 5 minutes into their work, the teacher comes around to see how the group is doing. The group has been working in the simulation, changing a number of different variables and trying many values (e.g., setting the gravity constant, changing the distance between planets, changing radians setting, etc.). She notices that the students have not written anything down in their notebook, nor do they have the Progress Portfolio open.

> Teacher: *How are you guys doing?*
> Student: *We're doing fine.*
> Teacher: *So are you guys writing down what you're doing? Whether you know what you're doing or not, you need to write down what you do.*

Here the teacher emphasizes that the students need to be documenting their work even if the things that they are trying are not working. One student then asks for a piece of paper from another student, and sets himself up to write things down, but does not actually write anything down.

Ten minutes later, the teacher comes back around. Again, the students have been trying different variables, and have not been successful in getting a planet to orbit the sun. (The names of the students have been changed.)

> Teacher: *John, are you writing down things that they're trying?*
> John: *I'm trying. I've got two things.*
> Teacher: *They've already tried 3 things since I've been here.*

John tries to write more things down, but is confused about what to write.

Twenty minutes later, the teacher returns to the group and has a discussion with the students about the variables that they have been trying. The students are still struggling with trying to get a planet to orbit the sun. In particular, the students are going off in the wrong direction trying to figure out what "radians" are and which value to use in the simulation. The students have only written down a few of the variables they changed on John's piece of paper. The teacher once again brings up the topic of documentation: "Perhaps at least you could write down some of the things you tried today so we could know what you've done? One of the things you could do is to try capturing some things in the Progress Portfolio and writing the results in there."

The students start up the Progress Portfolio and proceed to capture a picture of the current simulation screen. Without any prompting from the teacher or the researchers, one student spontaneously puts a sticky note on the captured screen. He writes: "We tried to plug in numbers to see the earth compared to the moon," and puts an arrow pointing to the earth. (They had previously used the Progress Portfolio with their literature search, and were taught to use sticky notes to point out interesting features on their captured pages).

A few minutes later, the teacher returns to do her end-of-the-day assessment on each group's progress. The teacher goes down her list of rubrics, giving stamps (a rubber stamp on a rubrics page indicating satisfactory completion of the rubric) for the day's work habits. She asks the group, "What measurements have you taken today?" The student points out his notes. The teacher then continues through her rubrics, noting that their measurements were not put into a data table, and giving the students credit for other aspects of their work, but not for their collected data (measurements). In this case, the teacher was looking for evidence that the students documented each run of the simulation and each variable that they changed. Instead, the students have only documented three of their simulation runs. [The key points in the teacher's communication are emphasized.]

> *Are they in a data table? You don't get that one.* Use of class time—you've all been busy, you're writing in your journal, you're keeping the project going. Teamwork can be improved guys. You really need to be working together. I'm going to give it to you for today, but never again if it's like that. Communication, alright. *Alright, so everything but measurements today.* Good job.

The students then continue what they were doing. The student writing down the observations has written: "We tried to plug in numbers to see the earth compared to the moon. We need to find the velocity and the gravity and other variables to plug into the simulation."

The researcher asks the students about which variables they still need to find, prompting the other two students to suggest "the distance between the satellites and planet," "mass of each," and "gravitational pull and formula for gravity," which are all typed into the observations field (see Figure 5).

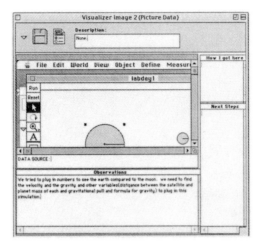

Figure 5. Students capture and annotate their work in the investigation environment (captured from Interactive Physics).

This example illustrates the students' progressive understanding of how to document and why they needed to document. At the beginning of the class, the students clearly did not adopt the documentation task they were expected to do. The teacher had tried to encourage them to document, and they seemed to respond to this directive, but by the middle of the class, it was clear that they did not know what to write down nor how to write it down. Near the end of the class, the teacher gave students a specific strategy for documentation—capture and write the results in the Progress Portfolio. This specific instruction seemed to motivate the students to begin more serious documenting. They began to recognize the value that the teacher had placed on the activity, and had some knowledge of how to do it. So they were beginning to understand how to create a record, and that that record had value in this particular classroom. They did not yet seem to recognize the value inherent in documenting their own investigation process however, as they seemed to be documenting their work primarily in response to the teachers' prompts. At the end of class, the teacher reinforced the value of documenting in her class through her use of end-of-the-day assessments, as she pointedly gave the group only partial credit for their work that day because of their lack of measurements and data tables.

The contrast between the two approaches to documentation can be attributed in part to the different nature of work involved in each groups' data-gathering phase. The different contexts led to very different behaviors and needs. For the music group, their data (e.g., pictures of waves, frequency values, etc.) were obvious and easily collected. They were able to construct an initial plan for collecting data that successfully yielded observations for analysis. In contrast, the things that needed to be documented in the planet group's work were not intuitively obvious to the students and required some extended interventions on the part of the teacher. The teacher needed to emphasize to the students the need to document their steps, even if they were trying different things and not getting the results that they expected. In this instance, the coordination of software affordances, teacher prompting, and assessment rubrics helped encourage students to document. The software made the documentation process easier and more apparent, the teacher prompting told the students when and how to document, and the assessment rubrics helped establish the importance of documenting, providing a motivator to document.

Monitoring

A key purpose for having students document is to help them monitor their own progress. The act of documenting itself can involve monitoring as it requires students to step back from their investigative work, identify particularly important steps in their process, and capture and annotate what they are doing. Do students monitor as they document? Can they use their Progress Portfolio records to monitor their progress? How can a teacher make use of these artifacts to help students monitor?

Laura tried to promote monitoring in a number of ways. Together with the researchers, she designed a page in the Progress Portfolio to encourage reflection and monitoring. As the students collected their data in the Progress Portfolio, their data was saved onto pages that prompt students to note "observations," about the data, as well as "how I got here" and "next steps." These passive prompts nudge students beyond thinking about the immediate activity of data collection to how their data relates to the larger goals of their investigation. But as the previous example demonstrated, passive prompts are also easily ignored, and are only effective when combined with teachers' intervention.

Monitoring and Revising Data Collection Strategies

There is some evidence that the students were doing some monitoring as they were collecting data. As the students in the music group were recording and analyzing the sound waves of the trombone, they were recording two sound waves for each note. In the process of creating a record of their work in the Progress Portfolio, one student noticed that the sound waves they were capturing looked very different from each other, when they should have been the same. This example occurs on the first day of their data collection, as they are still working out their data collection routine.

The students have already recorded and measured the first sound wave graph for one note. A student, Ken, is concerned about not playing the correct note, so he plays the note on the electronic keyboard and tries to match that note on the trombone. Ken then plays the note a second time on the trombone as the other students record the resulting sound wave for their second measurement of the same note, but the graphs of the waves look very different.

Norm: *I think these are different graphs.*
Ron: *Should we use that one?*

Even though the students seem to be capturing the "wrong" data, they keep trying to record the note until they get a graph that looks similar.

Ron: *Amplitude changes based on the volume?*
Norm: *Ken, you sure you doing the same note?*
Ron: *Do 'em back to back.*

Ron tells the students to record both graphs over again because the graphs are coming out so different. Previously they had been recording one note, stopping to make measurements, then recording the second note.

Ron: *(after the second graph is a little off) Do it one more time.*

They do it until the two graphs look very similar.

Norm: *Maybe he was playing the second one louder. Should we, uh ... get rid of this one?*
Ron: *Yeah.*

Students delete their first attempt, and capture the screen for the new graphs.

In this example, the students were monitoring the data that they were documenting, and noticed that the sound waves looked different when they should have looked the same. This seemed to be occurring as they were sampling the same note on separate recording occasions, so there was some variability in how the note was played (both in terms of proximity to the microphone and the intonation). So they revised their data collection strategy to minimize this variability and maximize the "sameness" of the two collected graphs. This example illustrates a strategy of reflective inquiry: monitoring data collection strategies, and revising them when they are not meeting goals.

There were also some missed opportunities for enhancing the investigation. The students were monitoring at the local level of their data collection activities, but missed the opportunity to reflect on the more global level of their investigation question. Their unexpected differences may have helped them understand some properties of sound. They were on the cusp of a more concrete understanding of how graphs of sound waves are related to the sound itself (e.g., Ron: "Amplitude changes based on the volume?"). But they overlooked the significance of this observation and its potential as a way to refocus their inquiry question. Instead of focusing on figuring out why the graphs were different, they tried to minimize the difference. There were two variables causing the differences in the sound waves: the relative sound level of the note (as measured by the proximity to the microphone, and as played by Ken), and the intonation of the note (Ken was playing notes in different octaves at some point, and Ken may not have played the note with the slide in the exact same spot). Both of these variations could lead to the different waveforms they observed, resulting in an interesting investigation into how waveforms differ on different instruments. Not only did they fail to think about the anomaly they observed, they failed to document it, even deleting "bad" data.

One possible explanation for this missed opportunity is that students' knowledge of waveforms simply was not "deep" enough for them to recognize anomalies and interesting patterns. This points to a more general challenge with inquiry projects of this type: they are very complex and may require a relatively deep understanding of the phenomena to pursue these sidetracks successfully. On the other hand, if we could teach students to be careful about documenting their work, including anomalies, then the teacher could potentially discuss these alternative explorations with the students when she reviewed their work.

Teacher Helps Students Evaluate Their Progress and Extend Data Collection

After their initial struggles with establishing a data collection routine, the music group settled into a relatively straightforward process of data-collection and stopped questioning what they were gathering. Although the students were making good progress in their investigation, the teacher noticed that they were becoming too data driven and felt that they needed to be pushed to pursue their investigation in more depth. The following discussion occurs at the end of the first day's data collection. Like the earlier episode with the planet group, the teacher is going around the room at the end of the day assessing student progress with her stamp rubrics. She opens up a few of the student's Progress Portfolio pages and reviews their work for the day. Based on what she sees, she makes some concrete suggestions to the students about their data gathering:

Teacher:	*How'd you guys do today?*
Student:	*We got three trials done.*
Teacher:	*Excellent! Can I do some stamps? You have data...that's good, that's nice...using your class time . . .* [she gives them a stamp] *You have a journal, somewhere where you wrote down what you've done today and...?*
Student:	*Yeah, we got all that stuff in uh...* [referring to the Progress Portfolio]
Teacher:	*Here? Can I see?* [The teacher opens up the students' Progress Portfolio document and looks at one of the pages that they captured, Figure 6] *...It would be really helpful if you start thinking about what...what you have to do with this afterwards. You have three different kinds of peaks, or maybe four different kinds of peaks on here. So you're going to want to figure out what the frequency of all those peaks is.*
Student:	*Okay.*
Teacher:	*Cause you got at least four different frequencies...I think...Looks like at least four different frequencies in just that note.*
Student:	*Okay.*
Teacher:	*So you're going to want to figure that out also. You might even want to write that in there...In under "next steps": "We need to figure out the frequencies of all four harmonics in this note."*

In response, the student writes: "We have to figure out all four harmonics in the notes," in the "next steps" text field (see Figure 6). After the teacher leaves, the students then seem to ignore her advice. They never get around to measuring the other peaks, although they do go back through the images they captured and put the positions of the trombone slide in the observations box.

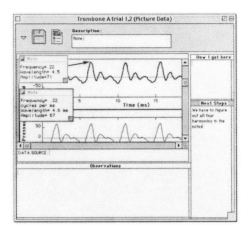

Figure 6. A page showing students documentation of their measurements of sound waves in the Progress Portfolio. The teacher used this to assess the students' progress, suggested some more measurements, and prompted them to record some "next steps."

This episode highlights a number of important instructional strategies. Because the students used the Progress Portfolio to create documentation artifacts, the teacher was able to use these artifacts to review the students' investigation strategies. Student work in the Progress Portfolio created learning opportunities as the teacher reviewed the students' work with them. Rather than merely having access to students' interpreted results, the teacher was able to review the students' raw data and help them reinterpret their data collection methods. Realizing that the students have not explored the data they collected very thoroughly (i.e., measuring the peak of only one wave, instead of all four peaks), she suggested new investigation strategies with the students to help them delve deeper into the data. Measuring the different peaks was the first step towards being able to make more sophisticated comparisons across the instruments. Encouraging the students to measure the peaks of all of the harmonics was the teacher's attempt to get the students thinking about and interpreting the content of what they were doing.

As this example suggests, while students kept track of which things they had recorded and which parts of their plan were pending, they did not assess their progress very thoroughly. The key skill here was knowing or recognizing when they needed to reassess their work process. In some cases, seemingly unresolvable problems—like the planet group's challenges with the simulation—can trigger reassessment. On the other hand, other problems may not trigger reassessment because students are able to continue down their existing inquiry path. So while the music group had some data collection problems (e.g., trying to make sure their samples matched), the problems did not point out the shortcomings of their approach the way they did for the planet group. To get the students to reassess, the teacher had to step in and prompt the students to explore alternatives. The record of work the students had collected in the Progress Portfolio provided the concrete trace of their data collection and interpretation necessary for this conversation.

Our challenge lies in instilling these reassessment strategies in students. They need to be able to recognize and trigger reflection themselves, making reassessment a habit of inquiry. One way to do this is to use the act of creating documentation to trigger reflection by building in more specific reflective prompts. For example, as students capture sound graphs onto their pages, they could be prompted to ask themselves if the wave pattern matched the previous wave pattern. However, as these examples suggest, a more powerful use of the Progress Portfolio is simply its ability to provide the teacher with artifacts with which to diagnose and guide student investigations. Using the Progress Portfolio artifacts, the teacher is able to help the students reinterpret their raw data, talk about their plans for their data, and suggest concrete next steps. In contrast, without the Progress Portfolio artifacts, the teacher would have had to rely on the students' own accounts of their activities.

Communicating

Presentations are an important part of project-based learning. A central aspect of doing research is communicating to others what you have learned. How can the Progress Portfolio facilitate communication between students, and between students and teachers?

Creating Presentations Can be Reflective

The students easily grasped the task of creating a presentation—they understood this mode of communication because they had been exposed to it previously in this class and in other science classes at the school. This ability to create and give presentations, like other school skills, is something that teachers help students develop over the course of the semester and throughout their school careers (Baumgartner & Reiser, 1998).

The task of creating a presentation was very different for our two Progress Portfolio groups. In spite of Laura's efforts, the music group never really progressed beyond collecting and measuring their sound waves. They did not really derive any principles of sound, nor make any generalizations. In the end, their project was primarily focused around data collection, and the act of putting together their presentation reflected this. In creating their presentation, they simply reviewed the sound wave graphs they had collected and put them together onto comparison pages, and added a few literature search pages, a title page, procedure, and a discussion page. The artifacts that they had created throughout their investigation made the task of creating a presentation very simple and effortless (see Figure 6).

In contrast, the main challenge of the planet group was literally reconstructing their investigation, and figuring out how to present an experiment that essentially did not have any conclusive results. By the end of their project, the planet group succeeded in the first of their four experimental trials: getting Pluto to orbit the Sun. Through a mix of trial and error (and help from the teacher and the researchers) the group had figured out that in Interactive Physics simulations (and unlike the real world), planets needed an initial velocity to set them spinning; otherwise, they would be gradually pulled into the sun. The students also worked out a set of values for initial velocity and interplanetary distances that would result in a stable orbit. However, they did not reach a point in their investigation where they could address the effects of other planets on Pluto's orbit. Despite not having an answer to their original question, the teacher was able to help the students understand that they could still create a presentation that focused on what they had discovered about planetary motion.

The planet group began creating their presentation only to discover that they had captured too few images from their many experimental trials, and that deciphering the images they did capture was difficult as they had not documented the variables being explored. So the group's time was spent trying to figure out what these images were, and getting confused about their naming scheme. They had originally set up four different trials in a data table, which they called Trial 1, Trial 2, etc. When they were struggling with the simulation, they would try to set up Trial 1, fail, change something, and call this second trial, "New Trial 1," (They were using the number "1" to refer to their first experiment, which was supposed to explore the Sun's effect on Pluto's orbit, rather than as a numbering scheme for their simulation runs). The following dialogue illustrates the students' initial confusion, and their efforts at reconstructing what they did. The students were paging through their captured screens trying to figure out what they had captured (see Figure 7):

Student 1: *I think this is …*

Student 2: *What is this, is this trial one?*

Student 1: *Oh, this is…where we tried the actual distance but tried to plug in velocity.*

Student 2: *Do you have [trial] four with just distance and masses?*

Student 1: *Yeah, they're in the workspace…*

Student 2: *This was the one where we were trying to decide what initial velocity was needed, right?*

Student 1: *Yeah.*

This example demonstrates the need to document the rationale for decisions along with the interpretation of results. Ultimately, if students adopt a reflective inquiry style of work, they can create a trace of their work that records not only what they did, but why they did it and what they learned from each step.

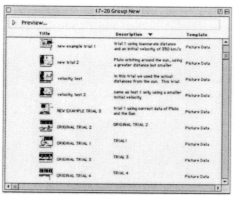

Figure 7. Students review a list of their captured images in the Progress Portfolio workspace to reconstruct what they did in their investigation, and choose images that best convey the tenor of their investigation.

As the planet group created their presentation, they had to reflect on many aspects of their work. As the dialog above suggests, the students had to reconstruct the various trials that they had investigated, noting which variables were changed, why they were changed, and the results of these trials. The students were not starting this reconstruction process from scratch. Although they did have to reconstruct a more complete description of their work, the record of the important steps captured in the Progress Portfolio enabled them to reconstruct the important decisions they made and the different approaches they had tried in order to achieve a working orbital simulation. They had a partial record of their work captured in the Progress Portfolio, so the reconstruction process centered on figuring out the nature of the trials they had captured.

Without the Progress Portfolio, the student group would have had only sparse records of anything they tried beyond what was in their original paper table of values, their meager notes, and their recollections of the trials.

Documenting in Presentation Creation Phase

There is an interesting change from the data collection phase to the presentation creation phase in how the students documented their work. During the data collection phase, the planet group students seemed to focus their documentation around simply recording the values of the variables they were trying. They rarely captured anything, and mostly wrote down things that worked. In contrast, during the presentation creation phase, they were more sophisticated in thinking about what to capture and how to annotate it. The students were careful about setting up the simulation so that it conveyed the essence of the trials, using sticky notes to label the astronomical objects, and writing detailed observations on each page. Rather than simply capturing the screen at the end of a simulation run, the students carefully set up the simulation screen to capture it in a state that best conveyed the results of simulation run. For example, to illustrate the results of one of their trials, they wanted to capture a screenshot that clearly showed that Pluto was about to collide with the sun (see Figure 8). One student tells another student how to capture as they work in the simulation, "I guess we should stop it [the simulation] before it gets to the sun."

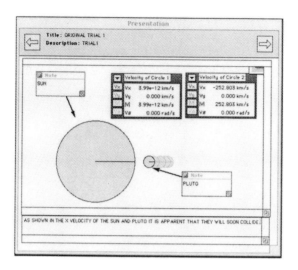

Figure 8. Students re-construct their simulation trial for their presentation. This page shows the result of one of their trials, depicting Pluto moving towards the sun.

In addition to thinking about what their pictorial representation should look like for their presentation, the students also approached their annotations in a more reflective manner. As the students created their presentation pages, they also annotated their pages (using the "observations" field) with notes that suggested an enhanced awareness of their own investigative process, as well as an awareness of conveying ideas to an audience. (These examples were drawn from the written artifacts and from various dialogs in which one student was telling another student what to type. See Figure 9.)

- How to interpret the images: "This is the path that Pluto followed in escaping ..."
- How the trial was set up: "This one was at a greater distance and a less velocity."[Written.]
- Shortcomings in their methodology: "Both new trial one and new trial two have a working orbit, but the actual distances from the sun are off in these trials." [Written.]
- Descriptive interpretations of the trial results: "We believe we have put in a velocity that's too high since the planet seems to have escaped ... the sun's gravitational pull."

• Relating the results to their larger inquiry questions and hypotheses: "We were correct in our theory that the initial velocity would create the right orbit. Correct in our new hypothesis ..."

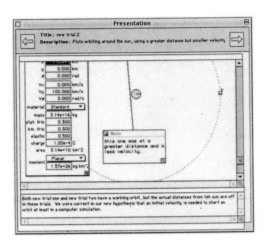

Figure 9. Students add a written explanation of the setup and results of a trial on a presentation page.

This difference in the way they approached documenting could be attributed to several factors. One possible explanation is that the combination of the teacher's constant prompting throughout their project and her use of rubrics that specifically assess documentation has paid off and the students are starting to understand the need to document their work, errors and all. For example, one of the students tells another student as they are putting together their presentation: "Save some where it doesn't work because we need to put some of that in our discussion of results. Go back and save some where it did mess up. These were sort of describing what we did ... Also save like what you inputted for velocity when it got away."

How did they come to this realization? In addition to the teacher's prompting and assessing, the students simply needed to have some concrete artifact to show during their presentation. Since they did not have any successful trials, they needed to show their unsuccessful trials, which the teacher had repeatedly told them was important. Another possible reason is that they better understood the model of work: creating presentation slides is a task that the students understood. They knew what the final product should look like (even if only approximately), they knew who the audience was, and they knew how to create such a product. Annotations describing the graphics were part of their model of this artifact, having been established earlier in their work. As the above examples show, the students also seemed to be more aware of the audience for their annotations. Their annotations took on the character of prose rather than cryptic notes. In contrast, during the data collection phase, the students did not seem to have a clear understanding of what a documented artifact should look like nor what purpose the documentation was supposed to serve. Unlike the data collection phase of work, the nature of the task during the presentation creation phase may have helped the students better understand the need and the purpose of documentation.

One way to look at the creation of the presentation is that documentation and reflection are the central skills that are needed during this phase of the activity. In contrast, during the data collection phases of work, documentation and reflection were ancillary to the central tasks of finding sources and gathering data. So although the students may have understood documentation and reflection better by the time they were creating the presentation, the nature of the task itself may have aided them as much, if not more, than their understanding.

Reflective Conversations During the Presentation

Reflective inquiry was also in evidence during the act of giving the presentation to the whole class. In their presentations, both groups made extensive use of their collection of captured and annotated data images as they explained their inquiry processes. Their presentations featured annotated data from all stages of the investigation, including their literature search, various trials in the simulator or data visualizer, early understandings, and final conclusions. Rather than simply showing "what we found," the students gave an account of how their ideas about their topic changed over the course of their investigation. In comparison to other groups using HyperStudio or Claris Home Page to create their presentations, the Progress Portfolio groups' presentations included more detailed descriptions of investigation trials, and more investigation-based rationale for conclusions.

For example, the planet group used the Progress Portfolio to show a sequence of images captured from four different trials they ran with the physics simulation. A student's introduction of these pages shows evidence of a number of different levels of thinking about their investigation process:

> This one we used, uh, the correct distance, but we used a smaller velocity, uh, we used a one—this is part of our trial and error method—and this one looked like it was going straight into the sun.

Here we see the student using annotated images to:

- Explain inquiry decisions: "This one we used ... the correct distance, but we used a smaller velocity...we used a one [km/s]."

- Characterize their inquiry strategies: "This is part of our trial and error method [for trying out different values to see which one worked]."

- Explain outcomes: "And this one looked like it was going straight into the sun."

The images and annotations captured in the Progress Portfolio also facilitated reflective conversations between the students and the teacher. During the presentation, having detailed images from trials allowed the teacher to have in-depth reflective conversations with the students about the setup of each trial as well as the meaning of their conclusions. For example, on the basis of the four different trials presented by the planet group, the teacher was able to engage the students in a conversation about their findings. As the group presented their data in the Progress Portfolio, their artifacts enabled the teacher to prompt the students to be more specific:

> I know you weren't able to answer your original purpose. If you were to revise, could you state clearly what your original purpose was and what you found out? Can you be more specific than that? ... The orbit of what? Any old planet? ... I want you to be really specific... What did you find out about the orbit of Pluto? ... Our revised purpose is this, our answer is this.

Discussion: Some Reflections on Reflective Inquiry and Its Support

It seems appropriate to end this chapter with some reflections on our own designs and experiences.

Students Show Evidence of Developing Some Reflective Inquiry Skills

This study provides a rich picture of the role of reflective inquiry in students' investigations. Both student groups found this data-rich and project-oriented style of work challenging, and were successful in some ways and not as successful in others. They were both successful in working through the whole inquiry cycle. They were able to generate questions, gather and read background materials, develop a methodology to address their questions, generate and analyze data, and talk coherently about their results. But both groups also had room for improvement. The music group could have benefited from a more refined question, and the planet group had only just gotten to the point in their investigation where they could begin to set up the experiments they had originally planned.

Overall, both groups of students demonstrated some level of facility as reflective inquirers. While they may not have started with a well-developed sense of reflective inquiry, through their work in their investigations, and through the guidance of the teacher and the affordances of the software, they started to develop some reflective inquiry skills. Both groups used the Progress Portfolio to create a record of their work, capturing their data, and annotating the data with some information about its relationship to their work. The act of creating this record helped the students to monitor their own work, and provided learning opportunities as the teacher reviewed and discussed their records with them. By the time the students created a presentation to communicate their work to others, the student groups (especially the planet group) showed evidence that they had progressed in their understanding of how and why creating a record of their progress was important.

It was not necessarily the case that the high achievers (the music group) were able to succeed where the average achievers (the planets group) struggled. The investigation environment being used by the planet group (Interactive Physics) was much more complex and difficult to use than software use by the music group (Sound 3.01). In fact, another group of high achievers in the same class was also using Interactive Physics in their exploration, and they had similar problems. Afterwards, in our conversations with the teacher, she said that the Progress Portfolio "saved" the planet group.

> They had a lot of ideas for how to get Pluto to go around the sun, and none of them worked. But by the end, they could tell a really good story about what variables they tried and how they tried to make it go around and stuff like that, and how they learned about the velocity and the start-

ing point of Pluto ... and how that helped... They could tell that story really easily ... Where this group couldn't [the non-Progress Portfolio high achievers group] ... They didn't succeed in the experiment, but they learned something about doing experiments.

The music group succeeded in part because they did a good job of establishing a good data collection routine. However, their advanced planning allowed them to fall into "auto-pilot" mode, forging ahead and not really monitoring their progress. In contrast, the planet group was practically forced to monitor their progress as a result of the complexity of the simulation.

Lessons Learned About Promoting Reflective Inquiry

In addition to having a richer picture of what reflective inquiry looks like in a classroom context, we were also able to identify some key leverage points for improving supports to promote reflective inquiry.

Understanding Why and How to Create a Record

Understanding why it is important to create a record of progress, and how to do so, is one of the main challenges that students face as they learn reflective inquiry. The implicit task model provided by the Progress Portfolio's tools is not sufficient to develop reflective documentation skills. Knowing how to document is not just a matter of providing "actions" that a student can take with software tools. Student conceptions of the task, their expectations, their understanding of its purpose, and its intended audience has a great impact on the nature of the work they do. This was very evident in the way that the students approached the task of creating a record.

We were overconfident in assuming that prompting students to write things down would be sufficient. The change in documentation behavior from the data collection phase of work to the presentation phase suggests that the students' conception of the task (especially awareness, purpose, and audience) had a significant impact on the quality of their documentation. During the data collection phase, students were hindered by a model of the task that suggested that "documenting" consisted of writing down what worked, and anything that did not work was not interesting. In the planet group's case, this approach to their work would have led to a failed project. But since the teacher was able to help them shift their task model, to see how they could tell a different story about their investigation that focused on the process of the investigation rather than only the results, they began to see the benefit of documenting all of their work, including "mistakes." This understanding was further developed as the students created their presentation. Their understanding of the product helped them to document in a way that they did not do while collecting data.

Making this shift in their concept of inquiry work is key to getting students to document. This has three potential implications for instructional practice. First, it is likely that understanding this new mode of work requires experiencing the whole cycle of inquiry at least once in order to fully appreciate how each of the components fit together. As students begin to see the value of documenting in the latter stages of their project, they may begin to approach the task of documenting differently. This suggests that reflective inquiry needs to be developed across multiple projects and repeatedly addressed throughout a school year. We have recently begun to explore these more extended implementations in a number of classrooms (Loh, Marshall, Radinsky, Mundt, & Alamar, 1999).

The other implication for instructional practice is that shifting student understanding of the task needs to be an explicit part of a teacher's pedagogical practice. In our original conception of the tool, we had envisioned the teacher's role as primarily that of using the records in the Progress Portfolio as a conversational prop for pedagogical discussions. We did not anticipate how much the teacher would be responsible for setting the expectations of use around the software. How the software was or was not used was determined by the value that the teacher placed on the activity through her use of assessments, and her conversations with students as they worked in their investigation. Teachers need to use examples, rubrics, and explicit teaching strategies that can help students develop an understanding of the value of creating a record.

A third implication for instructional practice is that we need to make data collection strategies an explicit focus for students. In project-based science, it is common to focus on developing a question, forming hypotheses, analyzing data, and communicating results. But documentation itself is also an important component of this process. Students need to learn explicit strategies for documenting, just as they do for the other phases of project work. For example, at the end of each day, a teacher might have students reflect on what they captured and explain why they captured it. Or she might encourage students to share their documentation strategies with others who can point out what is missing.

Problems as an Instigator of Reflection and Monitoring

Helping students to develop the necessary skills for monitoring and reflecting on their investigative process also requires a complex set of instructional strategies. Our basic approach was to put students in a pro-active monitoring role. The locus of control for most of these interactions lies with the students, rather than being software- or teacher-driven. Students are designing their own data-gathering strategies. Rather than being given worksheets with tables of numbers to fill in, the students are creating their own tables.

One of the design tradeoffs that we had considered early in our development was concerned with this notion of student control. One might think that the "ideal" inquiry support software would make it as easy as possible for students to make a record of their work, even automatically capturing all aspects of their work in investigation environments. However, because our goal is to have students take on the responsibility of actively monitoring their work, we felt that an important aspect of our design was to give students the responsibility of documenting and anno-tating their work, rather than doing it completely automatically. This way, students have an opportunity to learn not only how to document, but also to experience the pitfalls of haphazard documentation.

Putting students in control, however, is only a part of the solution. Students also need to recognize when they need to monitor their work, and how to monitor their work. As we said at the beginning of this section, the extensive monitoring that the planet group did was very much driven by their problems with setting up the simulation. This suggests perhaps that one way in which monitoring may lead to revising one's strategies is when there is a perceived problem. Indeed, this was the case with the music group early in their data gathering. Their perception of a problem with the two unmatched graphs of sound waves led them to revise their data collection strategies to record both sound waves at once. In a way, this supports our decision to make the process of creating a record an active, rather than an automatic process, as the act of creating a record can help students recognize problems.

The Process of Creating a Communicative Product is as Important as the Communication Itself in Fostering Reflection

Our original motivation in designing the presentation tool was to help students see the benefits of documenting as they worked, that the artifacts they were collecting along the way had some value in themselves and were not just worksheets to be filled out. We also thought that a presentation would really help facilitate communication among students and teachers. We did not really anticipate how much reflection would be promoted by the act of putting together the presentation. Creating a presentation turned out to be a very reflective process wherein students needed to reconstruct an investigation and make decisions about how to tell a coherent story, abstracting from the details. An awareness of the potential audience really seemed to help students to develop a much more coherent product.

There are some obvious implications for instructional practice. First, presentations can be as important to inquiry as the experiment itself. Presentations are often tacked on to the end of projects as an afterthought. Our experience suggests that the process of creating a presentation can be a powerful learning experience, helping students to develop a better understanding of the scientific process as a whole. Second, we may want to consider instituting multiple iterations of presentations in a project cycle. For example, students might be asked to present their project proposal, or their data collection strategies. This can potentially provide more opportunities for reflection throughout the project. This also has the added benefit of helping to establish a reflective task model earlier in the project's life cycle.

Final Remarks

Students do not learn to be reflective inquirers within the scope of a single project. Rather, students need to develop the habits and dispositions of reflective inquiry over time. The students in this study at first did not really understand how to create a record, monitor, and communicate about their work, nor really understood its purpose. But as the teacher guided the students through their project, and as the students began experiencing the need for and the benefits of their reflective practices, we saw evidence that they began to develop some of these skills, to internalize the habits of reflective inquiry. Reflective inquiry did not consist of disparate skills that students learned piecemeal. Rather, learning to be a reflective inquirer depended on the interaction of all of the components of reflective inquiry in the context of an authentic problem. Students documented in order to have something with which to monitor and review their work, and to have something to communicate about. Also, as we saw in the examples, the processes of monitoring and communicating (and creating communicative products) prompted students to document in more sophisticated ways.

Promoting reflective inquiry requires this confluence of multiple streams of instructional strategies: from the affordances of the software, to the rubrics that are used to guide student work, to the verbal prompts provided by teachers. Having tools that enable documentation is helpful, but not enough. Making the tasks explicit is also helpful, as is providing examples, and tying performance to grading rubrics. Instilling this mode of work requires giving specific prompts when students are in a position to act upon them, and more importantly, to provide students with the opportunity to reflect on what they did so that they can see the direct benefit that this reflective inquiry mode of work provides. It requires a long process of building skills, changing understanding of the nature of the task, repeated prompting and application of the skills in various contexts. It requires breaking many existing school habits that interfere with reflection, and acquiring new habits that encourage the thoughtful pursuit of investigations.

The Progress Portfolio was designed to support this process by making it easy for students to create artifacts that can represent their work processes and be used as objects for reflection. The tools help students to make the inquiry process itself visible so that they can review it and talk about it. Our pilot study has offered evidence that teachers can effectively use the tool to promote aspects of reflective inquiry, and that students can benefit from its use. Our current work now takes a longer developmental view of reflective inquiry, expanding reflective supports beyond a single project to explore the role of reflective inquiry across multiple projects throughout a school year.

Acknowledgements

We are grateful to our teacher-collaborator, Laura Baumgartner, and to the teachers and students of the science department at Glenbrook South High School; to Eric Russell, who has patiently programmed the Progress Portfolio through a myriad of redesigns; and to Diana Joseph, Iris Tabak, Eric Baumgartner, and the editors of this book for comments on drafts. This chapter was based on work previously presented at AERA and CSCL. This work is funded in part by DARPA/CAETI No. N66001-95-C-8630 and NSF Grant No. 9720377 and NSF Graduate

Research Training Grant 9454155. The views and conclusions contained in this document are those of the authors and should not be interpreted as necessarily representing the official policies, either expressed or implied, of these institutions.

For more information about The SIBLE (Supportive Inquiry-Based Learning Environment) Project and the Progress Portfolio, please visit: http://www.ls.sesp.nwu.edu/sible/.

References

AAAS (1993). *Benchmarks for science literacy.* New York: Oxford University Press.

Ball, D., & Cohen, D. K. (1996). Reform by the book: What is—or might be—the role of curriculum materials in teacher learning and instructional reform? *Educational Researcher, 25*(9), 6-8.

Baumgartner, E., & Reiser, B. J. (1998, April). *Strategies for supporting student inquiry in design tasks.* Paper presented at the Annual Meeting of the American Educational Research Association, San Diego, CA.

Collins, A., & Brown, J. S. (1988). The computer as a tool for learning through reflection. In H. Mandl & A. Lesgold (Eds.), *Learning issues for intelligent tutoring systems.* New York: Springer-Verlag.

Davis, E. (1996, April). *Metacognitive scaffolding to foster scientific explanations.* Paper presented at the Annual Meeting of the American Educational Research Association, New York, NY.

Edelson, D. C., & O'Neill, D. K. (1994). *The CoVis Collaboratory Notebook: Supporting collaborative scientific inquiry.* Paper presented at the NECC 94: National Educational Computing Conference, Boston, MA.

Glynn, S. M., & Duit, R. (1995). Learning science meaningfully: Constructing conceptual models. In S. M. Glynn & R. Duit (Eds.), *Learning science in the schools: Research reforming practice.* Mahwah, NJ: Lawrence Erlbaum Associates.

Linn, M. C., Songer, N. B., & Eylon, B. S. (1996). Shifts and convergences in science learning and instruction. In D. C. Berliner & R. C. Calfee (Eds.), *Handbook of Educational Psychology.* New York: Macmillan.

Loh, B., Marshall, S., Radinsky, J., Mundt, J., & Alamar, K. (1999, April). *Helping students build inquiry skills by establishing classroom norms: How teachers appropriate software affordances.* Paper presented at the Annual Meeting of the American Educational Research Association, Montreal, Quebec, Canada.

NRC. (1996). *National science education standards.* Washington, DC: National Research Council.

O'Sullivan, C. Y., Reese, C. M., & Mazzeo, J. (1997). *NAEP 1996 science report card for the nation and the states.* Washington, DC: National Center for Education Statistics.

Perkins, D. (1998). What is understanding? In M. S. Wiske (Ed.), *Teaching for understanding: Linking research with practice.* San Francisco, CA: Jossey-Bass Publishers.

Pintrich, P. R., Marx, R. W., & Boyle, R. A. (1993). Beyond cold conceptual change: The role of motivational beliefs and classroom contextual factors in the process of conceptual change. *Review of Educational Research, 63*(2), 167-199.

Scardamalia, M., Bereiter, C., McLean, R. S., Swallow, J., & Woodruff, E. (1989). Computer-supported intentional learning environments. *Journal of Educational Computing Research, 5,* 51-68.

Schauble, L. (1990). Belief revision in children: The role of prior knowledge and strategies for generating evidence. *Journal of Experimental Child Psychology, 49,* 31-57.

Schauble, L., Glaser, R., Duschl, R. A., Schulze, S., & John, J. (1995). Students' understanding of the objectives and procedures of experimentation in the science classroom. *The Journal of the Learning Sciences, 4,* 131-166.

Schauble, L., Glaser, R., Raghavan, K., & Reiner, M. (1991). Causal models and experimentation strategies in scientific reasoning. *The Journal of the Learning Sciences, 1,* 201-238.

Schauble, L., Raghavan, K., & Glaser, R. (1993). The discovery and reflection notation: A graphical trace for supporting self-regulation in computer-based laboratories. In S. P. Lajoie & S. J. Derry (Eds.), *Computers as cognitive tools.* Hillsdale, NJ: Lawrence Erlbaum Associates.

Schoenfeld, A. H. (1987). What's all the fuss about metacognition? In A. H. Schoenfeld (Ed.), *Cognitive science and mathematics education.* Hillsdale, NJ: Lawrence Erlbaum Associates.

Shute, V. J., & Glaser, R. (1990). A large-scale evaluation of an intelligent discovery world: Smithtown. *Interactive Learning Environments, 1,* 51-77.

Soloway, E., Krajcik, J. S., Blumenfeld, P., & Marx, R. (1996). Technological support for teachers transitioning to project-based science practices. In T. Koschmann (Ed.), *CSCL: Theory and practice of an emerging paradigm* (pp. 269-305). Mahwah, NJ: Erlbaum.

Suthers, D., Weiner, A., Connelly, J., & Paolucci, M. (1995). *Belvedere: Engaging students in critical discussion of science and public policy issues.* Proceedings of AI-ED 95: World Conference on Artificial Intelligence in Education, Washington, DC.

Tabak, I., & Reiser, B. J. (1997). *Complementary roles of software-based scaffolding and teacher-student interactions in inquiry learning.* Proceedings of Computer Support for Collaborative Learning '97, Toronto, Canada.

Tabak, I., Smith, B. K., Sandoval, W. A., & Reiser, B. J. (1996). *Combining general and domain-specific strategic support for biological inquiry.* Paper presented at the Intelligent Tutoring Systems: Third International Conference, ITS '96, Montreal, Canada.

Tobin, K., Tippins, D. J., & Hook, K. S. (1995). Students' beliefs about epistemology, science, and classroom learning: A question of fit. In S. M. Glynn & R. Duit (Eds.), *Learning science in the schools: Research reforming practice.* Mahwah, NJ: Lawrence Erlbaum Associates.

11
High Throughput Discovery: Search and Interpretation on the Path To New Drugs

Jeff Shrager
Afferent Systems, Inc.

The tale of science is very often one of attrition, with heroic endurance against disappointments.

-Frank Ryan (1990), p. 89

Search and interpretation occupy places of special importance in discovery. Search uncovers phenomena; interpretation gives them meaning. Search underlies the development of hypotheses from theories, and the design of experiments from hypotheses (Klahr & Dunbar, 1988); interpretation connects observations and experimental results back to hypotheses, and thus to theories (Shrager, 1990). In theory revision, search and interpretation work hand-in-hand: scientists search among possible abstract theories and then, in interpretive steps, revise their emerging concrete theories based upon the selected abstractions (Shrager, 1990).

In this chapter, I examine the roles of search and interpretation in drug discovery, one of the most important and exciting areas of modern science. Throughout history, medicinal chemists have relied upon massive search among candidate drugs, often trying hundreds or thousands of possibilities before finding a promising lead. This technique is so common that modern chemists give it a special name: High Throughput Screening (HTS), and conferences and books are devoted to it. The massive search involved in HTS can be easily automated by robots, permitting drug researchers to screen—that is, test for possible activity against disease—thousands of candidates in the space of a few weeks or even a few days. The result is uncountable quantities of data that must be analyzed to understand why an ongoing search is succeeding or failing so that it can be efficiently guided. Therefore, in order to be effective, HTS must be complemented by interpretive tools that help the researcher understand what is going on. But unlike search, interpretation is a poorly understood process, and computational approaches to it are poorly developed. The result is an "intepretive gap" that widens as data pours in from the ceaseless screening of new candidate drugs.

My analysis of search and interpretation in High Throughput Drug Discovery relies upon historical examples, and upon examples from my current work on drug discovery tools. I shall examine the sources of the drug search spaces for the case of the discovery of anti-tuberculin drugs, the ways in which search was guided in and among these search spaces, and the cognitive mechanisms that might have been involved in the discovery of these important drugs. I shall argue that a large role in revising search spaces and in guiding search within specific spaces is played by interpretation, as possibly implemented by a particular cognitive mechanism called "Commonsense Perception." Finally, I shall describe some ways in which interpretive computational tools can assist in modern drug discovery via HTS.

High Throughput Drug Discovery

Numerous important discoveries have resulted from dogged search. Indeed, search among candidate compounds is probably more important than careful reason in the case of drug discovery. Frank Ryan records many such cases in his history of the discovery of antibiotics (Ryan, 1990):

> [Paul] Erlich [1854-1915] devoted [his life] to the great program of experimentation, not hundreds but thousands of experiments, testing one dye after another against infectious diseases. (Ryan, 1990, p. 89)

> Using techniques that seem closer to gardening than the intellectual exercise of science, [Rene Dubos, 1901-1982] trowelled soil into pots, searched in farmers' fields, manure heaps, lawns and hedges, altered growing conditions, added and subtracted chemicals. (Ryan, 1990, p. 65)

These searches consisted not only of trying numerous natural compounds, but also, with the enormous advances in organic chemistry in the late 19th and early 20th centuries, search at the molecular level, among synthetic compounds, as well. Between 1937 and 1940, Gerhard Domagk

[1895-1964], an organic chemist with the resources of the pharmaceutical giant, Bayer, to draw upon tested more than two thousand permutations of one promising compound, collectively called sulfonamides, against tuberculosis (Ryan, 1990).

Such searches often lead to more than mere selections from among the candidates. Indeed, often the failure of search is a useful result in and of itself. An excellent example of this comes from experiments conducted by Domagk, and his colleague, Robert Benisch [b. 1908], in the late 1930's. Among the thousands of sulfonamide drugs they had tested, only two had shown any significant activity against tuberculosis. Therefore, reasoned Benisch, the common feature of these molecules that makes them sulfonamides could not be the part of the molecule that mattered (Ryan, 1990). This insight lead Benisch in short order, and through some additional search, to the discovery of a major class of anti-tuberculin drugs.

Mass search was so prevalent a method during this period that when, in 1943, Jorgen Lehmann [1898-1989] "without a stroke of experiment," proposed a new antibiotic based upon aspirin, called PAS:

[It] was a deduction so brilliant that his fellow doctors and scientists would refuse to believe it. How could Lehmann have possibly picked out this single chemical derivative of aspirin as the one to test before a single experiment had been performed? (Ryan, 1990, p. 242)

We shall shortly see how Lehmann accomplished this feat.

The method of manual mass screening persisted through these years:

[Albert's Schatz, b. 1920 hunted] for new strains of actinomyces in soil, in manure heaps, in drains, even from the culture plates that were being thrown away by colleagues working on other unrelated projects, indeed anywhere in the world that his imagination would take him—this was Albert's entire life. (Ryan, 1990, p. 215)

"It was salt mine, where, in order to pull a practical antibiotic producer out of Mother Nature, we literally have to work our asses off. The failure rate is about 99.99 per cent" (Doris Jones, quoted in Ryan, 1990, p. 218).

The technique of massive search for drug candidates continues to this day as the most common means of drug discovery, but technology has increased the throughput. For example, around 1976, researchers at Sankyo, in Japan, screened *8000* strains of microorganism to find *three* compounds that were active sterol inhibitors, eventually resulting in Mevastatin, a cholesterol reducing drug (Silverman, 1992, p. 159).

Whereas researchers historically conducted tens, hundreds, or thousands of experiments over the course of years, half a century of technological advance has brought large pharmaceutical companies to the point at which a single laboratory—sometimes a single chemist!—using robotics and various non-robotic methods, can conduct similar numbers of experiments in days!

Drug Discovery and Search

Let us now take a step back from the details of historical cases to examine the process of drug discovery more carefully, and to elucidate the role that search plays in this important activity. Drug discovery involves many steps, including several different sorts of search. First, a "lead" must be found. This is a product that exhibits some desired biological activity in an *in vitro* test of biological activity (called an "assay"). Lead discovery may include testing numerous compounds, which, as we have seen, may be selected from among existing natural products, or they may be synthesized in a laboratory. Historically, such synthesis required years of labor because in order to produce a number of different products, one had to follow a number of different chemistries. (A *chemistry* is a set of reactions, precursors, reagents, and protocols—that is, methods—that combine to produce a set of desired products.) In the past decade, however, the development of "combinatorial chemistries" has greatly accelerated the production of synthetic candidates for screening. The term *combinatorial* refers to the fact that the reactions of the chemistry are general: they can apply to more than one combination of compounds. As a result, the chemist can use combinatorial synthesis to produce the cross product of precursors to form a large set of compounds, called a "library" or "combinatorial library." We will see this in more detail shortly.

After a lead compound has been identified, an analytical step is often required to determine what precise compounds are responsible for the observed effect. If the lead is a natural product or compound, this step requires isolating and purifying the component compounds of the product, which may be extremely difficult. Next, one must produce enough of the material to conduct clinical trials, beginning with animal safety analyses to determine if the compound is poisonous, and then *in vivo* effectiveness of the drug against disease. This may be conducted in animals, if there is an animal model of the disease available. But if no animal model is available, which is often the case, as with AIDS, then the initial tests are run on humans, and are extremely dangerous. Finally, the drug is tested in clinical trials on humans. If these tests succeed, and the drug is to be marketed, another "production" chemistry must be developed in order to deliver the compound in quantities and with the purity required for market. This is almost always different than the chemistry through which the compound was originally produced, and is often the point at which a promising drug flounders.

I shall reserve the term *High Throughput Screening* (HTS) to refer only to the lead discovery part of this process. Some of the steps after lead discovery can also be conducted in a high throughput way, but I am not concerned with these at the moment. The "high throughput" part of the term high throughput screening refers to a parallel or pipelined process, in which multiple compounds or natural products are synthesized or assayed at the same time. When it is important to distinguish the cases in which natural products are being screened, from those in which synthetic products—possibly resulting from combinatorial synthesis—are being screened, I will use the terms *natural HTS* vs. *synthetic HTS*.

Natural HTS requires arduously collecting thousands of natural products, but combinatorial synthesis can easily produce thousands of compounds without ever leaving the comfort of one's laboratory. Indeed, in his retrospective article, appearing in the premier issue of the new *Journal of Combinatorial Chemistry*, Michal Lebl predicts:

> The new chemists graduating from schools in the next couple of years will not be surprised when asked to prepare *a couple of hundred thousand compounds for the screening project next week*. (Lebl, 1999, p. 3; emphasis added)

Two advances have brought Lebl—and, indeed the whole field—to such enthusiasm. First, there have been significant methodological advances that enable chemists to carry out the physical task of combining tens or hundreds of precursor chemicals to form hundreds or thousands of products. Indeed, combinatorial synthesis is now so efficient that it is outcompeting the more time consuming and costly search for natural products (Service, 1999)! Robotics, and many clever non-robotic technologies have helped in this task.

The second advance is in chemistry itself. In order to conduct efficient "parallel synthesis"—a neologism for the obvious approach of putting multiple cakes in the oven at once—reactions need to be developed that have two important properties. First, the reaction must be, to some degree, general—that is, it must apply to many possible combinations of precursor molecules to produce different products (thus the term *combinatorial*). Consider the very simple three-way problem faced by a chemist who needs to substitute an amino group (a nitrogen atom and two hydrogen atoms) in one of three possible positions on the salicylic acid core ring, as depicted in Figure 1: *ortho* (the 10 o'clock of the aspirin main ring), *meta* (8 o'clock), or *para* (6 o'clock). As we shall soon see, this is similar to the problem facing the chemists who first synthesized Lehmann's PAS molecule.

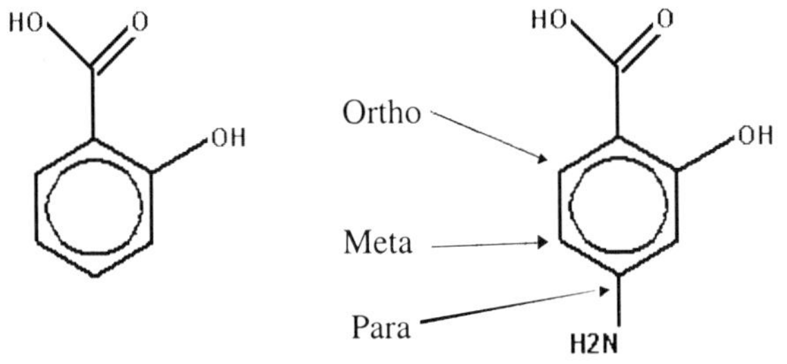

Salicylic Acid (2-hydroxybenzoic acid)   PAS (p-Aminosalicylic Acid;
                                            4-Amino-2-hydroxybenzoic acid)

Figure 1. PAS, para-amino salicylic acid (right) was the drug discovered by Jorgen Lehmann in 1943. It is built upon a salicylic acid core (left), which is the same core upon which aspirin is built, by adding an amino group (H2N) in the "para" position (6 0'clock) of the central ring. O=oxygen, N=nitrogen, H=hydrogen. Each kink in the ring represents the location of a carbon atom, and there are hydrogen atoms attached in various places. Hydrogen atoms are usually not shown in organic representation because organic chemists can tell right away how many there are and where they must go. The OH and H2N groups are organic "idioms," recognized by chemists. Lines connecting atoms represent single or double bonds.

Since there are only three possible molecules that need to be produced, the chemist will be at leisure to use three completely different synthetic pathways—three different chemistries—if necessary. However, one can easily imagine that in even slightly more complex cases there might be hundreds of possible manipulations required, resulting in thousands of possible products. This would require the development of reusable, generally-applicable chemical reactions. Many such generalized reactions have been devised in recent years, as, for example the reaction shown in Figure 2.

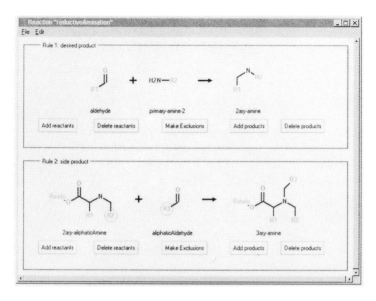

Figure 2. A reaction as represented in Afferent Systems' combinatorial chemistry software. Symbols as in Figure 1, but R# is a variable which will match any atom. The top rule specifies a desired product. It is essentially a production rule that matches any molecules that have the left-hand forms (R1 and R2 replaced by any atom), and combines them into the molecule on the right of the arrow. The second rule specifies a known contaminant, that is, a result that is not desired, but which is a likely accidental result of this reaction. (Circles around R# groups give special constraints that do not concern us in this chapter.)

The second important property of a combinatorial chemistry is that it enables the products to be recovered from the complex, and sometimes messy, process of their production. There are various ways that this purification problem has been addressed. One of the most common, and simplest, approaches is to conduct each reaction in a separate "reaction vessel" (what we would have called a "test tube" in high school), and employ chemistries that allow waste products to be washed off or filtered out. This is often accomplished by binding the desired product to a tiny particle of resin, so that anything not bound to the resin can be easily washed off, leaving only the desired product, which is then cleaved from the resin in a final step.

Another common technique is to combine all the compounds in complex mixtures in the same reaction vessel, and then to use a "separation column" to partial out individual types of molecules from the mixture on the basis of mass, charge, or other properties. After the molecules are separated, the different component "fractions" are collected as they leave the mouth of the column. (We will see this technique, called *chromatography*, again when we discuss analytical chemistry for HTS.)

Regardless of these advances, one might still question Lebl's enthusiasm on practical grounds: Chemicals are expensive—sometimes *very* expensive—and even robotic synthesizers can only produce on the order of hundreds of molecules over reasonable times; not because the synthesizers are particularly slow, but because chemical reactions take time, so that even if the physical manipulations were reduced to milliseconds, it might still take hours to conduct one experiment. Forming mixtures and then separating them can be more efficient, but separation still takes significant time, and is often imperfect, introducing impurities into the products. Technological advances might reduce these delays in synthesis and purification to minutes, on average, per product, but "a couple of hundred thousand minutes" will still put your homework 4 months overdue! Regardless, combinatorial chemistry is an efficient, safe, and easily controlled means of producing compounds for high throughput screening for drug candidates.

Reason and Experiment

At this point, the computationally sophisticated reader will ask why not, instead of actually doing the physical experiments by whatever means, just simulate them? Indeed, high-fidelity chemical simulations have been developed for just this purpose. Even if such simulations do not offer 100% fidelity, they can still significantly reduce the number of compounds that remain as likely candidates, and which have to be physically synthesized and screened.

Simulation, whether based upon high-fidelity physical models, or upon other principles, comes under the rubric of "reason"—something you may do before conducting physical experiments in order to reduce the number of experiments you have to do. Reason also comes into play *after* experiments, in order to figure out what happened, again in order to inform the direction of your search, or to conduct theory revision based upon the results of the experiment.

In making his striking discovery of PAS, Jorgen Lehmann reasoned from the principle of "competitive inhibition," without conducting any search at all. Some molecules facilitate biological reactions, but molecules that are structurally similar, but not identical, to these facilitators can compete with them to *inhibit* the very same reactions. Penicillin works in this way to inhibit the construction of the cell wall of bacteria. Lehmann had read a short paper showing that aspirin increases the metabolic rate of tuberculosis germs. Through the principle of competitive inhibition, he reasoned that a modification of aspirin should *reduce* the germs' metabolic rate, thus slowing or even killing them. But what modification should he make? The answer came from the recently discovered best example of an antibiotic: the "sulfa drugs," most of which are sulfonamides, discovered in the 1930s by Gerhard Domagk. A sulfonamide has an amino group in the para position of a ring that is similar to the core ring in aspirin, as I described above, near Figure 1. In Lehmann's words:

> [...] it was very simple. In the sulfonamide there was an amino group in the para position and if you changed the amino group for another group or put it into the ortho or meta position, then the effect diminished or disappeared. (J. Lehmann, quoted in Ryan, 1990, p. 244) [recall Figure 1]

Thus, Lehmann proposed putting an amino group in the para position of an aspirin core molecule (salicylic acid), resulting in para-aminosalicylic acid, or PAS, an extremely effective, and relatively safe antituberculin drug.

Lehmann had reasoned by a number of means to reduce the search space of molecules to a single candidate from three near possibilities on the aspirin core, but this reasoning had also enabled him to implicitly *reject* hundreds or thousands of more distant possible molecules, unrelated to aspirin.

The concept of competitive inhibition was due to Paul Erlich. Erlich was originally interested in the medicinal potential of dyes because they are useful in staining microbes for microscopic viewing. Since dyes differ in which microbes they will color, there must, he reasoned, be something about the surface of the microbe that interacts with the dye to bind it. So one could use dyes as differential drugs, to poison certain microbes while not affecting their human host. (Ryan, 1990, p. 89). Erlich examined the palliative properties of numerous dyes, eventually discovering that a dye called trypan red was effective against dysentery in mice (though not in humans).

> Erlich now had the most subtle, possibly the most important, inspiration of his life. What if by altering the slightest part of a dye molecule, it dramatically changed the effects within the body? He began a further

series of experiments, trying out a great many new chemical substances, all minor variations from one another. On the *606th permutation*, with the assistance of [...] Dr. Sahachiro Hata, he discovered Salvarsan, the first drug in the world to cure syphilis. (Ryan, 1990, p. 89, emphasis added)

Thus, both Lehmann and Erlich had used reason to reduce the search space from all the possible molecules that one could try, and all the possible modifications that one could make, to consideration of only a few, which led them efficiently to useful drugs.

Commonsense Perception in Search Spaces Choice

Search is at the heart of these important discoveries, but even in the very open-ended setting in which Erlich, Dubos, Schatz, Lehmann, and their contemporaries were working, they looked in particular places, and not in others. The way in which search proceeds is determine by the selection of a search space, but *where do search spaces come from*? In these historical cases there was already significant constraint imposed by the germ theory, and the concept of drug therapy, but why were Dubos and Schatz dredging through manure heaps instead of, for example, through the ocean? Why was Erlich searching among dyes instead of, for example, among cleaning agents? Why did Lehmann choose aspirin as his core molecule, and amino groups as the side group? The reasons that researchers choose particular search spaces are complex and contextually determined, but there is a common cognitive thread.

Selman Waksman [1888-1973], advisor to both Rene Dubos and Albert Schatz, was a soil biologist. Dubos had come to Waksman in 1926, before the frenzy of antibiotic research had begun in Waksman's laboratory. He was interested in the way that bacteria broke down cellulose. After his thesis work on this topic, Dubos moved to the laboratory of Oswald Avery. Avery, a medicinal chemist, was interested specifically in tuberculosis, which turns out to have a tough membranous outer polysaccharide wall, much like cellulose. Dubos' reasoning at this point is very interesting: "I'm convinced," he says to Avery, "that a microbe exists in nature that will attack those polysaccharides. If such a microbe didn't exist, polysaccharides would cover the earth, which they don't." (quoted in Ryan, 1990, p. 59).

Albert Schatz joined Waksman much later, in 1943, after Waksman had dedicated his laboratory to the search for antibiotics, and Schatz was immediately set to the task. In 1932, Waksman and Chester Rhines demonstrated that tuberculosis could not survive in normal soil when certain fungi were added to it. The problem, then, was to determine what it was about the fungi that had killed the tuberculosis bacillus. Waksman did not follow up these results until Schatz arrived in 1943, and within just a few months "Despite all the odds, Al hit paydirt!" (Doris Jones, quoted in Ryan, 1990, p. 218; pun noted if not intended), and Streptomycin was discovered![1]

We have seen that Erlich was interested in dyes because they differentially bind to microbes. Domagk, following closely on Erlich's technique, was able to produce thousands of chemical modifications, which quickly took him far from the concept of a dye into the realm of more general drugs.

Finally, we have Lehmann, who, much later (1943), reasoned from scant data but strong prior theory to the one structure of PAS which proved effective. One might argue that Lehmann was lucky. Indeed, Erlich's principle of small changes having large effects is largely correct; Lehmann might have missed the mark by merely missing by a single atom or position. Regardless, if Lehmann had only come close, we should probably still be reading of him, but instead of the "brilliant" one-shot discovery, he would probably have had to conduct tens or hundreds of experiments, ending up at the same place.

All these examples involve the reasoned choice of a particular space of compounds that must be searched. It is this choice that is the important cognitive content of these discoveries. Is there some common cognitive thread among these? I believe that the answer to this is "yes." Specifically, I will argue that each of these is a result of *incremental interpretive construction*, and that one of the principle processes contributing to such interpretive construction is commonsense perception (Shrager, 1990; previously called View Application, Shrager, 1987).

Commonsense perception is a mechanism of cognitive change, similar to the well-studied mechanisms of analogy, categorization (a.k.a. classification), and conceptual combination, but it differs from these in several important ways. In each case, there is some unknown "target" concept that describes something of interest—in the examples above, this is the

---

1. Selman Waksman was awarded the Nobel Prize for medicine in 1952, as was Erlich in 1908 and Domagk in 1939, although the Nazi regime did not allow Domagk to collect it, so he actually received it in 1947. Many others involved in the search for antibiotics around this time were candidates for awards, including Schatz and Lehmann.

particular space to be searched through HTS: soil microbes, dyes, etc. In the theory of search space construction, the target concept—the search space description—is obtained through a series of conceptual changes based upon knowledge from some prior concept or concepts. What differs between the four mechanisms is the source of prior knowledge, and what is done with it.

In *analogy*, the source is some particular prior concept. In effect, the reasoner says to him or herself: "This new thing is like some other thing that I already know about, therefore I can conclude something about the new thing based upon features of the other thing." Which particular conclusions apply once this proposal is made has been a matter of controversy for some time (Gentner, 1983; Holyoak & Thagard, 1989), and I believe that the right answer is probably that there is no single answer. What carries over depends upon the details of the instances and the goals at hand.[2]

In *categorization (a.k.a. classification)*, the effective claim is: "The new thing is a member of a previously understood class, and therefore any predicate that applies to that class applies to the new thing." The source is a *class* of things—an abstraction of some kind—and what carries to the new instances is *everything* applicable to that class.

In *conceptual combination* one asserts: "The properties of the new thing are a combination of the properties of prior known cases or concepts." (Medin & Shoben, 1988; Smith, Osherson, Rips, & Keane, 1988). This is less well studied, and so less well defined than analogy and categorization. Also, until very recently, few computational models of conceptual combination have been described (e.g., Cooper & Franks, 1996). As a result, the term is poorly pinned down, and is as often used to refer to a particular process as to refer to the results of any process that combines two concepts into a new one, as, for example, do analogy and categorization. Furthermore, conceptual combination is often studied in a linguistic context, such as how the meaning of phrases like "conceptual combination," "combinatorial chemistry," or "drug discovery" are understood (e.g., Murphy, 1990; Wisniewski & Gentner, 1991). This brings with it linguistic baggage that confuses our understanding of the cognitive processes involved. As a result of all this confusion, conceptual combination is a

---

2. The reader can prove this to him or herself by taking any two arbitrary objects or concepts, for example, by choosing random pages out of the dictionary and using the first concepts found on each, and then asking yourself how many ways you can list that these concepts as analogous—that is, like one another in some way. You will find that for any two objects, you will be able to discover, with very little thought, many, many ways in which they are analogous, thus calling into question the possibility of very effective use of constructive analogy in discovery.

more fluid concept than the others, and it is possible to see commonsense perception as a form of conceptual combination if one likes.

Commonsense perception is an *interpretive* mechanism of conceptual change. Metaphorically, one can think of commonsense perception as "seeing" something "through the lens" of some abstract concept. For example, as a result of the general acceptance of the germ theory of disease, the scientists involved in the historical discoveries above all "saw" tuberculosis as caused by a microbe. This can be thought of as a cross between categorization and conceptual combination. In this sense, a learner might be said to reason as follows: "This new thing is in some ways a member of a previously understood class, and so its properties are some combination of the properties of the thing as I currently understand it, and some of the properties of that class."

Aside from its interpretive function, there are differences in detail between commonsense perception and the other principle mechanisms of conceptual change. Unlike analogy, commonsense perception begins from abstract classes. Yet unlike categorization, commonsense perception does not require that the target object inherit *all* of the properties of the class. In these ways, commonsense perception is most similar to conceptual combination and, under some meanings of conceptual combination, commonsense perception can be seen as a special case of conceptual combination, where a class is used by the reasoner as a guide to reformulating the current instance.

Furthermore, commonsense perception is conceived of by the researchers who study it (Shrager & Klahr, 1986; Shrager 1987, 1990) as participating in an ongoing and *incremental* process of discovery. People may take many steps of commonsense perception in a short period of time. On the other hand, the research on (and anecdotes of) categorization, analogy, and conceptual combination paint these as a difficult, large-scale computations, and so we would not expect to find a person doing many of these in a single discovery session of, say, an hour. (Unless the person was explicitly searching, say, an analogy space by trying out one analogy after the other, and backing up upon each trial to the original concept, for example in a psychology experiment on analogy.) Commonsense perception is, to the contrary, conceived of as a very fast—possibly automatic—process. Since it does not require digging through particular instances, like analogy or conceptual combination, and since it is not a gross category change in the target, like categorization, commonsense perception can be carried forward with little regard for the costs, either in terms of resources or error. Indeed, people seem to take commonsense perception steps with almost no thought at all, sometimes completely reinterpreting their knowledge of the system under study "in the blink of an eye."

Commonsense perception folds together abstractions into a continuously changing "theory" of the system under analysis. Armed with this way of understanding theory change, let us examine the four cases that I have described: Erlich's investigation of dyes, Dubos' interest in soils, Waksman and Schatz' interest in fungi, and Jorgen Lehmann's invention of PAS. Can we identify the steps of commonsense perception—of *theory change through reinterpretation*—that led each to his choice of search space? To do so, we must begin with an analysis of the structure of search spaces in drug discovery.

Drug Discovery Search Spaces and Interpretive Change

A classical search space is defined by four components: a set of *states*, a set of *operators* that move between the states, one or a few of the states that are nominated as *goal* states, and a *goal test* that tells the searcher when he or she has reached the goal.[3] In finding a search space for modern drug discovery, researchers begin from germ theory, the postulate that microbes cause disease.[4] If they are lucky, they also know which microbes are associated with specific diseases.

What is the nature of the search space for drug discovery? Given the germ theory of disease, as was mentioned above, the goal statement is most easily determined through interpretation of the goal in these terms: "Negatively affect the microbe without negatively affecting the host." What is the goal test? How do we know when we have reached the goal state? Here there is great variability in what particular test was used; whether an animal model, a human model, or something simpler. Ryan describes the elegantly simple "streak test" devised by Schatz:

---

3. Since the goal test defines the goal, one might argue that there are only three components instead of four; the goal statement being redundant. But it is useful to name the goal, and so it is generally included, even if not strictly required.

4. There are other search spaces associated with the search for cures for disease, including spaces of alternative medicines and therapies, radiation therapies, vaccination, physical therapy, psychological interventions, and many others. Without deprecating these, my focus here is on drug discovery, and so I will stick to the search spaces that are relevant to that particular method.

[If] Schatz had a colony of actinomyces he wanted to test for antibiotic activity—say against streptococcus germ—he brushed a wire loop which had been dipped in the actinomyces down the middle of [an agar] plate, so that he eventually got a growth of actinomyces that took the form of a thick diagonal band bisecting the plate. Next he dipped a clean and sterile wire into a culture of the dangerous streptococcus, streaking this microbe across the plate at right angles to the line of actinomyces, so they crossed at right angles in the middle. [...]After he had cross-streaked, he would wait one or two days to give the test organisms time to develop. [...]If those cross-streaks refused to grow when they came near to the diagonal streak containing the test actinomyces, he knew he had something interesting. (Ryan, 1990, p. 215-216)

Next we need to describe the states of the search space. What form will each candidate take? This is given to us by the adoption of chemotherapy, the postulate that ingesting chemicals can cure disease.[5] Thus, what we are looking for in order to satisfy the goal is a molecule or mixture of molecules.

Next we need operators to move from state to state in the search space. How should the goal be obtained? Since the states are molecules, the operators must change from one molecule to another. The change may be at the molecular level by changing specific groups of atoms, as was envisioned by Lehmann, and accomplished by Domagk and others, or through testing many natural products, as was the pratice of Dubos, Schatz, and (initially) Erlich.

How can we understand this progression in cognitive terms? Through the lens of commonsense perception—of interpretive theory change—the sequence is simple: Germ theory leads one to "see" disease as caused by microbes, thus leading to the search for microbial causes of disease. The discovery of a specific microbial correlate leads one to "see" the specific disease as caused by this microbe, thus leading to a search for ways to influence that microbe without harming the human host. This search is broadly conducted, often largely in scientists' heads, and depends upon reason as well as experience. Erlich "saw" dyes as chemicals that bind to and attack microbes. Dubos "saw" the tuberculin bacillus as a disease agent wrapped in a polysaccharide coat, and reasoned that the coat must

---

5. Although the concept of ingesting or injecting various materials to cure disease is, of course, ancient, Erlich was the first to propose the ingestion of laboratory chemicals for this purpose. He coined the term *chemotherapy* for this, although we now usually use that particular term to refer to chronic treatment of cancer, and use the simpler term *drug treatment* to describe Erlich's vision.

be defeatable ("saw" it as defeatable?), and Schatz "saw" fungi as the product of choice as a result of the previous experimental successes in his advisor, Waksman's, lab. Finally, after these (and many other) interpretive refinements, the researcher is left with a particular search space within which screening will take place. From each of those points onward, discovery is largely a matter of HTS.

It is important to notice that there are numerous search spaces along the way toward a final goal, each with particular goal tests. For example, Schatz' streak test could not determine which of the many molecules associated with the actinomyces was responsible for the effect, nor whether, once that chemical was isolated, it would be effective *in vivo* against the infection, and safe for the patient. But the streak test was a necessary step from one search space into the next; from the space of all possible fungi, to the space of components of that one fungus that passed the streak test, ending up, eventually, with animal and then human trials. The numerous search spaces toward an overall goal might be concieved of as subordinate to one another (Newell, 1990), as interactive (Klahr and Dunbar, 1988), or as sequential. Regardless, the important point is that upon concluding one search, additional steps of commonsense perception might come into play to move into the next search space along the overall route.

Whether one makes the effort to "take stock" from moment to moment during an ongoing search is an important difference between historical HTS and modern HTS, usually involving combinatorial chemistry. Consider the case of Domagk, who was, for the most part, trying combinations randomly, or at least with little guidance, but always within the conception, handed down from Erlich, that a small molecule (initially, a dye) can bind to and attack a microbe. Since Domagk was conducting a mostly serial search (not specifically a high throughput search), he was able to refine where he looked as results came in. Indeed, if he did not do this, it could very possibly have taken thousands of *years* instead of thousands of experiments to discover the sulfa drugs.

Lehmann's case is a perfect example of this facility for commonsense perception to guide search by refining the search space "on the fly." Lehmann "saw" the problem as one wherein competitive inhibition could be put to good use. Given this, and the results of aspirin's effect upon tuberculosis, he "saw" the salicyclic acid core molecule as an appropriate basis for modification into a competitive inhibitor. The structure of sulfa drugs, with the para amino group, fitted the last piece into the puzzle. (Refer back to Figure 1.)

This is perhaps the most important difference between the historical practice of HTS, and modern synthetic HTS as carried out by chemical robots. Modern HTS is generally conducted in parallel, whether by human or machine, and no one (whether human or machine) looks at the progress of the process until it's over. As a result, there are fewer points for opportunistic guidance of the sort just described, nor for short-circuiting the process if a good lead appears before all the experiments have been conducted. One reason that one would like to have the process short-circuited is that although robot (or lab intern) time is cheap, chemicals are not, nor is the time and expense involved in assaying molecules for activity, which might cost in the lives of people and animals. However, there is also an advantage in overproduction. Many pharmaceutical companies now test *every* new molecule against *every* assay that they have in their repertoire, so massive overproduction makes a different kind of opportunistic discovery available.

Interpretive Tools for Modern Drug Discovery

How can the massive search involved in modern synthetic High Throughput Screening be efficiently guided? Computers are of necessity "in the loop," at least in the obvious role of database managers, in running synthesis robots. These computers might also serve the important additional role of search assistant. Taking advantage of this opportunity requires a good understanding of the modern HTS process, and of the general drug discovery problem. Given the importance of interpretation formation in theory formation, and the importance of commonsense perception in interpretation formation, one might reasonably expect to find good use here for commonsense perception. In this section, I examine one such approach.

A principal interpretation formation problem in synthetic HTS is in the interpretation of analytical data, as I have touched upon above: After a compound or mixture is synthesized, it often must be purified and analyzed. The specific techniques used to do this are rapidly evolving, but at the moment they usually involve some combination of Liquid Chromatography (LC or, sometimes: HPLC), Mass Spectrometry (MS or "Mass Spec"), and, less often, Nuclear Magnetic Resonance (NMR). Within each of these there are numerous submethods, and different analytical chemists prefer different combinations of methods and submethods. It is enough for now to understand these in their simplest, most general forms.

Liquid chromatography separates mixtures of many types of molecules (many "molecular species") into several groups, called "fractions,"
each component of which contains fewer molecular species with similar
properties, such as mass or charge. In the best case, the resulting fractions
will each contain a single molecular species. The methods of mass spectrometry and nuclear magnetic resonance analyze mixtures of molecules
to determine the exact mass (in the case of MS) or to provide information
about the molecular structure (in NMR) of its component molecules. LC,
MS, and NMR are most often used in a pipelined fashion: LC is used to
separate a complex mixture that results from a combinatorial chemistry
into fractions, each of which is literally piped into MS or NMR for analysis
of each fraction in terms of content and purity.

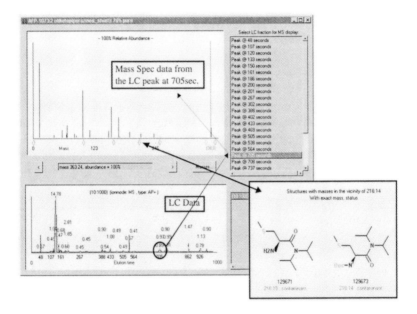

Figure 3. LCMS (Liquid Chromatography + Mass Spectrometry) data. This is data is from
an Afferent demonstration database (© 1999, Afferent Systems, Inc.). Each peak in the
lower pane represents a "fraction" (usually a mixture of molecules) that has "eluted"
(drained out) from the LC column. For each peak, there is an MS graph, such as the one
shown in the top pane for the peak at 705 seconds (light, unidirectional arrows). The bars
of the MS graph represent the intensity of the MS data at each molecular mass of each
appearing fragment species (see text). The diamonds represent plausible products appearing at each mass point, and one of these diamonds, representing two plausible contaminants with similar mass has been revealed. (Dark, bi-directional arrow.)

In fact, the combination of LC and MS is so common that it is given the shorthand name, "LCMS." Figure 3 is an example of the results of LCMS analysis of a single combinatorial reaction product. For the moment, we are concerned only with the main window, composed of two graph panes. The lower pane is an LC trace. Each peak represents a fraction separated from the combined mixture. These come off of the LC device over time, and so each peak is referred to by its "elution" time (the time at which it reaches a detector). A complete mass spectrum is associated with each peak. One such spectrum—the one associated with the LC peak at 705 seconds—appears in the upper pane (follow the light, unidirectional, arrows). We shall examine the rest of this figure shortly.

Knowing what combination of molecular species occupy a reaction vessel is crucial in synthetic HTS through combinatorial chemistry. First, when a chemist is developing the combinatorial reactions and protocols (the "chemistry") that will produce a large diversity of products, it is important to determine that this chemistry is working in the expected way. Therefore, even before a large scale run of a combinatorial library is attempted, the chemist will often produce a small test run, and analyze every product of this run to see that the expected products have been produced with relatively high purity. Once the chemistry appears to work well, the chemist may synthesize the entire library, probably using a synthesis robot. Before the library is subjected to costly and time-consuming biological assays, a subset of the library will often be subjected *again* to analysis, to ensure that the chemistry is still working, and perhaps to exclude questionable parts of the library (where, for example, some mistake was recorded by the robot). Many companies have a standard "passing grade" at this point, so that if the library is not, say, 80% pure, according to analytical measures, it does not go into the biological assay process. Finally, and most importantly, when one or more "good leads" are reported by an assay, indicating that some products appear to have the desired effect, all such lead products will usually be subjected to *yet another* analysis in order to find out what is *really* in the vessels, as opposed to what the chemist, database, and robot merely *believe should be* there. This last, apparently redundant step is often the most important one. There have been many cases where a chemist has obtained a positive assay result, only to discover upon re-producing the chemistry that the effect disappeared because some accidental side-product actually caused the positive result, and the same accident was not reproducible. In these cases, unless some of the original product was saved, it is quite possible that the lead will be lost forever.

What use is commonsense perception in this process? Isn't the decision of whether or not one has obtained a product simply a matter of reading the report from the analytical instrument? Not so! There are numerous complexities in analyzing LCMS data to determine whether the desired product appears and, if not, what might have gone wrong. Analytical chemistry is a massive interpretation problem. Specifically, given the various plausible hypotheses about what should or could appear in a series of reactions, build a theory about what has actually gone on, based upon the results delivered by the LCMS process. Such a theory is fundamentally important in guiding search, and commonsense perception offers a set of intelligent eyes, so to speak, that help one make sense of the morass of analytical data.

To see why this is so important, one must get an idea of the size of the interpretive problem here. The Mass Spectrometer fragments a molecule into many parts by randomly breaking its bonds. Each peak in an MS graph represents the relative abundance of the resulting fragmentary molecules with each particular mass (Figure 3, top pane). Therefore, even a pure product can produce many lines in an MS graph, and a complex mixture may produce *thousands* of lines. A chemist, expert in both analytical and synthetic chemistry, and familiar with this particular library, could, with some effort, interpret LCMS results in terms of the purity, and possible problems that took place in a given reaction. However, the analytical chemists and synthetic chemists are usually different people with different expertise. Also, recall that we are talking about hundreds or thousands—possibly *millions*—of products. It isn't possible for a person even to spot check, much less carefully understand, every result; even a small fraction of the results! Interpretive computing is clearly called for to help combinatorial chemists discover whether a library has worked correctly, and if not, what might have gone awry.

Just such a tool is embodied in the combinatorial chemistry system developed by Afferent Systems, Inc. The chemist specifies the reactions and protocols that define the chemistry of the combinatorial library (refer back to Figure 2), permitting the Afferent system to carry out four interlocked tasks. First, it can *operate a synthetic robot*, and keep track of what the robot actually did. Second, it can *simulate the chemistry*, so that it can tell the chemist what exact molecular species are expected in each vessel. Third, along with knowing what should have been produced, the system can *theorize about possible contaminants*—species that might have been unexpectedly produced. (More on this in a moment.) Finally, given these theories about what should have and should not have been produced, the

Afferent system assists the chemist in forming *interpretations of the analytical data*, as described above, inspecting the library for purity and contamination, and in figuring out what might have gone wrong when the purity of the desired product is low, or of the level of contamination is high.

The set of plausible contaminants is the most important knowledge used in the interpretation of analytical data. Where does the Afferent system get this knowledge? First, in describing the chemistry of the library, the chemist can explicitly indicate plausible contaminants that are already known, for example, as known side products of the reactions. (We saw this in Figure 2.) But there are many other sources of information about contaminants. The Afferent system can also guess about plausible contaminants that were not explicitly given by the chemist. A common source of such contaminants is left-over reactants and reagents, or partially reacted products. These can result either from incomplete reactions or incomplete filtering or purification steps. This is a non-trivial calculation, and the Afferent system must know more than just the list of reactants and reagents in order to figure out plausible contaminants of this sort, because they also include the *partial results* of those reactions. It must know the chemistry in order to compute plausible contaminants in this way, and must be able to simulate the chemical reactions involved.

The problem faced by the Afferent system is quite simple to express. We are given a set of "views" (in commonsense perception terms) that include the desired compounds, plausible contaminants, and possible problems, all derived from the *layout* of the library (which precursors are to be distributed to which reaction vessels), the *chemistry*, and the *protocol* by which the library will be produced. The ground data which must be interpreted are LCMS results from a subset of the vessels, giving the molecular mass of each fragmental product found. The problem is to figure out what happened. Did we get the expected products in reasonable purity? If there are significant contaminants, where did they come from? Were some reactions carried out incompletely? Was a filter step missed or incomplete? Was too much or too little of some product used? Was a reagent or precursor tainted?

Although easy to state, these questions are difficult to answer. As we have seen, mass spectrometers do not directly give the exact mass of the component products of a mixture, and there is much subtlety involved in its interpretation, but knowing what you are looking for is half the battle. Moreover, it could very well be the case that more than one of these problems took place. Indeed, when one thing goes wrong in a reaction, this often leads to a chain of problems, so forming an interpretation of what happened in a complex chemical experiment, even given lists of expected products and plausible contaminants, is not a simple task. Some of the complexity of the problem, and a small example an Afferent interpretation can be seen in Figure 3. The diamonds below the X-axis in the Mass Spec graph (the "mass" axis) indicate the masses of expected products or contaminants. One diamond's contents have been expanded in the lower right of the figure (follow the heavy, bi-directional arrow), indicating that two possible contaminants that appear in this region of the mass scale. Whether these contaminants are those represented by the appearance of a peak in the MS graph at this point is a part of the combined interpretive problem. The computational tools developed by Afferent Systems help the chemist make these, and other important interpretations.

Conclusion and Prospectus

Modern medicinal chemists have a clear need for the assistance offered by computational assistants, like the one developed by Afferent Systems, in understanding what is going on in their work so that they can make better decisions about how to proceed. But would this sort of assistance have helped Erlich, Domagk, Schatz, or Lehmann in their problem of forming an initial search space, and will it help the scientists involved in the Human Genome Project who are faced with the task of interpreting the function of the *three-billion* nucleotide sequence being produced by the 24-hour-a-day work of chemical robots (Cooper, 1994)? The answer is probably not, at least not in a simple, direct sense. The Afferent system is engaged in reasoning about the success of combinatorial chemistry, but, with the possible exception of the reasoning that led Lehmann to PAS, the interpretive problem for the discoverers of antibiotics, was not and is not one of *in-process search space guidance*, but one of *initial search space selection*. Once the search space was selected, their task was simply to try every possibility within that space; no further theory formation was conducted unless something surprising happened, or until the final goal, or an interim goal was reached.

On the other hand, when something surprising *did* happen, or when a goal was reached, software assistance in interpretation formation might have been of significant use. However, in these tasks: forming initial search spaces for drug discovery, changing search spaces when interim goals are reached, and forming interpretations for the function of the human genome, the concepts that are needed relate to properties of soils, of dyes, or of biological mechanisms that no one has yet envisioned, and arise from directions as yet unknown. This demands an extremely broad world knowledge base from which to draw views. How can this interpretive gap, between the development of data and the availability of knowledge with which to form interpretations, be closed?

Perhaps such a knowledge base exists in one or another currently available electronic resources: an encyclopedia, a database of biological literature, or the World Wide Web. Regardless of the source, what is needed to use such knowledge to good effect in forming theories that will help to guide search in biological discovery is a search assistant with a little commonsense perception.

Acknowledgements

Thanks to Kevin Crowley for encouraging me to write about my current work, and to David Chapman for the opportunity to work on analytical problems in combinatorial chemistry. David built Afferent's virtual chemistry system, and played the largest role in design of Afferent's analytical tools. Carrie Armel, Kevin Crowley, Allison Howard, Michal Lebl, Takashi Okada, Chris Schunn, and Mike Travers offered helpful comments on various drafts. I especially thank my father, Dr. Morton W. Shrager, M.D., for making me aware of Frank Ryan's wonderful history of antibiotics. He and my brother, Dr. Joseph B. Shrager, M.D., also gave me detailed comments on the chapter in draft form.

References

Cooper, N. (1994) *The human genome project.* Mill Va, CA: University Science Books.

Cooper, R., & Franks, B. (1996). The iteration of concept combination in sense generation. In G. Cottrell (Ed.), *Proceedings of the 18th Annual Conference of the Cognitive Science Society,* San Diego, CA (pp. 523-528).

Gentner, D. (1983). Structure-mapping: A theoretical framework for analogy. *Cognitive Science, 7*(2).

Holyoak, K. J., and Thagard, P. (1989). Analogical mapping by constraint satisfaction. *Cognitive Science, 13,* 295-355.

Klahr, D., & Dunbar, K. (1988). Dual space search during scientific reasoning. *Cognitive Science, 12,* 1-48.

Lebl, M. (1999). Parallel personal comments on "classical" papers in combinatorial chemistry. *Journal of Combinatorial Chemistry. 1,* 3-24.

Medin, D. L., & Shoben, E. J. (1988). Context and structure in conceptual combination. *Cognitive Psychology, 20*, 158-190.

Murphy, G. L. (1990). Noun-phrase interpretation and conceptual combination. *Journal of Memory and Language, 29*, 259-288.

Newell, A. (1990). *Unified theories of cognition*, Harvard University Press.

Ryan, F. (1990). *The forgotten plague: How the battle against tuberculosis was won—and lost*. Boston: Little Brown.

Service, R. F. (1999). Drug industry looks to the lab instead of rainforest and reef. *Science, 285*, 186.

Shrager, J. (1987). Theory change via view application in instructionless learning. *Machine Learning, 2*, 247-276.

Shrager, J. (1990). Commonsense perception and the psychology of theory change. In J. Shrager & P. Langley (Eds.), *Computational models of scientific discovery and theory formation*. San Mateo, CA: Morgan Kaufmann.

Shrager, J. , & Klahr, D. (1986). Instructionless learning about a complex device: The paradigm and observations. *International Journal of Man-Machine Studies, 25*, 153-189.

Silverman, R. B. (1992). *The organic chemistry of drug design and drug action*. San Diego: Academic Press.

Smith, E. E., Osherson, D., Rips, L. J., & Keane, M. (1988). Combining prototypes: A selective modification model. *Cognitive Science, 12*, 485-527.

Wisniewski, E. J., & Gentner, D. (1991). On the combinatorial semantics of noun pairs: Minor and major adjustments to meaning. In G. B. Simpson (Ed.), *Understanding word and sentence* (pp. 241-284). North-Holland: Elsevier Science Publishers B.V.

III

Evaluating
Scientific Thinking

12

Epistemologically Authentic Scientific Reasoning

Clark A. Chinn
Betina A. Malhotra
Rutgers University

In this chapter, we present a cognitive theory of scientific reasoning, and we discuss implications of this theory for instruction and research. We focus especially on experiments as one important form of scientific reasoning. Our basic premise is that experiments can be represented cognitively as models that incorporate several kinds of inferential connections, including causal, contrastive, inductive, and analogical connections. Reasoning about experiments involves constructing and critiquing these cognitive models of experiments. The theory presented in this chapter is a major extension of an earlier theory, the models-of-data theory developed by Chinn and Brewer (1996; 1999).

Although we focus mainly on experimentation in this chapter, our analysis can easily be extended to other forms of scientific research. Models-of-data theory was originally developed to account for data in historical sciences such as paleontology, geology, or archaeology. This chapter extends models-of-data theory to experimentation. We think that only short steps are needed to extend the theory from these two forms of data to other forms of data such as correlational studies or case studies. In later sections, we will briefly discuss these extensions.

Models-of-data theory provides a basis for examining the nature of reasoning about experiments and other scientific research. In this chapter, we apply models-of-data theory by contrasting the reasoning needed to think about two kinds of experiments: a) experiments typically conducted by scientists, and b) experiments typically conducted by students in schools or by participants in psychological studies of scientific reasoning. We argue that the models underlying actual scientific experiments are fundamentally different from the models underlying most of the simple experimentation tasks currently used in classrooms and psychological studies of scientific reasoning. As a consequence of the differences in cognitive models, reasoning about models of actual experiments involves different cognitive processes than does reasoning about models of these simpler experiments. Indeed, we propose that reasoning about actual experiments is based on a fundamentally different epistemology than reasoning about the simple experiments. Our analysis suggests a need to develop scientific reasoning tasks for use in schools and in psychological studies of scientific reasoning that come closer to reflecting the epistemology of real scientific research.

Throughout this chapter, we will call experiments typically conducted by scientists *authentic experiments*. Experiments typically found in schools and in psychological studies of scientific reasoning will be called *simulated experiments*. The reason for using the term simulated experiments is that these experiments are intended to simulate key components of authentic experimentation within tasks that can be completed with relatively limited time and resources. If simulated experiments are successful at simulating crucial features of scientific reasoning, then they can be used to teach students about scientific reasoning and to investigate processes of scientific reasoning.

The outline of the chapter is as follows:

1. We begin by briefly reviewing past work on the nature of data.

2. We outline models-of-data theory and then present our extension of this theory to experimentation. We also note how the theory can be extended to non-experimental research.

3. We turn to an analysis of the dimensions along which authentic experimentation and simulated experimentation may differ. We analyze: a) differences in underlying models, b) differences in cognitive reasoning processes needed to reason about the different models, and c) differences in epistemological assumptions that are implied by the different cognitive reasoning processes.

4. We discuss implications of these differences for research, instruction, and assessment. We emphasize the importance of developing simulated tasks that capture the epistemology of authentic experimentation.

What are Data?

Most scientists and philosophers of science would agree that theories explain data. But what are data? Philosophical work on data has been dominated by the issue of whether data are theory laden. The positivists assumed that data are based on direct experiences and are logically independent of the theories that explain them. Later work challenged the assumption that data are independent of theories. Philosophers such as Hanson (1958) and T. Kuhn (1962) argued that data are theory laden, so that the very way in which data are conceptualized is tainted by theories. If data are theory-laden, then data can never provide an unambiguous test of theories, which means that the validity of scientific theories is suspect. Much subsequent work has debated whether data really are as theory laden as Hanson and Kuhn suggested.

The issue of the theory ladenness of data long obscured the question of what data are. Data were most often treated in an unanalyzed fashion. Data were seldom analyzed as having a complex internal structure of their own, and the details of the data collection processes were not given much attention. In the past two decades, scholars have begun to redress the neglect of data. Both sociologists of science (e.g., Knorr-Cetina, 1981; Latour & Woolgar, 1986; Pickering, 1984; Rudwick, 1985) and philosophers of science (Franklin, 1986; Galison, 1987; 1997; Giere, 1988; Hacking, 1983) have developed detailed accounts of the work of scientists, paying careful attention to the actual process of gathering data, including detailed descriptions of how experiments are carried out and interpreted. Psychologists of science have also examined the experimentation of scientists as revealed in their laboratory records (such as Tweney's analyses of Faraday's work, this volume) and in their laboratory meetings (Dunbar, 1995). This work has provided a set of rich descriptions of the data-gathering procedures that lie behind what scientists report as "data." It has made clear that data are complex and that many inferences are needed to link data to theory.

Chinn and Brewer (1996; 1999) have developed a theory of evaluating data that assumes that people represent data cognitively as models. Their *models-of-data* theory was developed to account for how undergraduates evaluated nonexperimental data such as data supporting or opposing the theory that the mass extinction at the end of the Cretaceous period was caused by a meteor striking the earth. Models-of-data theory endeavors to present a systematic account of how data are connected to theories. In the next section, we outline this theory and then extend the theory to experimentation.

Models-of-Data Theory

Models of Data

Models-of-data theory was originally developed as an account of how individuals evaluate reports of data. The theory assumes that when individuals evaluate data, they begin by constructing a cognitive model of the data (cf. Kieras & Bovair, 1984). Suppose, for example, that a student reads the following report describing hypothetical archaeological data from the American southwest:

> One theory that has been advanced to explain why the Anasazi abandoned their cliff dwellings is the theory that the Anasazi were driven away by a drought. Evidence for the drought theory derives from analyses of tree rings. It is well established from the narrow rings found in tree rings that the Colorado Plateau suffered a severe drought between A.D. 1276 and 1299, and this interval corresponds with the time of the abandonment. Recent studies of tree rings from timbers in the ruins on Long House shows that the last construction took place in the late 1270s.

We assume that a reader constructs a model of the ideas in this report using standard comprehension and elaborative processes. The model consists of causal connections and generalizations that connect observed data with the explanatory theory that drought caused the abandonment of the cliff dwellings. Several pieces of the model of data are explicitly stated in the text. Other parts of the data are inferred by readers (cf. Collins, Brown, & Larkin, 1980), who will vary in how elaborate a model they construct (Chinn & Brewer, 1999). Models are thus mental constructions that will vary from reasoner to reasoner.

A hypothetical reasoner's model of the situation described in the text is shown in Figure 1. The model consists of three causal paths intended to explain two pieces of data. One of the two pieces of data is explicitly described in brief report: Archaeologists have observed that trees had narrow tree rings from 1276 to 1299. This first piece of data is explained by assuming that a drought occurred from 1276 to 1299.

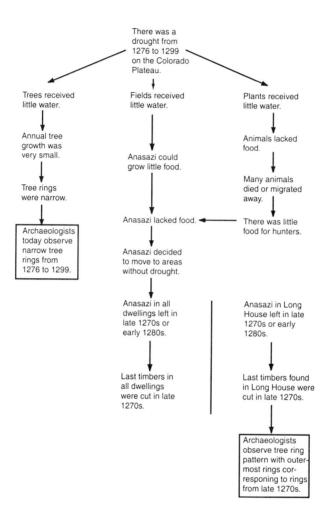

Figure 1. A model of tree ring data supporting the theory that drought caused the Anasazi to abandon their cliff dwellings.

The leftmost causal path in Figure 1 connects the hypothesized drought to the tree ring observation: Because of the drought, trees received little water, which caused annual tree growth to be restricted, which in turn caused tree rings for those years to be narrow. Thus, a drought provides a causal explanation for the observed narrow tree rings from 1276 to 1299.

A second piece of data can be easily inferred from the report: Archaeologists have observed that the outermost tree rings in logs in Long House correspond to rings found in the late 1270s. This implies that the last timbers cut by the Anasazi were cut in the late 1270s, and hence that the Anasazi left Long House in the late 1270s or early 1280s. Generalizing from Long House to other cliff dwellings (generalization occurs over the line segment in Figure 1), archaeologists infer that probably all cliff dwellings were abandoned at about this time. The report asserts that the drought caused the abandonment. Although the report does not specify the causal paths by which drought causes the abandonment, two causal paths can easily be hypothesized. One path traces the events by which a drought would cause crop failures; the other elaborates the process by which drought would drive game animals away. These events together would have left the Anasazi without food, a sufficient cause for deciding to move away and abandon the cliff dwellings.

The model of data in Figure 1 integrates the observed data into an explanatory web of connections, consisting of many causal connections and an inductive connection. Figure 1 displays the model of the data in a semantic network as a convenient shorthand for displaying key events and inferences. However, we are not committed to this representational format; mental models are another plausible format (see Chinn & Brewer, 1996).

Evaluating Models of Data

According to models-of-data theory, the reader of a research report constructs a model of data such as the one shown in Figure 1. If the reader's own theory is consistent with the interpretation embodied in the model, the reader is likely to accept the complete model. If, however, the reader's theory is inconsistent with the interpretation contained in the model, then the reader is likely to try to discount the model by finding alternative causes for one or more events in the model. For example, with the model in Figure 1, a skeptical reader might accept that the last timbers in Long House were cut in the late 1270s but deny that this was due to the Anasazi leaving. A possible alternative cause is that the Anasazi did not leave but stopped building rooms because their population was no longer growing. Alternatively, a reader might accept both that there was a drought and that the Anasazi left in the late 1270s but argue that the departure was due not to the drought but to other causes such as being attracted to new centers of culture that were growing to the south. If the individual can provide an alternative explanation for any event in the model, the individual can discount part or all of the model. If not, the individual will probably accept the entire model. (For more details, see Chinn & Brewer, 1996; 1999.)

Chinn and Brewer (1999) have presented evidence in support of this theory from undergraduates evaluating data in the domains of dinosaur metabolism and the cause of the Cretaceous mass extinction. Chinn and Brewer noted that the theory had been elaborated only for prehistoric data, as is typical in fields such as paleontology, geology, and archaeology. This chapter will extend the theory to account for other types of data.

Models of Experiments

In this section, we extend models-of-data theory to experimentation, presenting two examples of models of experiments. One purpose of presenting these examples is to provide concrete illustrations that we can use in our later discussions of the differences between authentic experiments and simulated experiments.

To illustrate how models-of-data theory can be extended to experimentation, consider first a fairly simple example, a clinical trial of a cancer-fighting drug. In this hypothetical two-condition experiment, patients take Drug X in one condition and a placebo in the other. Figure 2 presents a model of the experiment that might be constructed by someone with a moderately detailed understanding of the experiment. A scientist involved in designing or evaluating the experiment would certainly have a much more elaborated model.

The two conditions in the experiment are represented as two separate models, separated by a dotted line that denotes that the two models represent contrastive conditions. In the first condition, represented in the model in the left half of Figure 2, doctors tell patients to take pills that contain Drug X. Those variables that are known to be controlled are listed within brackets at each point of human intervention. For example, the recommended dosage and frequency of taking the drug are known to be controlled, as are the doctors' tone of voice and the wording used to provide directions to patients. The three dots inside the brackets indicate that there may be other unknown variables that have been or should be controlled.

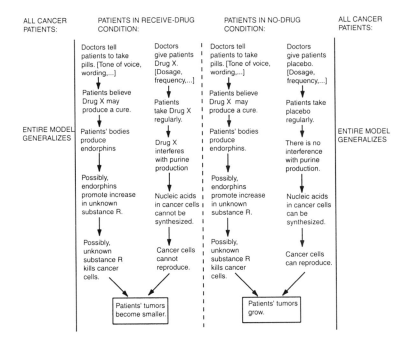

Figure 2. A model of conditions in a hypothetical clinical trial.

There are two causal paths by which the drug reduces the size of the tumors. The first path reflects the direct biochemical effects of the drug itself, in which the drug interferes with purine production and hence with the reproductive functions in the cancer cells, leading to a reduction in the size of the tumor. The second path specifies that patients' belief that the drug may be effective induces the production of endorphins, which in turn promote an increase in an unknown chemical substance that, it is speculated, kills cancer cells. Notice that models of experiments can include guesswork such as this.

In this experiment, the control condition (shown on the right half of Figure 2) experimentally alters one node in the model. Doctors still tell patients to take pills, but now the pills are a placebo. The causal path involving endorphin production does not change, because patients have the same degree of belief in the possible efficacy of the pills. But the causal path that traces the pharmacological effects indicates that the placebo produces no change in purine production or in the ability of cancer cells to reproduce. Overall, the absence of pharmacological effects outweighs the positive effects of patient beliefs, and tumors continue to grow.

The entire model for each condition is assumed to generalize from the sample of patients who participate in the experiment to the overall population of humans. This is represented as inductions across the single lines in Figure 2.

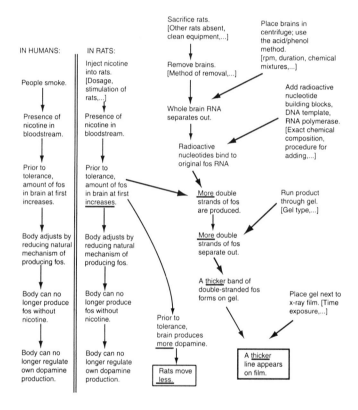

Figure 3. A model of the nicotine condition in the Parkinson's disease study.

We next analyze an actual neurobiological experiment that investigates the effects of nicotine on the development of Parkinson's disease (see Malhotra, 1991; Sharp et al., 1991). Like many contemporary scientific experiments, this experiment involved the use of complex experimental procedures and equipment. Figure 3 presents a model of one of the three conditions in this experiment; we do not present diagrams of the models of the other two conditions but will discuss these models in the text below.

As before, the model shown represents the incomplete model that a non-expert might construct; an expert would construct a more elaborated, more complete, more precise model.

The experiment began with the assumption that causal pathways that are established for rats can be applied to humans. This is an analogical relation rather than an inductive relation. Inductive relations involve generalizations from a subclass of entities to the entire class of entities (e.g., from humans selected for a study to all humans), whereas analogical relations involve generalizations from one class of entities to a different class (e.g., from rats to humans, or from tissue cultures to humans). The experiment was one of a series of studies testing whether the following hypothesized causal path is implicated in Parkinson's disease: a) Nicotine at first stimulates high levels of production of a type of messenger RNA (mRNA) known as fos; b) as the body grows tolerant to nicotine, nicotine stimulation of fos replaces the body's natural mechanisms for producing fos so that fos levels return to normal; c) when nicotine is removed, the body can no longer produce fos because the body has lost its ability to produce fos; d) reduction in fos causes a reduction of dopamine, which e) causes the lack of muscular control found in individuals with Parkinson's disease. The experiment being analyzed here focused on steps a and b.

The study was intended not only to provide information about a possible role of nicotine in Parkinson's disease but also to indicate whether Parkinson's disease in general might be caused by a breakdown in the body's ability to produce fos. Findings about this causal pathway in rats were intended to provide evidence that the same pathway operates in humans.

There were three conditions in the experiment. A control group of rats was injected with saline solution. A second group of rats was injected with nicotine and then examined soon after injection. In comparison with the control rats, the nicotine-injected rats were expected to have much higher levels of fos and, hence, higher levels of dopamine. A third group of rats was injected with nicotine and then examined after they had become tolerant to the nicotine. These rats were expected to show lower levels of fos and dopamine than newly injected rats and levels equal to control rats. The overall model for the entire experiment consists of three contrastive models, one for each condition.

Figure 3 presents one of three conditions in the experiment, the condition in which rats were injected with nicotine and examined before they developed tolerance for nicotine. The parts of this model that were expected to differ from corresponding parts in models of the other conditions are underlined in Figure 3. Variables known to be controlled are enclosed in brackets at each point of experimenter intervention. There was one behavioral observation, shown in one of the rectangles in Figure 3: The researchers observed the activity levels of the rats. As would be expected if fos and dopamine production were increased, the rats showed decreased movement. In order to determine the amount of fos mRNA in rat brains, the researchers employed a set of complex procedures. Some of the key steps are shown in Figure 3. The procedures require that the rats be sacrificed and the brains removed. Through a complex series of steps involving centrifugation (these steps are summarized as a single node in Figure 3), all the RNA for the entire brain was isolated. To this RNA the researchers added several chemicals, including radioactive nucleotide building blocks, a DNA template, and a binding agent. In the presence of the binding agent and DNA template, the radioactive nucleotides bound selectively to the fos from the rat's brain, yielding double strands of radioactive fos. When the resulting mixture was run through an agarose gel, a relatively thick band of radioactive double-stranded fos formed on the gel. When the gel was placed next to an x-ray film, the thick band of radioactive fos caused a thick visible line to appear on the film. Thus, the conclusion that levels of fos increased was based on the thickness of a line found on an x-ray film.

The model illustrated in Figure 3 is a nonexpert's model. An expert could elaborate many of the steps in more detail and add many additional steps. For instance, a more complete model would specify in detail the many steps involved in such processes as the procedure for isolating RNA, the process by which double strands of fos form, and the mechanism by which fos clusters on the gel. An expert would also know more of the variables that are controlled.

Models of Other Forms of Research

The models in Figures 1, 2, and 3 can be extended to many other forms of research. For example, nonrandom comparative studies can easily be treated as a contrast between two models in which the samples are not randomly assigned. Similarly, a comparative case study can be represented as contrasting models, one for each case. A single case study, whether in archaeology, paleontology, or ecology, can be represented as a single model as in Figure 1. Even correlational studies can be represented as contrasting models. For instance, a study showing a correlation between fatty diets and heart attacks may be explained in terms of the contrast between two causal models, one with a high fatty diet and one with a low fatty diet, each of which has distinctive biochemical effects. Thus, single models of data and contrastive models of data can be seen as underlying many different types of scientific research, in addition to experimentation.

Implications

A main theme of this chapter is that models of authentic experiments are different in several crucial respects from models of most of the simulated experiments that have been used in schools and in psychological studies of scientific reasoning. One obvious difference is that models of many authentic experiments are much more complex than models of most simulated experiments. However, it is important to recognize that simulated reasoning tasks must necessarily be simpler than authentic reasoning tasks. Most authentic experimentation in modern science requires time, equipment, and resources that are not available in the classroom or in the psychological laboratory (Chinn, 1998; Chinn & Brewer, in press). Moreover, scientists' experimentation is grounded in many years of study of relevant theories and research. Because schools lack the time and resources to recreate the full complexity of modern science, it is inevitable that educators must devise simulated tasks that are simpler than authentic experimentation.

Therefore, we are not arguing that simulated experiments are flawed because they are simpler than authentic experiments. Our argument is that many simulated experimentation tasks oversimplify the experimentation process in a way that alters crucial epistemological features of real experimentation. In other words, the basic cognitive processes needed to succeed in simulated experimentation tasks may be fundamentally different from the cognitive processes needed to succeed in authentic scientific experimentation. When such oversimplified tasks are used in schools, students may learn a form of reasoning that is in fact antithetical to authentic scientific reasoning.

In the next section of this chapter, we will examine the differences between models of real experiments and models of the simpler simulated experiments used in school instruction and in psychological studies of scientific reasoning. We will begin by discussing differences between models of authentic experiments and models of typical simulated experiments. Then we will examine differences in cognitive processes that are implied by these differences in models. Finally we will turn to broader issues of epistemology. Our claim will be that models of real experiments imply a different epistemology than do models of many of the experiments used in schools and in psychological studies of scientific reasoning. Our argument implies a need to develop simulated tasks that better reflect the epistemology of authentic scientific reasoning.

Contrasting Authentic Experimentation with Simple Multivariate Experimentation

In the next sections of the chapter, we contrast models of authentic experiments with models of a very common type of simulated experiment, which we will call the *simple multivariate experiment*. The simple multivariate experiment is one in which students investigate which of several variables affect a single outcome variable. As an example of a simple multivariate experiment, we describe a task that we ourselves have used in a recent study (Malhotra & Chinn, 1999). (By using our own task as an example, we want to emphasize that any criticisms in this chapter apply as much to our own work as to anyone else's.) The task was used in a classroom study investigating different approaches to teaching children to control variables when they conduct experiments. In the study, groups of four to six children investigated which of five factors influenced how fast Lego® cars roll down a ramp: The height of the ramp (which could vary along one of three heights), the material covering the ramp (wood or paper), whether the car was large or small, the presence or absence of a weight, and the presence or absence of a flag attached to the car.

Simple multivariate experiments are very commonly used both in instruction and in psychological studies of how people conduct experiments. In instructional interventions, Palincsar, Anderson, and David (1993) had students test variables that might make sugar dissolve faster. Zohar (1995) used an interesting task developed by Schauble (1996) in which students work out which of five variables affect the speed of a boat in a canal. In developmental studies, Schauble (1990; Kuhn et al., 1992) used a computer environment in which students work out how five variables affect the speed of a car. In studies of assessment, Germann, Aram, and Burke (1996) asked students to test the hypothesis that when hot and cold water are combined, they end up at an intermediate temperature. These tasks are representative of those used in many studies in developmental psychology (e.g., Metz, 1985; Kuhn, Garcia-Mila, Zohar, & Andersen, 1995), assessment (see Ruiz-Primo & Shavelson, 1996), classroom instruction (e.g., Adey & Shayer, 1993; Duggan, Johnson, & Gott, 1996), and commercial software (Houghton Mifflin Interactive, 1997; Theatrix Interactive, 1995).

Simple multivariate experiments are also found in K-12 science curricula as recommended science laboratories. In fact, simple multivariate experiments are among the *best* tasks found in many curricula. Germann, Haskins, and Auls (1996) reviewed 90 biology laboratories exercises in nine commercial high school biology curricula and found that most exercises were very simple. In fact, most of these exercises were even simpler than simple multivariate experiments. For instance, only 18% of 90 lab exercises asked students to identify experimental controls. Fewer than 6% of the labs required students to design experiments or predict results. In our own analysis of six textbooks for upper elementary and middle school students (Bernstein, Schacter, Winkler, & Wolfe, 1991; Danielson & Denecke, 1986; Mallinson, et al., 1993; Thompson, McLaughlin, & Smith, 1995; Warner, Lawson, Bierer, & Cohen, 1991), none had more than a few experiments that went beyond simple multivariate experiments. Most of the best tasks in these curricula are simple multivariate experiments. For example, a relatively advanced experiment found in one middle school text was a simple multivariate experiment in which students vary the weights placed on the end of a meter stick to investigate how adding weights increases the amount of bending of the meter stick (McFadden & Yager, 1993).

As the above examples illustrate, when we discuss simple multivariate experiments in this chapter, we are not discussing a type of task that is seldom used. We are discussing a task that has been a workhorse for investigating scientific reasoning in the psychological laboratory and for teaching reasoning in the classroom. Indeed, simple multivariate experiments are much closer to authentic science than many other tasks used in research and education. For example, simple multivariate experiments are much more similar to authentic science than another widely used task in psychological studies of scientific reasoning, the 2-4-6 task. Hence, the adoption of simple multivariate tasks in studies of scientific reasoning has actually represented a large stride in bringing simulated experimentation tasks closer to authentic experimentation.

Simple multivariate experimentation represents an endpoint along a continuum of experimentation, with authentic experimentation at the other endpoint. By analyzing the differences between these two endpoints, we gain insights into the dimensions along which authentic experimentation and all forms of simulated experimentation can differ. By clearly seeing where the endpoints are, it becomes easier to see how to develop simulated tasks that lie more on the authentic side of the continuum.

Models of Authentic Experiments Versus Models of Simple Multivariate Experiments

The models that underlie simple multivariate experiments are structurally very different from the models of authentic experiments displayed in Figures 2 and 3. Figure 4 presents a model of two conditions in a controlled experiment investigating whether the size of a Lego® car affects how fast the car rolls down the ramp. The causal model underlying this experiment is simple. The students are considering a single causal variable (size of car). They are examining a single outcome variable (which car rolls faster). They are not considering intervening variables of any kind; therefore, Figure 4 shows a single causal link connecting two nodes in each condition. The list of variables in brackets specifies all of the variables that are controlled for.

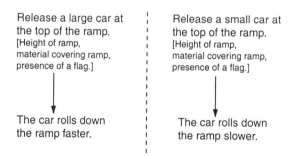

Figure 4. A model of an experiment using the car task.

A comparison of the simple causal model in Figure 4 with the more elaborate models in Figures 2 and 3 suggests a number of important differences. Table 1 summarizes the differences between the two model types along six key dimensions. The arrows in Table 1 are intended to emphasize that the values shown in the table represent endpoints along a continuum rather than a dichotomy. Although many experimentation tasks—whether authentic or simulated—may fall near the endpoints of these continua, many tasks undoubtedly fall nearer the midpoint on some or all dimensions.

Table 1. Differences between models of authentic experiments and simple multivariate experiments.

Dimension	Models of Authentic Experiments		Models of simple multi-variate experiments
Intervening nodes	Many	<->	None
Types of links between events	Causal, contrastive, inductive, analogical	<->	Causal, contrastive
Number of causal paths per model	Multiple	<->	One
Human intervention	At multiple points	<->	At a single point
Variables			
Number	Indefinitely many	<->	Few
Nature	Unknown in advance	<->	Known in advance
Possible values	Continuous	<->	Discrete
Complexity	Constructed	<->	Perceptual
Equipment and materials	Constrain models	<->	Little constraint on models

Intervening Events

In Figure 4, there are no causal events that intervene between the initial event and the final event. By contrast, there are many such intervening events in Figures 2 and 3. For instance, in Figure 2, there are many events between the administration of Drug X and the measuring of the tumor, such as the interference of Drug X with purine production and the effect of reduced purine production on the synthesis of nucleic acids.

Types of Links Between Events

In Figure 4, there are just two types of connections between events: Causal connections and the contrastive connection. In the more complex causal models of authentic scientific experimentation, there are also inductive connections and analogical connections. In authentic experiments, scientists infer that what is true of one class of studied entities (such as rats) would likely be true of other entities (such as humans). In the model of

Figure 4, it is not clear that the students are generalizing to any class of objects, unless they are generalizing to the overall class of Lego® cars. (If they are in fact making this generalization, then Figure 4 should be expanded to include an inductive connection.) However, any generalizations made are straightforward and do not involve uncertainties that may exist when generalizing from one group of humans to humans of other backgrounds or when generalizing from biochemical reactions in rats to biochemical reactions in humans. The lack of analogical connections in Figure 4 is especially noteworthy, because real experiments often involve reasoning from one situation (e.g., a tissue culture in a petri dish) to a very different situation (e.g., functioning tissues in living humans).

Multiple Causal Paths

In Figures 2 and 3, the causal events within each condition in the experiments fall into two or more causal paths. In other words, the models show complex branching and forking. Conversely, each condition in Figure 4 has just a single one-link path.

Researcher Intervention at Multiple Nodes

In Figure 4, children intervene at just one point in each condition, the release of the car. By contrast, in Figures 2 and 3, experimenters intervene at multiple points. For instance, in Figure 3, researchers intervene by injecting rats with nicotine, sacrificing rats, removing brains, isolating neurotransmitters, adding additional chemicals, and so forth.

Variables

In many of the simulated research tasks used in instruction and research, students are told in advance which four or five variables they can vary, and they are often given discrete variables (e.g., only two car sizes can be tried out, so that size is treated as a discrete variable rather than a continuous variable). By contrast, in authentic experimentation the number of potential variables may be very large, and many or most of them are not defined in advance. Many variables are potentially continuous (e.g., the amount of nicotine injected into the rats can vary continuously). Variables must be controlled at each point of human intervention. Moreover, scientists must often invent or define for themselves the variables to investigate and control, and these variables are often not perceptually obvious. For example, when scientists investigate the effects of purine production on the reproduction of cancer cells, the very concept of purine production is the product of complex research programs designed to establish the reality of substances such as purine (see Latour & Woolgar, 1986). Often the variables that are manipulated and controlled are complex theoretical constructions developed by scientists.

Equipment and Materials

Many of the causal connections in models of authentic experiments are constrained by the properties of equipment and auxiliary substances used in the experiments. Indeed, some causal connections embody a theory of how pieces of equipment work. For instance, a complete causal model of the centrifugation process would embody a theory of how centrifuges work. Similarly, the causal model makes assumptions about how chemicals such as fos, nucleotides, and binding chemicals interact. Many such assumptions go into the construction of a model of the experiment. The simple model in Figure 4 is much less dependent on such auxiliary theories of equipment and materials.

Summary

Table 1 summarizes key differences between models of authentic experiments and models of simple multivariate experiments. The dimensions in Table 1 define continua along which models of experiments may vary. In the next section, we discuss implications of these differences for the cognitive processes that are involved in reasoning.

Differences in Cognitive Processes Used in Authentic Experimentation Versus Simple Multivariate Experimentation

In order to teach students to conduct and interpret experiments, it is crucial to know what cognitive and social processes are involved in actual experimentation. We believe that some of the cognitive processes involved in authentic experimentation are very different from the cognitive processes involved in simple multivariate experimentation. We also think that our analysis of the differences between models of experiments provides a good basis for examining differences in cognitive processes.

Table 2. Differences in cognitive processes between authentic experimentation and simple multivariate experimentation.

Cognitive process	Authentic experimentation		Simple multivariate experimentation
Generating research question	Researcher must develop research question, often with societal purposes in mind	<->	Research question is provided
Designing Experiments			
Selecting variables	Select and even construct variables to investigate	<->	Choose among provided variables
Planning procedures	Creative act of inventing a model of an experiment	<->	Straightforward act of following the same procedure many times
	Decide on an appropriate analog	<->	No analogs are involved
Controlling variables	Multiple controls are needed	<->	Single control is needed
	What to control is not straightforward	<->	What to control is straightforward
Planning measures	Multiple measures of independent, intervening, and dependent variables are used	<->	Single dependent variable is used
	Each measure may involve a complex series of steps	<->	The one measure is straightforward
Making observations	There are checks on perceptual and other biases	<->	There are often no such checks
Explaining results			
Transforming observations	Observations are transformed into other data formats	<->	There is little or no transformation of observations
Finding flaws	Much worry about experimental error	<->	Little worry about experimental error

(Table 2 continued)

Indirect reasoning	Indirect paths of inference	<->	Straightforward inferences
Generalizations	Uncertain generalizations or analogies	<->	Simple or nonexistent generalizations
Type of reasoning	Multiple reasoning processes	<->	Simple contrastive causal reasoning
Developing theories			
Level of theory	Theories are about unseen mechanisms	<->	Theories are about observable phenomena
Coordinating results	Coordinate results from many studies of different types, including studies at level of observable phenomena and studies at level of underlying mechanisms	<->	Coordinate results from a single type of study
	Results are partially conflicting	<->	Results are generally consistent
	Theories are about unseen mechanisms	<->	Theories are about observable phenomena
Studying others' research	Researchers read or hear about other expert research reports	<->	There are no research reports

Again, as a point of departure to consider the full range of simulated experimentation tasks, we examine several of the differences in cognitive processes involved in authentic experimentation versus simple multivariate experiments. Our analysis of these differences is not intended to be exhaustive. On the contrary, we believe that this is an area in particular need of further work. In making our comparisons, we will consider the following general processes involved in experimentation: a) Generating a research question, b) designing experiments, c) making observations, d) explaining results, e) developing theories, and f) studying others' research. The key differences are summarized in Table 2, again with each dimension treated as a continuum rather than as a dichotomy. In the following section, we discuss differences in each of these cognitive processes in authentic versus simple multivariate experimentation. We also note how the differences in cognitive processes are related to the differences in the models that underlie the two types of experiments.

Generating a Research Question

In most simple multivariate experimentation, students are provided with the research question. In authentic experimentation, researchers must develop their own research questions. Among many criteria used to choose research questions, a common one is to select questions with a view toward solving societal problems. The desire to solve societal problems is reflected in the fact that models of many authentic experiments include causal paths that pertain to real world problems, such as the causal path that is intended to explain the progression of Parkinson's disease in Figure 3 and the causal path that leads to smaller tumors in Figure 2. The model of Figure 4 does not incorporate such societally relevant causal paths.

Designing experiments

We consider four aspects of designing an experiment: Selecting variables, planning procedures, controlling variables, and planning measures.

Selecting Variables

In simple multivariate experimentation, generating a research question is a trivial matter. Students simply investigate one or more of the several variables that are provided to them. For instance, in the car task, students simply decide whether they want to investigate ramp height, ramp material, car size, whether a weight is present, and/or whether a flag is present. In authentic experimentation, variables are not provided, and, as we noted earlier, they must often be constructed. This difference is reflected in the fact that models of simple multivariate experiments exhaustively list all variables to be included, whereas models of authentic experiments include partial lists of possible variables, many of which are complex cognitive constructions.

Planning Procedures

In the typical simple multivariate experiment, planning procedures is trivial. The model of the experiment is transparent, and manipulations are as simple as clicking several buttons on a computer screen or releasing cars from two ramps simultaneously. In authentic experimentation, planning a treatment involves inventing a complex model of an experiment such as the ones shown in Figures 2 and 3. Many steps may be needed in the procedure, such as the array of steps needed to isolate relevant chemicals. Designing an experiment can require considerable ingenuity because of the complexity of the models needed to generate interpretable data.

In addition, authentic experimentation often involves a difficult process of choosing a simpler system to function as an analog or simplified model of the system of interest. For example, the experiment on the effects of nicotine on Parkinson's disease used rat physiology as an analog to human physiology. Similarly, geologists use high-pressure laboratory experiments to simulate the pressures at the earth's mantle in order to support theories about mineral behavior in the mantle. These analogs are expressed through the analogical links in models of authentic experiments. Simple multivariate experiments do not employ such analogs.

Controlling Variables

In simple multivariate experimentation, controlling variables is a simple matter of varying one of the four or five provided variables while keeping the other variables constant. This task is much simpler than the task of controlling variables in authentic experimentation, in which it can be difficult to determine whether all relevant variables have in fact been controlled. In addition, controlling variables does not only mean holding unmanipulated variables constant; sometimes it means letting such variables vary randomly, a strategy that does not appear in simple multivariate experiments.

An example of the difficulty of controlling variables in authentic experimentation comes from the history of clinical drug trials. At first, controlling variables seemed to mean that half of the patients should receive the drug being tested, and the other half should not. These conditions reflected a contrast between a simple pair of models. In one, taking the drug produced biochemical changes that produced better health; in the other, not taking a drug produced no such changes. However, it was later realized that these simple models left out several crucial steps, including events such as the doctor being told who receives the drug and the patients being told whether they are receiving a drug. When patients know that they are receiving a treatment, this can lead to psychosomatic healing effects, and when doctors know that their patients are receiving the drug, they may behave in ways that promote healing. This change in knowledge can be viewed as generating a more elaborated model of the causal processes involved in healing. Once this elaborated model is generated, the need for new controls becomes obvious. Controls must exist not only for the use of the drug but also for the type of information available to doctors and patients. This example shows that devising controls in authentic experimentation depends on having a detailed and accurate causal model of all the relevant events in the experimental procedure.

Planning Measures

In simple multivariate experimentation, there is only one measured outcome variable. In the car task, the only outcome variable that students measure is the relative speed of the two cars as they roll down the ramp. In the contrastive models shown in Figure 4, this one outcome variable corresponds to a measurement taken at the only node that follows the release of the cars, which indicates the relative speed of the cars as they travel down the ramp.

In authentic experimentation, multiple variables are typically measured. Each variable that is measured corresponds to one of the nodes in the model of the experiment. For instance, in Figure 2 the various nodes on the causal path include events such as the size of the tumor getting smaller, increases or decreases in various chemicals in the body, and increased confidence of the patients. Measurements can be made to check expectations at each of these nodes. These various measures can include *measures of outcome variables,* such as the overall survival rate of patients or the size of tumors, *measures of intervening variables* that mediate the expected outcomes such as the presence of expected intermediary chemicals in the bloodstream or greater confidence exhibited by patients who believe that they are taking an effective medicine, and *manipulation checks* such as measures of whether patients actually took the drug as directed. Each of these variables corresponds to a different node in the causal path in Figure 2. The many nodes in the complex causal models that underlie authentic experiments suggest many different points of potential measurement. The simple causal models that underlie simple multivariate experimentation do not provide multiple nodes at which measurements can be made.

Each measurement can lead to complex branching of the model of the experiment. For example, in Figure 3, most of the model consists of the complex steps needed to measure the level of fos mRNA. Each measurement may potentially involve such complex branching causal paths.

In authentic experimentation, all four aspects of designing experiments—selecting variables, planning procedures, controlling variables, and planning measures—are ultimately intended to create linkages between theoretical and empirical components of a model that is so strong that other scientists are persuaded to accept the model. This differs from simple multivariate experimentation, in which persuading others is seldom part of the scientific reasoning process.

Making Observations

Scientists often employ elaborate procedures to ensure that their observations are accurate and not distorted by human bias (Bogen & Woodward, 1988). Indeed, many observations are automated so as to avoid any human bias at all. Such procedures show up in models as complex causal paths constructed to create unbiased measurements. This need to devise methods to control perceptual bias does not arise in most simulated multivariate tasks, where it is assumed that the observer can straightforwardly observe and register the outcome without any special perceptual aids beyond rulers and other simple measuring devices.

Explaining Results

The rules for explaining results of simple multivariate experimentation tasks are straightforward. Not counting interactions, there are basically three rules for correct reasoning:

1. *Identifying a causal variable:* If two causes are identical except for Variable X, and if there is a difference in outcome, conclude that X is causal.

2. *Identifying a noncausal variable:* If the two causes are identical except for X, and there is no difference in outcome, conclude that X is not causal.

3. *Concluding that no conclusion is possible:* If the two causes vary along two or more variables, then no conclusion can be drawn about the causal effect of any variable.

When interactions are included in the mix, the rules become more complex, but because all variables are known in advance and procedures are simple, the reasoning can be encapsulated in a small number of rules. This form of reasoning differs from reasoning about authentic experiments in at least five important ways, as discussed below.

Transforming Observations

Authentic experimentation often involves transforming observations into other data formats. Observations may be coded, recoded, diagrammed, tabled, summarized, mathematically transformed, or statistically analyzed before yielding the data that are in a format that can be interpreted. In simple multivariate experimentation, by contrast, there is seldom if ever any transformation of data into other formats. Students usually explain their observations without re-representing their observations in any way.

Finding Flaws

In simple multivariate experimentation, there is little consideration of possible sources of error in the experiment beyond rudimentary failure to control variables. In authentic experimentation, scientists scrutinize both their own experiments and others' experiments for flaws in methodology and interpretation (see Brewer & Chinn, 1994). According to models-of-data theory, when people evaluate data, they first construct a model of the data, and then they evaluate each node and link in the model to see if there are any plausible counterexplanations. For instance, in Figure 3, an individual might reason that the observed pattern of lines on the agarose gel was caused by errors in the centrifugation process rather than by the actual presence of high levels of fos mRNA, or the individual might agree that there was an increase in dopamine production but argue that other internal processes that do not directly involve nicotine could be responsible for this increase. Questioning inferences involves searching memory for plausible alternative explanations for events in the model of the experiment. Such processes are less likely to occur in simple multivariate experimentation, because the simple models that underlie these experiments have many fewer inferences that can be questioned.

Indirect Inferences

In most simple multivariate experimentation, the observation is straightforwardly linked to the research question. For example, in the car task, the research question asks which car moves faster, and the raw observation is which car moves faster down the ramp. In authentic experimentation, the observation is often linked to the research question by indirect paths of inference. In the experiment represented in Figure 3, the research question is whether nicotine causes an increase in fos mRNA in the brain. The raw observation is the pattern of lines on an x-ray film. The conceptual relationship between the observation and the theoretical claim is captured in the complex array of nodes and links in the model of the experiment. In classrooms that employ only simple multivariate experiments, children do not have opportunities to experience the indirect paths of inference between the observation and the research question.

Nature of Generalizations

As we noted earlier, the models of authentic experiments usually include inductive or analogical inferences. For instance, in the case of Figure 3, the experiment assumes that one can legitimately analogize from rats to humans. Such generalizations are uncommon in simple multivariate experiments. In the Lego® car task, students do not talk about the extent to which the results can be generalized. Schauble, Glaser, Duschl, Schulze, & John (1995) have presented evidence that many children do not fully understand analogies between experimental tasks and the real-world situations that the tasks are supposed to represent.

Types of Reasoning

In simple multivariate experimentation, the only form of reasoning needed is simple causal inference across contrastive conditions. In authentic reasoning, more complex reasoning is needed to develop explanatory models that integrate explanations with data. These forms of reasoning include such processes as inferring unseen mechanisms, ruling out alternative explanations, determining which explanation is simpler or has broader explanatory scope, and deciding how far a result can be generalized.

Developing Theories

At least two important aspects of the process of developing theories differ between authentic experimentation and simple multivariate experimentation.

Level of theory

Simple multivariate experiments are about empirical regularities such as the observable factors that influence the speed of a car or the observable variables that affect plant growth. These tasks do not afford any opportunity to investigate underlying mechanisms. Authentic experiments are often about unseen mechanisms that employ unobservable entities such as forces, molecules, and levels of fos mRNA. Such unseen entities and events are prominent in models of authentic experiments but are not found in models of simple multivariate experiments.

Coordinating Results

When scientists make choices between theories, they must coordinate results from different types of studies. For example, scientists investigating the effects of a pharmaceutical product can conduct clinical trials on humans, correlational studies with humans, studies with animals, and studies using tissue cultures. Each of these general types of experiments can include different types of specific studies. Moreover, different types of studies are directed at different levels of analysis. Reasoning involves coordinating research at the level of observable phenomena with research at the level of underlying mechanisms. For instance, medical scientists work to coordinate results of research at the observable level (e.g., a correlational study of the effects of a high-dairy-product diet on cancer) with the results of research at the level of underlying mechanism (e.g., an experiment on the effects of Vitamin D on the action of the enzyme alkaline phosphatase in cancerous cells).

Often the use of different methods leads to conflicting data. In the history of microscopic analyses of cells, some methods of preparing specimens indicated the presence of a structure called mesosomes, but only in gram positive bacteria, whereas the freeze fraction method of preparation showed no such structure in any kind of bacteria (Rasmussen, 1993). Scientists must sift through such conflicting results in order to reach conclusions. In terms of models of data, this means that scientists must draw conclusions from multiple studies, each having a unique underlying model.

In simple multivariate experimentation, students conduct just one type of experiment over and over. They can try different variables as they release cars down ramps, but each experiment has the same basic structure. Such tasks give students no experience with the reasoning processes needed to coordinate results from different kinds of studies. In simple multivariate experimentation, all experiments have essentially the same model, which precludes the need to engage in complex processes of developing mutually consistent models of different experiments.

Studying Others' Research

In authentic science, all of the cognitive processes discussed in this section employ a rich knowledge base of information about other scientists' research—their theories, their methods, their patterns of explanation. Scientists develop this knowledge base by reading and hearing about other scientists' research reports. Scientists build both on extensive knowledge of other scientists' theories and experimental procedures so that they do not have to construct new models of experiments from scratch but can instead refine previously developed models (cf. Dunbar, 1995). All of these processes present a sharp contrast with most school science, which involves little or no reading of research reports nor any building upon earlier models of experiments developed by others.

Differences in Epistemology

As we noted earlier, it is inevitable that simple multivariate experimentation will be simpler than authentic experimentation. When teaching children to reason scientifically or when investigating children's reasoning, the only feasible option is to use relatively simple tasks that fit within the available time and resources.

We suggest that a useful guideline for developing simulated tasks is to develop tasks that reflect the *epistemology* of authentic science to the greatest degree possible. By epistemology we mean the basic principles that guide decisions about when and how to change one's knowledge in response to evidence. Some simulated tasks share little of the epistemology of authentic experimentation; other tasks may share some or most of the basic epistemology of authentic experimentation. The goal should be to create simulated tasks that simulate the epistemology of authentic experimentation.

Unfortunately, many current simulated experimentation tasks appear to differ from authentic experimentation in several key aspects of epistemology. Many current simulated tasks (including ones that we have developed) do not simply create a simpler version of scientific experimentation; they create a profoundly altered version of scientific experimentation. This is certainly true of the simple multivariate experiments that we have been discussing. In this section we discuss several of the ways in which simple multivariate experimentation may actually foster a false sense of what scientific reasoning is. Once again, our purpose in making the contrast between authentic experimentation and simple multivariate experimentation is to get clear on dimensions that can then be used to analyze other types of simulated scientific reasoning tasks.

Table 3 presents several epistemological dimensions along which authentic experimentation differs from simple multivariate experimentation. We discuss these dimensions below and also note ways in which students who learn only from simple multivariate tasks might develop a nonscientific epistemology.

Purpose

The purpose of authentic experimentation is to develop, critique, and revise theoretical models that explain a wide variety of data. The models incorporate mechanisms with unseen theoretical entities such as molecules, hormones, and so forth. The choice of topics is often guided by human interests such as improving human health or building better space probes. Simple multivariate experimentation is directed at the surface level of determining empirical regularities, such as whether weight affects car speed. In this way, simple multivariate experimentation transforms science from a search for mechanisms into a Baconian enterprise of accumulating simple observations and drawing simple generalizations. Researchers have found that students often adopt such a Baconian view of science; simple multivariate experiments and other oversimplified school tasks can only reinforce this faulty view.

Table 3. Differences in epistemology between authentic experimentation and multivariate experimentation.

Dimension of epistemology	Authentic experimentation		Simple multivariate experiments
Purpose of research	Build and revise theoretical models with unseen mechanisms	<->	Uncover surface regularities
Theory-data coordination	Coordinate theoretical models with multiple sets of complex, multi-level partially conflicting data	<->	Coordinate phenomena with observations
	Seek global consistency	<->	Seek local consistency
Theory-ladenness of methods	Methods are partially theory-laden	<->	Methods are not theory-laden
Responses to anomalous data	Data are regularly and rationally discounted	<->	Data cannot be rationally discounted
Nature of reasoning	Heuristic, nonalgorithmic	<->	Algorithmic
	Multiple acceptable argument forms	<->	Contrastive causal inference is the only form of argument
	Uncertain	<->	Certain
Social construction	Institutional norms through expert review	<->	No such institutional norms
	Builds on existing research	<->	Seldom builds on existing research

Theory-Data Coordination

As noted earlier, in order to generate and revise theoretical models, scientists must coordinate their theories with results from many different types of studies that often yield partially conflicting results. Some studies are at the level of unseen mechanisms, and others are at the level of observable phenomena. No such complex coordination occurs with simple multivariate experimentation, which has just one kind of experiment restricted to the level of observable phenomena. Simple multivariate experimentation can thereby promote a false view that science is a relatively simple process. Students will certainly fail to understand the multi-layered complexity of scientific reasoning.

As scientists strive to coordinate data from many kinds of research studies, they seek global consistency between theories and evidence

(Chinn & Brewer, 1993; Reif & Larkin, 1991). Simple multivariate experimentation aims only for a local consistency among results from a single type of experiment. As a result, students who do not go beyond simple multivariate experimentation may fail to appreciate the importance of insisting upon a global consistency between beliefs and evidence. Introducing students to more complex scientific reasoning could show students that scientists strive for consistency (and sometimes fail) despite dealing with complex, partly ambiguous, partly contradictory data. If students recognize that such thinking could also be applied to the complex, confusing data of the real world, they may be more likely to seek rigorous consistency in everyday reasoning.

Theory Ladenness of Methods

Existing simulated tasks mask the constant tension between method and theory that has been noted by historians, philosophers of science, and scientists (Collins & Pinch, 1993; Duhem, 1954; T. Kuhn, 1962). In science, theories and methods are partially interdependent, so that methods have a degree of theory ladenness. (We do not think, however, that data are completely theory laden; see Chinn, 1998; Chinn & Brewer, in press; Hacking, 1983; Franklin, 1986; and Galison, 1987.) When an empirical test of a theory fails, one can preserve one's theory by making adjustments to one's assumptions about the method used (Duhem, 1954; Quine, 1951). For example, Latour and Woolgar (1986) have documented that different biochemical methods used by microbiologists led to different conclusions about the structure of a particular hormone. Scientists using one method criticized the reliability and validity of methods used by other scientists. This tension between theory and method does not exist in current simulated tasks because the reliability and validity of methods are not fundamentally at stake in these tasks. Students whose only experience with scientific method is simple multivariate experimentation will develop an oversimplified view of how science really works.

Responses to Anomalous Data

Closely related to this point is the way in which current simulated tasks transform the way in which experimenters respond to anomalous data. In simulated tasks with straightforward decision rules, the only rational response to anomalous data is to change one's theory. However, Chinn and Brewer (1993; 1998; Brewer & Chinn, 1994) have documented that scientists respond to anomalous data in many ways besides changing theories. They also a) ignore data, b) reject data (e.g., because of methodological flaws), c) express uncertainty about the validity of the data, d) exclude data from the domain of the current theory, e) hold data in abeyance, f) reinterpret data, and g) make peripheral changes to the current theory. All of these responses can be viewed as highly rational in the appropriate circumstances. By simplifying the task environment and ruling out many of these responses to anomalous data, many current tasks transform the nature of scientific reasoning. Students will not learn the full range of responses to anomalous data or when various critical responses are appropriate.

Nature of Reasoning

Simple multivariate experiments transform reasoning about experiments into an almost algorithmic process, utilizing the simple set of decision rules described earlier. The decision rules become slightly more complex if interactions are taken into account, but the reasoning remains algorithmic. By contrast, reasoning in authentic experimentation is profoundly non-algorithmic. Scientists are often faced with conflicting results from different studies using different methods. All theories under consideration may have substantial evidence, both pro and con. Results from one measure may not be completely consistent with results from another measure from the same study. Reasoning about experimental results such as these must involve non-algorithmic heuristics that must be weighed against each other rather than hard-and-fast rules (e.g., Newton-Smith, 1981).

As a related point, simple multivariate experimentation employs just a single form of argument—the argument based on a contrastive causal inference. Authentic experimentation employs many different forms of argument, ranging from arguments for ruling out experimental error to arguments for weighting evidence of difference types. By failing to introduce students to more authentic forms of reasoning, schools miss the chance to help students learn heuristics that can be used to reason critically about uncertain evidence—heuristics such as checking and double-checking for possible sources of noise or error, checking the results of different methods against each other for confirmation, and preferring theories that meet criteria such as simplicity and explanatory scope. Such heuristics could be broadly useful to students when reasoning about everyday issues as well as when learning about scientific results through the media.

In real science, theories and methods are uncertain, always subject to error and correction. By contrast, simple multivariate experiments yield highly certain results within their narrow limits. If students' experience with reasoning tasks is limited to such simple tasks, they might conclude that science is a highly certain process. Later, when they discover that scientists regularly disagree with each other and frequently change their minds, they may become disillusioned. If students do not understand that science progresses through argumentation about uncertain evidence, they may shift from a belief that science is certain to the belief that scientific ideas are just a matter of opinion. The failure to engender an authentic scientific epistemology in students may contribute to a view of science as mere opinion.

Nature of Social Construction

As a final dimension of epistemology, we consider the nature of the social construction of knowledge. One aspect of the social construction of knowledge that is shared by authentic science and by simple experimentation in the classroom is the use of collaborative groups. Both scientists (at work) and children (at school) frequently work in collaborative groups as they design, conduct, and interpret experiments. But authentic scientific reasoning includes an additional dimension of social construction involving the publication and perusal of expert-reviewed research reports. The expert-review procedures used to evaluate scientific reports in authentic experimentation ensures that research and explanations conform to institutionally supported norms (cf. Chinn, 1998). Scientists derive ideas about theory and methods from reading these published reports, and they conduct research with an aim to persuade other scientists that their methods are valid and their interpretations correct. Scientific knowledge is built on a structure of expert-reviewed work and in turns aims to contribute to that work. This aspect of scientific reasoning is absent from most, if not all, reasoning tasks used in schools.

Conclusion

Simple multivariate experimentation reflects a positivistic philosophy of science, in which trustworthy empirical observations are used to support general laws. Authentic science is post-positivistic. Method and theory are not fully separate. Reasoning employs heuristics that are anything but algorithmic. Institutional structures are central to the advancement of knowledge. To the extent that simulated tasks embody a positivistic philosophy of science, students have no opportunity to learn an authentic scientific epistemology.

Extending the Analysis

Extensions to Nonexperimental Research

The dimensions presented in Tables 1, 2, and 3 can readily be extended to nonexperimental research. None of the dimensions listed in the tables is specific to experimentation. Even the control of variables, which is a defining feature of experimentation, occurs in other types of studies as well. In comparative case studies, correlational studies, and nonrandom designs, there is a need to determine whether confounding variables are present. Thus, the analysis summarized in Tables 1, 2, and 3 can be treated more generally as an analysis of differences between authentic scientific research and simulated research tasks.

A theme that pervades the categories in the tables is that scientists construct, test, evaluate, and revise theoretical models on the basis of a wide variety of messy data that can be criticized in a variety of ways. The data are often messy. The data are subject to methodological criticisms and other forms of discounting, and different studies may yield differing results. This theme applies equally to all forms of scientific research, experimental and nonexperimental.

Extensions to Simpler Forms of Scientific Research

Our analysis of authentic scientific research has been based on instances of experimentation in contemporary science, with its reliance on powerful theories, refined procedures, and complex equipment. An important question is the extent to which our claims about authentic scientific research apply to historical instances of scientific research that were less complex, such as Faraday's work on electricity or the early research on heat transfer. Although some of these studies are much simpler than the study on Parkinson's disease described in this chapter, we think that the underlying causal models for most of this research remain more complex than the simple model of a simple multivariate experiment shown in Figure 4 (e.g., see Gooding, 1990). We expect that most of our analysis will apply to these somewhat simpler studies. However, further work on this issue is certainly needed.

Extensions to More Complex Simulated Research Tasks

In recent years, a number of new simulated tasks have been developed that are major advances on earlier tasks (e.g., Dunbar, 1993; Linn, Bell, Hsi, 1998; Maor & Taylor, 1995; Metz, 1997; Sandoval & Reiser, 1996; Roth & Bowen, 1993; Schunn & Anderson, 1997; White & Frederikson, 1998). Many of the chapters of this volume describe tasks or approaches to instruction that encourage students to engage in more authentic forms of reasoning (e.g., see the chapters by Azmitia & Crowley; Dunbar; Klahr, Chen & Toth; Loh et al.; Lehrer, Schauble & Petrosino; Penner; Schunn & Anderson). We suggest that careful task analyses be conducted of these new simulation tasks and instructional approaches to see which aspects of authentic epistemology are successfully captured. For instance, many new tasks allow students to investigate hypotheses about theoretical mechanisms, but it appears that it may be rather less common to incorporate the tension between method and theory. The framework presented in Tables 1, 2, and 3 provides a set of categories to analyze these tasks to determine the respects in which they approach the features of authentic science and the respects in which they retain more positivistic features.

Implications

In this chapter, we have argued that scientific studies of many types can be represented as models consisting of events connected by causal, contrastive, inductive, and analogical connections. Models of experiments are useful in illuminating important differences between authentic research and the simulated research tasks used in classroom instruction and in psychological studies of nonscientists' reasoning. The differences between models of authentic experiments and simulated experiments highlight differences in cognitive processes used to reason in these tasks. These differences in cognitive processes point in turn to important differences in the epistemology implied by such tasks. In this section, we discuss implications of our analysis for assessment, instruction, and research.

Implications for Assessments

There have been many efforts to improve assessment of students' ability to reason scientifically. Most of these efforts have emphasized assessing students' ability to reason scientifically (see Germann et al., 1996; Ruiz-Primo & Shavelson, 1996). The implication of our analysis for assessment is that when educators construct assessments of the ability to conduct and interpret experiments, these assessments should include tasks that reflect the epistemology of authentic scientific reasoning. This criterion implies that assessments should include tasks that examine whether students can carry out processes such as the following:

- Construct models of at least moderately complex experiments.

- Critique experiments by weighing alternative explanations for events in these models.

- Decide when it is rational to discount the results of research and when results should be accepted.

- Coordinate results from different types of studies.

- Comprehend and apply results from research reports.

- Investigate hypotheses about unseen theoretical mechanisms.

This list is far from exhaustive, but it indicates that knowledge of scientific reasoning includes much more than merely controlling variables in simple experiments. There are more recent examples of assessments that have begun to assess more athentic forms of scientific reasoning (see, e.g., Glaser & Baxter, 1997) and more advanced aspects of epistemology (e.g., Minstrell, this volume). Further work on improved assessments is certainly needed. The analysis provided in this chapter can provide a framework for developing and evaluating assessments that reflect the epistemology of authentic science.

Implications for Instruction

If the ultimate goal of instruction is to foster the development of authentic scientific reasoning, it seems clear that educators should develop an array of new experimentation tasks of intermediate complexity that do a better job of reflecting the epistemology of authentic science. By exploring these tasks, students will have an opportunity to learn authentic reasoning strategies and a more authentic scientific epistemology. But important questions about sequencing remain unanswered. What is the best way to proceed? Should schools begin with simple tasks in the early grades, even though these tasks do not reflect the epistemology of authentic experimentation, and later move to more complex tasks that reflect a more authentic experimentation? Or should schools introduce tasks reflecting a more authentic epistemology from a fairly early age? And if so, at how early of an age? Students who start with tasks that are not epistemologically authentic might develop an incorrect epistemology that is very hard to change later on. However, too much complexity too soon could lead to frustration and confusion.

Implications for Research

One pressing research need is to identify the cognitive processes involved in authentic scientific experimentation. This chapter has pointed to many differences between simulated tasks and authentic tasks, such as the more complex reasoning involved in coordinating information from diverse experiments, with sometimes contradictory results. However, much more research is needed to specify the exact heuristics that scientists use when reasoning about authentic research. Only then will it be possible to set appropriate goals for instruction and assessment. Researchers should also investigate how children and nonscientist adults reason using more complex reasoning tasks. How do students reason when given tasks in which methods are partially theory laden or tasks that coordinate different levels of analysis? Finally, research is needed on instructional methods that are effective at promoting complex reasoning about authentic experimentation. What instructional methods are effective at promoting understanding of how to coordinate theory and evidence?

Conclusions

Models-of-data theory provides a window into the nature of scientific reasoning. By examining the reasoning processes needed to construct and evaluate models of experiments, we gain insights into the nature of reasoning needed to carry out experiments. Because the models of authentic experiments are quite different from the models of simple multivariate experiments, the cognitive processes needed to construct and evaluate research are very different. The differences in cognitive processes are profound, reflecting a different epistemology at the root of the two tasks.

The analyses presented in this chapter provide a sound basis for analyzing other simulated experimentation tasks, as well as a variety of simulated tasks involving other forms of scientific research. Using the arrows represented in Tables 1, 2, and 3 as a guide, it is possible to analyze the features of the models that underlie the simulated tasks, the cognitive processes needed to carry out the tasks, and the epistemology implied by the tasks. Such task analyses are valuable for guiding the development of simulated tasks that reflect the epistemology of authentic science.

Acknowledgements

We are grateful to Brian Reiser, Rick Duschl, Brian White, and the editors for very helpful comments on an earlier version of this chapter. This work was supported in part by National Science Foundation grant number REC-9875485 to the first author.

References

Adey, P., & Shayer, M. (1993). An exploration of long-term far-transfer effects following an extended intervention program in the high school science curriculum. *Cognition and Instruction, 11,* 1-29.

Bernstein, L., Schachter, M., Winkler, A., & Wolfe, S. (1991). *Concepts and challenges in life science.* Englewood Cliffs, NJ: Globe Book Company.

Bogen, J., & Woodward, J. (1988). Saving the phenomena. *Philosophical Review, 97,* 303-352.

Brewer, W. F., & Chinn, C. A. (1994). Scientists' responses to anomalous data: Evidence from psychology, history, and philosophy of science. *PSA 1994, 1,* 304-313.

Chinn, C. A. (1998). A critique of social constructivist explanations of knowledge change. In B. Guzzetti & C. Hynd (Eds.), *Perspectives on conceptual change: Multiple ways to understand knowing and learning in a complex world* (pp. 77-115). Mahwah, NJ: Lawrence Erlbaum Associates.

Chinn, C. A., & Brewer, W. F. (1993). The role of anomalous data in knowledge acquisition: A theoretical framework and implications for science instruction. *Review of Educational Research, 63*, 1-49.

Chinn, C. A., & Brewer, W. F. (1996). Mental models in data interpretation. *Philosophy of Science, 63* (Proceedings), S211-S219.

Chinn, C. A., & Brewer, W. F. (1998). An empirical test of a taxonomy of responses to anomalous data in science. *Journal of Research in Science Teaching, 35*, 623-654.

Chinn, C. A., & Brewer, W. F. (1999). *Models of data: A theory of how people evaluate data.* Manuscript submitted for publication.

Chinn, C. A., & Brewer, W. F. (in press). Knowledge change in response to data in science, religion, and magic. In K. Rosengren, C. Johnson, & P. Harris (Eds.), *Imagining the impossible: The development of magical, scientific and religious thinking in contemporary society.* Cambridge: Cambridge University Press.

Collins, A., Brown, J. S., & Larkin, K. M. (1980). Inference in text understanding. In R. J. Spiro, B. C. Bruce, & W. F. Brewer (Eds.), *Theoretical issues in reading comprehension: Perspectives from cognitive psychology, linguistics, artificial intelligence, and education* (pp. 385-407). Hillsdale, NJ: Lawrence Erlbaum Associates.

Collins, H., & Pinch, T. (1993). *The golem: What everyone should know about science.* Cambridge: Cambridge University Press.

Danielson, E. W., & Denecke, E. J. (1986). *Macmillian earth science.* New York: Macmillian Publishing Company.

Duggan, S., Johnson, P., & Gott, R. (1996). A critical point in investigative work: Defining variables. *Journal of Research in Science Teaching, 33*, 461-474.

Duhem, P. (1954). *The aim and structure of physical theory* (P. P. Wiener, Trans.). Princeton, NJ: Princeton University Press. (Original work published 1914.)

Dunbar, K. (1993). Concept discovery in a scientific domain. *Cognitive Science, 17*, 397-434.

Dunbar, K. (1995). How scientists really reason: Scientific reasoning in real-world laboratories. In R. J. Sternberg & J. E. Davidson (Eds.), *The nature of insight* (pp. 365-395). Cambridge, MA: The MIT Press.

Franklin, A. (1986). *The neglect of experiment.* Cambridge: Cambridge University Press.

Galison, P. (1987). *How experiments end.* Chicago, IL: University of Chicago Press.

Galison, P. (1997). *Image and logic: A material culture of microphysics.* Chicago, IL: University of Chicago Press.

Germann, P. J., Aram, R., & Burke, G. (1996). Identifying patterns and relationships among the responses of seventh-grade students to the science process skill of designing experiments. *Journal of Research in Science Teaching, 33,* 79-99.

Germann, P. J., Haskins, S., & Auls, S. (1996). Analysis of nine high school biology laboratory manuals: Promoting scientific inquiry. *Journal of Research in Science Teaching, 33,* 475-499.

Giere, R. N. (1988). *Explaining science: A cognitive approach.* Chicago, IL: University of Chicago Press.

Glaser, R. & Baxter, G. P. (1997, February) *Improving the theory and practice of performance-based assessment.* Paper presented at a conferenceof the Board of Testing and Assessmentm National Research Council/National Academy of Sciences.

Gooding, D. (1990). *Experiment and the making of meaning: Human agency in scientific observation and experiment.* Dordrecht, The Netherlands: Kluwer Academic Publishers.

Hacking, I. (1983). *Representing and intervening.* Cambridge: Cambridge University Press.

Hanson, N. R. (1958). *Patterns of discovery.* Cambridge: Cambridge University Press.

Houghton Mifflin Interactive (1997). *InventorLabs Technology.* CD-Rom, produced in Somerville, MA.

Kieras, D. E., & Bovair, S. (1984). The role of a mental model in learning to operate a device. *Cognitive Science, 8,* 255-273.

Knorr-Cetina, K. D. (1981). *The manufacture of knowledge: An essay on the constructivist and contextual nature of science.* Oxford: Pergamon Press.

Kuhn, D., Garcia-Mila, M., Zohar, A., & Andersen, C. (1995). Strategies of knowledge acquisition. *Monographs of the Society for Research in Child Development, 60* (4, Serial No. 245).

Kuhn, D., Schauble, L., & Garcia-Mila, M. (1992). Cross-domain development of scientific reasoning. *Cognition and Instruction, 9,* 287-327.

Kuhn, T. S. (1962). *The structure of scientific revolutions.* Chicago, IL: University of Chicago Press.

Latour, B., & Woolgar, S. (1986). *Laboratory life: The construction of scientific facts* (2nd ed.). Princeton, NJ: Princeton University Press.

Linn, M., Bell, P. & Hsi, S. (1998). Using the internet to enhance student understanding of science: The Knowledge Integration Environment. *Interactive Learning Environments, 6,* 4-38.

Malhotra, B. A. (1991). *The molecular basis for the relationship between nicotine and Parkinsonianism.* Unpublished manuscript.

Malhotra, B. A., & Chinn, C. A. (1999). *A microgenetic study of learning to control variables in the classroom.* Manuscript in preparation.

Mallinson, G. G., Mallinson, J. B., Froschauer, L., Harris, J. A., Lewis, M. C., & Valentino, C. (1993). *Science horizons, Sterling edition.* Atlanta, GA: Silver Burdett Ginn.

Maor, D., & Taylor, P. C. (1995). Teacher epistemology and scientific inquiry in computerized classroom environments. *Journal of Research in Science Teaching, 32,* 839-854.

McFadden, C., & Yager, R. E. (1993). *SciencePlus: Technology and society.* Austin, TX: Holt, Rinehart and Winston.

Metz, K. E. (1985). The development of children's problem solving in a gears task: A problem space perspective. *Cognitive Science, 9,* 431-471.

Metz, K. E. (1997, March). *Scaffolding children's construction of fundamental statistics: Analysis of learning from extended class-based investigations.* Poster presented at the annual meeting of the American Educational Research Association, Chicago, IL.

Newton-Smith, W. H. (1981). *The rationality of science.* Boston, MA: Routledge & Kegan Paul.

Palincsar, A. S., Anderson, C., & David, Y. M. (1993). Pursuing scientific literacy in the middle grades through collaborative problem solving. *Elementary School Journal, 93,* 643-658.

Pickering, A. (1984). *Constructing quarks: A sociological history of particle physics.* Chicago, IL: University of Chicago Press.

Quine, W. V. O. (1951). Two dogmas of empiricism. *The Philosophical Review, 60,* 20-43.

Rasmussen, N. (1993). Facts, artifacts, and mesosomes: Practicing epistemology with the electron microscope. *Studies in History and Philosophy of Science, 24,* 227-265.

Reif, F., & Larkin, J. H. (1991). Cognition in scientific and everyday domains: Comparison and learning implications. *Journal of Research in Science Teaching, 28,* 733-760.

Roth, W-M., & Bowen, G. M. (1993). An investigation of problem framing and solving in a grade 8 open-inquiry science program. *The Journal of the Learning Sciences, 3,* 165-204.

Rudwick, M. J. S. (1985). *The great Devonian controversy: The shaping of scientific knowledge among gentlemanly specialists.* Chicago, IL: University of Chicago Press.

Ruiz-Primo, M. A., & Shavelson, R. J. (1996). Rhetoric and reality in science performance assessments: An update. *Journal of Research in Science Teaching, 33,* 1045-1063.

Sandoval, W. A., & Reiser, B. J. (1996, April). *Evolving explanations in high school biology.* Paper presented at the annual meeting of the American Educational Research Association, Chicago, IL.

Schauble, L. (1990). Belief revision in children: The role of prior knowledge and strategies for generating evidence. *Journal of Experimental Child Psychology, 49,* 31-57.

Schauble, L. (1996). The development of scientific reasoning in knowledge-rich contexts. *Developmental Psychology, 32,* 102-119.

Schauble, L., Glaser, R., Duschl, R. A., Schulze, S., & John, J. (1995). Students' understanding of the objectives and procedures of experimentation in the science classroom. *The Journal of the Learning Sciences, 4,* 131-166.

Schunn, C. D., & Anderson, J. R. (1997). General and specific expertise in scientific reasoning. In M. G. Shafto & P. Langley (Eds.), *Proceedings of the nineteenth annual conference of the Cognitive Science Society* (pp. 674-679). Mahwah, NJ: Lawrence Erlbaum Associates.

Sharp, F. R., Sagar, S. M., Hicks, K., Lowenstein, D., & Hisanga, K. (1991). C-fos mRNA, fos, and fos-related antigen induction by hypertonic saline and stress. *The Journal of Neuroscience, 11,* 2321-2331.

Theatrix Interactive. (1995). *Bumptz Science Carnival.* CD-Rom, produced in Emeryville, CA.

Thompson, M., McLaughlin, C. W., & Smith, R. G. (1995). *Merrill physical science.* New York: Glencoe/McGraw-Hill.

Warner, L. A., Lawson, S. A., Bierer, L. K., & Cohen, T. L. (1991). *Life science: The challenge of discovery.* Lexington, MA: D. C. Heath.

White, B. Y., & Frederiksen, J. R. (1998). Inquiry, modeling, and metacognition: Making science accessible to all students. *Cognition and Instruction, 16,* 3-118.

Zohar, A. (1995). Reasoning about interactions between variables. *Journal of Research in Science Teaching, 32,* 1039-1063.

13

Everyday Activity and the Development of Scientific Thinking

Kevin Crowley
Jodi Galco
University of Pittsburgh

Years before encountering their first formal science lessons in elementary school, children may already be practicing scientific thinking on a weekly, if not daily, basis. In one recent survey, parents reported that their kindergartners engaged, on average, in more than 300 informal science education activities per year—watching science television shows, reading science-oriented books, and visiting museums and zoos (Korpan, Bisanz, Bisanz, Boehme & Lynch, 1997). This strikes us as a lot, but it is likely to pale in comparison to what young children may experience five years from now. Encouraged by findings suggesting that children's out-of-school activities and learning environments are linked to motivation and success in the classroom (e.g., Gottfried, Fleming, & Gottfried, 1998), developers continue to expand the number of science-oriented museums, internet sites, books, and television shows specifically designed for young children. But what constitutes effective learning environments? What are the knowledge bases, processes, and practices that good informal science education should seek to develop?

It seems natural that at this moment, psychologists interested in cognitive development would step to the fore with their research-based knowledge of how children learn to think scientifically to work as partners with developers to produce effective informal learning environments. But, as many have noted with respect to classrooms and formal education, it is almost never the case that basic learning research can be translated immediately into effective practice. The complexity, extended time-scale, and socially-embedded nature of *in vivo* learning and development are not just annoyances to be controlled by an experimenter; they are fundamental, irreducible characteristics of how learning actually occurs (Brown, 1992).

Laboratory studies of children's learning have produced an important body of findings about the ways that children develop scientific thinking. However, those findings will remain inert and untapped unless there is also research that situates mechanisms identified in laboratory studies within the patterns and practices that actually occur as children develop everyday scientific literacy in the real world (see Stokes, 1997, for discussion about fruitful ways to reconsider issues of basic vs. applied research).

In this chapter, we overview a line of research designed to extend prior laboratory-based research on children's scientific thinking to the everyday contexts where it actually occurs. We describe analyses of naturally-occurring parent-child interactions as families use interactive science exhibits in children's museums. We describe how parent participation extends children's exploration of an exhibit and describe how parents sometimes offered brief explanations to frame the ongoing activity. We close by reflecting on what our findings suggest about everyday parent explanation and the development of children's scientific thinking.

Developing Scientific Thinking in Everyday Settings

In this chapter, we describe a line of work that has grown from the simple idea of looking to the cognitive ecology of children's everyday thinking for guidance on how to think about the development of scientific thinking. Developmental psychologists interested in cognitive development have a long history of research inspired by observations of children's thinking in everyday contexts. The foremost example is probably Jean Piaget, whose accounts of his own children's exploits still provide a conceptual touchstone for much of modern cognitive developmental research. It remains commonplace to hear researchers weave anecdotes about their own children into conference presentations and colloquia (Gauvain, 1997), and it is not unusual for new lines of successful experimental work to grow out of chance observations of children that, for one reason or another, strike a researcher as inconsistent with some aspect of a prevailing theory (Okada, this volume).

Yet, the vast majority of studies of children's cognitive development take place in the context of laboratory studies where individual children work alone to complete clever, but contrived, laboratory tasks. As Dunbar points out in this volume, *in vitro* studies are a powerful, albeit limited, scientific tool. Although they provide control, precision, and convenience, they provide no built-in reality check. There is always the possibility that, as researchers extend, elaborate, and perfect programmatic *in vitro* paradigms, they will develop increasingly specified, nuanced, and replicable answers to questions that may not be the best reflection of actual developmental processes.

As in the field of cognitive development at large, most of what is known about the development of scientific thinking is based on evidence from laboratory studies. The studies have been of two kinds. First, some studies have focused on children's scientific reasoning processes, including their abilities to design controlled experiments, make valid inferences, and generate new hypotheses. Compared to adults or adolescents, children are often observed to be less systematic when considering evidence, less likely to conduct informative comparisons, and more likely to see all of the relevant evidence when in engaged in self-directed scientific thinking (e.g., Schauble, 1996, Dunbar & Klahr, 1989; Kuhn, Amsel, & O'Loughlin, 1988). Developments in scientific reasoning are often described as general improvements in individual metacognitive abilities that enable children to deploy increasingly sophisticated experimentation strategies, to construct more accurate and complete encoding of incoming evidence, and to search for evidence that is inconsistent with their existing beliefs (e.g., Kuhn, 1989).

Other studies have focused on the content and structure of children's concepts, mental models, and naïve theories in scientific domains such as biology, physics, and psychology. For example, in the absence of any direct instruction, children appear to develop mental models of the shape of the earth (Vosniadou & Brewer, 1992) and theories about what fundamentally distinguishes biological and physical entities (e.g., Wellman & Gelman, 1998). In addition to describing age-related differences in concepts, mental models, and theories, research focused on the content of children's scientific knowledge has sometimes explored how the structure of knowledge constrains categorization of new instances. For example, Chi and Koeske (1983) described a young dinosaur expert who, through repeated reading of dinosaur books with his mother, had developed a well-organized semantic network of dinosaur knowledge that enabled him to categorize and recall novel dinosaurs more accurately when they were related in meaningful ways to his prior knowledge.

Although sometimes focusing on the process and sometimes focusing on the product of scientific thinking, extant work emphasizes internal cognitive mechanisms such as metacognition, knowledge-based constraints, or theory revision to explain learning and development. These are appropriate mechanisms given the situation of an individual child in a laboratory setting. It is probably true that, when working alone on a novel task, younger children are less systematic than older children due to less sophisticated metacognitive skill. It is probably also true that the surprisingly advanced performance of young children on certain categorization tasks suggests that they hold naïve theories that constrain how they interpret and organize new evidence.

But, are the mechanisms that appear to be central in laboratory studies the same mechanisms that appear to be central in everyday settings? It is logically possible that developing scientific thinking is best thought of as an individual struggle where breakthroughs occur as children develop internal metacognitive skills or as children tinker, gradually or suddenly, with the contents and organizations of their everyday scientific theories. But we think an alternative is at least worth testing: That parents actively involve their children in activities and conversations that directly shape children's early scientific thinking. After all, the kinds of activities where young children are most likely to encounter science are activities often embedded in the context of parent-child interaction—activities such as parents reading picture books to young children or families visiting a museum or zoo together on the weekend. What does this shared scientific thinking look like?

A Location for Research on Everyday Scientific Thinking

The first step in exploring the characteristics of children's everyday scientific thinking was to choose a location to observe it. We chose to focus on naturally occurring family activity at interactive science exhibits in museums. Similar to the computer microworlds that have often been used in laboratory studies of children's scientific thinking, interactive science exhibits use environments where children can generate evidence, interpret evidence, and build theories relevant to particular science or technology content. However, exhibits are also authentic artifacts used by families in the context of recreation and education independent of our research activities. Thus, interactive science exhibits seemed to be a fruitful location to explore whether and how findings from extant scientific thinking research are reflected in everyday activity.

As an example of an interactive exhibit, consider the zoetrope (Figure 1). This is a simple animation device with an animation strip on the inside of a drum that visitors can spin. If they spin and look through the slots, the exhibit produces the illusion of motion through a stroboscopic effect involving persistence of vision (the retina retains an individual image for about one-tenth of a second) and the Phi phenomenon (the visual system combines the series of successive individual images into a single smooth motion).

Figure 1. A zoetrope affords simple exploration, observation, and explanation.

The zoetrope affords simple manipulations and straightforward connections to animation—a topic with which children and their parents are likely to be familiar. Unlike some interactive science exhibits, it does not produce amazing, unexpected, and unique outcomes that surprise and astound visitors. Furthermore, it is easy for even toddlers to use the zoetrope without assistance. If a child is about 30 inches tall and can stand on her own, she is capable of spinning the cylinder and observing the animation through the slots. Thus, the zoetrope is a good example of everyday scientific thinking where children could explore and where parents could chose whether or not they will shape the path of exploration, help children to place the experience in a broader context, or step back and allow the child to do it by themselves.

The particular kind of scientific thinking that is most common at interactive science exhibits like the zoetrope is an informal kind of evidence collection and evaluation. Most children do not come to interactive science exhibits with well-organized plans to conduct systematic investigations to test specific hypotheses. Instead, they adopt an informal mode of exploration where the initial goal is often to poke around and see whether the exhibit does anything interesting. If something sufficiently intriguing occurs, children may decide to pursue it further, perhaps experimenting with different conditions that are necessary to produce the outcome or that modify it in an interesting way.

By normative definitions of scientific thinking, this may not sound much like scientific thinking. However, as many of the chapters in this volume note, including Simon's, Okada's, Dunbar's, Chinn's and Malhoutra's, and Tweney's, the actual cognitive processes of scientific thinking only sometimes resemble normative prescriptions. We think it is common for children in everyday settings to conduct informal, recreational exploration of their environment. We agree with Simon's argument (this volume), that seeking out evidence, noticing interesting patterns, and making inferences about evidence are natural features of the cognitive ecology of childhood. Such exploration requires no formal hypotheses or formal references to existing theories. Children are simply curious, attentive to novelty, and trying to make sense of their world as best as they can.

Characterizing the Exploration of Solo Children and Children with their Parents

What does everyday scientific thinking look like at interactive science exhibits? We present two examples of children using a zoetrope: One uses the exhibit solo, while the other uses it with her mother.

Before we describe these examples, we should pause to say a word about methodology. Both of these interactions, and all of the subsequent work we will present in this chapter, were collected with the same methodology, designed to be a low-impact, unobtrusive means to collect spontaneous use of exhibits during normal family museum visits. Before each day of data collection, video cameras were set up at target exhibits throughout the museum and wireless microphones were integrated into the exhibits to provide high resolution audio recording. Signs informing visitors of our research activities were hung at the museum entrance and at each exhibit being filmed. Researchers greeted families entering the museum, explained that we were videotaping as part of a research project, and asked families for written consent to participate. Most families (typically greater than 90%) agreed to participate. Children in consenting families were given large stickers identifying them as participants; ages of the children were determined by distinct stickers. If, in the normal course of their visit, children with stickers chose to engage one of the target exhibits, the camera operator turned on the camera for the length of the engagement.

	Looking through slots	Looking over top
Zoetrope spinning	**SlotSpin** Observer sees the illusion of motion	**TopSpin** Observer sees a spinning series of separate frames
Zoetrope stopped	**SlotStop** Observer sees one still frame	**TopStop** Observer sees a series of still frames

Figure 2. Evidence relevant to the illusion of motion can be described as a factorial space determined by observational vantage point and rotational state of the zoetrope. The animation has a unique appearance in each cell of the space. By comparing the evidence available from different cells, children could collect sufficient evidence to understand how the zoetrope works.

Now we return to our comparison of the children who used the zoetrope with and without their parents. To describe their exploration of the zoetrope, we adopted the convention of considering evidence collection as movement through a search space (e.g., Klahr & Dunbar, 1988). As shown in Figure 2, the search space for the zoetrope is a simple factorial space defined by whether the zoetrope was spinning or still and whether the child was looking at the animation through the slots or from over the top of the cylinder. In each of the four spaces, children perceive the animation differently. By collecting data in different parts of the space children could accumulate evidence to support inferences about how and why the zoetrope worked.

First, consider the exploration of a 5 year-old girl who was without her parents as she engaged a zoetrope at the Pittsburgh Children's Museum. As Figure 3 suggests, the solo girl's exploration was shallow and incomplete. She spun the zoetrope several times but never observed the true animation effect by looking through the slots. She only observed the animation by looking over the top of the zoetrope—a view that produces either a series of moving but separate frames or a blur, depending on how fast the zoetrope is spinning. As she spun the zoetrope, she often looked away from the exhibit. Midway through the engagement, she looked under the zoetrope—perhaps an attempt to find out if there was anything else to do or see at this exhibit. However, there was nothing to see under the zoetrope and the girl quickly lost interest, stopped the spinning zoetrope, and left.

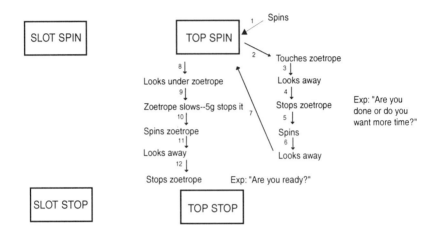

Figure 3. Tracing the activity of a 5 year old girl who explored the zoetrope by herself. The four categories of evidence that children could encounter are included as boxes in the center of the chart. Actions are transcribed as text connected with numbered arrows indicating the order in which they occurred. When an arrow enters one of the four cells of the exploration space, it indicates that the child was seeing that category of evidence at that point in the engagement.

Contrast the shallow and incomplete search of the solo girl with that of a 6 year old girl who engaged the zoetrope with her mother (Figure 4). While the solo girl had entered only one cell of the evidence space, the girl with her mother entered three of the four cells and spent the most time in the critical SlotSpin cell. The interaction began with the girl looking at the animation through the slots and calling her mother's attention to it: "Mom, look at this!" The mother began almost at once to guide the girl's exploration. She suggests an informal experiment, telling her daughter to "do it as fast as [she] can and see what happens." The girl takes up the suggestion and notes the outcome: "Yeah, they are running really fast. The mother then begins a brief episode of explanation. She starts with a question: "Do you have any idea how this works?" The girl does not answer the question, but stops the zoetrope from spinning and looks first through the slots and then over the top.

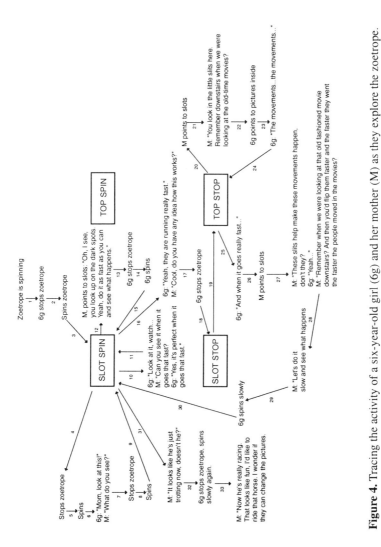

Figure 4. Tracing the activity of a six-year-old girl (6g) and her mother (M) as they explore the zoetrope.

The mother follows up the question by pointing to the slots and then asking the girl if she remembers the "old-time" movies that they saw downstairs. This is a reference to a faux-antique flip card device that happened to be on the lower level of the museum as part of a traveling exhibition. The mother also explicitly established a causal role for the slots— "These slits help make these movements happen, don't they?"—although she did not extend to a more complete explanation of why the slits help to make the movements happen. Next, the mother returned to the old-fashioned movie, connecting the speed of spinning experiment with a similar comparison they had they apparently conducted earlier at the old-fashioned movie.

The engagement wraps up with the mother suggesting: "Let's do it slow and see what happens." The girl complies and the mother volunteers an interpretation of the outcome: "It looks like he's just trotting now, doesn't he?" As the engagement comes to a close, the mother is making casual conversation, mentioning that it might be fun to ride the horse and wondering whether it is possible to change the pictures inside the zoetrope.

There are two things to note about these two examples. First, compared to the girl who engaged the zoetrope alone, the girl who engaged it with her mother spent more time at the zoetrope, entered more cells in the evidence space, re-entered cells more often, conducted pair-wise comparisons between cells in the evidence space, and spent more time in the critical SlotSpin cell. Second, the girl who used the zoetrope with her mother participated in an ongoing conversation about generating, interpreting, and explaining evidence as she explored the zoetrope. We know nothing about the inner dialog of the girl who used the zoetrope by herself, and it is possible that she may have made have engaged in some similar form of reflective commentary and self-explanation. However, her cursory exploration seems unlikely to have provided her with sufficient evidence to support much in the way of reflection.

A Broader Study of Shared Scientific Thinking

How general are the characteristics suggested by these two examples? We examined exploration and conversation among families who, in the normal course of a museum visit, decided to use a zoetrope at the San Jose Children's Discovery Museum (Crowley, et al., in press). We compared the activity of 49 families where parents and children happen to use the exhibit together, to the activity of 20 families where children happen to use the zoetrope by themselves while their parents were occupied elsewhere in the museum.

Exploration

Consistent with the two examples we already presented, findings suggested that children's search of the zoetrope was extended and more focused when they used the exhibit with their parents. Figure 5 illustrates differences in the evidence encountered by children who used the zoetrope either with their parents or by themselves.

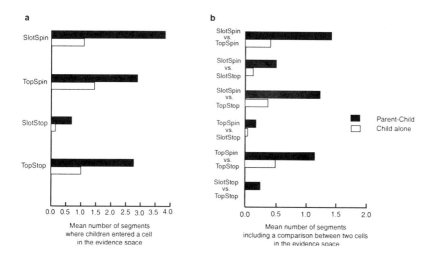

Figure 5. Children's exposure to evidence while using the zoetrope. a) Children using the exhibit with their parents encountered each kind of evidence more often than children by themselves, and b) were also more likely to make direct comparisons between different kinds of evidence.

To estimate the amount of exposure children had to each kind of evidence, we divided each interaction into 10 second segments and coded whether children had seen each category of evidence within each 10 second segment. As shown in Figure 5a, children who engaged the zoetrope with their parents visited each cell of the exploration space more often than children who were alone. Furthermore, notice that the most common cell visited by children with parents was the critical SlotSpin cell—the cell in the evidence space where children can observe the illusion of motion. In contrast, children alone spent less time, both in absolute and relative terms, viewing the animation. Children alone spent the most time in the TopSpin cell and equal amounts of time in the TopStop and SlotSpin cells.

In addition to counting how often children saw each kind of evidence, we also tracked how many paired comparisons children made, defined as children entering two cells within the same 10-second segment. For example, consider a child who looks through the slots of a spinning zoetrope to perceive the illusion of motion (SlotSpin), and then, with the zoetrope still spinning, looks over the top and to perceive a spinning series of non-animated frames (TopSpin). This is a controlled comparison with one variable (observation vantage point) manipulated and one variable (spinning) held constant. Comparing the two outcomes provides evidence to support the inference that looking through the slots is necessary to perceive the illusion of motion.

As shown in Figure 5b, children with parents were more likely than children alone to engage in each of the six possible paired comparisons. Consistent with the finding that children with their parents spent the most time in the SlotSpin cell, the most common kind of comparison for children with parents was between SlotSpin and TopSpin evidence. In contrast, the most common comparison for children alone was between TopSpin and TopStop evidence. It is worth noting that it was not necessarily the case that children with their parents would make more comparisons than children alone just because the earlier analysis revealed that they spent more time in each cell of the evidence space. If children with their parents had engaged in a serial, non-backtracking search of the whole evidence space, of if they had searched until they found the critical SlotSpin cell and then looked no further, they would have performed fairly few comparisons regardless of how much time they spent using the zoetrope. However, findings suggest that children using the zoetrope with their parents continued to collect different types of evidence and to make comparisons between them, even after they had achieved the initial effect of seeing the animation.

Thus, consistent with the two examples we presented above, children with parents explored the zoetrope more deeply than other children and were most likely to focus on the most interesting cell in the evidence space. Furthermore, their exploration included high levels of direct comparison between different cells in the evidence space, particularly between SlotSpin vs. the other kinds of evidence. In contrast, solo children appeared to distribute their attention more equally throughout the space.

Conversation

We turn next to consideration of the talk between parents and children who used the zoetrope together. Return for a moment to the conversation between the mother and daughter depicted in Figure 4. The pair keep up a fairly constant level of talk throughout the interaction and both mother and daughter participate in the conversation. However, the mother is responsible for most of the suggestions for how they might explore, for most the commentary on the evidence as it is encountered, and for all of the explanatory talk about the slots and the relation of the zoetrope to the old-fashioned movie exhibit downstairs.

The parent-child conversation in Figure 4 is in some ways typical of the conversations one can observe at interactive science exhibits. It is often the case that parents and children talk when they are engaged in collaborative activity at exhibits. In the broader study of family exploration of the zoetrope, we recorded talk in 92% of families where parents and children used the zoetrope together. Although it was almost always the case that both parents and children contributed something to the conversations, most of the talk was carried out by parents. Parents were twice as likely as children to talk about how to generate evidence—defined as talk about how to manipulate the zoetrope, such as, "Spin it the other way" or "Look through those slots." Parents were seven times as likely as children to describe evidence as it was being encountered—defined as talk about observable outcomes that did not established causal or analogical connections such as "It looks like he's galloping" or "Is he running backwards?"

Finally, parents were about five times more likely than children to explain. We coded parent talk to be explanatory if they talked to their children about causal relations, noted analogies between the zoetrope and related devices, or made general statements of the scientific principles underlying the exhibit. Causal explanations included talk about causal links within the local context, such as, "Look, if we slow it down, the pony runs really slow. And if you make it go fast, the pony goes really fast." Analogies included talk that made a connection between the exhibit and prior knowledge or prior experience such as, "Remember when we made the little comic book on the bottom of the page and you flip the whole notebook and it made it look like it was a moving cartoon? ...I think this is the same kind of thing." Principles included talk about underlying unobservable causal principles; for example: "They wanted to take a look at how pictures move, see how they drew the pictures, and they're all different, they're all in different positions, they move them … and if you look, look down here, you see?"

While reflecting some aspects of the average conversation at the zoetrope, the conversation depicted in Figure 4 is atypical in its completeness. While the mother in our example talked about how to generate, interpret, and explain evidence, less than half of the parents from the broader study provided each kind of assistance. Parents talked about how to generate evidence in 49% of interactions; talked about how to interpret evidence in 47% of interactions; and offered explanations in 37% of interactions.

Summary

We have described how parent participation shapes the path of children's naturally-occurring scientific thinking at one interactive science exhibit. When parents were present, children exploring the zoetrope saw more unique kinds of evidence, spent more time collecting the most informative kind of evidence, and were more likely to make paired comparisons between different kinds of evidence. Even if the development of scientific thinking is best explained by mechanisms "inside the head" of an individual child, our findings suggest that parents play an important role in enriching the evidentiary record on which individual children could make inferences, generate explanations, and construct new theories.

However, we also observed that parents often talked to their children about evidence while families used the zoetrope. Parents spontaneously provided assistance about how to generate new kinds of evidence by manipulating the zoetrope. They provided assistance about how to encode evidence and volunteered interpretations of evidence. Parents also provided explanation about causal connections within the experience, ways that the experience related to other experiences, and ways that the experience related to more general principles.

Explanatoids

What guidance might these findings provide for current accounts of the development of scientific thinking? We had made the argument earlier that the dominance of laboratory studies raises the question of whether current developmental accounts accurately reflect contexts where children think scientifically everyday. Our findings suggest that they may not.

In particular, current accounts of the development of scientific thinking may have underestimated the level of spontaneous parent assistance available to children in everyday environments. Studies of children's scientific reasoning have focused on young children's lack of systematicity during evidence collection. Studies of the content of children's developing scientific knowledge have, in large part, been interested in ontological organization and constraints, in part to account for the fact that even young children have surprisingly rich theories and are able to make adaptive decisions about assigning novel instances to appropriate categories. Our findings suggest that children may not have to solve problems of evidence collection and theory construction by themselves. We observed parents providing guidance in collecting and annotating evidence and parents offering explanations sufficient to facilitate at least some simple kinds of theory construction.

We think the most interesting insight might involve the finding that parents sometimes explain to their children while engaged in scientific thinking. Explanations are a privileged category of scientific discourse. At its core, science is a way of making sense of the world. It is a way of building up new theories to explain existing evidence, and a way of seeking out new evidence to revise existing theories. Current national standards for science education and current reforms in classroom science instruction emphasize explanation. Standards for science education proposed by the American Association for the Advancement of Science and the National Research Council advocate going beyond traditional science instruction to focus on facilitating the development of scientific "habits of the mind." These habits refer to general scientific reasoning skills, including coordinating evidence and logic in constructing and evaluating scientific explanations. In response to such guidelines, current science education reforms advocate hands-on classroom activities where students are actively involved in collaborating with classmates and teachers in explanatory activities such as forming hypotheses, interpreting empirical findings, and revising theories to account for new evidence (e.g., Lehrer, Schauble, & Petrosino, this volume).

Recent cognitive science research focused on the reasoning of practicing scientists reveals that effective explanation building between collaborators is often the source of scientific breakthroughs. In a multi-year cognitive ethnography of four molecular biology laboratories, Dunbar described the essential role of collaborative explanation in terms of scientists integrating findings, forming analogies to well-understood systems, and opening up new lines of inquiry (Dunbar, 1995). The labs that made important breakthroughs during the course of Dunbar's study were those that were best at constructing shared explanations during lab meetings. Consistent with Dunbar's findings, cognitive psychology studies of adults working on simulated science problems typically find that explanations are key mechanisms in creating and extending useful science learning (Chi, Bassok, Lewis, Reimann, & Glaser, 1989; Okada & Simon, 1997).

The unobtrusive observational methods of this study were necessary to capture natural moments of parent-child interaction. It is important to note that the findings we have presented in this chapter are observational and do not yet support causal conclusions about the effects of parent explanations on children's scientific thinking. However, recent laboratory studies suggest that adult explanations can facilitate both children's problem solving and theory construction. When adults explain as they demonstrate new problem solving strategies, children are better able to transfer strategies to novel problems (Crowley & Siegler, 1999). When adults provide causal explanations as children construct family-resemblance categories from novel instances, children are more accurate in categorizing subsequent instances (Krascum & Andrews, 1998). If adults do not provide such explanations or at least prompt the child to self-explain, it is unlikely that children will decide to do so on their own (Göncü & Rogoff, 1998; Siegler, 1996). Thus, available evidence from laboratory studies supports the possibility that the spontaneous parent explanation we observed could facilitate children's learning.

The finding that about one half of parent-child interactions at the zoetrope included an explanation struck us as a rather high level of explanation, given that previous studies had suggested that parents rarely explain in everyday settings. For example, Gelman et al.'s (1998) study of parents and children reading storybooks detected fairly few parent explanations. Perhaps the lower level of explanations relates to the fact that they studied reading. Reading with children is an activity primarily carried through language and pictures, primarily directed by the parent, and that does not involve extensive non-verbal explanation, manipulation, or creation. Although it may be ideal for studying certain categorization issues, book reading is not representative of a broad range of everyday activities where language may serve as a secondary layer to direct, encode, and connect non-verbal activity. Our research has focused on activity in a children's museum; however, the essential properties of museum activity characterize much of the everyday parent-child activity that goes on as children construct buildings out of blocks, help their parents cook, mix watercolors, garden, or figure out how a new toy or computer program works.

Similarly, Callanan and Oakes (1992) asked parents to keep a diary of children's questions and to note how they responded to the question. Parents reported an average of six explanatory discussions over the 2 week period; a number that seems somewhat low compared to the current finding that about one in four of the brief parent-child interactions in the museum included at least one form of explanation. However, there are two important differences in diary methodology and the methodology we have adopted. First, because parents were asked to keep track of children's questions, the study only revealed parent explanations that were responses to questions. Most of the explanations we observed in museums were offered by parents rather than requested by children. Second, in the diary study, parents needed to record conversations with their child off-line— sometimes hours after the actual conversation occurred. Thus, the diary methodology only detects conversations that are memorable and, from the parent's point of view, interesting enough to be reported to the researcher. In contrast, most of the explanations we have observed in our studies are no more than a few words uttered at an appropriate moment during the ongoing activity. Compared to the conversations reported in Callanan and Oakes (1992), the explanations we have observed seem brief, sketchy, and somewhat mundane. They were perhaps not the kinds of clever parent-child exchanges that a parent chooses to relate to grandparents, friends, colleagues, or, for that matter, developmental researchers.

We have coined the term "explanatoids" to characterize the simple, incomplete, and mundane explanatory talk that parents provide as they engage in collaborative everyday activity with their children. We hypothesize that explanatoids may have a broad impact on the development of children's scientific thinking. The family interactions we analyze here are sampled moments from a larger pattern of interaction that is woven throughout many different kinds of activities in which families engage. We do not conceptualize the most general kind of parent guidance as extended explanatory dialog that serves to catalyze, perhaps in a blinding flash of insight, the creation of a complete explanation that leads to large scale re-organization of a child's knowledge. Although such events may certainly occur, the more common kind of parent explanation is probably the kind we describe here. Although brief and incomplete, explanatoids are well-targeted to a moment of activity. Following from the idea of "active language" first suggested by Shrager and Callanan (1991), we hypothesize that explanatoids are powerful because they are offered when relevant evidence is the focus of joint parent-child attention and thus they serve the function of providing children an on-line structure for parsing, storing, and making inferences about evidence as it is encountered.

It is undoubtedly the case that parents sometimes produce explanations that are misleading or just plain wrong. This might happen because parents do not actually know the correct answer, because they do not think that children are ready to understand the correct explanation, or because, even if they know the correct answer, parents have difficulty constructing a good explanation on the spot. This could also happen if parents do not believe that correct explanations are necessarily the point of interacting with children in a museum. For example, in a recent study we asked families to look through some fossils together and talk about them. One mother encouraged her daughter to be creative rather than accurate. She asked her: "What do you think this one is?" while pointing to a velociraptor claw. The child put the claw on top of her head and said, "It's a horn!" The mother laughed and said, "Yes! It's a horn."

In the long run we do not think that it is much of a problem that parents are wrong. First, any single moment of explanation seems unlikely to have much of an impact given the thousands of explanatoids that parents probably pepper their children with in the course of a normal year. In both conceptual development and problem solving, one-trial learning is rare—it is more often the case that new knowledge is forgotten and re-discovered several times before it becomes an established part of a child's theory or a child's collection of problem-solving strategies (e.g., Siegler & Crowley, 1991). We doubt that encouraging parents to explain in museums or elsewhere will lead to great misconceptions that will have to be later unlearned in science classrooms.

Second, it seems to us much more likely that parents will get closer to a good explanation than children will on their own. The kinds of statements we observed at the zoetrope were not very advanced—the most complete explanation we observed about principles of the exhibit fell far short of what would be an acceptable explanation in a science class or a textbook. This observation is at the heart of what we believe explanatoids are. Explanatoids provide simple but helpful prompts which shape children's theory building and strategy development; they are not fully formed explanations that are to be internalized as a completed product. And, simple but helpful prompts are not that difficult for adults to generate correctly. In a recent study we asked adults to generate conceptual, analogical, and principled explanations for the zoetrope: Over 75% were able to produce what we considered to be accurate examples of all three.

Conclusions

More generally, we think the most important implication of our findings is not that parents are providing declarative content for their children's theories, but that parents are modeling a specific kind of meaning-making for their children. Scientific thinking, like the specific thinking that characterizes other disciplines, might be considered a specific kind of causal reasoning with its own rules about what constitutes acceptable theory, evidence, and argument. When we observed parents talking to children about explanations, we saw them not only shaping the interpretations possible for their child at that moment, but also perhaps scaffolding their children's transitions from general causal thinkers to early scientific thinkers. A parent who explains an interactive exhibit to their children may increase the likelihood that the children understands the exhibit and may also demonstrate that constructing a causal, analogical, or principled explanation is an appropriate activity when one is manipulating a device either to engineer an outcome or just to see what happens.

In many ways, this argument echoes those that have been made about the development of literacy. Findings suggests that early out-of-school parent-child activities such as story book reading are linked to reading and writing outcomes once children enter school. Among the causal mechanisms proposed to explain this link is that parents who involve children in out-of-school literacy activities not only support the direct development of literacy skills but also instill in children the value that practicing the habits of literacy is an important priority throughout life.

It seems likely that a related scenario exists in the case of scientific literacy: Parents who involve children in informal science activities not only provide an opportunity for children to learn factual scientific information, but also provide opportunities for children to engage in scientific reasoning, to develop an interest in learning more about science, and to develop a sense that practicing the habits of scientific thinking is an important priority. Similarly, children are learning a lot about science years before they are taught official science curricula in classrooms. Whether children are visiting museums, watching television shows like "Bill Nye the Science Guy," surfing the Web, or using a chemistry set, parents are often available to children to act as guides and interpreters. In terms of future classroom success or later choices about science as a career, the most important outcome of everyday parent-child scientific thinking may not be the content children acquire, but the interest, habits, and identity they form as someone who is competent in scientific thinking.

Acknowledgements

Supported by a grant from the National Science Foundation (ESI-9815021). Special thanks to our museum partners, including Sally Osberg, Jenni Martin, and Tom Nielsen at the Children's Discovery Museum of San Jose, and Jane Werner and Chris Siefert at the Pittsburgh Children's Museum.

References

Brown, A. L. (1992). Design experiments: Theoretical and methodological challenges in creating complex interventions in classroom settings. *The Journal of the Learning Sciences, 2,* 148-171.

Callanan, M., & Oakes, L. A. (1992). Preschoolers' questions and parents' explanations: Causal thinking in everyday activity. *Cognitive Development, 7,* 213-233.

Chi, M. T. H., Bassok, M., Lewis, M. L., Reimann, P., & Glaser, R. (1989). Self-explanations: How students study and use examples in learning to solve problems. *Cognitive Science, 13,* 145-182.

Chi, M. T. H., & Koeske, R. D. (1983). Network representation of a child's dinosaur knowledge. *Developmental Psychology, 19,* 19-29.

Crowley, K., Callanan, M., Jipson, J. L., Galco, J., Topping, K., & Shrager, J. (in press). Shared scientific thinking in everyday parent-child activity. *Science Education.*

Crowley, K., & Siegler, R.S. (1999). Explanation and generalization in young children's strategy learning. *Child Development, 70,* 304-316.

Dunbar, K. (1995). How scientists really reason: Scientific reasoning in real-world laboratories. In R.J. Sternberg & J.E. Davidson (Eds), *The nature of insight.* Cambridge: MIT Press.

Dunbar, K., & Klahr, D. (1989). Developmental differences in scientific discovery strategies. In D. Klahr & K. Kotovsky (Eds.), *Complex information processing: The impact of Herbert A. Simon.* Hillsdale, NJ: Lawrence Erlbuam Associates.

Gelman, S., Coley, J. D., Rosengren, K. S., Hartman, E., & Pappas, A. (1998). Beyond labeling: The role of maternal input in the acquisition of richly structured categories. *Monographs of the Society for Research in Child Development, 63 (1).*

Göncü, A. & Rogoff, B. (1998). Children's categorization with varying adult support. *American Educational Research Journal, 35 (2)*, 333-349.

Gottfried, A. E., Fleming, J. S., & Gottfried, A. W. (1998). Role of cognitively stimulating home environment in children's academic intrinsic motivation: A longitudinal study. *Child development, 69 (5)*, 1448-1460.

Klahr, D., & Dunbar, K. (1988). Dual search during scientific reasoning. *Cognitive Science, 12*, 1-48.

Korpan, C. A., Bisanz, G. L., Bisanz, J., Boehme, C., Lynch, M. A. (1997). What did you learn outside of school today? Using structured interviews to document home and community activities related to science and technology. *Science Education, 81 (6)*, 651-662.

Krascum, R. M., & Andrews, S. (1998). The effects of theories on children's acquisition of family-resemblance categories. *Child Development, 69(2)*, 333-346.

Kuhn, D. (1989). Children and adults as intuitive scientists. *Psychological Review, 96 (4)*, 674-689.

Kuhn, D., Amsel, E. & O'Loughlin, M. (1988). *The development of scientific thinking skills.* New York: Academic Press.

Okada, T., & Simon, H. A. (1997). Collaborative discovery in a scientific domain. *Cognitive Science, 21(2)*, 109-146.

Schauble, L. (1996). The development of scientific reasoning in knowledge-rich contexts. *Developmental Psychology, 32 (1)*, 102-119.

Shrager, J., & Callanan, M. (1991). Active language in the collaborative development of cooking skill. *Proceedings of the Cognitive Science Society*, Cambridge, MA: MIT Press.

Siegler, R. S. & Crowley, K. (1991). The microgenetic method: A direct means for studying cognitive development. *American Psychologist, 46*, 606-620.

Siegler, R. S. (1996).*Emerging minds: The process of change in children's thinking.* New York: Oxford University Press.

Stokes, D. E. (1997). Pasteur's quadrant: Basic science and technological innovation. Washington, DC: Brookings Institute.

Vosniadou, S. ,& Brewer, W. F. (1992). Mental models of the earth: A study of conceptual change in childhood. *Cognitive Psychology, 24*, 535-585.

Wellman, H., & Gelman, S. (1998). Knowledge acquisition in foundational domains. In Kuhn & R.S. Siegler, (Eds.), *Handbook of child psychology: Cognition, perception, and language.* New York: Wiley.

14
Facets of Students' Thinking: Designing to Cross the Gap from Research to Standards-Based Practice

Jim Minstrell
Talaria, Inc.

Understanding complexity in the physical world necessitates a "focus on the right level of description... Use the right level of description to catch the phenomena of interest. Don't model bulldozers with quarks"

-Goldenfeld & Kadanoff, 1999

The Need for a Practical Language to Describe Students' Thinking

To model the complexity of teaching and learning in the classroom, we need to use the right level of description for the purpose. The description of students' thinking needs to be understood by teachers, by scientists, and by researchers on learning. Thus the purpose of this chapter will be to suggest a description level that will serve classroom teachers as they make instructional decisions. Teachers are the primary target consumers. In this chapter, I will briefly review what I learned from alternative levels of description. Then, I will describe what experience suggests is a level of description with which teachers can work. We call the descriptions Facets of Thinking. I will next describe how educators are presently using facets in designing science assessment and instruction. Finally, I will conclude with some guidelines for research and development of facets and facet-based learning environments.

Lessons from Learning Research Perspectives

There exist the results from research on students' conceptions. How might the results be organized to be useful to teachers? As a classroom teacher-researcher, I explored various organizations of the research and what I could use from each. Some organizations involved characterizing students' thinking as theoretical in the large-scale sense of organizing a lot of phenomena. Are the students' ideas more consistent with Newtonian theory or Impetus theory of motion, for example (McCloskey, Caramazza & Green, 1980)? Other characterizations involved identifying tiny phenomenological primitives that arise from the perception of features of particular situations. For example, from the "knowledge in pieces" perspective, students looked for whether the objects involved in a particular situation were perceived to be rigid or springy (diSessa, 1993). Still other characterizations looked at logic of ontological categories of conceptions used by learners. For example, do students think of force as an "action" on the object or as a "property" of the object (Chi, Feltovich, & Glaser, 1981)?

Each of these research perspectives has its validity. At some level, each research perspective describes its proponent's beliefs about the nature of student thinking. Each suggests a particular view of a learner's knowledge. But I am interested in a description that can inform issues and decisions of curriculum and instruction. From diSessa's work it is important to attend to the salience of features in problematic situations. From these features, learners choose intuitive mechanisms and elements that seem relevant and construct an explanation or description from those intuitions. The "knowledge in pieces" perspective is a useful construct for thinking about the disassembling of learners' existing understanding and reconstruction of new knowledge built from the intuitive pieces. Chi's work suggests that we watch for ways in which learners construct knowledge in categories that prevent them from understanding the logic of science. McCloskey's work, taken with that of diSessa and Chi, suggests that an overall goal for learning may be in developing a different theoretical perceptive. But, the development should involve reconstructions from the intuitions with care in clarity of the logical organization of ideas.

Aspects of each perspective have their applications in the classroom, but each by itself was not seen to be sufficiently practical for my day-to-day planning and teaching in the classroom, nor for communicating to my fellow teachers the purposes in our day-to-day activities. These are all theories of knowledge organization on the part of learners. The language and issues in the perspectives do not speak directly to how to respond to what learners have just said or done or to identifying what to do next with students. The goals need to be more immediate and need to relate to the content teachers are expected to teach and kids are expected to learn.

Lessons From Standards Documents

The national standards are exhibited primarily by the Benchmarks for Science Literacy (Project 2061, 1993) and the National Science Education Standards (National Research Council, 1996). Similar standards have been created in many of states and districts, and teachers and students are being held accountable to these standards. These are not so much a characterization of students' thinking as they are statements of learning targets to be achieved by the educational system.

   Although many of the standards statements are not sufficiently specific or clear as to what is expected, they are much more clear than what has typically existed before them. They usually include learning goals that involve processes of scientific inquiry. For example, the following statement from the National Research Council (NRC, 1996) document suggests that students: "Formulate and revise scientific explanations and models using logic and evidence" (NRC, 1996, p. 175). They go on to say, "... discussions should be based on scientific knowledge, use of logic, and evidence from their investigation." This statement says both what students should be able to do as a result of the instruction and also suggests what students ought to be doing during their instruction to accomplish the skill of developing scientific explanations. The NRC also suggests that "Eliciting and analyzing explanations are useful ways of assessing science achievement" (NRC, 1996, p. 92). But, in this statement, the result of such assessment might be whether or not the students were able to give a correct explanation. It does not say much about what constitutes a good explanation, or what sort of troubles students might have with the concept of explanation.

   The goals that are more directly related to specific subject matter describe more specifically what students should know. For example, regarding force and motion, "If more than one force acts on an object along a straight line, then the forces will reinforce, diminish, or cancel one another, depending on their direction and magnitude. Unbalanced forces will cause changes in the speed or direction of an object's motion" (NRC,

1996, p. 154). "The change in motion of an object is proportional to the applied force and inversely proportional to the mass" (Project 2061, 1993, p. 91).

Although vague, these descriptions are at a level that is somewhat understandable to teachers. If the teachers' content understanding is sufficient, they probably can tell if the student seems to "have" the idea or not. If students do not yet have the idea, teachers may be able to choose more lessons that give students some opportunity to learn, or at least practice using, the idea. But, assessment based on description of learning goals only facilitates knowing whether students "have it" or not. These learning goal descriptions give no advice about what alternative understandings might be exhibited and what the evidence for those understandings might look like. They give no assistance in determining what understandings the students do have if they don't have the goal understanding. Also, they do not give advice for how to bridge the gap from the preconceptions to these targets of learning, except to do more activities in which students practice the proper thinking. However, that tends to yield "school science" and does not foster conceptual change on the part of the learner.

Requirements for a Description of Students' Knowledge Based on These Lessons

We need a system of description that both incorporates what we have learned from research on students' understanding and learning. I believe that we need descriptions of students' understandings that help teachers and developers form bridges to the goals (standards) for science learning. I suggest the following requirements:

- The system of description should be based on research on students' understanding and reasoning.

- It should include explicit learning goals.

- It should build from the intuitive ideas of students toward the targets of learning.

- Various sorts of reasoning difficulties, conceptual difficulties, and procedural difficulties should be made explicit as well as making the learning targets specific.

- The language of the descriptions should be understandable to discipline experts and to teachers who may not have the domain expertise but who are responsible for creating the classroom environments to foster development toward the learning targets of the discipline.

A characterization of students' understanding and reasoning that makes the most sense to me and to my fellow teachers is middle level in the sense that it is between elemental psychological primitives on the one end and alternative (or naïve) theories of knowledge on the other. We want to describe the learning targets and the problematic conceptions and actions in what students said and did in the classroom. Knowledge of these initial and intermediate alternative understandings allows us to identify them and design lessons to motivate students to reconstruct more successful understandings. We are creating a description called Facets of Thinking to serve our desire to incorporate results from research in a middle language to that which both scientists and teachers could relate. The description is intended for use in making day-to-day decisions in the classroom.

Facets of Thinking: A Middle Language to Describe Students' Thinking

Although the Facets of Thinking perspective is now being used in several content areas (e.g., introductory physics, university statistics, middle school mathematics, environmental science, and issues in eldercare), I will primarily use the context of introductory physics to describe the approach, since that is the context in which the perspective was first developed. The purpose of this section is to describe what is meant by the phrase "facets of students' thinking" and to present some examples.

Facets are used to describe students' thinking as it is seen or heard in the classroom or other learning situations. Facets of students' thinking are individual pieces, or constructions of a few pieces, of knowledge and/or strategies of reasoning. While a *facets* perspective assumes a "knowledge in pieces" perspective, the pieces are generally not as small as the phenomenological primitives (p-prims) suggested by diSessa (1993). Facets have been derived from research on students' thinking and from classroom observations by teachers. They are convenient units of thought for description and analysis in serving teachers and developers as they make instructional decisions. Since facets are only slight generalizations from what students actually say or do while learning, they can be identified by teachers and used by teachers to discuss the phenomena of students' ideas. Some are content specific, e.g., "horizontal movement makes a falling object fall more slowly." Others are strategic, e.g., "average velocity is half the sum of the initial and final velocities" (in any situation). Still others seem to reflect more generic reasoning approaches like "more implies more," e.g., "the more batteries, the brighter the bulb." Typically they are (or may seem to be) valid, depending on the context of usage.

While teachers can participate in "discovering" facets, their primary task is in designing or choosing appropriate activities and in implementing instruction in the most effective way possible. For the most part teachers do not have the time to conduct the research or to accumulate and organize the research results themselves. We consider that to be our contribution to constructing more effective learning environments.

Facet clusters are sets of related facets, grouped around explaining or interpreting a physical situation (e.g. forces on interacting objects) or around some conceptual idea (e.g. meaning of average velocity). Within the cluster, facets are sequenced in an approximate order of development from most problematic to least problematic. There is numerical coding correlated with the assumed ranking of development. Those ending with zero or one in the units digit tend to be appropriate and acceptable understandings for introductory physics. The facets ending in eight or nine tend to be the more problematic facets in that if this is not dealt with during the design and implementation of instruction, the student will likely have a great deal of trouble achieving the specific learning goal. Those facets with middle digits frequently arise from formal instruction, but the student may have over-generalized, or under-generalized, its application. The numerical code is intended as a descriptive aid, not as a scoring system. Although there is an intention to rank the problematic understandings, the ranking is done more for sequencing instruction than for evaluating one answer as better than another answer. The real purpose of the coding is to indicate qualitatively different understandings that will likely require different lessons to address them.

Examples of Facets and Clusters

Facets to Describe and Monitor Procedures

This first example is a cluster describing the ideas students have or strategies they use to determine a best value in measurement. Consider the cluster in Table 1, including seven facets, describing what students say or do with respect to determining a best value resulting from measurement in laboratory work in introductory physics at the high school level.

Table 1. Facet cluster: Best value in measurement.

*100   Use a procedure appropriate to the context to obtain a number representative of the possible measures one might get.

*101   Measure the quantity several times (possibly using different scales) and take the average of the several measures (perhaps using appropriate rationale to eliminate extreme outliers) to determine a number that best represents the actual value.

103   Always average all the measures obtained (regardless of outliers).

104   Always eliminate the high and low values and average all the rest (even in cases with only three measurements).

105   Average the highest and lowest measures inappropriately, such as when data is skewed.

106   Use the median when the data is mulitimodal.

108   "Mine" (single measure made by the student doing the reporting) is the only valid measure.

109   Some one authority made one measurement and the student reports it as "the" actual, true value.

Facet number 100 represents a conceptually appropriate action. It is a brief statement of a learning goal relative to determining best value in measurement. What action is appropriate depends on the context. In some situations, such as weighing oneself in the morning, it might be a single measurement that will satisfy the situation. At other times, such as determining the maximum acceleration of a car, multiple measures might be more appropriate. Depending on the data resulting from multiple measures and how the result is to be used, the most appropriate method might be to report the mean or the median or even the mode(s) for the data. Facet 101 represents a more formulaic method to determining the best value in measurement. It is the usual preferred algorithmic method in laboratory work, even though a simpler method might well also apply.

Notice in both cases the word "appropriate" is involved. Thus, some judgement is involved on the part of the teacher user.

Notice that there are no codes 102 and 107 for this cluster, and there are only possibilities for eight problematic codes in the system. In our experience in the physics class, the facets indicated were the primary problematic facets which we felt our students tended to use frequently. We also limited the number to about ten facets in a cluster because that was about all the teacher could attend to in instruction.

Facets numbered 103 through 109 may each be appropriate in certain contexts. But, each becomes problematic if it is the only strategy used by the student or if the strategy is used in inappropriate contexts. For example, I gave my students a situation involving five measurements of Blood Alcohol Content (BAC) taken from the same sample for the same individual. The measurements were assumed to have been made by five different people, including a head MD, a nurse, a technical assistant, an intern, and themselves (assuming they had been trained to use the apparatus). Students were asked what should be reported as the BAC for the individual. One reading was clearly an outlier, but in the scenario, it was the measurement made by the head MD. A significant proportion of the class defended their choice of the number obtained by the MD, "because he knows the most." Even though there were five measures, other students chose some measure made by one of the other people making the measurements, "because they are the expert." Thus, for this question, their response was coded 109. In subsequent class discussion, other students argued against taking the value from one "expert" given the several other measures. They suggested several ways that the "expert" might have been wrong. For example, some said, "My dad is a doctor and he wouldn't even know how to take the measurement." Others said, "Since there are other measures probably no single measure is necessarily the 'right' one. You need to take into account the other numbers." When students with the 109 idea heard the experiences and arguments from their fellow students, they were dissuaded from overuse of the "expert" doing the measurement once. Through similar arguments, other students were dissuaded from believing that "mine" (facet 108) must necessarily be the correct measurement.

In this cluster, the codes 103–106 represent various emphases on using multiple measures, but inappropriately. The BAC problem provides a context in which to discuss each of these strategies and the sorts of contextual situations in which each strategy might be appropriate and the sorts of situations in which they would not be appropriate. With the 100/101 learning target in mind, the teacher should choose problems and other activities that offer opportunities to use *and* to misuse some of these other strategies. In order to assess whether students have problematic ideas, we need to present them with tasks wherein taking the problematic approach might initially seem appropriate to the learner. Also, we need to assess what students do in naturally occurring situations in which the idea might inappropriately be applied. For example, ask students to correctly handle measurements in subsequent lab activities. Then, observe whether they are using appropriate procedures. How are they handling outliers? What do they do with bimodal data? When do they decide they can get by with one measurement and when are they careful to measure multiple times and resolve the several readings into a best value? Give them problems that have skewed data, bimodal data, or cases in which only one measurement was made and ask them how the data should be handled? Give them data that comes from their life experiences. "In any of your classes, should you be graded on the basis of the results of one test? Why or why not?" "What should the grade be if a student had the following scores: …?" "How sure are you that the SAT score you got represents a prediction for your success at college?" Then, how do the students reason about the data? What facets of their understanding are exhibited? Have they moved toward a more flexible view of determining "best value in measurement?" Do they choose a procedure appropriate for the purpose of the measurement? If not, what is their facet of thinking about best value?

Sometimes there are procedural facets within a cluster of facets about the meaning or application of an idea. For example, in the cluster on the meaning or application of average velocity, there are facets in which the misapplications are buggy procedures. A student may invert the ratio and calculate delta time divided by delta position. This is a rate, and it involves the changes in the appropriate quantities, but it results in a quantity that better describes "slowness" than "fastness." As it turns out, that is a useful concept in considering the rate of sedimentation of solid particles in a body of water. The point here is that some of the facets are mis-procedures rather than mis-conceptions.

Facets to Describe and Monitor Explanations in General

As noted earlier, generating scientific explanations is a focus of the current science education reform efforts. We developed facets to describe what learners do in general when it comes to explaining various phenomena. Peoples' explanations generally progress from a description of the phenomenon or description of procedures for creating the effect, through identification of relevant concepts, to understanding particular mechanisms of causality, to a more model-like weaving of concepts, mechanisms, and relations among factors. When teachers are monitoring how students explain or interpret phenomena in general, they can use the general cluster in Table 2.

Table 2. Facet Cluster: Explaining and interpreting phenomena.

*050   Explanations or interpretations involve conceptual modeling of multiple related science or math concepts, using experimental evidence and rational argument to address questions of "how do you know...?" or "why do you believe...?" the results, observation, or prediction.

*051   Explanation involves a mathematical modeling approach, incorporating principles subsumed under that model.

053   Explanation involves identifying possible mechanisms involving a single concept causing the result and the relation between that variable and the result.

056   Explanation involves identifying and stating the name of a relevant concept.

058   Explanation constitutes a description of procedures that led to the result.

059   Explanations or interpretations are given by repeating the observation or result to be explained.

My past observations in science museums suggest a similar, general sequence in development of meaning and use of explanation. Visitors, especially children, when asked what sense they make of an exhibit, typically first respond with a description of an observation (59), e.g., "The thing went pop," "The color changed," or "The fish came to the top." After spending more time at the exhibit, they may express the procedure by which they can create the observed effect (58), e.g. "When I did this, it made that happen." Many visitors stop here to run off to another exhibit. Some try to identify a relevant concept or at least a word to represent the related concept (56), e.g., "It happens because of air pressure." Some may identify a mechanism and the relation between the associated variable and the dependent variable (53), "The bigger the glancing angle, the more the surface makes the light bend." Eventually, when learners have a deep, model-like understanding of a situation, they can identify several related factors and the relation between the independent factors (some maybe even unseen) and the outcome.

Facets to Describe and Monitor Students' Understanding of Particular Situations

Many of the facet clusters are created around classic events in the learning of the discipline. When the class is investigating particular content, such as explaining falling bodies, teachers may use the cluster in Table 3. The two facets, 349+ and 349++, almost never occur at the high school level but frequently happen with young children. The other facets represent the sort of statements given by students prior to and during learning activities involving dropping various objects and explaining the results. Although typically most students begin the unit exhibiting lower level facets (349 or 348), with good instruction, nearly all students move up the roughly ranked ladder of facets. Over half (59%) of our students used explanations 342, 341, or 340 on the end-of-year test, several months after instruction on falling bodies. On interim exams, discussions, problems, or other class activities involving falling bodies, a teacher can follow the development of understanding of individual students or the class as a whole by charting the codes for relevant clusters as they occur.

Table 3. Facet cluster: Explaining falling bodies.

*340	Gravitational pull by earth on falling object and mass of object compensate for each other. The resistance by the medium through which the object is falling increases with speed and will decrease the rate of acceleration.
*341	$(Fg - Fr)/$ mass = acceleration (instantaneous rate) of fall. With no resistance, near the earth, things fall, accelerating at about 9.8 m/s/s.
342	Gravitational pull and mass compensate, but greater air resistance on the lighter object, making it fall behind.
343	Gravitational pull and mass compensate with no accounting for air resistance.
344	Greater drag effects compensate for greater gravitational pull explaining equal accelerations. No apparent accounting for inertial mass of the object.
345	Drag effects of medium will exist even when there is no motion relative to fluid medium. The resistive force exists even when the object is not yet falling.

Table 3 continued

346   All things fall with equal acceleration of about 10m/s/s.

347   All things fall equally fast regardless of medium effects. For example, vertical fall is at a constant velocity of 10 m/sec.

348   Weight makes it hard to move things. The more weight, the slower they fall. It takes time to get them going. Heavier things will lag behind until they can get going.

349   Weight makes things fall. The more weight, the faster they fall.

349+   When you let things go, they fall.

349++ Things fall down.

For the cluster "explaining falling bodies," the facet ending in 0 again represents a more conceptual understanding and the facet ending in 1 represents the more mathematical modeling of the situation. Ideally, eventually physics students would have both the scientific conceptual reasoning and the equations, and the understandings would be integrated with their everyday knowledge based on intuitions (Larkin & Chabay, 1989). They would have links between their final, more formal, principled understanding and their early intuitions.

One caution needs to be leveled when one considers interpreting results from different clusters. In the present version of facets, the facets in different clusters can not be assumed to be at an equal level just because the codes end with the same digit, and likewise similar levels of understanding presently may have different units digits from one cluster to another. For example, the code 058 is a generalized explanation that just repeats procedures, whereas in the falling bodies cluster, 349+ corresponds to the procedural explanation. Ideally, at some point in time, we might have enough knowledge and experience to go back and equalize levels between cluster. At present it would be a mistake to assume that it had been done.

The Relation Between Facets and Standards

Standards say what we *want students to know and be able to do*. Facets describe the sorts of things that students *do seem to know and do*. One can think of the standard as the facet ending in 0 or 1. But, the standards do not identify student difficulties based on research. Facets coded with digits other than 0 or 1 are intended to identify what is problematic about the students' understanding on their way to the learning target standards. The following analogy may help the reader understand the relation between standards and facets:

> "Benchmarks are the islands of understanding to which we want our students to sail. The problematic facets are like the reefs on the way to the islands. To be able to navigate between the islands one needs to have a deep understanding of the reefs which themselves may seem to be firm enough to stand on."

Thus standards and facets can be integrated to incorporate the results of learning research with the standards. For example, Table 4 includes some of the Project 2061 benchmarks for understanding force and motion along with the relevant clusters of facets.

Table 4. Integration of facets with AAAS benchmark standards for grades 9-12.

AAAS benchmark: "When one thing exerts a force on another, an equal amount of force is exerted back on it." (Project 2061, 1993, p. 92).

Cluster 470: Forces during interactions (developed).

*470	All interactions involve equal magnitude and oppositely directed action and reaction forces that are on the separate interacting bodies.
474	Effects (such as damage or resulting motion) dictate relative magnitudes of forces during interaction.
474-1	At rest, therefore interaction forces balance.
474-2	"Moves," therefore interacting forces unbalanced.
475	Equal force pairs are identified as action and reaction but are on the same object.
476	Stronger exerts more force.
477	One with more motion exerts more force.
478	More active/energetic exerts more force.
479	Bigger/heavier exerts more force.

AAAS benchmark: "Change in motion of an object [v/t] is proportional to applied [unbalanced] force and is proportional inversely to the mass." (Project 2061, p. 91).

Cluster 420: Forces to explain linear accelerated motion (reviewed from grades 6-8 or redeveloped here).

*420	Acceleration is proportional to Fnet and inversely proportional to mass.
*421	*421 $A = F_{net}/m$
423	Acceleration is the result of any force applied to the object (not F_{net}).

Table 4 continued

424   F_{net} depends upon potential (or on what's about to happen to it). If it is going to accelerate eventually, then it has a net force on it.

425   Objects do not have mass in space, they can accelerate without force.

426   Objects do not have "hold back" inertia in vertical situations, they just accelerate down.

428   Explaining any accelerated condition with an excess force proportional to the velocity acting on the object.

429   While the object is accelerating, it "has" force proportional to its velocity. Force is perceived as a property of the object.

Benchmarks at grades 9-12 include knowing Newton's Second and Third Laws. Achieving both of these learning targets is difficult. Many of the alternative ideas exhibited by students are described in facet clusters 420 and 470. Each facet is the description of a different idea. For example, facet 429 describes the idea that force is a property of the object, and facet 428 describes that the force acting on the object needs to be proportional to the velocity of the object. Facets 479, 478, 477, and 476 each describes a different salient feature to which the student seems to be attending when considering situations in which two objects interact, such as in a collision. These are ideas that stand counter to the identified learning targets, the particular 2061 benchmarks (Project 2061, 1993).

Although it is probably not appropriate to think of the facets at equal increments along an interval scale, the rough ranking may serve as some measure of progress. For example, the student who is focusing on effects (474) or the student who at least is looking for an action-reaction pair (475) seem to have some knowledge that students who gave the responses coded as 476 through 479 do not seem to have. Facets coded as 474 and 475 represent some formal learning. In most of the facet clusters, there are facets which typically represent pre-instruction understanding, one or two facets that represent the targets, and then one or more groups of facets that represent some middle ground. Thus, these facets seem to group into what might be something like a three-position scale. However, it is more important to think of facets as important way-points on the way to understanding the targeted standard. Each facet is a different idea that probably requires somewhat unique instruction.

Instructional Design Based on Facets

Using Facets to Design a Facet-Based Learning Environment

The purpose of a facet-based learning environment is to build from students' initial and developing ideas towards a richer, more principled understanding, to bridge the gap from research on students' understanding and reasoning to learning goals or benchmarks. Facets are used to diagnose students' ideas and to direct the choice or design of instructional activities (Minstrell, 1989; Minstrell & Stimpson, 1996; Minstrell, in press).

If teachers are only given the learning targets, the focus of their assessment is likely to be whether the student is right or wrong. Since most have not had time or opportunity to study the research on students' conceptual difficulties, and they have not had tools to help them identify specific ways that students might have gone "wrong," "correct" or "not yet correct" is all we can expect of teachers. If students are not yet correct, without the knowledge of just what is problematic about students' thinking, the teacher is left to ask the student to not think like that, "think like I have been telling you to think." That sort of instruction does not address the specific positive or negative aspects of students' present thinking. Having facets allows the teacher to a) identify the sort of thinking on which the student may be stuck and b) focus instruction on what is problematic about the student's understanding.

Suppose we are going to begin a sub-unit of instruction focused on learning Newton's Third Law, the action-reaction law. Our learning goal is some form of the top benchmark in Table 4, e.g., facet 470. Having the other facets in that cluster gives a teacher (or a developer) some of the design features for an assessment task. Posing a task with two interacting objects such that one object is clearly bigger/heavier (479), more active (478), moving more (477), stronger (476), and/or produces more apparent effects (474) will likely assist the teacher in diagnosing the extent to which these facets are salient for her students. One example situation for asking about relative forces during interaction includes two skaters, one of whom is bigger and stronger than the other. Suppose they face each other and push each other away, who exerts the greater force? Always asking students to explain how they decided allows the teacher to diagnose more reliably the facet(s) of thinking exhibited by this student.

Each diagnosed facet suggests features that need to be included in subsequent first-hand learning activities for students. Indeed, each facet can be thought of as an hypothesis suggested by the student. For example, if students are thinking that the one skater will exert the larger force because she is stronger, they need activities that allow them to test the effects of the variable of relative strength. Strength becomes a variable around which the students can design experiments. Some of my students have designed situations in which a person known to be strong is pitted against a frail person. Each holds a bathroom scale and puts it against the bathroom scale of the other person. Each pushes and observes the readings of the scale. They are typically surprised to find that the scales read the same, within limits of precision. Other students attach a strong spring to a weak, very stretchy rubber band. They put their fingers through the free ends of the rubber band and the spring and feel (and further test with laboratory spring scales) the force to stretch each, reasoning that they are indirectly reading the forces that the rubber band and spring exert on each other at the point of contact. They end up concluding that the forces are not distinguishably different, even though they predicted one hand would feel more force because the spring was so much stronger.

As a variation of this last experiment, I created two magnetic boxes that seemed in every respect the same, except that one would pick up a paper clip from the table while the box was a couple of centimeters from the clip, and the other would not pick up the paper clip until the box was brought within a couple of millimeters of the clip. Clearly one of these magnets is stronger than the other magnet. But, when the magnetic boxes were brought near each other so they repelled, the hands holding the boxes could not detect any difference in the forces. This experiment was done in the interest of controlling all hypothesized variables except magnetic strength.

In a similar way, the students investigated each of the other features they had identified through the elicitation questions involving the skaters. Relative weight was tested as a possible relevant variable by having two students of obviously different weight pulling or pushing on scales that were back to back between the pair of students (Camp & Clement, 1994). The scales read the same. Greater activity was tested by having one cart with a protruding spring push away from another identical cart but without the "active" spring. Regardless of which cart has the active spring pushing, the resulting motion of two otherwise identical carts is the same.

Greater effects were tested with students riding on different carts and pushing off on each other, again with scales between them. One cart had low friction wheels and the other would barely roll. Again, the scale readings are not detectably different.

Although the students were attempting to control all variables other than the one they were testing, several of the experiments were fraught with possible confounding variables. But, by this point the students were seeing the pattern that the forces interacting objects exert on each other seem to be equal in magnitude but in opposite direction. They were beginning to generate and understand the meaning of equal and opposite action and reaction forces.

Some students have picked up on the pattern of what to say (equal and opposite) but have not yet grasped the real meaning. As a developer, or as a teacher, I now need to structure situations in which it would be inappropriate to say that the forces are equal. For example, I need to ask questions about the forces on one accelerating object as well as asking about the forces during the interaction between two objects. "How do the forward forces on the accelerating object compare with the resistive forces on the object?" In this situation, students need to recognize that there needs to be a net unbalanced force in the forward direction on the accelerated object, so the forward forces must be greater than the backward forces. However, that is asking about the forces on one object to explain acceleration of that object. (Note we are now asking questions relevant to cluster 420, a cluster of ideas that came before the 470 in the sequence of development of ideas in the class.) If students truly understand these aspects of force, they will distinguish between when we are talking about the forces to make an object accelerate and when we are talking about the forces that interacting objects exert on each other. These are subtle distinctions that many beginning physics teachers and their curricula have not made, but having the facets from research helps cue the teacher to the need to make these distinctions in the activities made accessible to the students in order to go for depth of understanding.

During a series of activities lasting a few days, teachers in a facet-based learning environment typically have a page with the relevant facet cluster(s) handy as they prepare and implement lessons. As they design or choose laboratory activities, they design them to challenge the problematic facets as well as support the goal facets. In discussions and problem assignments, teachers listen and watch for expressions representative of a particular facet and guide the students into activities designed to address that facet. If through hands-on experiences and discussions, the problematic ideas are shown to be unsuccessful, then students are more willing to seek and adopt new ideas that work, e.g., the learning goal facets (Posner, Strike, Hewson, & Gertzog, 1982).

Early in my experience in action research, I thought I could "give" these problematic facets to students and they would see the troubles with them and move toward the goal facets. That was not effective. The alternative facets needed to come from them. When they identified what they thought was going to happen, or what they thought were the relative forces, they were more able to see the relevance of the experiments they did to test the idea. It was their idea they were testing. Later they remembered their original idea did not work and they remember the experience that showed the idea did not work.

Using Facets and Facet Clusters to Design Assessment

When designing assessment activities teachers use facets within a cluster to predict the sorts of answers students might give. If the assessments are embedded within the instruction, teachers can identify the facets that are still representative of students' present ideas. Then they choose or design other activities that address those particular problematic facets. Colleagues and I designed a computerized Diagnoser to assist with ongoing assessment (Hunt & Minstrell, 1994; Levidow, Hunt, & McKee, 1991; Minstrell, 2000; Minstrell, in press). The questions come in pairs. The first question typically asks, "What would happen if...?" Although it involves multiple choice answers, each choice is associated with one or another facet. Thus the system makes a preliminary diagnosis of a specific, potential difficulty. The second question follows up with "What reasoning best justifies your answer?" Again each answer from which the students choose is associated with a particular facet. From this answer, the system makes a secondary diagnosis and gives feedback fitting the particular facet diagnosis and the problem addressed. These sorts of tools help classroom teachers monitor and address students' thinking in time to address problematic thinking.

The design of subsequent assessment can also be informed by revisiting the facets. For example, long after students have forgotten the slogans that they may have memorized for tests, strong assessment items can be used that incorporate many of the features students intuitively invoked. For example, there is a question that Clement used in his Mechanics Diagnostic that will be very difficult for students whose ideas about interacting objects have not yet changed. A bowling ball rolls down an alley and hits a bowling pin. How do the forces that the ball and the pin exert on each other compare? In this case, the bowling ball has all the advantages from the students' intuitive notions. It is heavier, made of harder material (stronger), moving when it hits the pin, more active as it moves along toward the passive pin, and certainly creates the greater effect, in the sense that the pin gets knocked way back while the ball simply continues to roll along, apparently with little change.

This is an example of the difference between traditional assessment and facet-based assessment. In the former, we tend to look for affirmation that students will respond correctly or not. In facet-based assessment, the questions are what students call "tricky"—in that they offer seductive situations from which we are trying to find out what learners do not yet have as part of their understanding. In this example, we do not want to know that students have learned to parrot an "equal and opposite" answer as a result of being trained in "school science." We want to see if students have changed their thinking about the world around them. Thus, the "tricky" questions that may be found along side questions asking about the forces on the pin. (Force by bowling ball on pin is bigger than resistive force of friction by floor on pin, but force by ball on pin equals force by pin on ball.) For a deep understanding, learners need to understand when the slogans "equal and opposite" and "net unbalanced forward force" apply. The relation between the action-reaction idea (facet cluster 470), the forces on an accelerating object (facet cluster 420), and the forces on objects moving with a constant velocity (facet cluster 430), and forces on an at rest object (facet cluster 410) suggests that for a true understanding, students will need an ecological relationship between multiple clusters. Lasting development in one cluster will require building a new model for understanding motion, but the construction can happen with a focus on one cluster at a time (Halloun & Hestenes, 1987).

Facet-based assessment and related instruction pushes students to learn what they do not yet understand as well as what they do seem to understand. Learning is a gradual and ongoing process. Diagnostic assessment can tell us where the student's understanding seems to be at a particular time, so teachers can know what might still need to be addressed in instruction.

Results from large-scale, on-demand assessments based on facets could inform educators and policy people on where resources are needed (Minstrell, 2000). If students in a particular school are stuck on a particular facet, that school can be made aware of the curriculum and instruction used by another school that specifically addresses that facet. Effective lessons can be shared between schools and teachers to address particular learning difficulties, provided we have been able to identify the particular problematic thinking. Typical large-scale assessment tells us only generally where the troubles lie. It tends not to help us know specifically what needs to be addressed and how.

Facets Research and Development

Research to Discover, Collect and Organize Facets and Facet Clusters

In this section I will describe several approaches taken to discover, collect, and organize facets in several content areas and at several age levels. Then I will summarize the general principles behind the process for development of a facet base that can serve instructional decision making. The research has ranged from very systematic to quick, "on the fly" methods. In either case, the facets and clusters produced represent tentative descriptions of thinking by that group of learners. Through use by teachers, the drafts get revised. Notice also the diversity of the topics in which the facet research and related instructional development have been done. I now believe a facet-based approach can be used in any learning situation in which learners have alternative ideas or alternative procedures and associated reasoning.

Introductory Physics and Beyond

As briefly described earlier, the facets in learning introductory physics were derived from an attempt to organize the "misconceptions" research. In the 1970s, I was a co-investigator of a project for assessing conceptual development in introductory physics at the university level. At the same time, I was investigating the thinking of my high school students in the interest of effecting better learning in my classes. The list of "misconceptions" became very long and many of the ideas expressed by students had positive aspects as well as negative aspects. By the middle 1980s I had quite a long list of conceptual difficulties of my high school students. This was the beginning of facets of students' thinking. As suggested earlier in this chapter, *facets* was my term to sidestep the issue of whether they were misconceptions, procedural errors, mistakes in reasoning, etc. Regardless of the type of difficulty, as a classroom teacher, I needed to deal with it. Facets of thinking was my way of acknowledging and describing students' thinking so that I could begin addressing it in the classroom.

Also, because the list of facets was getting long, I needed a way to organize facets to make them manageable for me to attempt to address them in my high school instruction. After grouping facets into sets that seemed to show up together, I noticed that the sets were either about students' understanding of some big idea or about students' attempts to explain classic events in the teaching of physics. These sets of related facets evolved into the facet clusters for introductory physics. Examples of the physics facet clusters have been shown earlier in this chapter.

Based on the early work on facets, computerized tools have been developed to assist teachers in facet-based learning environments. Earlier in this chapter, I described the computerized Diagnoser. Variations of Diagnoser have also been developed in modules for assessment of ratio reasoning in mathematics by Aurora Graf and for assessment of understanding environmental issues of water quality by Alice Barnes and Earl Hunt, all in the Psychology Department at the University of Washington (Barnes, 1998). These tools have been effective for delivering multiple choice questions and quick facet analysis of students' responses.

Steve Tanimoto and colleagues in Computer Science at the University of Washington have been developing a tool for on-line assessment reading responses to open-ended questions. The system is called Interactive Facet-Assessment Capture Tool (INFACT). To use the system, a set of relevant clusters of facets must be installed, such as the facets and clusters for introductory physics. Then the application of the tool for the assessment process begins with an imported set of electronically submitted responses. On the screen the instructor can read each student response, highlight evidence for a particular facet, and record that evidence in the student record. The accumulated records for students can then be reported to the teacher and display the students' development within a cluster across time or display the status of the whole class with respect to an individual cluster or set of clusters. The vision involves automating the reading of short and extended answers by students to help reduce the analysis time by teachers in order to free them up to help groups of students address their particular learning needs.

Physical Science and Mathematics, Grades 6 through 10

At the time of writing this chapter, Earl Hunt and I, with colleagues in the public schools, in cognitive science at the University of Washington, and at Talaria are identifying facets associated with Washington State learning goals for grades six through ten in physical science and mathematics. We have months instead of years to describe the associated facets and clusters. With this time constraint, we are applying more "seat of the pants" approaches. We are incorporating some of the facets and clusters from the earlier introductory physics study. Literature on students' thinking provides grist for constructing other facets and clusters (Driver, Squires, Rushworth, & Wood-Robinson, 1994; NSTA, 1994). But, for big ideas or critical events to explain, we are also conducting our own research to find out about students' thinking with respect to the state guidelines. We create relevant, open-ended questions and teachers in the field collaborate by obtaining responses from their students and helping us interpret the results. Somewhere between 40 and 100 responses seems to give us sufficient data. As we read students' answers and rationale, we put the papers into piles representing similar reasoning. After summarizing what is similar about the papers in each particular stack, we draft a facet description for the apparent thinking exhibited by those students. The set of facets "discovered" in this way becomes a draft facet cluster. The draft cluster is circulated to resource teachers who comment on and suggest additions or revisions to the draft cluster. This interim version will likely be further revised after classroom use. One example of a middle school level cluster is shown in Table 5.

Table 5. Science strand: Properties Washington Benchmark 2. Facet Cluster: Meaning and use of Density.

0   An appropriate conceptual modeling of density as the number of units of mass (of substance or object) associated with each one unit of volume (of substance or object).

1   A mathematical modeling of density, appropriately using the relation D=M/V.

2   Density of object is the average density of the densities of the materials out of which the object is made.

3   Density is close packing. It is the number of things in a region of space.

4   Different densities, if and only if, different materials. Uniqueness of density number with unique material.

5   Density is associated with floating, means not dense and sinking means dense.

7   Density means how heavy—the heavier the greater the density.

8   Density means size/volume/liquid displacement. E.g., if displace same amount of water, then same density

8a   The bigger the more dense.

8b   The smaller, the more dense without reference to keeping the mass the same.

9   Density is a function of shape. Different shape implies different density.

University Statistics

Colleagues Andrew Shaffner and David Madigan developed a facet-based learning system called Diana for the World Wide Web. It was patterned after Diagnoser in Physics. To identify learner's facets of understanding in statistics, Shaffner and Madigan did a review of literature on students' understanding of statistics. But, since much of their statistics course involved learning about experimental design, they needed to learn about students' thinking in those topics. Being time-constrained, they needed to gather lots of responses to various questions quickly. By putting open-ended questions on the internet, they were able collect as many responses as they needed to draft a set of facets for their course (Shaffner, et al., 1997). Within less than a year, they had redesigned their statistics course based on facets and had evidence of improved student learning about clusters related to designing and conducting scientific studies. See Table 6.

Table 6. Statistics Cluster: Sample size and precision in estimating population means.

0	The sample size, together with the inherent variability in the population from which the sample was drawn, determines how certain we are about our estimates of the population mean.
4	The size of the sample alone determines how certain we are about our estimate.
5	The sample size relative to the population size together with variability determines how certain we are about our estimates of the population mean.
7	The sample size relative to the population size alone determines how certain we are about our estimate.
8	Only the variability in the population determines how certain we are about our estimate.
9	Neither the size of the sample nor the population variability is considered.

Eldercare

To push the envelope in the creation of facet-based learning environments, colleagues at Talaria, a small research and development company in Seattle, are identifying facets of thinking on the part of caregivers who work with the elderly. To identify potential facets of thinking the researchers interviewed about 50 subjects. Each subject was interviewed about his or her understanding of the cause of the disease, the description of symptoms of the disease, and the treatment of one or more of 21 diseases typical in the elder population. Each interview lasted a bit over 1 hour per disease. A few of the subjects were novices in the eldercare field, and a few had 15 or 20 years of nursing assistant experience. Most had 3 to 5 years experience as a nurse's assistant working in eldercare. During the interviews, field notes were taken. Although there were several interviewers for each disease, one interviewer took responsibility for summarizing the potential facets for each cluster. Other interviewers then suggested revisions, and a final draft of facets and clusters was constructed.

Table 7 presents a tentative facet cluster related to learners' understanding of the primary cause of emphysema. The next phase of the research will be to run a trial using Web-served diagnostic questions related to the diseases wherein the expected answers are taken from the proposed facets. This will allow us to test and subsequently revise the facets and clusters. Finally, a computerized facet-based learning environment is the expected product.

Table 7. Elder Care Cluster: Cause of emphysema. The cause of emphysema is considered to be...

0	Environmental toxins, like cigarette smoke.
2	A contagious infection in the lungs.
3	Weakened lungs, due to a history of frequent colds or flu.
4	Asthma or some other chronic lung disease.
5	A genetic defect.

In General

Facets can be determined through interviewing learners, through paper and pencil questions and elicited responses, and through responses to questions on the Web. Questions used to elicit facets need to be carefully crafted to engage learners' thinking with respect to identified learning targets. Since the purpose of facet-based learning environments is to guide assessment and instruction at the learning site, teachers of the discipline need to be involved in reviewing and revising facets and in evaluating their utility.

The following represents a summary of guiding principles for designing a facet-based learning environment:

- *General goals.* Identify the understanding and process skills that represent the learning goals for the particular target audience.

- *Specific goals.* Identify specific ideas and events critical to what the learner needs to know and be able to do.

- *Elicitation questions.* Design questions which will engage the thinking of learners with respect to the learning goals.

- *Identify tentative facets.* Collect sufficient number of responses to questions to determine various approaches to thinking about each of the critical ideas and events. (About 20 in-depth interviews, and 40 extended written responses to 100 short responses seem to be a good sample for a first pass).

- *Rank order facets.* If possible, order the facets from those most problematic to those more consistent with the learning goals. Use intellectual development and instructional efficacy as guiding criteria.

- *Diagnostic questions.* Design more specific questions from which students' apparent facets can be identified.
  - Questioning contexts need to relate to the critical thinking in the goals.
  - Questioning contexts need to be seductive to eliciting some problematic facets
  - Write specific answers associated with relevant facets in multiple choice format or rubrics for facet diagnosis in open response format.
  - Leave an option for learners to respond with an unanticipated answer.
  - Facet revision. Revise the tentative facets and clusters on the basis of how well they describe students' responses and apparent thinking.
- *Question revision.* Revise questions on the basis of how well they elicit students' thinking.
- *Feedback.* Design feedback that fosters open sharing of learners' ideas and yet stimulates critical thinking on the part of learners.
- *Prescriptive lessons.* Design lessons informed by instruction known to effect movement from particular problematic facets of thinking toward thinking more consistent with the learning goals.
- *Test and revise the facet-based learning environment.* Design and conduct studies to test the effects of the learning system. Weigh costs against benefits of using the system. Re-engineer/revise the system to improve benefits and lower costs.

Identifying facets and facet clusters is an ongoing, iterative research and development process. As we try to extend the contexts of questions around one cluster, we find what we have actually done is increase the complexity of the knowledge and understanding required to appropriately address the question. And, we get responses we had not anticipated. We identify new facets. That may result in dividing one cluster into two. But, meanwhile, we try to remember that the tools we are developing right now are for learners who are relatively new to the topic. We first want to address their learning needs and their teachers' needs for tools to foster the learning at that level. Later, more elaborated clusters can be created for the learners who are going on to become experts in the field.

Meanwhile, we encourage our teachers to keep their eyes and ears open for different facets that may need to be addressed. At one point, while investigating forces and gravity, I suggested to my students, "Suppose there was no friction acting on the wheels of the cart. Suppose there was no air resistance acting on the cart, no air in the room..." And then I heard quiet voices in the corners of the classroom saying, "Why, then everything would just float off the table." This meant I needed a facet cluster dealing with the effects of the surrounding fluid (air) as well as a cluster about the nature of gravity and other actions at a distance. Thus, the process of facet finding will likely never be complete. The more complex the learning we expect, the more practical tools we will need to describe what is happening with respect to students' thinking.

Summary

In this chapter, I suggest a need for a middle language to bridge the gap between learning research and classroom practice. Facets of students' thinking bridges from what students do know to the learning goals we want them to achieve. From a facets perspective, assessment items can be designed to diagnose particular problematic facets, and instruction can be designed specifically to address each facet diagnosed. Finally, my colleagues and I have now done sufficient research and development from a facets perspective to believe that the research and development can be conducted in any realm of human experience that involves developing understanding from observational facts to rich conceptual frameworks. We finished by suggesting a draft of guidelines for the research and development of a facet-assessment based learning environment. We welcome other participants in the process. Please see http:://www.talariainc.com/facet.

Acknowledgements

I would like to thank David Madigan and other colleagues at Talaria Inc. for their assistance in preparing early drafts of this paper. I also wish to thank Earl Hunt, Steve Tanimoto, and colleagues at the University of Washington for their critical review of theoretical ideas and for their assistance in the transfer of the facets framework into technological tools. I especially appreciate assistance from our teacher collaborators and their students. Without their help, the facet perspective would not have been tested. Together I know we have constructed a practical, research-based framework that can assist students and teachers in effecting better learning. Finally, I want to thank the editors of this book for their thoughtful, constructive comments. Research and development of the facets perspective has been supported by grants from the James S. McDonnell Foundation Program in Cognitive Studies for Educational Practice (CSEP). The writing of this paper was partially supported by grants from the National Institutes of Health and the National Science Foundation Program for Research in Educational Policy and Practice (REPP). The ideas expressed are those of the author and do not necessarily represent the beliefs of the foundations.

References

Barnes, A. (1998). A *field study of school computer use: Examination of the effects on student learning and perceptions of learning*. Unpublished doctoral dissertation, University of Washington, Seattle.

Camp, C., & Clement, J. (1994*). Preconceptions in mechanics: Lessons dealing with students' conceptual difficulties*. Dubuque, IA: Kendall Hunt.

Chi, M. T. H., Feltovich, P., & Glaser, R. (1981). Categorization and representation of physics problems by experts and novices. *Cognitive Science 5*, 121-152.

diSessa, A. (1993). Toward an epistemology of physics. *Cognition and Instruction, 10 (2 & 3)*, 105-226.

Driver, R., Squires, A., Rushworth, P., & Wood-Robinson, V. (1994*). Making sense of secondary science: Research into children's ideas*. London: Routledge.

Goldenfeld, N., & Kadanoff, L. (1999). Simple lessons from complexity. *Science 284*, 87-89.

Halloun, I., & Hestenes, D. (1987). Modeling instruction in mechanics. *American Journal of Physics, 55*, 455-462.

Hunt, E., & Minstrell, J. (1994). A cognitive approach to the teaching of physics. In K. McGilly (Ed.), *Classroom Lessons: Integrating cognitive theory and classroom practice*. Cambridge, MA: MIT Press.

Larkin, J., & Chabay, R. (1989). Research on teaching scientific thinking: Implications for computer-based instruction. In L. Resnick & L. Klopfer (Eds.), *Toward the thinking curriculum: Current cognitive research*. (Yearbook of the Association for Supervision and Curriculum Development.)

Levidow, B., Hunt, E., & McKee, C. (1991). The Diagnoser: A HyperCard tool for building theoretically based tutorials. *Behavior research methods, instruments, and computers, 23 (2)*, 249-252.

McCloskey, M., Caramazza, A., & Green, B. (1980). Curvilinear motion in the absence of external forces: Naïve beliefs about the motion of objects. *Science, 210,* 1139-1141.

Minstrell, J. (1989). Teaching science for understanding. In L. Resnick and L. Klopfer (Eds.), *Toward the thinking curriculum: Current Cognitive Research.* (Yearbook of the Association for Supervision and Curriculum Development.)

Minstrell, J. & Stimpson, V. (1996). A classroom environment for learning: Guiding students' reconstruction of understanding and reasoning. In L. Schauble & R. Glaser (Eds.), *Innovations in learning: New environments for education.* Mahwah, NJ: Lawrence Erlbaum Associates.

Minstrell, J. (2000). Student thinking and related assessment: Creating a facet assessment-based learning environment. In J. Pellegrino, L. Jones, & K. Mitchell (Eds.) *Grading the nation's report card: Research from the evaluation of naep.* (Committee on the Evaluation of National and State Assessment of Educational Progress, Board of Testing and Assessment.) Washington DC: National Academy Press.

Minstrell, J. (in press). The role of the teacher in making sense of classroom experiences and effecting better learning. In D. Klahr & S. Carver (Eds.) *Cognition and instruction: 25 Years of Progress.* Mahwah, NJ: Lawrence Erlbaum Associates.

National Research Council (1996). *National Science Education Standards.* Washington DC: National Academy Press.

NSTA (1994). Gabel, D. (Ed.) *Handbook of research on science teaching and learning.* New York: MacMillan Publishing Co.

Posner, G., Strike, K., Hewson, P., & Gertzog, W. (1982). Accomodation of a scientific conception: Toward a theory of conceptual change. *Science Education, 66,* 211-227.

Project 2061 (1993). *Benchmarks for Science Literacy.* New York: Oxford University Press.

15

The Role of Hypothesis Formation in a Community of Psychology

Takeshi Okada
Takashi Shimokido
Nagoya University

When we interviewed scientists about their collaborative processes (Okada, et al., 1995), a computer scientist who had collaborated with a cognitive psychologist mentioned the following:

> The most important benefit of participating in this interdisciplinary collaboration is that there are scientists who have a different sense of value on science. For example, when working with researchers in the same discipline, we share a common ground and a common language. We can make progress in our project very quickly without wondering about what the co-researcher meant. Now, I think that my co-researcher in this interdisciplinary project and I didn't share that common ground when we started our project. Therefore, we could not make any progress for about one year. We could not understand what confused us... The difference of disciplines related to the differences in the sense of value on science, methodology that we use, and more concretely speaking, evaluation criteria. Those differences made me feel this interdisciplinary collaboration was very interesting! [Translated from Japanese]

We have also had similar experiences when working with computer scientists. It seemed that the computer scientists were more concerned with creating phenomena on a computer system, while we, as psychologists, were concerned with understanding phenomena in the real world, through experimental design, hypotheses, and manipulating variables.

These episodes suggest that scientists have beliefs about how science should proceed and be evaluated, and that these beliefs are discipline specific. These beliefs influence scientists' research activities, such as conducting research projects, writing research articles, and advising students' research projects. In this chapter, we will focus on our discipline-specific belief about science that is widely shared in the psychology community.

Our conclusions are based on historical case studies and a questionnaire survey addressed to the Japanese psychology community.[1]

Hypothesis-Testing Style as a Prescriptive Method in Psychology

Psychology encompasses a diverse range of topics and methodologies. However, scientific aspects have been important in characterizing mainstream psychology. The word *science* appears in the titles of many psychology and psychology-related journals: i.e, *Psychological Science, Behavioral Science, Cognitive Science, Human Science,* and *Social Science.* Furthermore, scientific psychology has emphasized the importance of justification as a measure for being scientific. The hypothesis-testing style (i.e., entertaining clear hypotheses and testing them based on data) has been adopted as a prescriptive means for justification. When conducting scientific research, many psychologists believe that they must first develop clear hypotheses before testing them against the available data.

This hypothesis-testing style seems to be an offshoot of several dominant movements that emerged in Western psychology in the 1930s and 1940s. There were several major movements that may have influenced the adoption and spread of the hypothesis-testing style: logical positivism and operationism, hypothetico-deductive method, and inferential statistics (Ikeda, 1971).

Logical positivism aims to clarify the language of science and investigate the conditions under which empirical propositions are meaningful, then verify the propositions by means of a concrete procedure. This movement in the philosophy of science was introduced to the psychology community in the 1930s by Stevens (1939). His papers triggered debates on this issue in the community. *Operationism* (Bridgeman, 1928), which claims that a scientific concept should be defined by concrete operations to achieve the concept, was integrated into the logical positivism movement. These movements served as a strong theoretical background for the formation of scientific psychology.

The hypothetico-deductive method (H-D method) is a scientific method in which investigators are required to adopt a postulate tenta-

---

1. This study has been presented at the Designing for Science Symposium held at University of Pittsburgh in April of 1998, the Symposium on "Thinking about Science" held at Nagoya University in February 1999, and the Annual meeting of the Japanese Psychological Association in 1999. A part of this chapter has been described in a Japanese publication (Okada, 1998). The details of these historical case studies and the questionnaire survey are described in Okada & Shimokido (2000).

tively and deduce its logical implications, and then check the validity of them by observation. This system had been discussed in the philosophy of science for quite a long time, but it was not well known in the field of psychology until Hull, a founder of neo-behaviorism, adopted it as a core research method for his studies (Hull, 1943). As neo-behaviorism became dominant in psychology for the next several decades, Hull's emphasis of the H-D method had a strong influence in the psychology community.

With the development and introduction of inferential statistics to psychological research, investigators then had tools to implement logical positivism and the H-D method in their research (Fisher, 1925; 1935). Before inferential statistics were developed, the psychology community had been limited to descriptive statistics.

It is difficult to tease apart the effect of these philosophical and statistical movements on the formation and adoption of the hypothesis-testing style in psychology. However, these movements had strong influences on the psychology community, the effects of which are still being felt today. In the rest of this chapter, we will address the following questions related to the hypothesis-testing style of research in the community of psychology: How and when was such a belief formed in the psychological community in Japan? What kind of role does this belief about science play in shaping research activities?

The primary data are from the Japanese psychology community. However, we feel that this data reflects the situation of psychology in the Western community as well, since the Japanese psychology community has been strongly influenced by Western psychology, particularly by the United States. Moreover, Kerr (1998) found a similar pattern of researchers' beliefs on the hypothesis-testing style in the psychology community in the United States using a similar questionnaire survey with somewhat a different focus. This work will be mentioned later in the chapter.

Three Aspects of Research Activities in Science

We will focus on three important aspects of scientific research: 1) Writing journal articles; 2) educating psychology students, and, most importantly; 3) conducting research projects. We chose these three activities because they have been emphasized as important aspects of scientific communication by philosophers of science, such as Barnes (1985).

On Writing Journal Articles

When submitting articles to psychology journals, authors sometimes receive comments that may have been motivated by the belief that research papers without hypotheses are unscientific. Following are examples of comments that our colleagues received from journal reviewers:

> "The authors do not make any predictions or provide the foundation for predictions." (*Cognitive Science*)

> "The most serious problem of this paper is that there is no clear hypothesis mentioned. . . You should predict what kind of result you would acquire and describe what the paper would contribute if the result is obtained." (*Japanese Journal of Psychology*) [Translated from Japanese]

In order to verify whether or not these examples reflect the current situation of the psychology community in Japan, we conducted a questionnaire survey of psychology researchers in 1998. Participants were first and second authors of articles published in the *Japanese Journal of Psychology* and the *Japanese Journal of Educational Psychology* over the previous year. Those two journals are bulletins of the two major scientific psychology societies in Japan. A questionnaire was mailed to 137 authors. We received replies from 111 authors—a response rate of 81.2%! The questionnaire included questions about the timeline of developing the hypotheses mentioned in each article and authors' past experiences of hypothesis formation in research activities. Each question will be described in detail in later sections of this chapter.

Participants were asked if they had ever received reviewer comments that recommended revising the article to clarify the hypothesis: 25.7% of respondents answered *yes*. Considering the fact that this question only applies to authors who have previously submitted at least one paper to a journal without including any hypotheses, this rate should be regarded as quite high! This suggests that the Japanese psychology community encourages researchers to write articles with clearly stated hypotheses. On the same issue, Kerr (1998) conducted a similar study, giving a questionnaire to 156 behavioral scientists in the United States. It asked them to estimate what percentage of publishable research articles should state an explicit hypothesis, according to journal editors and reviewers. Respondents thought journal editors and reviewers would say that research articles should state an explicit hypothesis about 80% of the time. Though this research did not focus on respondents' actual experience with reviewers, it does suggest that beliefs about the hypothesis-testing style in journal review processes are widely shared among psychologists, not only in Japan, but also in the United States.

In order to see how such journal review processes affect the style of journal publications, we coded the empirical articles (i.e., articles with data) in the 1997 volume in the Japanese Journal of Psychology (Okada & Shimokido, 2000). If any hypotheses, predictions, or expectations were stated in an article, it was coded as an "article with hypothesis." Sometimes, hypotheses were clearly stated in the articles: "The hypothesis of this research is..." or "We have three hypotheses. The first one is..." Sometimes, the expression in an article was more subtle such as, "...was expected" or, "If it is true, this result would happen." We included all of them as "article with hypothesis" because, with this analysis, we wanted to capture how authors were influenced by the hypothesis-testing style of writing. Using this criterion for hypotheses, we divided the empirical articles into four categories. The first category is *articles with no hypotheses mentioned*. The second category is *articles with hypotheses mentioned after the first experiment*. The third category is *articles with one or more hypotheses mentioned in the introductory section*. The fourth category is *articles with two or more hypotheses mentioned in order to distinguish a correct one from wrong ones* (i.e., a diagnosis test). The third and fourth categories were regarded as "articles with hypotheses."

The results showed that, in 1997, 58.8% of the empirical research articles in the *Japanese Journal of Psychology* had some kind of hypotheses written in the introductory section. Note that the other empirical articles that did not have any hypotheses focused mainly on clinical case studies, testing the validity of a questionnaire, or psychophysics, which traditionally are types of articles written without hypotheses. Taking this into account, we can say that the hypothesis-testing style of writing articles is currently dominant in the Japanese community of psychology.

Do research articles in other disciplines follow the same hypothesis-testing style? We checked the 1996 volumes of Japanese science journals; these were the most recent volumes available in our university library at the time. It was not easy to identify important journals in each field, but we looked at the publication lists of the faculty members of each discipline in our university, then chose journals in which they were frequently published. We used the same coding scheme as the one previously mentioned, for the 1997 volume of the *Japanese Journal of Psychology*.

Table 1. Articles with hypotheses in various scientific disciplines.

JOURNAL	ARTICLES WITH HYPOTHESES IN THE VOLUME
Solid-state physics	0% of papers had hypotheses
Earth science	0% of papers had hypotheses
Analytical chemistry	0% of papers had hypotheses
Environmental medicine	0% of papers had hypotheses
Neuroscience	0% of papers had hypotheses
Ocean and sky (meteorology)	0% of papers had hypotheses
Analytical chemistry	2.8% of papers had hypotheses
Polymer chemistry	24% of papers had hypotheses

The main result of this analysis is shown in Table 1. As we can see, many research articles in other scientific disciplines do not follow the hypothesis-testing style of writing. Despite the belief about a scientific writing style that our psychology community shares, it seems that many scientists in natural science disciplines do not adhere to the hypothesis-testing style of writing. Are we willing to say that these articles without hypotheses are unscientific?

The next question that occurred to us was whether or not psychology articles have always used the hypothesis-testing style. If movements such as logical positivism, H-D method, and inferential statistics had influenced research activities in psychology, the hypothesis-testing style of writing should have emerged at some point thereafter and spread throughout the psychology community. In order to answer this question, we conducted a historical analysis of the *Japanese Journal of Psychology*. It has been published since 1925, is the official journal for the Japanese Psychological Association, and is the oldest and most prestigious psychology journal in Japan. We coded the journal articles using the same coding scheme as previously described.

Figure 1 shows the results of the historical analysis of empirical articles in this journal. We examined every tenth volume of the journal from 1935 to 1998. (The most recent volume was Volume 69 at the time of this analysis.)

As shown: a) There were almost no articles with hypotheses in the introduction published prior to WWII; b) the number of articles with hypotheses gradually increased after WWII; and, c) the majority of the articles in the current volumes have hypotheses.

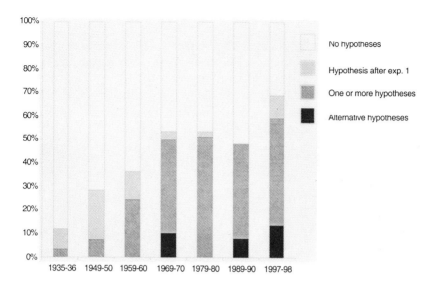

Figure 1. Historical analysis of hypotheses in the Japanese Journal of Psychology.

These results suggest that after Word War II, Japanese psychology researchers formed the standard that scientific articles should have hypotheses clearly stated in the introduction. This standard is quite different from that of the journals in other scientific disciplines. (Currently, we are conducting the similar analysis with American scientific journals so we can verify whether or not this trend is unique to the Japanese psychology community.)

The results of the historical analysis of the *Japanese Journal of Psychology* agree with the historical evidence regarding the import of the aforementioned movements—logical positivism, H-D method, and inferential statistics—from Western psychology to Japan. Although those movements emerged in Western psychology in 1930s and 1940s, World War II prevented Japanese psychologists from being exposed to them. When World War II ended, these movements were introduced and gradually adopted into the Japanese psychology community by those who were eager to catch up with the new trends in Western psychology. Theoretical articles on logical positivism and operationism appeared in the 1948 (the first volume after Word War II) and the 1949 volumes of the *Japanese Journal of Psychology*. Before Word War II, there was very little research in behaviorism in Japan. After Word War II, neo-behaviorism was introduced. For

example, symposia on behaviorism were held at the 13th annual conference of the Japanese Psychological Association in 1949, entitled "Behaviorism and operationism" and "Causal Inference in Behaviorism." With
these efforts, neo-behaviorism and its primary research method, the H-D
method, spread throughout the Japanese psychology community in the
following years.

According to analyses done by Omi (1997), the history of statistics in
Japanese psychology has four phases: Phase 1 (1926-1944) was a descriptive statistics era in which psychology researchers used only descriptive
statistics, including analysis of correlation. Phase 2 (1948-1950s) was an
inferential statistics era in which various methods of inferential statistics
emerged. Phase 3 (1960s-1970s) was called the "ANOVA era" in which
ANOVAs dominated the field as the main method of statistical analysis.
Phase 4 (1980s-present) could be described as the "multivariate analysis
era" in which the development of computers enabled psychology
researchers to employ complicated statistical analyses. As mentioned
above, inferential statistics were introduced to Japan right after Word War
II. For example, in the *Japanese Journal of Psychology*, the first theoretical
article on inferential statistics appeared in 1948.

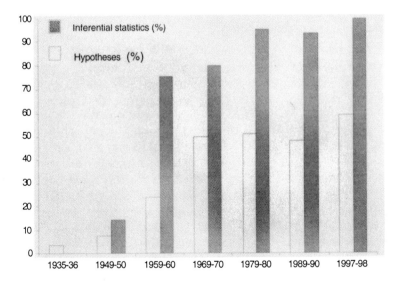

Figure 2. Historical analysis of the use of statistics in the *Japanese Journal of Psychology*.

Our historical analysis of the empirical articles in the *Japanese Journal of Psychology* also showed that the percentage of articles with inferential statistics increased dramatically during the 1950s (see Figure 2).

From this evidence, we believe that it would be a fairly valid inference that a new belief about the hypothesis-testing style of writing articles among Japanese psychology researchers was influenced by logical positivism, H-D method, and/or inferential statistics.

On Teaching How to do Research

During 4 years of teaching in the psychology department at Nagoya University in Japan, the first author found that many psychology majors were taught that they must form clear hypotheses before collecting data. An undergraduate student in a research methods course complained, "Although I want to study this topic, I cannot come up with a clear hypothesis. So, I cannot study this topic." A graduate student writing a master's thesis came to his office one day and confessed, "Though I conducted three experiments for my master thesis, I could only come up with a clear hypothesis in the last experiment. So, I may not have the ability to conduct scientific research."

In the process of learning about psychology, many students seem to acquire the idea that they have to form a clear hypothesis in order to conduct a psychological research study. In the questionnaire survey mentioned in the last section, we asked the following questions:

1. When you were a student, had you ever received advice from someone telling you that you should start a research project by developing clear hypotheses? *77.4% of respondents answered yes.*

2. When writing papers, had you ever received advice telling you that you should write clear hypotheses in the paper? *65.1% of respondents answered yes.*

3. Have you ever read a textbook on research methodology of psychology suggesting that you should start with clear hypotheses when conducting research? *70.8% of respondents answered yes.*

4. Have you ever given advice to someone telling him or her that when conducting research they should develop clear hypotheses before collecting data? *69.8% of respondents answered yes.*

Overall, the percentage of the respondents who answered yes to at least one of the above questions was 90.1%. Thus, the hypothesis-testing style seems to be the dominant practice in the Japanese psychological community.

The results of this survey are not surprising because many research methodology textbooks in psychology also mention that psychological research should proceed by finding questions and entertaining clear hypotheses first, then by collecting data. Following are excerpts from popular Japanese textbooks about research methods in psychology.

> *Research Manual for Educational Psychology,* Tatsuno, Arai, & Tanaka (1982): After clarifying a research question, you have to make a clear hypothesis. Experimentation is the method with which to verify the hypothesis. [Translated from Japanese]

> *How to Conduct Research and Write a Paper,* Shirasa (1987): The research process is the process of testing hypotheses. …Thus, entertaining hypotheses is a very important first step to start research. If you think that you can discover something when conducting a survey or experiment with vague ideas, you will never succeed in your research. [Translated from Japanese]

The same trend was found in textbooks in the United States (Kerr, 1998). It seems that both in Japan and in the United States, psychology undergraduate and graduate students have been taught to use the hypothesis-testing style of research and to write articles following that style.

On Conducting Research Projects

It has been suggested that psychologists value the hypothesis-testing style when they write articles and when they teach others how to conduct research. What about their own styles in conducting research projects?

Our questionnaire survey was individualized for each respondent (Okada & Shimokido, 2000). We identified the hypotheses in an article they had published and asked the authors specific questions about the hypotheses. If no hypothesis had been stated in their article, the same question was asked without identifying any specific hypothesis. The question was regarding whether they had developed the hypothesis written in their paper before they had collected the data. Respondents had to choose one of the following answers: a) The *same hypothesis was entertained throughout*; b) a *different hypothesis was entertained*; c) a *vague hypothesis was entertained*; d) *no hypothesis was entertained*; or (e) *others*.

In the case of articles with hypotheses, 70.6 % of the respondents said that the same hypotheses had been entertained throughout the study. However, 23.5% of the respondents admitted that they had different hypotheses, vague hypotheses, or no hypotheses at all before collecting data. Thus, we found that even if there are hypotheses clearly written in journal articles, it does not necessarily mean that the authors used the hypothesis-testing style when conducting their research. That is, in some cases hypotheses may have been developed between data collection and the writing of the paper. When interpreting the data, we have to consider that this survey was addressed to authors who have successfully published articles in mainstream psychology journals in Japan. It is highly possible to imagine that many psychologists who conducted research without hypotheses either could not publish their work in those mainstream journals or did not have the courage to submit them.

The practice of coming up with hypotheses after data collection, but implying that they had been developed prior to data collection, is referred to as HARKing (i.e., Hypothesizing After the Results are Known) by Kerr (1998). In his survey of behavioral scientists in the United States, Kerr found that HARKing is widely observed in the US behavioral science community.

These results tell us somewhat contradictory stories about psychologists' research activities. While researchers in psychology conduct research in diverse ways (i.e., sometimes starting with a hypothesis and sometimes without), when they write journal articles they often imply that they had conducted the hypothesis-testing style of research. When researchers teach others how to conduct research, they strongly emphasize employing the hypothesis-testing style. Does this mean that those psychologists who could not come up with any hypothesis before collecting data are not practicing the "correct" method of scientific research? Is the hypothesis-testing style really the best and the most scientific method of conducting research?

Potential Problems with the Hypothesis-Testing Style of Research

Many philosophers of science have pointed out that scientists are not necessarily using the hypothesis-testing style of research when conducting scientific research (e.g., Hanson, 1958). Although it is a complex phenomenon, to make the story simple, we could say that scientific discovery processes have two main phases: discovery of an explanation and justification for it. The hypothesis-testing style of research is strongly related to the justification side of scientific discovery processes, but not as much to the discovery side. Therefore, it does not completely reflect the actual process of scientific discovery. For example, Hanson (1958) stated in his famous book, *Patterns of discovery:*

> Physicists do not start from hypotheses: They start from data. . . H-D accounts begin with the hypothesis as given. ...The H-D account describes what happens after the physicist has caught his hypothesis; but it might be argued that the ingenuity, tenacity, imagination and conceptual boldness which has marked physics since Galileo shows itself more clearly in hypothesis-catching than in the deductive elaboration of caught hypotheses.

Like Hanson, it seems that the majority of philosophers of science abandoned the concept that the hypothesis-testing style of research was the ideal scientific method a long time ago. However, as we have described, many psychology researchers still believe that this method is the best (and sometimes the only) scientific method that psychology should follow.

Various Styles of Research in Science

Some scientists have pointed out that they are actually conducting research and producing prominent findings using other research styles. For example, Herbert A. Simon (1996), one of the founders of the fields of cognitive science, artificial intelligence, and cognitive psychology, has written about his research style as follows:

> The experiments described up to this point all compare performance under two or more different conditions, by manipulating an independent variable. When I examine my other experimental research, I find to my embarrassment that this fundamental condition for sound experimentation is seldom met. What have I been up to? What can I possibly have learned from ill-designed experiments? The answer (it surprised me) is that you can test theoretical models without contrasting an experimental with a control condition. And apart from testing models, you can often make surprising observations that give you ideas for new or improved models...
>
> Perhaps it is not our methodology that needs revising so much as the standard textbooks on methodology, which perversely warn us against

running an experiment until precise hypotheses have been formulated and experimental and control conditions defined. Perhaps we need to add to the textbooks a chapter, or several chapters, describing how basic scientific discoveries can be made by observing the world intently, in the laboratory or outside it, with controls or without them, heavy with hypotheses or innocent of them. (pp. 383-385.)

Simon (this volume) describes a case study of Faraday and further argues that curiosity and careful observation, which often lead to surprising results, are centrally important values to the scientific enterprise.

In another scientific discipline, the director of the Institute of Earth Science at University of Alaska and one of the leading scientists in Aurora research, Shunichi Akasofu (1998), described the way that scientists in earth science conduct research: First, they collect solid data on the phenomena they are interested in and do preliminary analyses on them. Then, they integrate those data to form hypotheses or theories. Then, they test the hypotheses or theories with the same data set conducting quantitative analyses.

These examples tell us that, at least in some scientific disciplines, scientists conduct research without using the hypothesis-testing style. They form hypotheses after observing phenomena. Are we willing to say that they are not doing science? Instead of clinging to a prescriptive idea that has been uniquely adopted and shared in the psychology community, it is better for us to open our eyes to see what the scientists (including ourselves) are actually doing.

Research Findings from the Cognitive Psychology of Scientific Thinking

This point is supported by further evidence from studies in cognitive psychology. In the field of cognitive psychology, there have been substantial numbers of studies focused on scientific discovery processes. These studies typically use micro-world discovery tasks in which subjects, usually undergraduate students, are required to discover a mechanism implemented in the task (for example, Dunbar & Klahr, 1988; Klahr & Dunbar, 1988; Okada & Simon, 1997; Schunn, 1995). Subjects in these studies were asked to talk aloud while participating in the study. Although findings from such studies using micro-world tasks may not necessarily be the same as findings from studies focused on actual scientists' activities, it is likely that such micro-world studies, if carefully used, reflect at least some parts of actual scientific discovery processes (Klahr & Simon, 1999;

Okada, 1999).

These studies suggest that: a) Subjects frequently design experiments without hypotheses; b) the frequency with which subjects design experiments without hypotheses is higher at the beginning of research; c) there are individual differences in whether people tend to design experiments without hypotheses (experimenters who start experiments without hypotheses vs. theorists who start experiments with hypotheses); and d) experimenters were just as likely to discover the correct hypothesis in the end, although perhaps not as quickly as theorists. These results fit with our findings from the questionnaire survey. Together, they converge to tell us that there are various research methods and styles in science.

Advantages and Disadvantages of Various Scientific Styles

Hypothesis-testing styles of research, which are based on the H-D method and strong inference (Platt, 1964: i.e., develop alternative hypotheses and devise a crucial experiment that excludes one or more of the hypotheses, then carry out the experiment so as to get a clean result), are probably useful when the research field has been well developed or the research project has progressed up to the level that the researchers do not need to create any new paradigm or theory. Although the percentage of articles which used strong inference in psychology journals is not high (see Figure 1), Platt (1964) claimed that this scientific method is the most productive way to conduct scientific research.

However, we feel that his claim is probably too strong to generalize. In certain situations, the H-D method (especially strong inference) might not work well. For example, when the research field is not well formed yet, or the research project is at the starting stage, the hypothesis-testing style of research might force researchers to form a hypothesis prematurely. Toyoda (1998) pointed out that even a study with a precise statistical analysis to distinguish rival hypotheses might only be able to distinguish the rival hypotheses that are located very close to each other in a highly complicated hypothesis space. Therefore, when there is no valid reason to form hypotheses with the currently available data and theory, there is a possibility that the researchers will focus on hypotheses that are far apart from the correct hypothesis. In such a case, they might be stuck with irrelevant questions or irrelevant hypotheses that might not lead to any major discovery.

Conducting Good and Interesting Research

As Simon (this volume) points out, we need to pay much more attention to the hypothesis discovery phase of research instead of, or at least in addition to, the hypothesis justification phase. One of the most important goals for a psychology researcher is to conduct good and interesting research that may lead to new discoveries. Although the H-D method and strong inference are useful to justify hypotheses that already exist, we might need something more than those methods to find new hypotheses before we can begin justifying them.

How can we come up with new ideas and conduct good and interesting research? Okada and Crowley (2000) interviewed ten prominent psychologists in the two approaches that have had strong influences in developmental psychology recently: The information processing approach and the sociocultural approach. In this study, we asked the following questions to the interviewees: a) What kind of features does good and interesting research have? and b) What are the important things to do in order to conduct good and interesting research? Some of the psychologists mentioned the importance of observation of everyday phenomena and of pilot analysis of data in order to come up with new research questions and new hypotheses.

For example, Robert Siegler, a developmental psychologist using the information processing approach, emphasised the importance of starting research with observation:

> One thing that I think that is important is relying more on issues that are important in children's everyday lives both in and out of school, and less on issues that are getting attention in the literature, because it's very easy to get captured by the literature. So, you read lots of studies, about the latest fad, and you say, "Oh well, this must be very important," and when there are a lot of studies, you can always think of ways they can be extended or alternative interpretations, confounds that were present, and you can do more and more, but it makes less and less of a contribution. I think a better way to go about is to ask yourself: "What is really interesting that I see children doing, what are the real problems that they confront, and how do they go about them?" So a lot of times I think the best studies are ones that take as their fundamental phenomemon something that everyone has seen, but that no one has analyzed or understood very well, and I think that that's a way to be creative on one hand, but also linked to reality on the other.

Jaan Valsiner, who is a developmental psychologist following the sociocultural approach, also talked about the importance of observation:

> I decided I should look for settings that are meaningfully organized before my ever trying to organize them without my intervention. So from that follows the interest in looking at everyday life contexts that are so ordinary that we fail to notice them. We don't see them. And meal-time contexts are contexts which are so ordinary that we do not pay attention to the fact of how they are culturally organized. So I decided to look at children during breakfast and lunch time, accepting the kind of organization that the given family had given to this, and analyze that structure of organization and then analyze the actual conduct by children and parents in that context. And that was the starting point for the meal-time study. It was the starting point also for the study looking at how American parents try to get children to say bye-bye to the departing visitor. That is, I noticed during these meal-time home visits, which started at 6 months of age and continued to 26, that when I left the house, the mother would take the child with her to the door, carrying the child, then takes the child's hand and waves bye-bye to me. And I became curious, this was a perfectly nonsensical act from the point of view of any aspect of the child's development except one, that of the socialization of the child toward politeness to visitors. The child of course was the simple object of moving through the motion, but for the mother, this was an important act to introduce the child to the departure context. So we went on to study that in the child's own home, looking at how a child would be asked to say bye-bye, and how the child does it. This was in the 12 to 18 months range. But again the starting point was an ordinary everyday observation of something that is so ordinary that we usually don't pay attention to it.

As these researchers pointed out, one of the useful ways to find new ideas about research questions and hypotheses seems to be starting a research project with an observation of an everyday phenomenon. However, psychologists' beliefs about the hypothesis-testing research style may prevent them from starting research with observations. For example, the gap among the sub-components of the research activities (i.e., conducting research projects, writing research articles, and advising students' research projects) might mean that such a prescriptive belief about the hypothesis-testing style of research distorts psychologists' view of research activities. Moreover, psychology students, who are just starting to learn how to conduct research projects, may be strongly discouraged from starting their research projects with observations. Researchers, who are at the beginning stages of their research careers, may also be intimidated by conducting exploratory research without hypotheses if their submissions are rejected from mainstream journals because of a lack of hypotheses in the introductory section of their articles. Many young researchers who are searching for jobs and working for tenure may have been concerned with conducting publishable research instead of innovative research. If the systems in the psychology community, such as education systems at the undergraduate and graduate levels, review systems in journals, and hiring and promotion systems in academia, are changed, psychology researchers and students could be more motivated to conduct innovative research using various methods.

Conclusion

In the historical and social context of Japanese psychology, many psychology researchers in Japan acquired the belief that the hypothesis-testing style was the best, and sometimes the only, scientific way. Such a belief creates a cognitive constraint (Brown, 1990; Miyake & Hatano, 1991; Siegler & Crowley, 1994;) on the way that psychology researchers participate in research activities such as conducting research, writing research articles, and teaching research methods. Such a belief, on one hand, has a positive effect in enhancing effective research activities; many research articles have been published using this hypothesis-testing style. However, on the other hand, there could be situations in which such a belief has negative effects on research activities. As we have shown above, it was suggested that some articles without hypotheses have been rejected by journal reviewers as non-scientific even though such articles might have made a great contribution to the community of psychology, had they been published. It was also suggested that such a belief shaped types of research procedures that might have distorted researchers' views on scientific discovery. As for the educational aspect, it was suggested that some of the psychology students felt discouraged to explore new research directions because they received advice emphasizing the hypothesis-testing style of research.

Recently, textbooks introducing non hypothesis-testing styles have emerged. Also, it seems that some research methods courses in psychology departments started to teach research styles other than the hypothesis testing style. However, it seems that the time is not yet ripe for articles with such styles to be published in mainstream Japanese psychology journals.

We believe that awareness of this cognitive constraint is the first step in overcoming the negative aspects of it. This chapter aims at making a contribution towards such an awareness in the psychology community. Since this cognitive constraint was formed socially, culturally, and historically, it would also be possible for us to change the role of the constraint once we become aware of it and attempted to work on it. For that sake, some of the suggestions made in other chapters of this book are very useful. For example, Simon (this volume) offers insight about the role of curiosity, and Lehrer, Schauble, and Petrosino (this volume) emphasize the importance of models and inscription rather than hypothesis testing. We believe that more work on these scientific activities needs to be done in future.

Acknowledgements

This chapter was written while the first author was a visiting scholar, supported by the Japan Foundation, at the University of Pittsburgh, Learning Research and Development Center. This research was partially supported by the Ministry of Education, Science, Sports and Culture, Grant-in-Aid for encouragement for young scientists, 1997-1998, and the grant of the Tokai Science Academy, 1999. We thank Kevin Crowley and Christian D. Schunn for useful comments on an earlier draft. We also thank Herbert A. Simon, Kazuhisa Miwa, Hitoshi Tamura, Kazuhisa Todayama, Takashi Murakami, Rose Russo, and many others who gave us valuable comments on our conference presentations.

References

Akasofu, S. (1998, March). *Science and paradigms.* Colloquium lecture at Nagoya University.

Barnes, B. (1985). *About science.* Oxford, England: Basil Blackwell.

Bridgeman, P. W. (1928). *The logic of modern physics.* New York: Macmillan.

Brown, A. (1990). Domain-specific principles affect learning and transfer in children. *Cognitive Science, 14,* 107-133.

Dunbar, K., & Klahr, D. (1988). Developmental differences in scientific discovery processes. In D. Klahr & K. Kotovsky (Eds.), *Complex information pro-*

cessing: The impact of Herbert A. Simon (pp. 109-143). Hillsdale, NJ: Lawrence Erlbaum Associates.

Fisher, R. A. (1925). *Statistical methods for research workers.* London, England: Oliver & Boyd.

Fisher, R. A. (1935). *The design of experiments.* London, England: Oliver & Boyd.

Hanson, N. R. (1958). *Patterns of discovery.* Cambridge, MA: Cambridge University Press.

Hull, C. L. (1943). *Principles of behavior.* New York: Appleton-Century-Crofts.

Ikeda, H. (1971). *Kodokagaku no houhou* [Methods of Behavioral science]. Tokyo: Tokyo University Press.

Kerr, N. L. (1998). HARKing: Hypothesizing after the results are known. *Personality and Social Psychology Review, 2,* 196-217.

Klahr, D., & Dunbar, K. (1988). Dual space search during scientific reasoning. *Cognitive Science, 12,* 1-48.

Klahr, D. & Simon, H. A. (1999). Studies of scientific discovery: Complementary approaches and convergent findings. *Psychological Bulletin, 125.* 524-543.

Miyake, N. & Hatano, G. (1991). Nichijoteki ninchi katsudo no shakaiteki bunkateki seiyaku [Socio-cultural constraints and beyond]. In Japanese Cognitive Science Society (Ed.), *Ninchi Kagaku no hatten,* 4. Tokyo: Kodansha.

Okada, T. (1998). Kasetsu wo meguru ikutsukano kasetsu: Kagaketuki kenkyu ni okeru kasetsu no yakuwari [Hypotheses on hypothesis: The role of hypothis in scientific research]. In S. Maruno (Ed.), *Series Shinrigaku no nakano ronso. [Volume 1] Ninchi shinrigaku ni okero ronso.* Kyoto, Japan: Nakanisiya Shuppan.

Okada, T. (1999). Kagaku ni okeru kyodou kenkyu no process:Interview, shitsumonshi chousa, oyobi shinrigaku jikken niyoru kentou. [Scientific collaborative research processes]. In T. Okada, H. Tamura, K. Todayama, K. Miwa (Eds.), *Kagaku wo kangaeru: jinkouchinou kara shiten.* Kyoto, Japan: Kitaoji-Shobo.

Okada, T. , & Crowley, K. (2000). Omoshiroi kenkyu no yarikata: Hattatsu shinrigaku ni okeru futatsuno approach no kenkyusha eno interview ni motoduite. [How to conduct interesting research: Based on interviews with psychologists in two approaches in developmental psychology]. In H. Kojima, T. Hayamizu, & S. Honjo (Eds.), *Ningenhattatsu to shinrigaku.* Tokyo: Kaneko-Shobo.

Okada, T., Schunn, C. D., Crowley, K., Oshima, J., Miwa, K., Aoki, T. & Ishida, Y. (1995, June). *Collaborative scientific research: Analyses of historical and interview data.* Paper presented at the 12th Annual Conference of the Japanese Cognitive Science Society.

Okada, T., & Shimokido, T. (2000). *Hypothesis-testing style of research in psychology.* Unpublished manucript, Nagoya University, Japan.

Okada, T. & Simon, H. A., (1997). Collaborative discovery in a scientific domain. *Cognitive Science, 21,* 2, 109-146.

Omi, Y. (1997). Kenkyuhou no hensen [Change of research methods]. In T. Sato & H. Mizoguchi (Eds.), *Tsushi Nihon no shinrigaku.* Kyoto, Japan: Kitaoji-Shobo.

Platt, J. R. (1964). Strong inference. *Science, 146,* 347-353.

Schunn, C. D. (1995). *A goal/effect trade-off theory of experiment space search.* Unpublished doctoral dissertation, Carnegie Mellon University, Pittsburgh, PA.

Shirasa, T. (1987). *Kenkyu no susumekata matomekata* [How to conduct research and write a paper]. Tokyo: Kawashima-Shoten.

Siegler, R. S. & Crowley, K. (1994). Constraints on learning in nonprivileged domains. *Cognitive Psychology, 27,* 194-226.

Simon, H. A. (1996). *Models of my life.* New York: Basic Books.

Stevens, S. S. (1939). Psychology and the science of science. *Psychological Bulletin, 36,* 221-263.

Tatsuno, C., Arai, Y., & Tanaka, H. (1982). *Kyoiku sinrigaku kenkyuho manual* [Research manual for educational psychology]. Tokyo: Kyouiku-Shuppan.

Toyoda, H. (1998). *Kyoubunsankouzobunseki nyumonhen: Kozohoteishiki modeling* [Introduction to Covariance structure analysis: structural equations modeling]. Tokyo: Asakura-Shoten.

16

Internet Epistemology: Contributions of New Information Technologies to Scientific Research

Paul Thagard
University of Waterloo

Internet technologies, including electronic mail, preprint archives, and the World Wide Web, are now ubiquitous parts of scientific practice. After reviewing the full range of these technologies and sketching the history of their development, this chapter provides an epistemological appraisal of their contributions to scientific research. It uses Alvin Goldman's epistemic criteria of reliability, power, fecundity, speed and efficiency to evaluate the largely positive impact of Internet technologies on the development of scientific knowledge. The chapter concludes with a brief assessment of the potential impact of such technologies on science education.

A Day in the Life of a Cyberscientist

Here is how a workday unfolds for a scientist who makes use of the full range of Internet technologies. Consider an imaginary scientist, Marie Darwin, who works in a field like physics or biology where the Internet provides many resources. She arrives at work in the morning and immediately checks her electronic mail, finding that she has numerous messages. Some of these are from her students asking for advice on how to run the experiments they are planning, and she responds with technical instructions that they can read the next time they check their own e-mail. Another message is from Charles Curie, a collaborator of Marie's working at another research institute in a different country, who has some ideas for developing the new theory that he and Marie are trying to construct to explain their experimental results. Marie responds with some improvements to Charles' hypotheses, and she e-mails him a first draft of a paper she is writing in collaboration with him, so that he can revise it and e-mail a second draft back to her. In addition, Marie has e-mail from a journal editor telling her that her most recent paper is accepted if she is willing to make a few changes suggested by referees who e-mailed their reviews to the editor.

Marie now accesses the World Wide Web, first checking her local institute Web page for news about visiting speakers. More important to her research, she links to the preprint archive for her field, which contains electronic versions of papers not yet published. Marie is quickly able to see that ten new papers in her special area of research have been posted to the archive since the day before. She clicks on the names of the papers to read the summaries, and makes a note to download several of them for more thorough examination later. Marie then sends a new paper that she finished the day before to the preprint archive, knowing that it will be quickly available to all the other researchers working on similar topics. Now she is ready to use the Web for her ongoing research.

Marie begins her most important work of the day by using a Web link to an internal site at her institute that is accessible to her research group. Immediately she can see that her students and research assistants working late the previous night have collected some new experimental data that she examines on her screen. These data raise a question about similar observations made in Charles' laboratory, so she finds the link to that lab's Web site and goes into a data base that contains the results of their experiments from the previous year. To find the particular data that interest her, she uses a search engine that Charles' lab has conveniently provided to take her immediately to the part of the very large database that contains the information she wanted.

This information, along with the new experimental results from her own lab, raise some interesting questions concerning the structure of the objects that she and Charles are investigating. Fortunately, another research institute has provided a Web site that vividly displays what is known about such structures, so she moves to that site and uses a search engine to call up the relevant objects. There she can examine their structure using several valuable tools that go well beyond the presentation of simple 2-dimensional pictures found in textbooks. First she runs a special "Virtual Reality" browser to examine 3-dimensional representations of the objects, using her mouse to navigate through the 3-D representation to view the objects from different angles. Then she downloads an animation that enables her to watch the objects moving together over time. Together, the animation and the 3-D model suggest a new theoretical insight into how these objects might produce the experimental effects that she has been getting in her lab. Because testing her new theoretical ideas requires some new software that has just become available for interpreting the kind of data she has collected, Marie follows a link to another Web site that makes the software available. She is pleased to see that she does not have to download the software, but can immediately run the program on her own computer as a Java application that is automatically set up for her by her Web browser. Excited by what the program suggests about her data, she e-mails Charles and her students a sketch of her new ideas and results, proposing a time when they can have a collective Web conference where they can interactively discuss new research directions.

The story I have just told is not speculative science fiction: every technology it mentions is currently available on the Internet and is in use by scientists, although of course not all scientists use every technology. The Internet, particularly the World Wide Web, is now an essential part of scientific communication. By examining the ways that scientists are now using them to further the development of scientific research, we can see how new technologies can contribute to the spread of knowledge.

Revolutions in Scientific Communication

In the 1450s, Johan Gutenberg used his new invention of the printing press to produce hundreds of copies of the Bible. In the following century, the printing of books had a dramatic influence on the development of scientific knowledge (Eisenstein 1979, vol. 2). The printing and distribution of astronomical observations contributed to the downfall of Ptolemy's theory that the sun revolved around the earth. Copernicus and others noticed discrepancies between the predictions of Ptolemy's theory and actual observations and constructed an alternative theory that placed the sun at the center of planetary system. Similarly, widespread publication of books on Galen's anatomy brought into question the accuracy of his descriptions of the human body, leading Vesalius and others to produce and publish more accurate depictions. The first scientific journals were started in 1665 and provided a means for scholars to communicate their findings that was far more efficient than the personal letters previously used.

In the 1990s, communication underwent another dramatic revolution with the development of the World Wide Web and other Internet applications. Conceived in the 1960s as a U.S. military communications system called the ARPANET, the Internet became in the 1980s a convenient means of scientific communication, enabling scientists at major research institutions to send e-mail, participate in news groups, and transfer files. Working at the European particle physics laboratory CERN, Tim Berners-Lee proposed in 1989 a networked project for high-energy physics collaborations, employing hypertext to provide a flexible means of linking words and pictures. By 1991 his group had produced a simple browser for their "World Wide Web" project, which was superseded in 1993 by a more sophisticated browser, Mosaic, produced in the U.S. by the National Center for Supercomputer Applications. Mosaic was, in turn, quickly supplanted by more sophisticated browsers such as Netscape Navigator and Internet Explorer. The number of hosts on the Internet grew from 213 in 1981 to 313,000 in 1990, then to more than 43 million in 1999; and the number of Web sites grew from 130 in mid-1993 to an estimated 650,000 in 1998.[1]

These tools have inspired thousands of scientists to create Web sites and Internet tools that are dramatically changing how science is done. To show how the Internet is transforming scientific research practices, I will describe how the Web is used at CERN, where it was first invented, as well as how it makes possible rapid and effective communication in the Human Genome Project and other research. Like the application of the printing press to scientific publishing, use of the World Wide Web has enabled scientists to increase the reliability, speed, and efficiency of their work.

Science on the Web

By 1999, the Internet guide Yahoo! listed more than 12,000 Web sites for biology, along with thousands of sites for other sciences such as astronomy, biology, earth sciences, physics, chemistry and psychology.[2]

1. This information is due to Network Wizards and is available at http://www.nw.com/. Historical information about the Internet is available on the Web, for example at http://www.w3.org/ History.html.
2. http://www.yahoo.com/Science/

Although many of these sites are used to provide general information to scientists and the public, some sites have become integral to research activities. In 1991, a physicist at the Los Alamos National Library, Paul Ginsparg, created a database of new physics papers. By 1996, this archive served more than 35,000 users from over 70 countries, with 70,000 electronic transactions per day. Physicists use the World Wide Web daily to check for newly written and not-yet-published papers in their research areas.[3]

The Web has also become a regular tool used by many scientists in the production of their research. Especially in fields like high-energy physics and genetics, contemporary science is a huge collaborative enterprise involving international teams of scientists (Thagard, 1997, 1999). It is not unusual for published articles in physics to have more than 100 co-authors, reflecting the diversity of expertise needed to carry out large projects involving complex instruments. Located near Geneva, CERN is a collaborative project of 19 European countries involving several nuclear accelerators and dozens of experimental research projects. Each project involves numerous different researchers from a range of different institutions in the participating counties. Since it began in 1954, CERN has been the source of many of the most important discoveries in particle physics, such as the 1983 finding of evidence for the top quark.

The World Wide Web was invented at CERN to improve information sharing among scientists from diverse institutions working on joint projects. It was conceived as a hypermedia project so that scientists could exchange pictorial information such as diagrams and data graphs as well as verbal text. Today, CERN has a World Wide Web team to support experiments, using numerous Web servers.[4]

The basic idea of the World Wide Web originated in a document written in 1989 by Tim Berners-Lee.[5] He argued:

> CERN is a wonderful organization. It involves several thousand people, many of them very creative, all working toward common goals. Although they are nominally organized into a hierarchical management structure, this does not constrain the way people will communicate, and share information, equipment and software across groups.

---

3. A paper by Ginsparg is available at http://xxx.lanl.gov/blurb/pg96unesco.html. The physics preprint site is http://xxx.lanl.gov/.
4. http://www.cern.ch/.
5. http://www.w3.org/pub/WWW/History/1989/proposal.html.

The actual observed working structure of the organization is a multiply connected "web" whose interconnections evolve with time. In this environment, a new person arriving, or someone taking on a new task, is normally given a few hints as to who would be useful people to talk to. Information about what facilities exist and how to find out about them travels in the corridor gossip and occasional newsletters, and the details about what is required to be done spread in a similar way. All things considered, the result is remarkably successful, despite occasional misunderstandings and duplicated effort.

A problem, however, is the high turnover of people. When two years is a typical length of stay, information is constantly being lost. The introduction of the new people demands a fair amount of their time and that of others before they have any idea of what goes on. The technical details of past projects are sometimes lost forever, or only recovered after a detective investigation in an emergency. Often, the information has been recorded, it just cannot be found.

If a CERN experiment were a static once-only development, all the information could be written in a big book. As it is, CERN is constantly changing as new ideas are produced, as new technology becomes available, and in order to get around unforeseen technical problems. When a change is necessary, it normally affects only a small part of the organization. A local reason arises for changing a part of the experiment or detector. At this point, one has to dig around to find out what other parts and people will be affected. Keeping a book up to date becomes impractical, and the structure of the book needs to be constantly revised.

Berners-Lee recommended that the information at CERN should be handled, not as a linear book or a hierarchical tree, but as hypertext. He had previous experience with hypertext, having written in 1980 a program for keeping track of software that he later adapted for use at CERN. He outlined how CERN could benefit from a large non-centralized hypermedia system, linking graphics, speech, video, and text in an unconstrained way that would enable users to jump from one entry to another. He stated that researchers needed remote access for the many computers used at CERN, independent of the particular kind of computer used. Berners-Lee presciently noted that CERN's diverse computer network was a miniature of the world in a few years time, anticipating that the World Wide Web would not merely be a local application.

CERN's various research groups now make extensive use of the World Wide Web. For example, the DELPHI (DEtector for Lepton, Photon and Hadron Identification) project at CERN involves about 550 physicists from 56 participating universities and institutes in 22 countries.[6] These scientists can use the Web to access data acquired over the past 8 years, including pictorial representations of important experimental events. Also available are DELPHI news bulletins, a discussion forum, and electronic versions of papers by the project's participants, as well as links to preprint servers, participating institutions, and other physics information sources.

After CERN's programmers initiated use of the World Wide Web for scientific research, they made the software they had developed freely available and international Web use expanded rapidly with the development of more sophisticated browsers. One of the most effective scientific users of the Web has been the Human Genome Project, an international consortium of research institutions working since 1989 to identify all of the approximately 100,000 genes that are responsible for human development. This project is medically important, because many diseases such as diabetes and some forms of cancer have a large genetic component. The identification of all human genes should be a substantial aid to finding genes responsible for diseases, which can potentially lead to new medical treatments.

Scientists working on the genome project are producing an astonishing amount of information. If published in books, descriptions of the DNA sequences of all the human genes would require more than 200,000 pages.[7] However, books would be a poor technology for keeping track of such information, not just because of its quantity, but also because new genes are being mapped daily and a printed text would be instantly obsolete. Fortunately, genome scientists have turned to computer databases to store the rapidly expanding information about gene locations. Storing this information would be useless, however, without effective means for accessing it, which search engines provide. Like CERN, the Human Genome Project is highly collaborative, involving dozens of different institutions in various countries. The arrival of the World Wide Web has been an immense boon to international collaboration on the genome project, with more than 25 contributing institutions making their data available on the Web for general access.

---

6. http://www.cern.ch/Delphi/Welcome.html.
7. http://www.ornl.gov/TechResources/Human_Genome/publicat/primer/intro.html.

One of the major contributors to the genome project is the Human Genome Center at the Whitehead Institute at MIT.[8] Since its creation in May 1994, the number of weekly accesses to their Web site has grown to over 200,000 (Figure 1). Internal users from MIT and external users from various institutions access the gene mapping information available at the site, as well as various documents and software available there. Like other genome project sites, the MIT site contains searchable databases that researchers can consult to find the latest information.

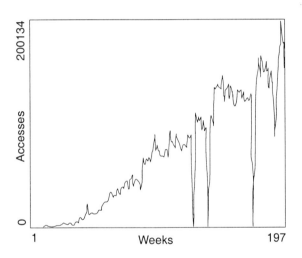

Figure 1. Web site accesses at the MIT Human Genome Center from May 1994 to February 1998. (Source:http://www.genome.wi.mit.edu/www/uage/index.html)

For medical researchers, a more directly useful database is Online Mendelian Inheritance in Man (OMIM), available since December 1995.[9] The reference book, Mendelian Inheritance in Man (eleventh edition, McKusick & Francomano, 1994), has been a valuable source of information on genetic traits and diseases, but the World Wide Web version is even more useful. Whereas the reference book was updated approximately every 2 years, OMIM is updated almost daily. It has an excellent search engine that enables users to quickly access entries about

8. http://www-genome.wi.mit.edu/.
9. http:// www3.ncbi.nlm.nih.gov/Omim/.

characters, genes, and diseases, and the entries provide links to relevant information such as genome maps and journal references. Whereas the reference book is expensive ($165) and typically found only in research libraries, anyone with Internet access can quickly obtain the information available on OMIM.

CERN, the Human Genome Project, and OMIM illustrate only some of the technologies available to scientists over the World Wide Web (Renehan, 1996). Various sites provide animations and videos that enable viewers to see nature in motion. The Virtual Reality Modeling Language is beginning to be used to enable scientists to view objects in 3 dimensions, for example in the Image Library of Biological Macromolecules.[10] A different kind of virtual reality environment is AstroVR, a multi-user networked environment with access to many astronomical tools and databases (URL currently not available). It enables astronomers and astrophysicists equipped with the proper software and hardware to talk, work together on a whiteboard, share images, make data plots, and look up astronomical data and literature. The goal of AstroVR is to enable users to interact and do collaborative research almost as if they were in the same room. Sites such as the NCSA Biology Workbench make computer programs and other tools readily available to scientific researchers.[11]

These exciting scientific uses of the World Wide Web provide examples of how it is contributing to the development of knowledge. To examine this contribution more comprehensively, we can use five standards proposed by Alvin Goldman (1986, 1992) for evaluating how well different social practices lead to true beliefs. These standards are reliability, power, fecundity, speed and efficiency. I will show how each of these standards enables us to see more clearly why the printing press was so important for communication, and then apply a similar assessment to the Web. Reliability, the most important standard for looking critically at the Web, is saved for last.

Goldman's criteria are all "veritistic," presupposing that science aims at and sometimes achieves truth understood as correspondence between beliefs and the external world. Truth is not the only aim of science, which seeks integrative explanations as well as the accumulation of truths, but the assessment that follows would be little affected by considering explanatory power as well as truth acquisition as the aim of sci-

---

10. http://www.vrml.org/ and http://www.imb-jena.de/IMAGE.html.
11. http://biology.ncsa.uiuc.edu/.

ence. The assessment would, however, be very different if the aims of science were taken to include other kinds of goals such as political power and personal domination, but I have argued at length elsewhere that science primarily aims at explanation and truth (Thagard, 1988, 1992, 1999). If these are in fact the primary aims of science, then Goldman's standards provide appropriate ways of evaluating scientific practices.

Power

The *power* of a practice is measured by its ability to help people find true answers to the questions that interest them. After the printing press made many more books generally available, people could use them to increase the total amount of their knowledge. The printing press eliminated the tedious chore of copying books, giving scholars more time to produce new knowledge rather than merely duplicating the old. They could compare and cross-reference different books, rather than producing commentaries on isolated works. The sixteenth century Danish astronomer Tycho Brahe took advantage of the printing press to detect anomalies in old records, to enlist collaborators, and to make corrections in successive additions. Scientists are concerned not only with observational truths, but also with finding explanatory theories which tie together numerous observations. Placing books in the hands of scholars provided them with information that made possible assemblages of information that unite to form new theories. Darwin's realization that natural selection could be the mechanism of biological evolution was inspired by reading Malthus's work on population growth. The printing press thus contributed to the capacity of science to produce theoretical explanations by providing more scientists with more of the conceptual pieces needed to assemble new theories.

The World Wide Web is similarly powerful in helping scientists find answers to the questions that interest them. The full range of representational techniques now available on the Web can help people find answers that would otherwise be unavailable. Suppose, for example, that you want to understand binary pulsars. A new electronic astronomy journal will include a video simulation: "You will see how two stars rotate around each other: They evolve; one star sucks up matter from the other, explodes in a supernova explosion, and so on. It is a very beautiful way to illustrate a theoretical model" (Taubes, 1996). Similarly, if you are curious about the operation of the new kind of bacteria that have recently been found to be a major cause of stomach ulcers, you can view an animation of *Helicobacter pylori*.

Web sites can use hypertext organization to facilitate the ability of researchers to find answers. For example, the Tree of Life provides information on many species of animals and plants, organized so that browsers can easily traverse the tree up from a species to a genus or down from a genus to a species.[12] Following hypertext links can serendipitously lead to new sources of information previously unknown to the user. The immense and rapidly increasing size of the Web, however, can limit its power. People can get so lost in following one link after another that they become "Web potatoes," so caught up in chasing the next bit of information that they lose track of the questions they wanted to answer.

Unlike printed materials, digital databases can be searched quickly and thoroughly. The entire Web can be searched for information using numerous search engines such as Yahoo! and AltaVista that have become available in the past few years. Scientists can use such search engines to find sites that are presenting information relevant to their own work. For researchers on such projects as the Human Genome Project, huge data bases containing genetic information can yield useful answers because they are accompanied by search engines that enable users to find answers to their questions about particular genes and diseases. It is not just that search engines enable people to find information more quickly—in large scientific databases they enable people to find answers that they would otherwise not find at all.

E-mail and news groups are also potential sources of power when they are used to solicit answers to interesting questions. Many Internet users subscribe to list servers that enable them to send e-mail automatically to people with similar interests. For example, I subscribe to a list on the psychology of science to which I can send queries or announcements. Many news groups are available for people to participate in discussions that interest them. Unmoderated news groups, to which anyone can send any message, often fill up with junk, but there are science news groups that have a moderator who screens out worthless postings, leaving entries that are likely to be relevant to a researcher's work. (Compare the difference between moderated news groups such as sci.physics.research and unmoderated, junk-laden groups such as sci.physics.) Web conferences provide an even more immediate way in

---

12. http://phylogeny.arizona.edu/tree/phylogeny.html

which researchers can communicate with each other to generate answers to questions of common interest.

Software easily available on the Web is another source of power when scientists use programs thereby obtained to generate answers to statistical or other questions that would be unanswerable otherwise. Software availability will rapidly increase when more Java applications become available. The advantage of Java programs is that they run on any computer with a Web browser, eliminating the need for separate programs for Unix computers, PC's, Macintoshes, and so on, although there is sometimes variation in runtime performance.

Electronic preprint archives of the sort now available for physicists also increase the ability of scientists to find answers to interesting questions. The physics archive can be searched by author and title, enabling scientists to find papers related to their questions. A similar archive has been established for cognitive science.[13] Even without a special archive, scientists can use the general search engines on the Web to find answers to questions on an astonishing array of topics, from aardvarks to medicine to zoos. Increasing numbers of scientific journals are available online, with searchable tables of contents and links from article to article that make it very easy to hunt down sources of information.

The Internet can encourage the development of new theoretical ideas also, as in the following example reported by Herb Brody (1996):[14]

> Physicist Andrew Strominger wrote a paper that suggested a radical departure from Einstein's conception of space-time as a smooth and continuous surface. Strominger e-mailed a question about the subject to Brian Green, who pursues similar research at Cornell. Green started to answer Strominger's question, then read the article, which Strominger had just posted on the Internet. The two scientists entered into a brief interchange of e-mail, joined by David Morrison of Duke University, and three days later all three had cowritten and posted a second paper that further refined their theory showing that tiny black holes can be transformed mathematically into infinitesimal vibrating loops of energy, called superstrings.

There are undoubtedly numerous other examples of new theoretical contributions arising from Internet-based collaborations.

---

13. http://cogprints.soton.ac.uk
14. 1996; http://www.techreview.com/articles/oct96/brody.html

Fecundity

The *fecundity* of a practice is its ability to lead to large numbers of true beliefs for *many* practitioners. This standard says that a practice should lead to truths for many people, as the printing press clearly did by making books available to far more people than previously had access to them. The number of books available jumped to more than 30,000 editions by the year 1500. Astronomers, anatomists and other investigators could publish their observations for use by others. Books no longer needed to be kept locked in chests or chained in libraries.

The Internet and the World Wide Web satisfy the standard of fecundity to the extent that they provide answers for many people. Some critics have seen these technologies as providing information for the technological elite but generating yet another barrier to economic and social opportunity for residents of underdeveloped countries and the underprivileged in developed countries. But just as the printing press made books available to many whom previously lacked access to university collections, so the World Wide Web makes information available to those who previously lacked access to good libraries. Physicists in underdeveloped countries whose libraries cannot afford increasingly expensive scientific journals can have the same instant access to papers that their peers in developed countries enjoy. Computers and Internet connections are not free, but they are much cheaper than travel to libraries or purchasing or copying numerous books and journals (see efficiency). When Java applications become more widely available, people will not require special hardware or software to run them, so many people will be use them to help answer their questions. News groups and e-mail lists reach many people simultaneously, so that they can contribute to the ability of many people to find answers to their questions. Web conferences and on-line forums have the potential to increase the knowledge of many people.

Speed

The *speed* of a practice is how quickly it leads to true answers. People aim to acquire knowledge quickly as well as reliably, and the printing press contributed enormously to the speed with which knowledge could be disseminated. No longer did scholars need to travel to distant libraries to consult rare copies of books, since printed books were produced in sufficient numbers that they could be held in numerous places. Scholars could even have their own copies of books, enabling them to increase their knowledge without the time needed to consult libraries. Printed tables of logarithm functions spared astronomers much calculating time. Production of printed books increased the size of libraries and encouraged the use of full alphabetical order and indexes, leading to speedier searches for information.

The Internet and the World Wide Web have enormous advantages with respect to the speed of producing answers. Electronic mail can transfer information around the world in seconds or minutes, in contrast to the days or weeks required for communication by traditional mail. When scientific information is posted on a Web site such as OMIM or sent to a preprint archive, it becomes available instantly, in contrast to the months or even years that publication in books and journals can take. The entire Web and many Web databases have search engines that provide information with a speed that was unimaginable a decade ago. New applications such as Java offer the potential for speedy use of new software.

Of course, as everyone who has used the Web knows, the speed of Internet use is heavily affected by the extent of usage at a particular moment. Information that might be almost instantaneously available at 6 a.m. may be painfully slow to load later when many more people are accessing the Internet. The WWW has been called the "World Wide Wait." Information seekers may waste time chasing one link after another when a trip to the library would tell them what they want to know more quickly. The many entertaining sites on the Web may distract people from looking for the information they need and slow down their work rather than speeding it up. But used intelligently, the World Wide Web can be the most rapid source of information ever available.

Efficiency

The *efficiency* of a practice is how well it limits the cost of getting true answers. Copying books by hand consumed huge amounts of labor, whereas printing made possible distribution of books at a fraction of the cost.

A friend once told me that "WWW" stands for "Wicked Waste of Wesources." Using the Internet is indeed costly because of the computers and information storage required, but nevertheless it fares very well on the standard of efficiency. E-mail, news groups, and electronic archives are much cheaper than sending paper mail. It is much less costly for CERN's international research groups to communicate electronically and access information from a common Web server than to try to meet frequently and to exchange data using physical tapes. Storage of papers electronically can now be done for less than 1/1000 of a cent per page, far cheaper than paper storage and reproduction. Expensive computer and network connections are not efficient for an organization whose people are using them to download recipes, play multiple user games, and learn more about their favorite TV shows. But the increasing amount of valuable information on the Web, including scientific information, makes it a highly efficient source of true answers if used intelligently.

The power, fecundity, speed, and efficiency of the Internet are impressive, but they raise problems about the quality of information that are even more severe than those that arose with print and television. Anyone with a Web site can post virtually anything, and a random look at what Joe Hacker has to say about the origin of the universe may be worse than useless. Web pages and postings to unmoderated news groups (for example the claim on alt.conspiracy that flight TWA 800 was shot down by the U.S. Navy) undergo no screening and evaluation, whereas even a profit-driven book or magazine publisher or cable TV provider has to apply some standards of taste and credibility. Libraries and other purchasers apply standards when they decide what is worth buying and making available to readers. In contrast, the lack of screening on the Web is accompanied by an unprecedented degree of access by anyone who has a connection to the Internet. Compared to print and television, the Web provides less scrutiny and more access, so the problem of distinguishing knowledge and nonsense is even more acute.

Reliability

The *reliability* of a practice is measured by the ratio of truths to total number of beliefs fostered by the practice. Science aims to achieve truths and avoid errors, and the printing press increased reliability in several ways. The previous method of producing books by hand-copying inevitably introduced mistakes, whereas once a press was set up it could produce many copies of a book without introducing any new errors. Moreover, the wide availability of printed books encouraged readers to consider the extent to which the contents of the book were accurate reflections of nature, rather than taking the contents of the books as sacrosanct. When errors crept into printed books, errata could be published and distributed to scattered readers. Illustrations could be duplicated exactly, instead of depending on the varying ability of each copier to reproduce drawings exactly. Before printing, maps were frequently unreliable since copying by hand introduced distortions and inaccuracies. Thus the printing press greatly increased the reliability of scientific communication.

Of course, the printing press was and is a mixed blessing. From the beginning, it was used to promulgate nonsense as well as knowledge. Shoddy books on worthless topics could sap the time and energy of thinkers and fill their minds with error. Books on astrology were as likely to attract the printer looking for a profitable product as books on empirical astronomy; in fact, horoscopes were published shortly after Gutenberg's bible, well before the publication of astronomical observations. Nevertheless, the overall contribution of the printing press to the production and availability of scientific knowledge is clear, according to the standards of reliability, power, fecundity, speed, and efficiency.

How do the Web and other Internet technologies improve the reliability of the research of scientists like Marie Darwin? Various technologies can help her to avoid erroneous beliefs. By e-mailing notes and drafts of papers to her students and collaborators, she can get immediate feedback that can correct misconceptions before they become entrenched in her thinking. Similarly, sending her preprints off to an electronic archive gives other researchers a chance to examine her work and suggest improvements. Conferencing over the Web provides another way in which the reliability of Marie's work can benefit from the critical response of her collaborators. Science, like knowledge in general, is an inherently social enterprise in which achieving truth and avoiding error gains enormously from feedback which Internet technologies can help to provide.

Seeking information generally on the World Wide Web is not always a reliable practice. But in the hands of scientists and other careful users, posting information on the Web has several features that can increase reliability. Unlike books and journals that are sent out into the world permanently, it is very easy to update and correct information on the Web. Whereas printed information needs to wait for further publications or new editions to correct errors, changes to a Web site can be made quickly to prevent propagation of erroneous information. Experimental databases such as those used at CERN and in the Human Genome Project can undergo continuous expansion and correction. Preprint archives are a potential source of misinformation, since the papers sent to them do not undergo the careful reviewing process that precedes journal publication. This problem may turn out to be more acute for psychology than for physics, whose journals have lower rejection rates than psychology journals: a physics paper is probably going to end up published anyway. But the potential for introduction of errors is to some extent compensated for by the ease with which new preprints and e-mailing among researchers can help to correct earlier mistakes. Archives can also indicate which papers are reprints of papers that have undergone reviewing and been published in scientific journals.

Many scientific fields, such as chemistry, involve objects whose 3-dimensional and dynamic character are inadequately captured by verbal and 2-dimensional representations. More reliable information may sometimes be provided by special Web tools such as Virtual Reality browsers that provide much richer 3-dimensional information. Videos and animations can provide more realistic depictions of the motions of a system under investigation. Like any picture, virtual reality displays and animations can provide erroneous impressions, but they have the potential for giving more accurate representations of the inherently 3-dimensional and dynamic aspects of the world that they are intended to describe. These examples show that the World Wide Web can increase reliability as well as diminish it. But even more than readers of printed sources, Web users need intellectual tools for discriminating between reliable and unreliable sources of information.

Implications for Science Education

My main concern in this chapter has been to assess the contributions of the Internet to scientific research, but similar issues arise with respect to the use of the Web and other technologies in teaching science. Students, from elementary school to Ph.D. programs, can also use e-mail, surf the Web, and access archives. But the epistemological issues are even more acute, because most students are not so strongly motivated as Marie Darwin to pursue scientific knowledge. The key question is the extent to which the scientific knowledge of students is enhanced or hindered by their use of the Web and other technologies.

Reliability is a serious problem because students are less likely than scientists to be aware of the difference between scientifically reputable sources and bogus ones. For example, a student using a Web search engine to get information on vitamins is much more likely to get a commercial site selling vitamins than a medically authoritative site that uses scientific information to assess their contributions to health. Hence science educators must not simply turn their students loose on the Web, but must provide them with lists of scientifically sound sites and warnings about the abundance of unreliable sites. Even more importantly, students need to be furnished with criteria for assessing the likely reliability of sites they find on their own, so that they pass over sites dominated by commercial or other interests and make use of ones based on scientific evidence. Whereas a science textbook assigned for a class is easily distinguished from a popular book on a friend's shelf, at first glance one Web site looks much like another.

Power and fecundity are also potential problems for students, since use of the Web may not necessarily lead to large numbers of true answers for large numbers of people. Scientists are not immune to the many distractions of the Web, and students may be even more inclined to visit sites that reflect their personal interests rather than the drier but more informative scientific sites. The Web can be highly efficient for people strongly motivated to get valid answers to scientific questions, but not for people who are easily distracted by abundant sites for their favorite sports teams, TV shows, or sexual activities. Students need to be cautioned that the Web can not only provide them with false answers to scientific and other questions, it can also massively waste their time on the way to getting them.

On the other hand, the Web can be enormously useful to students as well as scientists if they can respond affirmatively to the following questions:

1. Are you getting information from sites produced by legitimate authorities such as scientific and educational organizations?

2. Is your information based on scientific evidence?

3. Are you avoiding being distracted by sites irrelevant to your educational goals?

4. Are there other more traditional sources of information (e.g. printed ones) that would provide the desired information more directly?

Students can thus be encouraged to provide their own epistemological assessments of their Internet practices.

Conclusion

Table 1 summarizes how various Internet technologies can contribute to scientific research. There is great variation in the extent to which these technologies are now being used.

Table 1. Summary of the positive contributions of Internet technologies to scientific research.

	RELIABILITY	POWER	SPEED	FECUNDITY	EFFICIENCY
E-Mail, News Groups	feedback for corrections	many answers available	faster than mail	multiple recipents	cheaper than paper mail
Hypertext	easily revised	follow links, use search engines	instant publishing, no wait for access, searching	widely available, distance irrelevant	storage cheap
Animation, Video, VRML	more accurate depiction of structures and motion	lots of visual information not otherwise available	picture or animation may convey information quickly	multimedia may be useful for visual learners	no need to order video tape
Java	software provided without local alteration	provision of software to perform scientific computation	no wait for software	use by everyone, regardless of kind of computer	no need to buy software, or spend time on getting it
Databases	updatable, checkable	huge amount of information available	fast searchers, instant availability	accessible to many	storage is cheap
Preprint Archives	potentially quick feedback	find out latest research results	instant access	journal access unnecessary	total cost lower than print
Conferencing	immediate corrections	combine new ideas	no need to meet	everyone involved	cheaper than meeting

Every scientific field now has available to it electronic mail, news groups, and World Wide Web sites, but only physics has an extensive preprint archive. Within different fields, there is also great variability in the extent to which different scientists use technologies such as Web-based databases. For the Human Genome Project and particle physics at

CERN, such databases have become essential, but other scientific projects that are less collaborative can handle their data locally in more traditional ways. Visualization using graphically oriented browsers is becoming important for fields such as biomedicine, but may have little impact on other fields. Some of the technologies I have mentioned, such as Java applications, Virtual Reality browsers, and Web conferencing are newer and have so far received more limited use, although all have promising futures.

In describing these various ways in which Internet technologies such as the World Wide Web can contribute to scientific knowledge, I have provided a positive model of how the technologies can be used to foster the development of knowledge in anyone, including nonscientists such as students. At the other extreme, there is the real and frightening prospect of students and other people wasting electronic resources to fill their heads with nonsense gleaned from the many worthless sites on the Web. Internet Epistemology includes the highly critical task of examining and evaluating the large quantities of pseudoscience that the Web is being used to promulgate. My purpose in this chapter has been more positive, to describe the Internet at its best in aiding the development of scientific knowledge.

Acknowledgements

This paper is an expanded and updated version of chapter 13 of my 1999 book, *How Scientists Explain Disease*, and is reprinted with the kind permission of Princeton University Press. Live links for most of the Web sites mentioned can be found in an older version of this paper at http://cogsci.uwaterloo.ca/Articles/Pages/Epistemology.html. This research has been supported by the Social Sciences and Humanities Research Council of Canada and by a Canada Council Killam Research Fellowship. I am grateful to the editors of this volume for useful suggestions.

References

Brody, H. (1996). Wired science. *Technology Review, 99*(October), 42-51.
Eisenstein, E. L. (1979). *The printing press as an agent of change.* Cambridge: Cambridge University Press.
Goldman, A. (1986). *Epistemology and cognition.* Cambridge, MA: Harvard University Press.

Goldman, A. (1992). *Liaisons: Philosophy meets the cognitive and social sciences.* Cambridge, MA: MIT Press.

McKusick, V. A., & Francomano, C. A. (Eds.). (1994). *Mendelian inheritance in man: A catalog of human genes and genetic disorders.* (11th ed.). Baltimore: Johns Hopkins University Press.

Renehan, E. J. (1996). *Science on the Web: 500 of the most essential science Web sites.* New York: Copernicus.

Taubes, G. (1996). Science journals go wired. *Science, 271,* 764.

Thagard, P. (1988). *Computational philosophy of science.* Cambridge, MA: MIT Press/Bradford Books.

Thagard, P. (1992). *Conceptual revolutions.* Princeton: Princeton University Press.

Thagard, P. (1997). Collaborative knowledge. *Noûs, 31,* 242-261.

Thagard, P. (1999). *How scientists explain disease.* Princeton, NJ: Princeton University Press.

Author Index

Magnani, G., 12, 20
Mahoney, M. J., 85, 114
Mainzer, J., 124, 140
Malhotra, B. A., 359, 363, 391
Malhoutra, B., 398
Mallinson, G. G., 391
Mallinson, J. B., 364, 391
Marshall, S., 317, 321
Martin, L., 43, 48
Martindale, C., 55, 80
Marx, R., 282, 283, 322
Mataric, M. J., 180, 207
Matusov, E., 58, 80
May, M., 16, 20
Mayer, R. E., 151, 172
Mazzeo, J., 281, 322
McCloskey, M., 416, 443
McCormick, M., 21, 48
McDaniel, M. A., 213, 248
McFadden, C., 364, 391
McGilly, K., 210, 248
McKee, C., 432, 442
McKusick, V. A., 472, 485
McLaughlin, C. W., 364, 392
McLean, R. S., 283, 322
Medin, D. L., 336, 348
Meltzoff, A., 23, 45, 47
Mervis, C. B., 84, 113
Metz, K. E., 363, 391
Millar, R., 258, 276
Minick, N., 57, 81
Minstrell, J., 94, 429, 432, 434, 442, 443
Mistry, J., 23, 48
Miwa, K., 463
Miyake, N., 461, 463
Moll, L. C., 35, 48
Montgomery, R., 52, 57, 58, 78
Moore, A., 275
Moore, J. L., 22, 46, 169, 171
Mosier, C., 23, 48
Mugny, G., 53, 78
Mundt, J., 317, 321
Murphy, G. L., 336, 348
Mynatt, C. R., 116, 140, 156, 173

National Research Council, 281, 321, 417, 443
National Science Education Standards, 211, 243, 248, 417
Neisser, U., 117, 140
Nersessian, N., 156, 160, 172

Newell, A., 149, 172, 340, 348
Newton-Smith, W. H., 382, 391
Novick, L. R., 84, 114
NSTA 436, 442

O'Loughlin, M., 57, 79, 413
O'Neill, D. K., 283, 321
O'Sullivan, C. Y., 281, 322
Oakes, L. A., 409, 412
Oakes, L. M., 22, 23, 26, 27, 29, 30, 46
Okada, T., 51, 58, 80, 98, 394, 398, 408, 413, 445, 446, 449, 454, 457, 458, 459, 463, 464
Olson, D. R., 264, 277
Olson, G. M., 57, 79
Omi, Y., 452, 464
Osherson, D., 336, 348
Oshima, J., 463
Ost, D. H., 177, 207

Palincsar, A. S., 363, 391
Paolucci, M., 283, 322
Papert, S., 205, 207
Pappas, A., 24, 47, 412
Penner, D., 177, 207, 268, 277
Pérez-Granados, D., 26, 46
Perkins, D., 283, 322
Perkins, D. N., 70, 80, 172
Perret-Clermont, A. N., 53, 80
Petrosino, A. J., 110, 246, 254, 275, 276, 278, 462
Phelps, E., 51, 56, 57, 69, 79
Piaget, J., 22, 25, 48, 85, 114
Pickering, A., 251, 260, 263, 278, 353, 391
Piéraut-Le Bonniec, G., 243, 248
Pinch, T., 381, 389
Pintrich, P. R., 283, 322
Platt, J. R., 458, 464
Posner, G., 432, 443
Post, T. A., 149, 173
Project 2061 418, 443
Putz, A., 262, 277

Qin, Y., 7, 20, 172
Quine, W. V. O., 381, 391

Radinsky, J., 317, 321
Raghavan, K., 204, 207, 283, 322
Rasmussen, N., 377, 391
Ray, T. S., 179, 207
Reed, E., 173
Reese, C. M., 281, 322

Subject Index